"Stay close, children." Rebecca was ......, ... misunderstandings.

"We must keep moving, we are not the only things in the dark." Her voice wavered a little.

Arthur squeezed his mother's left hand, making her wedding ring dig deep into his skin. Emily hugged Hugo's matted fur, his freshness long gone. This teddy had been a gift from her father and nothing was going to separate them now.

Rebecca wiped her forehead with her right hand; God only knew how long they had been in the catacombs.

"Will Father be alright? He's out there with them."

Rebecca brought their lantern closer to her face. Emily could see her mother's head move up and down.

The wick in the lantern flickered a little and then steadied itself. Rebecca pushed Arthur behind her to be next to his sister.

"We must keep moving, children."

Some of the passageways were larger than others; it was a maze that had to be negotiated correctly. A wrong turn could result in hours lost in darkness and the knowledge that going up to the surface would not be without consequences.

The catacombs had been used as burial grounds for the dead Parisians who could not afford a proper place of rest. The tunnels that spread under Paris ran for miles in each direction; they had been quarried for limestone for buildings and used in many different ways.

Rebecca and the children had originally gone down into the catacombs with everyone who was escaping the flesh-eaters at the church. These civilians were then split into groups by a handful of French soldiers and told to be as quiet as possible as they made their way under Paris. Rebecca and the children had been moving rapidly with their group, until they had come to a junction. This junction had an exit point to the surface, with a rotten wooden ladder leading all the way up to the top.

A shell had landed, causing the roof around them to collapse. On one side had been Rebecca and the children, plus a French soldier. He insisted he would try and dig his way back to the others using a small army backpack spade. They were trying to do the same from their side. It was going to take some time and Rebecca began to help whilst Arthur and Emily sat and watched. Arthur occasionally tried to help a little, but was not able to assist in the same way as his mother.

No one had heard the soft shuffling coming through the side tunnel as the damp soil masked the sound. It wasn't until the teeth grinding and snarling echoed into the chamber that Rebecca looked around. Three flesh-eaters were now within metres of them. Long, blood-soaked, grey hair was flung back, as one of the flesh-eaters made a lunge for Emily. Rebecca moved with speed and kicked the creature in the side of its chest, causing it to stumble back. Spinning around with his spade, the French soldier planted a savage blow into the old woman's forehead. The flesh-eater twitched for a second and then stopped moving. The remaining two closed in as the children moved behind their mother.

The soldier moved forward with a direct assault. Swinging low and hard, taking away the legs of the "would-be" attackers. In spite of falling awkwardly, he wasted no time pounding the twitching bodies. Looking briefly towards Rebecca and then at the children, he sighed.

"Madam, you must take the children and continue whilst I dig."

He paused as if to catch his breath.

"I have a map of the catacombs, follow the marked route and it will lead you out of the city."

Fumbling around in his army tunic, his hand emerged with a tatty piece of paper. It was brown, with bits falling off it. The children looked at their mother. Their eyes searched for reassurance in this underground world.

Arthur took a sidestep away from his mother.

"How will you find your way out?" He spoke confidently to the man.

The soldier looked down at Arthur. "You'll make your father proud, young man." He told him he would find a way.

Arthur half-smiled, whilst his mind wandered to where his father was. He prayed he had not been killed or eaten by the monsters now stalking above.

Rebecca took the map and looked at this burly man in front of her. "Thank you for helping us, I pray we meet you again soon."

The digging from the other side was more frantic. The chambers around them started to carry more noises. The soldier picked up his spade and then reached for one of the lanterns they had. He passed it to Rebecca and urged them to go.

She had a quick glance at the brittle map. The route was marked in red and weaved its way through the catacombs. The soldier had pointed out on the map where they were, before starting to dig again. He urged them to keep moving and said they would all catch up soon. Rebecca and the children looked back once as they used the lantern's dim light to direct them in the darkness.

"Remember, children, whatever you hear, keep moving." These words stuck in the children's head as they moved along the tunnels under Paris. It had been an age since they were split from the soldier and the main group. The only sound to break the silence was Rebecca's words of "Keep close, children."

Arthur was rubbing his tummy, but said nothing. He knew his mother was very tired and probably hungry herself. She was doing her very best to keep them all alive.

The further they followed the map, the more anxious Rebecca became. She looked down at her feet, which were now sodden and covered ankle-deep in mud. The children were looking tired and as she brought the lantern closer to their pale skin, she saw Arthur rubbing his tummy.

"My dearest angels, I know you are hungry and tired, but we are nearly at an opening. We can rest there for a while."

The children looked at her with blank faces.

Emily eyes focused on her mother.

"Where are the others and the soldier?"

Rebecca lowered the lantern even more and crouched down.

"They're coming, but we must keep moving." She paused for a second to think about her next sentence. "Those things are following us and we cannot let them stop us from seeing Daddy again."

Brushing hair away from Emily's face, she leant forward and kissed her on the cheek. Arthur moved closer, as he wanted some affection as well. His mother responded with a kiss on his forehead. With both of them semi-recharged from this show of affection, she turned around and led them forward.

Walking with wet sore feet was not easy; an hour passed in the darkness of the tunnels. The occasional thunder and shaking from the ground above broke up the silence.

"Mummy, I've lost Hugo."

Rebecca placed the lantern onto the soil beneath her feet. The strong smell of dampness filled the air, a soil odour which was mixed with rotting wood and the water puddles which surrounded them.

"My beautiful Emily, I know Hugo is very important to you, but we cannot stop now."

As soon as the words left her mother's mouth, Emily's eyes welled up. She did not cry like a child who had lost her favourite teddy bear, these were silent tears slowly streaming down her face and then effortlessly falling to the ground below.

"He's lost in the darkness like Daddy."

Rebecca shook her head.

"I'll never see him again, will I?"

Rebecca did not know whether she was talking about Charles or the teddy.

"Oh Emily."

A growl and hiss followed Rebecca words.

The base of the lantern slowly sank a little into the soil beneath it. The wick inside flickered violently to the left and then to the right before steadying itself. Rebecca slowly pulled the children close to her side. Emerging from the darkness in front of them was a giant bald man. His skin was not soft or vibrant; it was yellow and discoloured. The flesh was rotten and the smell coming from his direction was disgusting. His mouth half-opened, revealing broken teeth and a detached tongue. The eyes of these flesh-eaters carried the darkness of the night. They no longer belonged to this world and Rebecca knew what was coming.

"Children, stay strong."

With that she drove forward, pushing the children behind her. Emily took her brother's hand and they pressed together.

The flesh-eater picked up speed, sensing fresh meat. His size kept his speed down, though. Rebecca used this to her advantage. His eyes focused on the children standing by the lantern, theirs on him. As he bore down on his prey, a kick to his left leg sent him tumbling. What followed was a series of kicks to his body and head. He was not reeling from the punishment that was raining down on him, but trying to lash out and grab at any flesh available.

Rebecca had one idea in mind and knew that only destroying the head could stop these beasts. With that she launched herself in the air and came down with both feet on his head. The crunching snapping sound echoed around the chamber they were in. Emily buried her head into her brother's side.

There was no time to stop. Again, Rebecca launched herself into the air and came down on his head. The gurgling lasted a second or two and then there was silence.

Without making a fuss, Rebecca quickly gathered the children and the lantern, and continued down a side tunnel.

"Mummy, did you use us as bait?" Arthur looked perplexed.

"I had to save us; I would never use you or Emily."

He looked at the ground as he moved along, trying to make sense of this new world. The warm baths and scrumptious roasts on Sundays were long gone. This was a world of darkness and death now. He no longer knew what to wish for; his father was missing and his family clinging onto life in the catacombs under Paris.

After two hours of walking, they found a small shack in a chamber off the tunnel they were travelling down. The door could be shut and it was big enough to lie down and shut their eyes. Rebecca wanted to keep moving, but the children could not go on further without rest.

***

The backpack which Rebecca had packed ever so carefully was now pushed up against the door. Its contents were put on a small table to the side of the entrance. The blankets had been warmly received by the children when their mother produced them. It had not taken Arthur and Emily long to fall into a deep sleep. The silence in the shack was only broken by heavy snores from the children. Rebecca kept her guard up for as long as she could; her bones ached, which was not helped by the cold floor she was lying on. She had used some wooden planks for the children to sleep on, but this left little for herself. Perched up against the door, her back helped keep a constant weight there. It did not take too long for her to fall into a deep sleep.

Something moving over loose stones broke the silence outside. Rebecca came around in a flash. Her adrenaline kicked in quickly. She threw a glance over at the sleeping children. Her first thoughts were to stay still and not move. She hoped whatever was out there would just pass them by and they could carry on resting. The noise moved about the tunnel outside.

Slowly but surely, the door she was perched up against started to be pushed from the outside. It was a strong force, moving Rebecca in her sitting position. Suddenly, the closed-in shack felt like a deathtrap with no other escape route.

"Children, wake up."

Arthur and Emily started to stir. Rebecca readjusted her weight and began to dig in her heels.

"Mummy, have the monsters arrived?" Emily was holding her brother.

"Just be ready, children."

Clutching a piece of broken wood, Rebecca prepared for whatever was coming through that door.

"Madam, Madam, are you in there? It is Lauren, the French soldier from earlier."

He asked her to open the door and join the others. Regaining her composure, she relaxed the pressure on the door and allowed it to open. Her eyes fell upon the soldier. He was smiling and gesturing them to come out. The children gathered their things and joined their mother behind him. He led them further up the tunnel until they came across the group they had started with. Smiles and hugs were given out freely and it was warming for the family to feel this attention and affection.

Lauren wasted no time and told them they must push on out of the catacombs. He believed the tunnels would soon be totally controlled by the flesh-eaters.

Rebecca thanked him for checking in the shack. He just nodded his head and smiled.

Arthur and Emily had rested well and Rebecca was grateful to now finish this journey in a larger group. The other members of their party looked tired and hungry. They had not been able to sleep since coming into the catacombs.

Hours slipped away in darkness; only the flickering lanterns lit the way in the murkiness of the tunnels. Arthur's eyes watched for movement every time they came to a junction. He studied the paths that led off into different directions, and tried to keep his mind from focusing on the living dead and their unquenchable desire for flesh. He could not help but reflect on how his father was and whether he would ever see him again.

A tear rolled down his cheek; for that brief moment he wanted everything to be back to normal, back to how it was. It was hard for him to understand this new world and what was happening to it.

"Quiet!" A French soldier called out for everyone to stop and be silent.

Rebecca turned and cuddled the children. Her warmth was powerful and her motherly touch meant so much to them.

"We're nearly out, my dearest ones."

There were small discussions going on ahead. Then the call to continue moving came along the line. An older woman stumbled a bit to the side of Emily, but a younger man, possibly a former factory worker in his overalls, grabbed her before she hit the side of the tunnel.

Rebecca could taste fresh air in her mouth and nostrils. It was sweet and energising. The group was then taken to a limestone stairway. It looked strong and robust, with stairs leading up in a spiral fashion.

The French soldier, who had helped them before, had his map out and spoke to another comrade who was nearby. In French, he declared they were now on the outskirts of the city and from here they would push on out of France. The coast was the destination of choice, but these were dangerous times and every action had to be thought out.

As they all left the tunnel, Rebecca looked back at Paris burning in the aftermath of the invading forces. She glanced down at her locket – which hung around her neck – and opened it up to reveal a picture of the family. Charles was standing with them, looking smart and dashing in his Engineering uniform. She would not give up hope of seeing him again, and slowly closed the locket and led the children into the woodland they were now entering.

Chapter 2

Charles Hayward felt a sharp pain around his ribs. It was hard to move from the position he was lying in. The linen sheet beneath him was pressing against his bandages, causing a slight irritation. His eyes rolled around the room, surveying the soft blue painted walls and the white coving.

The room was fairly sparse. It had a wardrobe pushed into its right-hand corner and a small table with a chair to the side of it. Sunlight crept in through an opened window close to the bed. Its warm rays added comfort to Charles's feet.

His thoughts quickly turned away from the room. Rebecca and the children were in France and he felt a deep sickness coming over him. He felt his heart drop and a piercing pain shot through his whole body. He did remember coming back on a boat from Jersey, but his memories were all very sporadic. The true horror of Paris slowly started to flood back. It forced him to sit up, instantly making red patches appear on his bandages. He swung his legs around and used the side of the bed to raise himself slowly. The room spun for a moment or two, before the dizziness subsided.

He then stepped forward, each step carrying a small price. The pain stung, but he wanted to seek advice. As he stretched out his hand toward the handle to open the door, it started to turn. The captain stood still, almost in apprehension at what was going to come through.

"So, you're up, Charles." It was the matron.

He looked at her whilst holding his side.

"Look, I need to get back to Paris. Who is in charge here?"

The matron had already taken him by the arm and started to lead him back to the bed.

"You've only been in bed for a day or two. It will take you another week until you're up and about."

The captain sat on the bed, shaking his head.

"My wife and children are in France. I must try and find them."

The matron looked at him with sorrowful eyes.

"Captain, I'm sure the British government are doing their upmost to get as many survivors out of France as they can."

She was fluffing up a pillow behind him whilst updating him on the situation. Putting her hand behind his back, she lowered him back onto the bed. This was a painful process for the captain and he winced whilst it was undertaken.

"Your supper will be along shortly."

As she turned to go, Charles's hand grabbed her forearm. "I need to see a doctor and an officer soon." Charles's eyes carried a deep concern in them; the air in the room suddenly filled with anxiety and tension.

The chirpy matron's demeanour changed; she could see he was not willing for this to be brushed off. Looking down, she glanced at her forearm. "Please, you're hurting me."
He let go, leaving a red swelling on her skin. "I will ask the doctor to come and see you. There are no officers in the hospital at the moment, but the doctor will know more."

She then turned and left the room.

Charles had not meant to be as forceful, but inside he was a mess. Letting himself sink back into the bed, the memory of Paris came back more vividly. He saw his family in front of him, the sheer panic in their eyes. The only hope lay with them going under the church. He had not known too much about the catacombs at that time, but he had been informed more in Jersey. A doctor there said it would be possible with the right guide to escape Paris that way. It was a long shot, but it gave him something to hold onto.

He let a few tears run down his cheek. His chest felt tight, which caused him to rub it with his left hand. His emotions were getting the better of him. The question of not seeing Rebecca and the kids drifted in and out of his thoughts. There would only be one outcome. Charles glanced at his gun holster. He then let himself relax on the bed and gently fell into sleep.

Chapter 3

Two weeks passed by. Captain Hayward was visited regularly by an army doctor. He was a big man, possibly 6ft5in and almost as wide. His hair was cut neatly with a slight flick at the front, and this was complemented by a well-trimmed moustache.

He was from the North East of England and had served in India and Africa before being recalled due to the fact of the war which was taking place on mainland Europe. Many overseas forces had now been recalled to Great Britain. The problem now was the British Army was overstretched.

"Captain, you've got remarkable healing qualities."

The captain looked up, and then slowly rubbed his ribs with his left hand.

"I feel strong again. I need to return to my men and see what is happening with the war."

The doctor looked at a piece of paper in his hand and then checked a clipboard at the end of the bed.

"We've asked many of the local county halls and refugee officials for any news of your family." The tall man scratched his head.

"Nothing has come back yet."

Charles looked at him with despairing eyes. He wanted to hold onto the moment he saw them in Paris and the last image of them going into the catacombs. Charles let himself sink into a side chair, the light of a mirror on the wall causing him to blink.

"How many people have made it across from Europe, Doctor?"

"Millions, Captain. We are facing the biggest crisis since the Black Death hit these shores hundreds of years ago."

This giant of a man wasted no time explaining the problems they were having housing so many refugees, and the pending winter would prove a massive headache. Food was not stored to help this many. With so many languages and demands, it was all proving too much for the Empire to deal with. "They have come across in such numbers; we just do not have the resources to cope."

The doctor let himself sit in the other chair in the room.

"You know this will play into enemy hands." Charles tried to gauge the man's knowledge of what was coming.

"We've heard stories of monsters and the walking dead. This must be madness?"

Charles reached into his pocket and pulled out his locket. With his right-hand thumb he flicked it open. Rebecca and the children looked out from the small photograph neatly tucked inside.

"The stories are true, Doctor. You cannot imagine what is in that darkness."

Charles wiped his left hand across his face. The army doctor stopped reading the charts, and waited with bated breath, as if he were an old spinster just on the verge of finding out where the family inheritance had gone. His eyes fixated on the captain.

"It's coming, you know."

The doctor looked puzzled.

"Who's coming?"

Charles looked him straight in the eyes. "Death."

Chapter 4

Time passed as Charles recuperated in the army hospital. During those weeks, he would spend as much time as possible sitting in the rose garden sipping tea. That morning started as usual, getting a paper and a fresh pot of tea.

"Captain Hayward."

"Nurse."

"I have your release notes here. It's been a month since you've arrived and you have done remarkably well."

He thanked her for his help and finished his tea whilst watching a bumblebee land on a rose flower. After letting the moment sink in, he left for his room.

Charles gathered his clothes from his wardrobe and placed them on the small chair by the bed. A shadow started to creep in from the entrance to the room. Captain Hayward looked up quickly and relaxed in the same instance as he saw the tall, army doctor. He had come to wish him well. Nothing was mentioned about their last discussion. The army doctor went on to explain that he had requested leave for the captain, but a new Royal Engineer major had arrived on the scene from South Africa and did not grant this permission, stating that every soldier should be mobilised ready for combat. This was an order which had been proclaimed from the high command. Major Douglas Sherborne intended to get his men to honour it.

Charles bit his lip. He wanted to scour the British ports for refugees from France, but he knew that if his family had arrived in England, they would have made their way to their family home in Sunninghill. His own mother and father, and even Rebecca's father and mother, had been evacuated to America, which by all accounts was still safe. He had several letters passed on to him, written by his mother and Rebecca's father. They explained how measures were being taken to free up space because large estates and housing were needed on a grand scale to house Europe's refugees. In truth, wealthy families and individuals had a better chance to leave the country, as money would always ease their passage.

Rebecca's father had only gone after being ordered to gain support from America and help smooth the flow of refugees now flooding their shores. He wanted to return as soon as he could to help find his daughter and support the Empire against her new enemy.

The captain thanked the doctor for all his help over the past few weeks. As he left, he looked around at the room which housed him. He was glad to be leaving, but had felt secure in this small white room. The horrors of what he had seen in Europe had left him for a while there, but not the thoughts of his family's absence. He knew he had to keep a positive mind, even though dark thoughts lurked at every corner. He fantasised a little about ending his life and how he would do this. The one thing he made himself promise was to find out if they were alive first and if he could get to them.

***

Charles had a carriage waiting for him at the hospital entrance. He was handed a letter from an officer who came to see him off. He was instructed to open it straight away; it read that he had been granted several days to return home and gather his things before reporting to Aldershot barracks for debriefing. Many regiments had been moved all over the country due to the soldiers being brought back from overseas. There were also issues regarding the retreating armies of Europe, which had landed in Great Britain and needed to be housed.

Charles grabbed the side of the carriage and winced in anticipation as he pulled himself up. Surprisingly, the pain was minimal. Once he sat down, the driver gave a crack of the whip and the horses started to take the strain of the carriage, slowly beginning to pull them away. Outside, many of the large oaks around the hospital had leaves which were a bright mixture of yellow and red. Charles looked at them through the glass door window. Fortunately, the carriage was a closed one, which meant it kept some body heat in it. Charles still wrapped a large blanket around his tunic and legs. He was dressed in a parade uniform as his original attire had been thrown away in Jersey.

The journey did not take too long, which allowed him to think about his men and what was happening to them. He hoped they had been reunited with their families and were making arrangements to get them out of England. Letting his mind wonder for a short while helped time slip away. They slowly crept along the cobbled streets and empty lanes. He managed to look out at the landscape as they passed an open grass meadow. There were hundreds of tiny fires burning brightly. The cab driver almost sensed what was on his passenger's mind and said without being asked, "Refugees from Europe." This was part of the distribution of them around Great Britain.

Captain Hayward lowered himself back into the carriage seat, his eyes closing with the impact of the soft leather on his back and the warmth generated from the blanket over his knees. He knew a short nap would do him good.

Thirty minutes passed.

"Mr Hayward, sir, we've arrived in Sunninghill."

Charles rubbed his face. The sleep had felt good, but maybe not long enough. His eyes fell on the family home. It looked friendly and welcoming. The lawn was overgrown, but he knew that all labourers and gardeners would now be utilised for the war effort. Lawns were not the Empire's priority anymore.

The cab had been paid for already, but the captain gave the man a tip for the excellent service. He was helped to his door with his belongings. Once the man had wandered down the pebble path from the house, Charles turned and looked at the door. He wanted to believe that as he pressed his hand against the bronze handle, a face would appear on the other side. Rebecca would welcome him in with open arms and then the children would join them in a family embrace.

The large brass key sunk into the lock and he began to turn it. The door creaked as Charles used his body to lever it open.

Once inside, his nostrils picked up on the air smelling a little musty and he wasted no time in opening a side window to let some fresh air in. The cottage had been empty for well over a year and the housekeeper who had normally kept things shipshape may have been summoned to help elsewhere in the country.

He fumbled around finding some matches and a lantern that was tucked inside the front entrance, and with a swift strike, the match was lit and the room came to life.

Charles looked around at the paintings on the wall. There were many family portraits and pictures. He was instantly reminded of Paris and the church. Placing the lantern on a side table, he held his head with both hands and let himself slide back against the drawing-room wall, beginning to weep. It was uncontrolled and desperate. He knew that if news were to come that they had not made it, he would use his revolver. But nothing had been confirmed and whilst there was hope, he would fight every demon within him to keep going.

The grandfather clock in the hall struck midnight and a weary Charles took himself upstairs into the master bedroom. He made the bed from sheets stored in a corner cupboard and sat there for a short while looking at the clouds floating by the window. The moonlight lit up the room enough for him to see shadows dancing around. He placed his revolver to the side of his pillow and then let his eyes close.

Chapter 5

A torrent of water rushed up a gully on a small escarpment. The seaweed moved freely in its natural environment.

"My lord; Queen Oksana is waiting in your quarters."

Nazar turned from the cliff's edge and made his way slowly up a narrow path. He stopped to look out across the sea and the valley below;

thousands upon thousands of tiny lights flickered in the evening air.

"We are back on course, sire." A drone general stood in front of him, with his officer's cap in hand.

Nazar turned his head slightly. "This delay has not been good. The enemy will be reinforcing their defences for every month that passes."

Nazar's right hand lowered towards his sword. The drone general saw what was unfolding and quickly renewed his apologies and explained that he would push the men, women, and children harder to have the Armada ready for a spring offensive.

"Work them through the night; work them until they drop dead. Then feed them to the flesh-eaters." He then turned and carried on walking up the path.

The officer left Nazar's side with great purpose, knowing that failure was not an option.

At the top of the hill, Nazar focussed on his tent. It had several poles which had been made out of pine supporting its heavy canvas structure. Around the tent were several fires burning and an elite regiment of destroyer drones. They were no longer just human in appearance – that feature had gone. They were now a mixture of creature and man, their jaw lines had stretched and their noses extended. Their teeth had grown out at the front of their mouths and their hands carried nails which resembled claws. They could still stand on their feet and talk with a deep gravelly voice.

Nazar was greeted by his personal guard's commander.

"My lord, the queen is bathing and awaiting you, sire."

He flung off his evening robe and undid his belt, which had two swords attached either side. It fell to the ground, thumping into the soil. The commander nodded to two soldiers to pick up their king's garments and weapons. The tent's entrance was pulled to the side without Nazar having to change step. Inside, he undressed slowly. The guards on the entrance quickly moved outside.

Lanterns lit this huge chamber he now stood in; from there, six other entrances awaited his choice.

"My lord, you've been gone too long. Your body must rest." The voice was coming from behind a silk door hanging to his left.

"My body will rest, but first it must feed on flesh."

A silhouette of a woman appeared behind the silk drape.

"Then let us feed together."

She slowly brushed against the silk as she moved forward, revealing her naked body. The queen clapped her hands as she moved towards Nazar's.

Two elite guards came in carrying a sack, which was moving around in their grasp. They stopped briefly to cut the rope which was binding it together. One of the guards then bent down and dragged out a woman, who had been tied up. Her eyes were bloodshot from crying and sheer panic covered her pale face. Her uniform was ripped and torn. On her shoulder, hanging by a thread, was a lapel emblem. You could just make out she was an Austrian nurse.

The guards left the woman curled up on the floor. She twisted around in earnest to break free from the ropes which were binding her, but something caught the corner of her eye. She looked up and saw the queen moving towards her at speed. She was using her hands and legs as if she was an animal. The nurse stopped wriggling and let her eyes follow this thing that was now moving towards her. It was then that the queen opened her mouth, revealing large, sharp teeth, and a jaw that seemed to extend extra wide. Dripping from these savage teeth was saliva. The nurse then doubled her efforts. She thrashed around using her last bit of strength to try and break free.

As the queen closed in, a voice rose up.

"Oksana, wait."

The queen looked around on hearing her name. Nazar had stood up and moved towards her. The nurse was still fighting to get free. She felt one hand break loose and then another. The queen looked around at Nazar coming over to her. She was only metres away from her victim.

The nurse wasted no time and bent forward and released the ties around her feet. Nazar did not seem to worry about what was unfolding. As the nurse stood up, she looked around for something to use as a weapon. There was a small pole being used as a divider of fabric in the tent. She unhooked it and began to wield it in their direction.

"Oksana, I like it better when the prey fight. The meat has fear in it."

Nazar moved to the left of the queen, who now stood up. The nurse looked anxiously from side to side. She kept the pole moving in the direction of the queen and Nazar.

"Please, I'll do anything. Just leave me be."

Oksana let her oversized tongue come out of her mouth and slowly work its way around her lips.

"You are a pretty thing." Her voice had a slight growl to it.

She then launched forward and knocked the nurse backwards in the attack.

The nurse reacted as quickly as she could and managed to hit Oksana in the ribs, causing her to fall to her side. As Oksana fell, the nurse saw the opportunity to strike a decisive blow on the queen's head. The pole was swung back and brought forward at tremendous speed. An arm came out of the darkness, breaking the pole's momentum and causing it to snap in half. The nurse's eyes quickly turned to Nazar, who was smiling at her. He then leaned forward and grabbed her with his other arm, lifting her off the ground.

Oksana came around, licked the blood which was coming from her side, and let out a yelp and then a squeal of happiness.

"My dear Oksana; let's feed."

With that, Nazar bit into the nurse's chest. His teeth had altered since arriving in the tent and his jaw extended. He was now in feeding mode, and what followed was a frenzied attack on the now mortally injured nurse.

She tried one more time to push her attackers off, but they were like rabid dogs, biting and tearing at every opportunity.

Slowly the life drained out of her, as bones were broken and blood was gulped down at a furious rate. The queen looked up at her king, smiling as blood dripped down from her face. She then carried on eating.

Nazar tore off a leg and threw it out to the guards at the front entrance. There was a moment's silence, before some growls could be heard accompanying a short fight. One of them then settled down to eat the leg, whilst the other guard licked his wounds.

Nazar walked over to their cushions and bear pelts. Oksana was still feeding; her naked body was covered in blood. Nazar reached for a jug of wine and poured himself a large glass. His face twitched as it reverted back to its normal size.

"My queen, come here and let me now feast on you." He was naked and lying on the cushions.

Oksana looked up and took one more mouthful of flesh before going over to Nazar. She put her blood-soaked breasts into his chest. Lifted her left leg over his right and lowered her mouth to his. Their eyes were now level.

"You look more alive once you've fed."

Oksana smiled, snarling a little with her teeth. She then began to kiss Nazar wildly. This excited him and he pushed her back and bit into her shoulder. She let out a yelp, and then a squeal of delight. The guards outside the tent looked at each other and smirked. They then returned to face forward.

The noise coming from the tent carried over the hilltops and down onto the lower prison camps by the sea.

The prisoners were being taken to their holding pens. Some were being used for food, others for pleasure. The main bulk of them were builders for the Armada now being assembled along the French coastline.

Drone soldiers patrolled around the pens with giant wolves at their side. One of the drone sergeants made a beeline for an English soldier pen.

"Don't make me execute more of you tonight!!"

He was a chubby bald man, with a short, trimmed moustache. From his left hand, he was eating a chicken leg. Bits of food fell out of his mouth as he barked out his orders.

The British soldiers huddled together. The sea breeze licked around their torn uniforms, it carried with it an autumn chill. Mixed in with the British soldiers were Austrian soldiers and nurses. Amongst them were John and Heidi.

"Heidi, stay close."

She looked at John with adoring eyes; her uniform was worn and dirty. They had been caught escaping the final push. The captain of the Lancers had held off a large attack which had seen most of the original fort survivors from the Carpathian Mountains enter boats bound for Great Britain. Heidi, John and William were caught as the riders of the north cut them off from the boats. Fierce hand-to-hand battles raged, but their numbers were too many. John did not know if the Lancer captain survived. William had been separated from them once they were taken to the work camps. He had been spotted a couple of times by Heidi, but it had now been a while since then.

"John, my legs are so tired, I'm not sure I can make this."

John's body was nearly broken, but he knew if she were to fall down, they would take her and feed her to the long limbs or flesh-eaters. He mustered up the strength in his arms and pulled Heidi in close. Her eyes looked lifeless, her skin pale. She managed to look up at him and smile.

"Sleep standing, I'll hold you." John's words were softly spoken.

The Drone officer walked around the enclosure letting his stick rattle against the wooden stakes that were keeping the prisoners in. Two drone soldiers patrolled behind him with a giant wolf; as they relaxed their grip on this beast, it lunged forward at the British pen, causing it to shake. It took both of the soldiers to pull it back. Saliva dropped from its mouth and a rasping growl aimed at the prisoners echoed around the shoreline.

"Commander, should we not let her feed on one of these prisoners?"

The chubby officer looked at them.

"She can wait."

John manoeuvred his arms around Heidi's waist and pulled her as upright as he could. If the guards thought she was ill, or dying, they would fish her out in an instant. His eyes followed the guards as they walked around the pen and then onto the next one. Once they were out of sight, he slowly lowered Heidi down. The other prisoners began to sit as well.

Torches stood burning on each corner of the enclosure. Cinders from these rose erratically up into the night sky. They were giving off some heat, but not enough to satisfy the tired and weary prisoners. John looked around at the other captives; their faces carried a forlorn look, pale and malnourished and lacking hope. He muttered to himself and then let his head rest on Heidi's shoulder. The sound of waves brushing against the sand brought some solace.

He knew they would be awoken early and the division of labour would start. The construction delivery time had been increased tenfold. Landing ships were needed to take Nazar's army across the English Channel. He had boatyards all along the French coast. General Georgiy was in charge of making sure the deadline was achieved. Nazar had applied pressure on his officers by executing several of them. This he believed would show them there would be no room for failure.

Nazar's armies had been amassing for months now. He had vast swathes of drone soldiers and large detachments of cavalry. The flesh-eaters now numbered in their millions. Europe had been a good converting ground. They were added to with long limbs, wolves, bears, and razor tooths. All of these formed the backbone of his army. He had added other creatures, and was always looking for anything that could give him the upper hand.

Jon finally succumbed to sleep; even if it was only for a number of hours, his weary body needed it.

Chapter 6

"Welcome to Aldershot, Captain Hayward."

"Good morning, Major Sherborne."

"I hope you had enough days to recuperate at your house?"

"I did, sir, thank you."

The major looked him up and down. They were both standing in the parade square; the sun had crept around from the east and was now illuminating the light brickwork of the officers' mess behind them.

"I've heard so many things about this enemy." He paused. "I've also heard many things about you, Captain."

Charles looked at the major. He was a middle-aged man who still looked in good shape. His hair was starting to go grey in places and he had a moustache that sat on his face as if it was his pride and joy.

"It's a difficult time for the British Empire, sir." Charles was straight to the point.

The major's eyes closed a little.

"You're talking about the greatest Empire in the world, Captain. No modern army should succumb to some horde from the east."

A door opened from the officers' mess and a private started to make his way over to them. He stopped a short distance back, whilst the two men spoke.

"With all due respect, this horde has already wiped out most of the British task force sent to Europe and nearly all of the European armies. Its next port of call will be this great country, sir." The captain lowered his arm and picked up his case, which had been sitting next to a large chest.

"Damn it, man, that's a defeatist attitude. If that was the general thought amongst the men serving in the battle of Reims, no wonder you bloody well lost."

Charles knew this was not a great start and did not have the willpower to confront this issue further. "Shall we take a drink, sir, and discuss this more over a whisky later?"

The major nodded his head and then beckoned the private forward. The soldier had been standing patiently, waiting to collect the chest, which contained the rest of Captain Hayward's belongings. The captain saluted the major and then started to follow the soldier to his quarters.

"Captain, don't get too comfortable. We have a mission for yourself and your men to undertake. I will be leading it. Debrief tomorrow; 9 a.m. sharp."

He then turned and left the parade square.

Charles was fairly familiar with the barracks at Aldershot. He knew his officers' quarters would not be too shabby and he could get some hot meals served on a regular basis. There was one question rattling around in the back of his mind. What was this mission the major was speaking of?

He was shown to his quarters, which were of a good standard and looked well kept. The walls were white and the furniture a little more tailored, more like to a fine house rather than an officers' quarters. On the far-side wall across from the bathroom hung a huge painting. It depicted a battle scene from the Napoleonic era; at a quick glance Charles could see it was the Scots Greys charging a French line. Battle scenes now had a different effect on him since the war in Europe had started. He had witnessed the horrors of battle first-hand, the suffering and the despair. He saw fear and anguish in the picture now, something he had not noticed before.

He was then left to unpack and make himself at home.

Fifteen minutes had passed when there was a loud knock on the door, the sound of which vibrated around the room.

"I've brought some tea, sir, and a message from the major."

"Come in, soldier."

The captain was still unpacking his things. The NCO put down a silver tray on a small table by the window. Sitting smartly on it was a green teapot and china cup. He then picked up the teapot and began to pour out the warm tea into the cup. "Milk, sir?"

"Yes please, and one sugar."

A copy of *The Times* newspaper was placed on his bed.

"The message, sir …" The NCO almost looked a little awkward in telling it.

"Yes?" The captain wanted to know.

"You have a debrief in thirty minutes, sir."

"What?" He then looked up to the ceiling and down again.

Charles turned around and walked over to the silver tray. With his right hand, he picked up the cup. His first reaction was to move his fingers away, but they soon acclimatised to the heat.

"Shall I say you will be there shortly, sir?"

The captain nodded his head. This new major was starting to be a real pain in the arse. It made him reflect back to his good friend Harry Richmond and their last meeting at Reims. How he wished he had made it out of France alive. So many men had given their lives to help Europe fight this army of darkness that was now sweeping across its lands.

***

Captain Hayward made his way along to the major's office. To either side of the door was standing a large Royal Marine. They were both carrying rifles and brought them to the present once the captain approached the door. He lowered his left hand onto the door handle and squeezed it slowly before turning. The door did not creak as he pushed it open. A roaring fire greeted his eyes to the far left, and officers were discussing tactics in earnest to the right.

Major Sherborne came forward from the shadows.

"Captain."

"Major."

He then used his right hand to dip in his smoking jacket nearside pocket, pulling out a pocket watch.

"You're a minute late, man."

The captain looked at him with a puzzled expression.

"I wasn't expecting it to be so formal, sir."

The major turned around and walked over to a table, which was perched against the wall next to the fireplace. On it was a silver ashtray.

"Bloody hell, man, that is exactly why we lost the war in Europe with that lackadaisical approach to timekeeping."

His face puffed up. This made his moustache twitch and look larger than it was. He then knocked back the remaining brandy he had in his glass with one quick swoop.

"With all due respect, sir, this is no ordinary army. They have conquered Europe and have creatures we have never even seen before."

The major raised his right hand to stop him mid-sentence.

"I've heard this nonsense about the dead walking and eating flesh. If they've already been killed once, I'm sure it will be easy to kill them again." He let out a chuffing sound as if to reinforce his own statement.

"Well, I'm sure you will get to meet the enemy soon."

The major came in close to the captain.

"Too bloody right!"

He then went on to explain he was now in charge of a division of Royal Engineers and Royal Marines. The captain could see how this had obviously empowered him and he was now out to make a name for himself.

"Right, let's cut to the chase."

The mission was then unveiled to Charles. They had written down hour by hour how it would unfold and even had small-scale dioramas to show the ports and harbours along the French coast. They knew they could not hit all the workshops or scuttle every ship, but it would buy time for the British Empire. Captain Hayward would lead one of the small attack groups, along with the several other officers in the room. They had several ships to take them across the Channel and then they would row to the ports/harbours and cause mayhem. The navy was developing its ironclad fleet and they felt they could patrol the English Channel sufficiently to stop a major landing taking place. That being said, sabotage missions would be essential until that fleet could be ready.

Each officer would lead twenty men. They would be a mixture of Royal Marines and Royal Engineers. Captain Hayward had not had time to fully meet up with his men or get the complete story of what had happened to the survivors of the fort and where they ended up. It played on his mind constantly.

"Major, I'd like to select some of my own men to accompany me on this mission."

The major chewed his mouth. This made a sucking sound and was followed by some small clicks.

"We do not normally let officers pick and choose in a situation like this."

He then looked at the other officers in the room. A captain came forward and whispered something in the right ear of the major. He was a tall man with blond hair and an oversized moustache, which he tweaked as he spoke to the major. This young officer had menace in his eyes. Charles only heard his name once, but he remembered it. Captain Brewer.

Since the battle of Reims, a lot of the officers who wanted to move up the ladder were seeing the perfect opportunity to elevate their standing in the army and society. With the heavy casualties suffered in France, the British Army had to be re-jigged. Some units were being merged, whilst a massive mobilisation of troops was under way. This was still taking time; the influx of refugees and their need to be housed and fed was a grave concern. The government was in a fluster about the cost and keeping Queen Victoria abreast of what was happening to her country.

There were twelve different laws going through parliament about the concept of allowing foreign armies on British shores to be mobilised. It had been requested that the remaining soldiers of Europe should be formed into a European force and take part in the preparation of the defences, for the forthcoming invasion.

With the government dragging their feet, there were massive delays in organising this. Defence work had started along the south coast and partly along the east coast, but resources were under constant pressure.

Rioting had broken out in many of the large European camps. The food quota had been argued against, as they felt more food was being saved for the British people. The government was indeed holding back food, but it was only marginally allowing more rations to the British civilians.

The South Downs had a battalion of Royal Engineers based there. They were working on the hill defences should the coast fall. Sergeant Butcher was one of the soldiers in charge of a unit at Box Hill. Captain Hayward wanted the sergeant next to him at his side should he take this mission.

The major turned around and walked over to the corner of the room. Standing pressed against the wall was a drinks cabinet. He bent down and opened a small drawer. Pulling out a key, he then slid it into the lock on the wooden cabinet. Once the door was opened, he pushed his right hand inside, pulling out a single malt whisky bottle. He looked around and let out a belly laugh, before pouring himself a large glass. After that, he placed the bottle down on a table in the middle of the room.

"Gentlemen, enjoy."

He wasted no time walking over to his drawing table. Sitting quietly to one side was a teak box with a dragon pattern engraved on the lid; he flicked at the bronze catch which was holding the box tightly closed and it slowly opened to reveal cigars underneath. The major took out a cigar and rolled it between his fingers.

He picked up the box and walked around the room offering it to the officers there. When he got to Captain Hayward, he paused.

"I don't really understand why you have to have the same men as you commanded before in Europe. They failed there once, why would they not fail there again?"

He said this with a smirk on his face. Some of the other officers were also grinning. Captain Fairbrook and Captain Brewer stood either side of him. Captain Hayward took his time. He moved closer to all three of them.

"Gentlemen, I would take any of my men over a hundred that have not seen the enemy yet."

This did not lighten the mood. Captain Fairbrook struck a match and then sucked at the cigar he had just taken from the teak box. With smoke slowly wafting out of the side of his mouth, he looked Charles in the eye.

"I think you should have your own men and not risk any of mine. I've heard about your willingness to have Austrians and Prussians in your ranks."

Charles looked to the side, and then made his way to the table, where the whisky bottle was now standing. Crystal glasses had been brought out for the officers to use. Three turns to the left and the cap became loose. He rested the neck of the bottle against the glass and let the whisky slide effortlessly out. To the side of this was a small jug of water. Captain Hayward brought the whisky glass to his mouth and in one quick movement swung his head back, taking all the whisky in one go.

He put down the glass hard on the table, causing the other officers to look around.

"The soldiers who fought with me across Europe are the reason I'm here. They know what is coming to Great Britain. You will get a chance soon to prove your worth on the battlefield."

The major slammed his glass down.

"I do not appreciate your tone with my men."

Charles started to pour himself another glass.

"My tone is in response to this unnecessary dialogue regarding the soldiers who fought in Europe."

He knocked the second glass back as he did the first.

"Remember, Captain, I can have you court martialled for this outburst. Harry Richmond is dead and I'm in charge now."

With that, Charles moved forward and leaned his face towards the major's. Fairbrook and Brewer closed in.

"Harry was a friend of mine and an excellent soldier. Choose your words carefully."

The major was angry, but pushed the other two captains back.

"Maybe we have got off on the wrong foot. You can choose the men you like, but on one condition. You follow my rules and my plans."

Captain Hayward nodded his head. Major Sherborne brought his lips to Captain Hayward's ear. "You have six weeks until the mission. Get your men trained and ready to go. I do not except failure."

He told Charles he could now leave, as the serious drinking was about to start. Captain Hayward saluted the major, turned and left the room. He could hear laughter as the door was shut behind him. It made him think more about Harry and how the army was a tough world to live in. The problem was a lot of good officers were dead and the ones left in Great Britain were not experienced enough to take on this sort of challenge. The senior commanders wanted to improve their status at any cost. Politics was always waiting to rear its ugly head at any given opportunity.

Charles did not give the meeting too much more thought. Having met the enemy, he did not hold out much hope for those who took them lightly. One thing did please him and that was the fact he could get his own force together. This he knew would be invaluable in keeping them alive on the forthcoming mission. There had been rumours of Paris survivors making it to Denmark. It was not the time or the place to go AWOL, but he was keeping his family close to his plans.

The next day, the captain was up bright and early. He shaved and washed before receiving his pressed uniform from the orderly assigned to him. Breakfast was a boiled egg and a slice of ham. *The Times* paper was folded neatly to the side of his teapot. Its headlines focused on woe and troubling times ahead for the British Empire. The level of anxiety sweeping across the land was epidemic. Charles did not let himself get too bogged down in the stories. He had always enjoyed reading the news, but since his family was missing, and this ever-consuming war grew, he no longer yearned for it.

Once he had finished breakfast, he had arranged a carriage to take him to the station, and from there he would then take a train to Dorking, before being met and escorted to the defences at Box Hill.

The autumn sun bounced off the golden leaves and carried with it a solid warmth. Captain Hayward could understand why the South Downs would be a good strategic last line of defence before London. Its long line of hills acted as a barrier for the London plains and would give the artillery being manoeuvred there a real chance of hitting the enemy from distance.

Charles observed the troop movements as the carriage pulled him close to his destination. Guards were placed at the base of Box Hill. He had to show his papers before they were allowed to continue. He noticed a new machine gun to the side of the guard hut. It was slightly different to the Gatling guns he had seen before.

"Excuse me soldier, but that machine gun looks different to the Gatling gun."

The soldier looked over at it and smiled back at the captain.

"It's been upgraded, sir, it's a Maxim gun. The enemy will sure know about this if they dare to land on British shores."

He said it with a nonchalant smile and nod to back it up.

"I hope you're right, soldier."

This brought a slight disrespectful look back from the guard. The captain had seen first-hand the European firepower being slowly overwhelmed and realised that machine guns alone were not going to save this Empire.

Chapter 7

As the carriage climbed the winding road which led up to Box Hill fort, Charles could see there was a hive of activity going on. Trees had been felled to allow fresh artillery posts to be set up. Howitzers and fixed artillery were being put in place along the Downs. Muzzle-loading guns had been brought back into action in 1871. This was down to the reliability and the fact that gas breech-loading guns had been temperamental. The problems with fighting a conventional force had not really been thought out. The main campaigns of the Victorian era had so far focused on armies which did not really have the same sort of weaponry as the British Empire. This now was of course different. The enemy had heavy artillery and mortars. They also had creatures which were new to the battlefield.

The wheels came to a halt at the top of the hill. Captain Hayward did not wait for the door to open. He instinctively pushed down on the handle and stepped out. Royal Engineers were busy at work. He could not stop himself smiling when he saw an old familiar face. Sergeant Thomas Butcher. The driver of the carriage saluted him and then geed up the horses and left to return to Dorking.

Sergeant Butcher had not seen him; his focus was giving instructions to soldiers on defences around the hill fort. Captain Hayward made a beeline for him. When he was close, he just stopped. The soldiers around the sergeant left to carry out their tasks and it was then he looked in the direction of Charles.

His eyes told a story of happiness. A huge grin stretched from one corner of his face to the other. There was even a small sucking in of air through his nose and a quick swallow to hold his emotions in tack.

"It's bloody good to see you, Charles."

The captain stepped forward, breaking protocols to embrace him.

"Likewise, Thomas."

Sergeant Butcher turned and led the captain towards the hill fort. It was swarming with soldiers taking munitions and shells into it. They had also built a raised viewing point, and both men climbed the wooden steps to the top. It was a crisp morning and the sun was shining down upon them. Sitting on a shelf made of oak was a pair of binoculars. Captain Hayward could see his friend looking at them and took up the gesture to pick them up. Taking a moment or two to adjust the focal points, he looked out from the hill fort. All along the South Downs defences were being built. Heavy artillery was being moved into place. Wooden stakes were being hammered in the ground and trench lines dug around the highest points. It was a breathtaking sight as the scale of the operation was of the like he had never seen in Great Britain before.

This was going to be the last defensive line before London. If the hill defensives fell, then London would be at the mercy of the invading force.

Taking the binoculars away from his eyes, he saw Sergeant Butcher place a map on the shelf in front of him. Marked in red were Hastings, Eastbourne, Brighton, Worthing, Portsmouth and Southampton. They were the main coastal towns that would be the first line of defence. Reserve regiments were being stationed in the New Forest.

They would be used to bolster the frontline force should the coastal towns fall and need reinforcements.

"It's an impressive sight, Sergeant, but you know what's coming!"

The sergeant nodded his head.

"This sort of work has been going on for a while. The beach defensives are equally impressive." The sergeant had a positive tone in his voice.

The captain studied the map.

"If I was the commander of the enemy, and knowing the force I had, I would hit across multiple areas at once."

The sergeant and captain exchanged ideas, both of them agreeing that it was going to take a heroic defence to keep the country out of the reach of this dark force.

No one really knew when Nazar planned to invade. This was a huge concern for the government and the people of Great Britain.

Spies had been sent over to France and reports were sporadically coming back regarding the building of a huge fleet of ironclad war ships. Landing vessels had also been seen in the many makeshift docks now scattered along the French coast. Some reports even suggested docks being set up in Norway, Belgium and Spain, which sent worrying signals to the British High Command.

Everything was being treated with caution. How much was bluff and how much was real? They had heard of refugees being used as slaves and those that had a purpose – which in this case were shipbuilders – being treated better than the rest. Fear was a driving force amongst the prisoners, with first-hand accounts of thousands being fed to the flesh-eaters and long limbs. Nazar had a plan for them, and that was to get the most out of them that he could. Once they became dispensable, their fate was sealed.

The Royal Artillery were manoeuvring a field battery along the road towards the defences. Shells were being stored underground in the hill fort and would be brought to the batteries on a small train track. The track was almost the same as miners would use to dig out coal, but this track would carry carts full of shells.

The captain paused from their conversation and looked out from the hill.

"It's a beautiful view, Thomas."

The sergeant was a little taken aback; he thought about the state of Charles's mind, with his family missing, possibly dead. Then he let himself gaze out across the green patchwork fields and the golden woods, stretching as far as the eye could see.

"It certainly is, Charles."

"Captain!!" Another voice broke the silence.

Both of them looked down from the viewpoint. Standing next to an iron gate was Corporal Heinz. Captain Hayward wasted no time in leaving the fort and going down to meet him.

"Bloody hell, Heinz, you're in a Royal Engineer uniform." He said this with a huge smile on his face. "It's great to see you, my old friend." They shook hands, which turned into a spontaneous arm around the shoulder.

"If I keep on hugging men, they will ask questions on what happened in the Carpathian Mountains!" All three the men laughed. It had been a while since a good belly laugh had come out.

Corporal Heinz went on to explain that some of the foreign forces had been amalgamated into the British units. The fact he was an Austrian Engineer and served with Captain Hayward meant he was fast-tracked into the regiment. With the heavy casualties sustained in France, many thought this would be a perfect way to bolster depleted regiments. Unfortunately, this was not the case as a whole; red tape and politics were slowing down the process. Vast foreign armies that were now spread out around Great Britain were being used to help with farming or the building and maintaining of the refugee camps.

Sergeant Butcher had been lucky, as had many of the soldiers who had fought in Europe. Their families had been evacuated to America. Corporal Heinz had now been told his family would be transported shortly. Many of the refugees in Great Britain were not that fortunate. There were simply not enough ships to transport people to the United States of America – they were buckling under the demand. Money had been a lubricant, but the sheer volume was causing concern. They also pointed to the fact that no invasion had started, even if they had seen hard evidence of an armada being built.

The British Empire and Europe were running out of worthy funds, as Europe no longer existed in its old state, and there was nothing forthcoming worth trading. Diplomats were being sent weekly to convey news of the situation. Senior cabinet officials had gone over to beg for an American army to help join the British Army to repel an invasion and possibly push on to attack Europe itself. Time was of the essence.

Captain Hayward asked Sergeant Butcher if there was a place they could have a quick meeting. He suggested they take some tea to a viewpoint on the hill. An orderly was summoned and shortly after that, tea appeared with a slice of Victoria sponge cake.

"My lord, you gentlemen have landed a cushy number up here" Corporal Heinz smiled as he said this. "Tea and cake, very British."

The Austrian was taking to his new regiment well. The sergeant had tried to keep together most of the soldiers that had been with them in the Carpathian Mountains fort. The British Army had at least recognised that they had achieved an amazing retreat through Europe and wanted to keep that unit together and draw on its skills. They had drafted in new recruits for those that had fallen in battle, or were captured on the beaches of France.

The three of them sat on a bench overlooking the towns and villages below. A steam train sped by, leaving an impressive trail behind it.

"What happened on the beaches after we split up?" Captain Hayward held his tea in his left hand as he looked at both soldiers.

Sergeant Butcher stroked his beard.

"We were ambushed by the enemy, who were wearing our uniforms."

Corporal Heinz sighed.

They then went on to retell the story of how they had been awaiting a ship in Cherbourg when they were approached by what looked like a detachment of British mounted cavalry. It was a trap; as they grew closer, they saw that their uniforms were ripped and blood-soaked. Clone soldiers had been using them to carry out raids on the retreating European forces. Oksana's cavalry was now terrorising the fleeing soldiers. Her giant northern riders were mixed in with drone Lancers and mounted soldiers. She had long limbs creatures and wolves, with a detachment of razor tooths being ridden by Nazar's personal guard.

"The captain of the Lancers instructed for the women and children, including his son, to get on the boats first." Corporal Heinz swallowed saliva in his mouth as he paused. His eyes narrowed. He explained that the Lancer met them head-on in a heroic charge. His unit only numbered a few, but their skill and bloody determination saved many that day. As the fighting unfolded, the transport ship came into sight. The boats, which were being used to ferry people to the rescue ships, were now loaded with the women and children from the fort and those they had picked up along the way. The Lancer's son was on the boat, and he watched his father continue the fight as they were rowed to safety.

"John, William and Heidi were with us as we formed a line to volley fire," Corporal Heinz said. Heidi had asked for a rifle and joined the soldiers and other civilians as they looked to stop the enemy from getting to the boats.

The fighting had been fierce; the initial waves of cavalry were mowed down by the line fire, but this could not be sustained as the long limbs broke into their ranks. It became a hand-to-hand battle. The Lancers were being overwhelmed and could not retrieve their position to help the infantry. The small crumb of hope was the ship coming into sight, meaning the fleeing women and children would be rescued.

Corporal Heinz recalled how Sergeant Butcher had brought down a long limb with a lance he had taken from a fallen cavalryman. The creature had reared up on to its hind legs; in doing so, it let its stomach become vulnerable. Sergeant Butcher did not waste a moment and rammed the Lancer through its stomach and out the other side, bursting organs and ripping skin along the way. The long limb fell forward, gasping and squealing in pain. It did not suffer long as a bayonet was pressed against its throat and drawn from one side to the next.

Eventually the line had been broken, and the bugler had sounded the retreat. The only thing left to do was swim for the ship which was mooring out in the bay.

It sent a volley fire over the battlefield and into the small woodland set back from the beach. Some of the enemy broke momentarily, but were quickly rounded up by the mounted priest commanders.

Corporal Heinz had been close to the sergeant and they gathered what men they could and started to wade in the water. Rifles and kit were abandoned on the sand. Nothing of extra weight could be taken on such a swim.

Captain Hayward lowered his head, breathed in and then gently let it out. He scratched his head and asked to hear more.

Sergeant Butcher took up the story. He went on to explain that no one knew whether the Lancer captain made it. There were stories of some of the cavalry making it into Denmark, but nothing substantial. Colonel Kiesl and Captain Müller fought side by side and managed to get some of their men to safety.

"Did they make it to Britain?" Captain Hayward asked hopefully.

"Yes, they did." Corporal Heinz smiled and told him they were in a fort in Portsmouth. This brought a smile to the captain's face.

"What about Alexander Chamberlin?" There was a pause.

"Rumour has it, the sniper went back into the war zone, helping soldiers and civilians alike." Sergeant Butcher shook his head as he told him. "Brave young man that one."

Charles looked up and then back at the men. "John, William and Heidi – are they in Portsmouth?" Sergeant Butcher shook his head. "They were cut off on the beach. I do not believe they made it."

Charles took a moment; he was thinking about all of the men and women who had come so far with him through Europe, only for some of them to fall at the final hurdle. He prayed some were still alive in France, along with his family.

Captain Hayward spoke cautiously about the mission ahead. He told them that he had been chosen to lead an attack party to scuttle boats along the French coast. He needed to have about twenty soldiers to land and destroy what they could. Explosives would be provided and a new prototype rifle – the Lee—Metford. This was a magazine bolt-action firing rifle. It had eight rounds in the magazine which loaded from the bottom. It was a new design, but the captain said they would get some time to practise around with it.

He discussed the mission in more detail over the next hour and then asked if they were in. Both men had a slight look of concern returning to France, but they knew that these missions would help prolong the amount of time the British had to fortify the country.

The commanding officer of Box Hill fort had been given a letter from Major Sherborne. This had been signed from further up the military hierarchy; in no uncertain terms, Captain Hayward could hand-pick his team. The captain had asked to address his unit in the morning. There were enough survivors from the Carpathian Mountains retreat and he only wanted to take those who felt ready for this risky operation. Those selected would be given a day's rest, before embarking to Portsmouth for training. Captain Hayward had sent a few letters out since his arrival back in Great Britain. One of those was to his brother-in-law Lieutenant Colonel Adams; he had served in the Royal Engineers before being transferred to Africa and the 24th Regiment of Foot. They had seen some action in the Zulu campaign, but were recalled to fight the war in Europe. Their ship had arrived too late for them to join in the battle of Reims, so they were now helping out along the south coast.

Captain Hayward wanted to meet his brother-in-law before he set off on the mission. There were not many of his close family left in the country and Charles wanted to leave a letter for him to safeguard. After speaking to the sergeant and corporal, Charles was shown to a cabin where he would be staying temporarily.

Chapter 8

A sharp whiteness greeted a blurry-eyed Charles as he awoke in the makeshift cabin. The crisp white grass and icy wind reminded all that winter would soon be upon them. A guard called over to the captain as he passed. "Jack Frost visited here last night." Charles nodded and pulled his winter coat tighter against his chest.

After a wash and shave, he had breakfast. The temperature was rising as the Autumn sun burst through the clouds and onto the ground below. A makeshift parade square had been cleared in a patch of woodland at the top of the hill. There were wooden barracks set back from the fort and other defences around the top of the hill. Sergeant Butcher had been instructed to get the Royal Engineers out on the parade square.

Captain Hayward arrived and greeted the men. His presence was warmly received as he was an officer much respected by his men. Doctor Brown, who was with them during the retreat from the Carpathian Mountains, joined them at Box Hill. He had travelled up from London and was glad to see Charles alive.

Captain Hayward made a comment to the sergeant about how well he had done keeping them all together. He then stopped to address the men.

"Good morning, men. We've been through a lot together, and I want to apologise for not being with you on the beaches in France."

The men nodded and looked interested in what he had to say. He went on to tell them about the mission ahead and that he only wanted men who could handle going back to France; he reiterated that no soldier should feel pressurised into accepting, as the mission could be a one-way ticket. Captain Hayward explained what would be needed from them and how they would be reinforced by the Royal Marines. The decision sadly could not be dwelt on, as they would depart for Portsmouth the next morning at 10 a.m. Sergeant Butcher then announced they had until after supper to come and sign up for the mission. The first twenty men would be taken.

The soldiers then had a quick inspection from the captain and sergeant, before falling out. They had a new bugler named Jack Thornton. He was a young lad from Berkshire. Jack wasted no time at all telling the captain that his father had known his at one point when they were at school. He said that his name was getting known amongst the different classes, and the escape from Austrian-Hungarian Mountains was becoming a military legend.

"Listen, young Jack. Please remember stories become taller the longer they go on."

Private Thornton listened intently.

He told him to keep up his work with the bugle and to only sign up to the mission if he was ready. The captain whispered to the sergeant as they left for the artillery battlements that maybe Jack needed another six months before joining a mission like this. His thoughts told him he might not get that long, but the captain knew that young lads dreaming of becoming a hero often got themselves killed, or worse, themselves and the men around them.

***

Supper came and went just as the clouds passed overhead at a speed. Walking towards one of the long cabins, where the enrolment was taking place, Captain Hayward was shocked and warmed to see a queue to sign up for the mission ahead. It was nearly every soldier who had escaped with him from the Carpathian Mountains and even the new recruits. Sergeant Butcher and Corporal Heinz were allowed to whittle down this group to twenty men.

Once the selection was complete, every man was thanked for their attendance.

That night, Captain Hayward let himself relax fully. A million thoughts were racing through his head, some negative, some abstract. He saw Rebecca and the kids and their time in England. The long walks they would take in Windsor Great Park and an occasional pint of beer with Rebecca when they could get a nanny to look after the children.

He did not know if his family was still alive or not. He had a plan of what he would do if they weren't, but until he was 100 per cent sure, he would keep looking and searching. In a way, this comforted him a little. Pulling his blanket up to his face and then dragging the thick woollen rug on top of that made the bed feel very cosy. The odd cough outside could be heard, as guards walked around trying to keep warm. Even a cart passing along the cobble road near the cabins caught the captain's ear; maybe it was a farmer coming home late from tending his animals, he did not know. One thing was for sure, it all made up the evening's background noise, which helped his mind drift to happier times.

Chapter 9

The journey to Portsmouth had been smooth. They arrived in good spirits at Fort Cumberland. It was an impressive structure, a mixture between a hexagon and star, but not quite so symmetrical. Some sides jutted out, whilst others were round. The idea being it would be more robust against enemy artillery fire. Gunpowder had changed the way forts had been built and with weaponry constantly changing, new designs were always needed.

This fort was finished in 1810 and had up to eighty-one guns as part of its defence. A battalion of Royal Marines had been moved in there to man the fort. Some of these soldiers would be joining Captain Hayward's men on this mission to France.

Major Sherborne was there to greet them. He had Captain Fairbrook with him and some other officers who would be landing in France as well. Captain Fairbrook was a short, stocky man. He played rugby scrum-half and was known to be a bit of a brawler and ladies' man. He was born into money as his family owned many farms in Surrey. His brown hair was cut short and his beard was well groomed. He sought power with an unquenchable thirst

The soldiers were taken to the barracks and told to settle in before supper and an evening debrief. The Marines were welcoming enough, but they made it clear they saw the Royal Engineers as behind the scenes soldiers and not frontline. They did not realise the amount of action the soldiers had seen.

Captain Hayward went to a local inn with Sergeant Butcher and Corporal Heinz. They enjoyed a pint, before having supper. After they had eaten, Major Sherborne got the officers and NCOs together for the final mission details. He handed over the briefing to Captain Fairbrook.

"Gentlemen, we leave within a week."

Charles looked at Sergeant Butcher.

"I understand this is short notice, but the Marines are ready." He said they had been training for several months now. The Royal Engineers were there to take down what structures they thought would be the most devastating to the enemy invasion plans. The Marines would cover them whilst this was taking place.

They would travel over on several troop-carrying ships, the main ones being HMS *Orontes*, HMS *Jumna* and HMS *Apollo*. The others were smaller vessels, carrying fewer men. This fleet would be guarded by six ironclad battleships.

They hoped to sail in as close as they could without being detected and then launch rowing boats with the attack units landing and doing as much damage as possible before returning. It was pointed out that this mission was a highly dangerous one and it would leave them little time on land should the enemy get their gun batteries firing. The British intelligence had pointed towards minimal harbour and beach defensives. The enemy focus was on invading, not defending.

This intelligence did not pick up whether Nazar's army had a navy worth mentioning. The British were counting on this being the main stumbling block to their whole invasion plan. The British Navy ruled the waves and it would take something out of this world to beat them at sea warfare.

Captain Hayward would be landing in Dinard. His orders were to destroy all temporary docks and harbours in the area, basically anything that was of value to the Nazar's forces. Captain Brewer would be with him commanding the Marines. There were rumours that Major Sherborne would be joining the landings at St Malo. He would have a force that was maybe five times the size of Captain Hayward's.

The idea behind attacking St Malo was not to take the town, but to cause enough confusion that they thought the British were trying to start a land invasion. It would then make the enemy send reinforcements to this area, when in fact the sabotage missions were happening all along the coast.

The logic behind the operation was sound. Charles's main concern was about the amount of naivety coming from the commanders leading it. It was as if they had heard nothing of the horrors that had befallen Europe. It was as if the battle of Reims had been swept under the carpet and the loss was primarily down to the European armies not being good enough. Having been there, Charles knew otherwise. They had to embrace what was coming, or it would consume them as well.

The briefing went on for two hours. Maps were handed out locating the targets and sheets of paper detailing the main objectives of this mission. Training was scheduled to start after breakfast the next morning.

After a cup of tea and a full English breakfast, Charles kitted himself out in his combat military attire. He put Adams revolver in its holster and attached his sword to his belt. With a quick look in the mirror, he aligned his helmet and went outside to join his men. Sergeant Butcher had them lined up for a quick inspection. Corporal Heinz was at the end with the bugler. Young Jack was not chosen this time.

"Lads, hopefully Sergeant Butcher has given you the details of the mission." The captain went on to explain they had only a week to get familiar with the operational plans and would have to also get used to working closely with the Marines.

Captain Brewer was taking the first day. He started them off with a gruelling 10-mile hike, followed by an assault course, which finished with bayonet charges. Even the sergeant was feeling the pace. The Marines' pace was tiring, but this made sure the Engineers knew this was the level they were at.

"Your men are not as fit as I thought they would be, after surviving Europe" quipped Captain Brewer.

Captain Hayward looked at him in a displeasing manner.

"Your men haven't seen Europe yet."

Both officers stood there looking at each other.

Corporal Heinz broke the silence and informed the men lunch was going to be served.

Days two and three were focused around attacking mock-up docks and harbours on land. The Marines looked sharp in this manoeuvre, using grenades to shake up the place before firing through the window with blank rounds and storming in. There were fake bodies made out of straw for this exercise. No mock-up long limbs or flesh-eaters were made. Captain Hayward and his men spoke about the new creatures that were on the battlefield, and if the soldiers had not encountered this before, it would take them some time to adjust.

Each day ended with shooting practise. Captain Brewer was not over impressed with his own men's accuracy, as the Royal Engineers had shown remarkable skills on the firing range. Charles pointed out that nearly a year of fighting – from the Carpathian Mountains, to the beaches of France – had sharpened their skills. "Don't forget you are Engineers, not warriors like us," Brewer proclaimed.

"Obviously," was Charles's response.

"Listen here, Hayward. I'm moving up the bloody ladder, so don't try and steal my thunder on this mission. I would hate for a stray bullet to go the wrong way."

Charles moved in close to the captain.

"Before the mission is over, I'm sure you'll be praying that I help save your sorry soul from the darkness."

They turned and went back to their men.

Days four and five were now on the water. They had a small ship stationed off the Isle of Wight. It was good to spread out the different practise landings as they knew spies could be lurking within the refugees that had come over during the evacuation of Europe.

In some ways, the high command had wanted the enemy to feel that a counter invasion could take place and that they should waste time building up their defences rather than building an armada to take Great Britain.

Mock-up docks and harbours were built for training purposes along the beaches near Cowes. The rowing boats on the ship were the ones they would use to land in France. The weather was good for late November and, considering they would leave Saturday early afternoon, all prayers that were made hoped it stayed that way.

Thursday morning and afternoon they practised during daylight. Captain Hayward's and Captain Brewer's men could all fit into one lifeboat. It could hold up to 65, they would number around 60. The exercise went well, in the daytime. The men had got used to the drill, and the docks and harbours had mini explosions attached to them and were destroyed accordingly. Nothing was done on a major scale, as they did not want to attract too much attention.

Captain Hayward had asked about the sea batteries and what sorts of precautions were being taken regarding them. His answer had been that the Royal Navy had bombarded French ports several times over the last few months. Nazar's ships had come to meet them on many occasions and suffered for it. The main worry had been the alarming rate in which he could re-stock these ships, and have a reasonable crew and captains back in place to defend the next time the British Navy arrived. Nazar had also moved some heavy field guns to strategic ports and points along the coast. It was by no means a full coastal defence network, but it did offer them a bit of respite from coastal bombardments.

That evening, they attempted a raid. It went fairly well considering the winds had picked up and there was a strong current working against them. One of the main aims was to keep the explosives dry and they achieved that. Landing 500 metres further down the beach exposed what could happen. There were Royal Navy sailors used as guards along the beaches. Their role was simple, to spot an attempted practice landing. It was all done to add authenticity.

The attack still went smoothly. Captain Brewer and Captain Hayward stayed clear of each other when they arrived back at Fort Cumberland. Major Sherborne wanted to hear how the evening excise went and was very pleased to find out there were no major mishaps.

The soldiers were given some time to relax in the evening and Captain Hayward managed to sort out an evening pass to visit his brother-in law Lieutenant Colonel Adams in Portsmouth.

The town was bustling with life. Fruit and vegetables were being carted off and there was a general mood of calmness. Policemen had been given extra shifts due to the large number of refugees in the country. They had most of the camps outside the major cities and towns so to not congest the very fabric of everyday life. Charles had taken a carriage into town and went to a local tavern where he and his brother-in-law agreed to meet. Inside, a fire was crackling away in the corner of the room. Its heat radiated everywhere, instantly warming the flesh on Charles's cheeks. An Irish wolfhound lay curled up near the fireplace.

Sitting in the corner was James. He had short brown hair and was sporting a small moustache.

"Charles, good to see you."

Charles shook his hand.

"Good to see you, James."

"You look like you have been looking after yourself, James." Charles had made this reference to his physique. His shoulders were broad and forearms had veins showing.

"It's all the bloody defence work, Charles. It's non-stop." James said this with a smile on his face. "The ladies like it old, chap." he added.

They had a lot to catch up on, but both knew time was against them.

Charles let the small talk finish before informing him about the escape from the Carpathian Mountains and the demise of Europe. When he got to Rebecca and the children, James could barely listen. It brought tears to his eyes hearing about his sister, and his nephew and niece. He remarked how well Charles was doing considering he did not know the outcome of his family. Charles held in his emotions and changed the subject to the mission ahead. After discussing tactics, they spoke about James taking over the fortifications at Box Hill.

"I have a letter for you, my dear friend. If I should not return, please give it to Rebecca and the children."

Charles knew they may never return themselves, but something had to be written down in case they did. It was details of everything they would need, should he be killed in action. Charles's 'will' was already written and stored in a bank in London.

"I still hear their voices, James. I can't really get that vision of Paris out of my head."

James paused before answering.

"Do not give up hope on them yet, Charles. Rebecca was raised a fighter, and she'll die trying to save them."

Charles needed those words of comfort and they had more weight coming from her brother. They discussed the war and life before it. They did manage to laugh at some old stories of misadventure and family life. Even if it did have an undertone of sadness, there was at least also hope there now.

After having several pints, Charles knew he should be heading back. James embraced his brother-in-law and remarked that they would meet again. "Stay safe, my friend."

"You too, James."

James had ridden in on horseback and had his horse tethered locally. Charles found a cab and asked to be taken back to Fort Cumberland.

He thought about James and his family. They had been evacuated to America many months ago, and Charles did wonder in times like this how much easier it was to have a partner to share your worries and concerns with. He understood James would be missing his children and wife dearly.

With the fall of Europe came an urge for the British citizens to understand their future role in the world and what would happen to them. Many started to lean towards Queen Victoria rather than the government. She had worked with the government closely, but her loyal subjects questioned their political motives and decisions to date.

**

Charles awoke with a slight sore head. He wasn't used to drinking, but it had been worth it meeting Rebecca's brother. For a small moment, he had got lost in another world. Portsmouth's busy nightlife had helped him detach himself for a short while. He opted for another full English breakfast and a pot of tea.

Captain Brewer must have been tipped off about Charles's current state and started the day with a 5-mile march. The Royal Engineers weren't too impressed knowing that they would be doing a couple of night runs that evening.

The weather was with them, though, and the day passed without problems. The evening was not so smooth. A scuffle had broken out between a Royal Marine and one of Captain Hayward's men. A cut lip and a sore jaw were fortunately the worst of it. Tensions were rising as the mission drew closer.

To add to the woes, they were spotted landing on the beach near Cowes in training. It brought back the reality of the dangers of the mission that lay ahead. On their return, they were both summoned to Major Sherborne's office. He was waiting there, sitting in a reading chair with a glass of port in one hand and a smouldering cigar in the other.

"We can't afford any more mistakes, fools make mistakes."

The major looked down, rubbed his head and then slowly looked up.

"Captain Brewer said it was one of your Engineers that caused us to be seen."

Captain Hayward looked across to Captain Brewer.

"With all due respect, sir, it was no single man's action, we were just caught out."

The major stood up abruptly, throwing his glass to the ground, sending slithers into the air. His greying blond hair ruffled.

"This fiasco does not happen on my watch." He almost slurred his words out.

Captain Hayward snarled back. It was a moment, when a thousand thoughts sped through his mind and one of them was to strike Sherborne in the face and then tackle Brewer. Common sense meant he would face a court martial and, in this current climate, things could be manipulated to make it even worse for the captain. The course of action was to stand still and take it.

"We leave tomorrow afternoon for France. I will be landing at St Malo." As the major said this, he poured some more port into a fresh glass.

"Captain Brewer will now take full charge of the Dinard operation." Sherborne looked in the direction of Captain Brewer, who had a huge smug grin on his face. Charles shook his head in disbelief.

"I guess he'll lay down the dynamite as well?"

This brought the major in close to the captain. The alcohol on his breath wafted up into Charles's nostrils. "Don't try me, soldier. You think yourself a hero, but to me you're nothing."

He knocked back the port and slumped back in the chair, taking in a deep drag on his cigar as he did so. "Leave me now."

With that, both captains left the room. As they turned to walk back to their officers' quarters, Brewer reminded Charles he wanted his men ready by noon for them to make their way to the troop-carrying ships. Charles nodded his head. Inside himself he now feared for the safety of his men.

Chapter 10

A blackbird's dawn chorus brought Charles out of his slumber. It was a cold morning, with a light frost covering the ground and trees. Charles pulled his double blanket up to his jaw. The stubble on his chin brushed away at the tiny fibres of the blanket. The bed creaked as he moved around, making him yearn for his own bed.

After breakfast, he joined Sergeant Butcher and Corporal Heinz in the barracks. They took a walk up to the battlements at the fort. Charles explained that he did not trust the major or the Marine captains that surrounded him. They were interested in moving up the career path and would do whatever it took to get there; even if it meant getting an officer court martialled that stood in their way. He pointed to how the loss of so many good commanders in Europe had allowed the void to be filled with self-absorbed personalities. He regrettably informed them that Captain Brewer was in complete command of the landing that evening.

"Should he have an accident during the landings, sir?" Sergeant Butcher's eyes were cold and the words slipped effortlessly out.

"No, Thomas. Not unless he is trying to kill one of us." Captain Hayward did not want to go down the same line as his new commander. He told the both of them to tell the men to keep close together.

The rest of the day was spent preparing weapons and readying the kit. Bayonets were sharpened and rifles cleaned. The Lee-Metford was a new piece of weaponry. It had responded well in training thus far, the odd jam being quickly overcome. All of the Engineers were issued Adams revolvers. This was done under Captain Hayward's request. It had been met with disapproval from Captain Brewer and Fairbrook, but he had insisted none the less.

A hearty lunch was served early afternoon. The men were in good spirits, even if they knew what it was like on the other side. After lunch, a local vicar came down and blessed the soldiers. They welcomed his prayers and kind words of hope.

Outside, it had grown dark quickly, the winter's sun leaving long shadows as it sunk slowly into the earth.

The weather seemed fairly good onshore, which made Charles tick off a prayer in his mind. Their red tunics were hidden beneath sturdy winter jackets. The Engineers had been split into three groups by Charles. They still fell under the command of Captain Brewer, but Charles knew his men and wanted Corporal Heinz, Sergeant Butcher and himself leading his men.

Explosives were packed in sealed boxes. They would have to be opened with care, not just because they could all be blown to kingdom come; it was the fact that water could also stop them from igniting.

The attack groups were getting ready along the south coast. The ships were leaving from Portsmouth and Southampton.

Charles looked at his pocket watch and the picture he had of Rebecca and the children. He slid them both back into his coat pocket and prepared to board the wagons with his men. The stars were magnificent, with the odd cloud floating by. A half-moon poked its head out, keeping it from becoming pitch-black. The high command was happy there were some clouds, as a totally clear night would bring its own problems. The last thing they needed was to be spotted before landing.

The men sat quietly as the wagon trundled along towards the harbour. Some of the Marines were in there with them. The different units were dispersed between several wagons; this was to remain that way until they got to the ship. They would then go into their attack groups.

Not all expressions on the soldiers' faces were calm. Some told another story, beads of sweat dropping from a Marine who sat directly across from Sergeant Butcher. "Your first bit of action, son?" The sergeant was to the point.

The young soldier nodded his head. His face was white, and he looked like he could throw up at any moment. His fellow comrades moved him to the end seat in the wagon. The covers were on, on the wagons. This served a dual purpose. Clear nights meant the temperature was dropping fast, and the covers helped to keep the warmth in. The second purpose was not to give any spies a chance to record large troop movements. Secrecy was the key to any surprise.

As they arrived at the harbour, Major Sherborne was seen talking to Captain Fairbrook. When the wagons stopped, Captain Brewer jumped down and went over to him. Charles took his time as he spoke to men and officers under his command. He could hear Major Sherborne getting impatient, and made his way over.

"Bloody hell, man, we haven't got all day." His face was red and his breath smelt of whisky.

"I wanted to put the men at ease, sir, before we start on this precarious mission." Captain Hayward kept a soft tone throughout his discussion. He knew it was not the time to stir up a hornet's nest and it could lead to unnecessary risks for himself and his men.

"Remember, Captain Brewer is in charge of your attack group. I do not want to hear you have taken control because of his age and lack of battle experience." The major fumbled around in his winter coat, but seemed to think twice before bringing anything out. "As you say, sir." Captain Hayward saluted him, turned and marched back to his men.

Moored proudly at the quayside was HMS *Orontes*. She was a fine-looking vessel. The next hour was spent loading the men onto her.

Boats were checked and readied. The sea air filled Charles's lungs, shrieks from seagulls circling above adding to the tension. Walking up the gangway, Captain Hayward looked down below at the dark, cold water. It licked and crashed into the harbour sides. The troop carrier ship was moored firmly and only gently lifted as the water underneath it rose, and then it gently sank down again as it subsided.

A call went out for anchors to be drawn up and the ropes to be cast off. They were leaving for France. Once they were on board, they gathered in their correct groups. Captain Brewer wanted to talk to the soldiers before they took time to rest and have an evening meal. He barked out orders to his sergeant and corporal to bring the soldiers together. They gathered in an open area about fifteen metres from the mess hall. The ship was in good condition and had recently been painted. HMS *Orontes* had been used to take soldiers to South Africa and was a good seafaring vessel.

Captain Brewer looked smart with his hair freshly cut and his moustache trimmed. He had on a dark blue uniform with a red stripe down his trousers and blue tunic. "Gentlemen, it gives me great honour to lead you fine soldiers on my first mission." One of the Royal Engineer soldiers gasped, which brought a disapproving look from the sergeant of the Royal Marines.

He went on to explain what he expected from them during the mission and how even though some of them may have seen more action than him, he was a fine leader and a first-class soldier. His eyes glistened as he spoke about himself and his achievements in life. There was a hint that this mission would lead him to a higher rank. Charles could hear Major Sherborne speaking between the lines.

"Remember, Captain Hayward is an officer, who reports to me on this exercise."

Captain Hayward stood there taking the young officer's words and kept himself calm inside, even if he was at breaking point. Captain Brewer finished off by wishing them all well and saying he would see them next when boarding the landing boats.

Their journey would take around eleven hours to Dinard. This meant attacking at early morning. Some of the other attacks were planned further along the coast, their departure being delayed to take into account the longer journey to St Malo and Dinard. Simultaneous attacks would be imperative to stop the alarm and gun batteries swinging into action.

Some of the attack groups were going to target the main gun defences, but Captain Hayward thought they would be heavily garrisoned and difficult to get near.

As the soldiers broke away after the speech, the Engineers waited behind to speak to their captain. Their concerns were evident. They were deeply troubled by this young commander. His lack of experience was unsettling them.

Keeping his diplomatic head on, he wanted to make sure the soldiers knew they would be following Captain Brewer's orders, but he would be keeping check on what those were. The punishment for not following Captain Brewer's commands could be a court martial and in some cases a firing squad. He wanted them to understand he was not happy about how this had unfolded, but there was not much they could do. The advantage they had over the Marines was that they knew what was on the other side.

After the pep talk, the men went to their quarters to settle in. Supper was not going to be served until eight o'clock. Charles's cabin was next to Sergeant Butcher's, who was sharing with Corporal Heinz. The bunks were firm and the sides slightly raised to stop them rolling out on rough seas. Charles put his belongings down, and unclipped his belt and gun holster, placing them on the table bolted to the side of the cabin. His Lee-Metford rifle was placed in a gun rack, and again was fastened in tight. He took the magazine out and made sure there were no bullets in the breech.

Charles sat back in his chair; looking around at the small cabin, he thought of his time travelling by sea. He wasn't the biggest fan of the sea; he loved taking his family to the seaside, but didn't like being on the sea for any length of time. As he let his family holidays flow into his mind, there was a knock at the door. Sergeant Butcher and Corporal Heinz were waiting outside. They had a cup of tea for him and suggested they went on the outer decks to see Great Britain's coast before it went out of sight.

The steamship was making good progress; the sea was calm and the cloud cover adequate. Charles breathed in the fresh air and turned to the others, who were doing the same. Both men had a slightly forlorn look on their faces.

"It doesn't seem that long ago that we were doing our best to escape this country. Now we're going back to those things." Corporal Heinz was almost lost in own thoughts as he said this. Sergeant Butcher nodded, as did Captain Hayward.

"Stick together and we will be fine." Captain Hayward knew it was never good to make promises. This was going to be a perilous assault and should the enemy get wind of it, things could turn nasty very quickly.

The lights of Portsmouth started to fade as the ship veered around the Isle of Wight on course for St Malo. The plan was to get the ship in as close as possible, so that both attack parties could be launched. There were going to be more men needed for Major Sherborne's operation, so he would have to get the ship into a better position for that to happen. The fortunate thing was, Dinard was not too far from St Malo.

The men stayed out on deck for thirty minutes or more before coming in to have supper with the others. It was done on a rotation basis, and the Engineers found themselves eating last. It was still appreciated, as a warm broth was brought round with fresh bread and butter.

Once the last dregs were mopped up, it was time to return to their quarters before the 3 a.m. call to arms was signalled.

Charles lay on his bunk thinking about his family. He blew out his lantern and tried to get some rest.

Chapter 11

The cabin door was knocked on twice. It was his morning wake up call. He had asked an orderly to come around twenty minutes early to give him time to get himself composed and ready for what lay ahead.

Splashing cold water onto his face gave him a sharp shock. Charles had placed out his uniform and his weapons. He had the same sword which had been a trusty companion since the Carpathian Mountains retreat.

He then heard a voice at his door – it was Sergeant Butcher. Standing next to him was Corporal Heinz.

"The French coast is within sight." Corporal Heinz had two revolvers, one on each hip.

Charles looked at both guns.

"You're starting to look like a cowboy." He said this with a smile on his face.

"flesh-eaters, sir. Sometimes one is not enough." Corporal Heinz was smiling, but he had a serious look as well.

The ship had sailed between Guernsey and Jersey. That had been a precarious part of the mission as Nazar's forces had taken the islands, shortly after the fall of Europe. They had then installed gun batteries along the coastal areas. Luck and good seamanship had played its part as they slipped through. It was predicted on the return journey that they would go around as the explosions along the French coast would have alerted everyone there.

HMS *Orontes* crawled along making as little noise as possible. No one was allowed on deck until it was time to board the boats. Below deck was a mixture of excitement and nerves. The young Marines who had not seen action were expressing both ends of the scale when it came to emotion, from overexcitement to throwing up and feeling faint.

The Dinard attack group was standing ready. Major Sherborne was making quick visits to the captains in charge of the operations. The other troop carriers were hopefully getting ready for a synchronised disembarking of landing boats, for attacks on the ports, docks and make-shift harbours of: Le Havre, Dieppe, Boulogne-sur-Mer, Calais and Dunkirk.

Captain Brewer came over to Captain Hayward and asked whether he thought his men were ready. There was an air of tension as explosives were being carried up to the various groups. Major Sherborne came over to speak to Captain Brewer for a minute or two and then bypassed Charles. He did not mind as he had nothing to say to the man. His thoughts were now focussed on making sure he kept as many of his group alive as he could. The operation so far was going to plan.

A call went up for the men to start boarding the boats. Sergeant Butcher looked at Captain Hayward, and then Corporal Heinz.

"Good luck, lads."

The weather outside had changed a lot since they left Great Britain. The stars had gone and the wind was much stronger. Waves crashed into the side of the ship and she tilted from one side to the other.

"Bloody weather." Captain Brewer looked anxious as the boats were loaded with explosives and ammunition for the operation.

Captain Hayward had his rifle tucked over his shoulder. The sea spray occasionally sprayed up and coated his face. Cackles echoed around them from the gulls above, as if they could sense an easy meal coming their way.

Sergeant Butcher checked the soldiers' ammunition pouches and straps to make sure they were all done up tight and correctly. Corporal Heinz was doing the same. He had a large hunting knife strapped across his chest. The men had taken to his excellent scouting skills and good leadership under pressure. Captain Hayward was glad to have them and some of his men from the fort in Austria with him.

Either side of the ship, boats started to fill with Engineers and Marines. Once all the attack groups were loaded onto the boats, the sailors started to winch them down to the water. With the sea being choppier than when they left Portsmouth, extra care was needed to lower them in. Calls and shouts rang out as orders and directions guided them into the water.

Captain Hayward looked at HMS *Orontes* as the boats slid down her side. The wind chill brushed off the water and hit his hands and face. He glanced over at the glimmering lights on the shores of Dinard and St Malo. St Malo was a walled town and it was not part of the operation to attack it. They would need a far greater force and more firepower to overcome it. Major Sherborne was going for the gun batteries and port nearby.

Once their boat hit the water, a wave smashed over the side. It knocked several men back, but lady luck played her part and no one went overboard. Using the oars, they pushed the boat away from the ship. Once clear, the rowers began to pull forward and head in the direction of Dinard. The other boats left in different directions as each would have been given a target. It was hoped this was happening all along the French coast. The high command wanted this operation to give them more time to think of what to do with the impending invasion. They also hoped it would send a clear message not to attack Great Britain.

Half an hour passed and the beach was coming into sight. They had drifted slightly down from the original target beach, but it was still enough for them to land and make their way to the temporary docks and shipyards. The boat rode in on the waves; some good rowing skills were used to make sure the boat did not go side on and capsize. Once they were able to get into shallow water, several men jumped out and helped guide the boat in. Then all personnel disembarked.

Captain Hayward shivered as the cold water went up to his waist. The sand sunk a little under his boots as he made his way out of the wash. They pulled the boat onto the beach and then dragged it to a collection of rocks inland, so as not to give its location away. The tide was going out, which meant they did not have too long, as they would have to drag the boat back to the water to get back to the ship.

Captain Brewer led the men from the boat and towards their destination. Three guards had been left behind to protect the boat.

There were no camp fires burning at the beach they had landed at. This was a good sign, as it allowed them time to get up the beach and into the surrounding fields. The makeshift docks and shipyards were east of their current position. Once they had made their way into a field which bordered the beach, Captain Brewer called the group together. Lookouts were placed at the four corners around them. The light was adequate enough for them to see what was going on. They knew their eyes would adjust after thirty minutes.

"Men, we will now split into two groups. I will attack the docks and shipyards to the east and Captain Hayward will take the ones nearer to Dinard." As he spoke, a thunderous explosion happened in the distance across from them. The attack around St Malo had begun.

"We must move now." Captain Hayward was forceful in his statement. Captain Brewer was not happy with his forcefulness but knew time was of the essence.

Before they got up to move, a hissing, groaning sound crept through the long meadow grass, a distinct rotting smell following with it. The spine-tingling noise was all too familiar to the Engineers, but the Marines wore a puzzled look, one of trepidation and anxiety. Captain Hayward looked over to Corporal Heinz; he slowly withdrew his hunting knife.

Captain Brewer held the men back and waited.

"What is it, Captain?"

The noise was drawing closer.

"It's the new enemy. It's a flesh-eater." Charles kept his voice low.

There standing on the edge of the beach was a wretched soul. The eyes were sunken and the body twisted. Parts of its torso had been eaten, probably before it changed. Its teeth were sharp and larger than normal, the nails on its hands long and curled. The rest of its body was a mixture of rotten flesh and shredded clothes. The creature's breathing was erratic, up until it tilted its head to one side and spotted the men. Then it twisted on the spot and started to come at them. The speed increased the closer it got to its intended victims.

With the creature transfixed on the soldiers, it didn't see Corporal Heinz come in from behind and he stuck his blade into the oncoming flesh-eater's head. Blood splattered from the wound, sending the head tumbling to the floor. Corporal Heinz did not take any risks and stuck the blade into its skull again to make 100 per cent sure. As he pulled out the blade, he wiped the fragments of flesh and hair off onto the creature's clothes.

"Remember, there are worse things than flesh-eaters out there. Be on your guard."

Captain Hayward led his men away. Captain Brewer stood still for a moment, as if he now realised the enormity of what lay ahead.

Sergeant Butcher looked back, and then after a short time saw them move on to their targets.

Charles kept the men moving at a reasonable speed. Explosions in the distance meant the action had fully kicked off in St Malo. There were also rumbles from further east. This was hopefully a good sign, and that everything was moving in the right direction.

Corporal Heinz went ahead. Captain Hayward brought the men to a halt; they had ventured a little further into the fields adjacent from the beaches. It was a network of small fields and hedgerows in Brittany, which had its own merits and failings. Whilst they waited, a wagon appeared on the horizon, and it was going at some speed. A Marine in the captain's group looked up and reached for a grenade. Sergeant Butcher shook his head.

"Don't bring the whole world down on us yet, laddie." His voice was calm and controlled.

The wagon veered off down a lane which was around 100 yards away. Corporal Heinz appeared out of the shadows. "I've seen the target, sir." He pointed in the direction of a stony outreach. The rocks there rose proudly from the ground and jutted out towards sea.

"What sort of numbers, Corporal?" Charles needed as much information as possible.

It was reported to be around forty drone soldiers, a handful of flesh-eaters and two tethered long limbs. They had a small field cannon on a rotating turntable at the top of the hill overlooking the dry docks and harbour. He also saw behind stacked sandbags an unarmed machine-gun nest.

Captain Hayward called the men into a circle. He spoke to them about attacking from the top of the hill downwards. Corporal Heinz was to take the machine-gun nest and Sergeant Butcher would come in from the west of the dock. He would come in from the east. Grenades could be used, but with caution.

Bayonets were fixed and the men crept off into position. Sergeant Butcher shook his old friend's hand. "See you on the beach, Captain." He smiled back in return, responding, "You will, Sergeant."

They had taken out their pocket watches and allowed all attack groups five minutes before commencing operations.

Charles had ten men with him: five Engineers and five Marines. Knives were to be used where possible. Two guards came into view as they moved down an escarpment. A Marine and Charles moved in behind the men, who were looking out to sea and chatting away. Using his knife, he brought it quickly into the ribcage of one of the guard's and with his left hand covered the drone soldier's mouth. The Marine did the same to the other guard. They both fell softly to the ground. Charles looked down briefly at this man he had just killed. Death was something he never took lightly.

A shout then called out from close to the machine-gun nest. The docks and harbour now burst into life. Drone soldiers were coming out of tents and rushing for their rifles. The British soldiers were in place to open fire on them. The Lee-Metford rifle gave them a chance to lay down a constant fire. The bolt-action rifle with magazine gave them eight rounds before they had to reload.

The sights on some of the rifles had been adjusted slightly, as the aim seemed to veer to the left in early tests. The thunderous claps echoed around the enclave. Drone soldiers were knocked over when hit. The larger .303 round had a devastating effect on the body of its victims. Some lost arms; others had ribcages ripped open and bones shattered.

Sergeant Butcher and his group came around the other side; soon they were in the thick of it. Charging down from their position, they were now in the dry dock, fighting hand-to-hand through the half-built boats. It was not totally going Captain Hayward's way. Some of the enemy started to get themselves in cover and returned fire. Two Marines were hit and one Engineer.

Corporal Heinz had overpowered two guards who were rushing towards the machine-gun nest with his small unit. They then brought the gun into use. The drone soldiers further down in the harbour were now trying to release the flesh-eaters and two long limbs. Before this could happen, the crackle of the machine rained down terror on its victims below –cutting through the closely bunched flesh-eaters and killing instantly the two long limbs where they stood.

"Charge!"

Captain Hayward led his remaining unit down the slope into the harbour. The machine gun was now turned to face a section of drone soldiers holding out in two wooden cabins. Again, the rapid hail of bullets tore into the buildings. Grenades were then thrown from Corporal Heinz's men onto the smouldering remains. The explosions shook the dry docks and harbour.

Sergeant Butcher moved forward slowly. He had a Marine to his left and an Engineer to his right. A drone came out of the darkness and swung his knife at the burly sergeant. Blocking it aside with his rifle butt, he then brought the butt around and impacted it into the side of the attacking drone's head. This sent the man flying to the floor; once he was down, the sergeant stuck the bayonet into his stomach. The drone let out a gasp and blood came out of his mouth and through his teeth. The sergeant then withdrew it and stuck it into the drone's head.

The Marine next to him gave him a look as if to say "That was over the top," which the sergeant could see.

"They come back if you don't."

The Marine looked puzzled and the sergeant didn't have time to explain more.

"Stay close, men." He then instructed the Engineer to plant the explosives.

Captain Hayward had come down from the slope, treading carefully so as to not fall on any loose rocks or broken ground. They then began to dart in and out of buildings to make sure there were no enemy soldiers in there. A drone soldier ran from a stack of planked wood and towards a sandy path leading out of the dry docks. Charles pulled the rifle into his shoulder, and pushed forward the bolt, sending the round into the chamber. He then looked down the sights, breathed in and squeezed the trigger. The drone fell. His body twisted and rolled down the slope a couple of times before coming to a halt in long meadow grass.

All the men had been advised to shoot or use a knife to the head of a dead drone soldier. If they did not do this, the drone would come back as a flesh-eater.

Charles sent an Engineer to finish the job. The remaining pockets of resistance started to come out with their hands held up. Their sergeant had been killed and their commanding officer was away at another coastal dry dock. They were quickly rounded up and taken to a wooden storage shack. Corporal Heinz was checking the hill tops for movement – the explosions and gunfire would bring in reinforcements. The idea was to destroy what they could and move on to the next target.

A Marine came forward and asked what they should do with the prisoners. He hinted at executing them, but Captain Hayward said they would be left in the shack. Sergeant Butcher gathered the men together, whilst the captain and several Engineers finished laying the charges. The wounded were moved up the hill and assessed. They had lost five men in the attack.

Unfortunately, the dead could not be repatriated. It troubled Captain Hayward as the bodies were gathered and put in the buildings. He knew they could not take them back, but he couldn't help but feel for them and their families.

Once this was done, fuses were lit and the men retreated to the machine-gun nest. The sound of cracking, splitting wood and disintegrating brick filled the air. All the men ducked down, and then felt the debris fall from the sky onto them. Charles told them they could not wait around. They left with a fiery backdrop behind them. The drone soldiers were still in the shack; it was intact and locked down.

The Marines in the group looked at Charles; they had now found a new respect for this Royal Engineer captain. There were three wounded soldiers to go back to the boats. This would take three soldiers to help them back. The ten men left would now move to the next dry dock and harbour.

Corporal Heinz was sent ahead to scout around. They kept close formation as they moved along the beach path. The grassy sward around the path had been eaten down by grazing cattle. Private Calvin Jones was a Marine who had been put on point. He had been in the Marines for two years and this was his first real combat role. The lad was 20 years old and was of medium build. His height had led to him being selected as a front-row forward in rugby. Calvin had tried to grow a beard before leaving on the mission, but it wasn't the time to really get anywhere with it. The other Marines in his unit pointed to his brown hair and reddish-brown beard. He then trimmed it down to support a small moustache instead.

His orders were to keep an eye out for anything that looked like the enemy. This made him a little on edge. When a silhouette appeared on the horizon coming towards them he brought the unit to a halt; it stopped and moved behind a hedge. A deathly silence followed for a second or two.

"Corporal Heinz here." The corporal was taking no chances and announced himself before approaching the unit.

He was given permission to come to them, and when he did he went straight to Captain Hayward.

"They're starting to reinforce the whole area, Captain." Corporal Heinz was concerned about the number of enemy soldiers arriving near the beach. The unit crouched down, whilst the discussion went ahead.

"I'll go with six men and the rest of you head back to the boats." Captain Hayward didn't want to risk any more lives. In the background, more explosions and loud bangs filled the night air. The whole of the French coast was coming alive to these attacks.

He asked a Marine corporal to lead the men back. Sergeant Butcher & Corporal Heinz would come with him and three others – two Marines and one Engineer – with explosives. The night sky was starting to lighten. Dawn was creeping in.

The smell of burning wood and gunpowder lingered around them. Charles took his smaller unit a little further infield, as the beach path was now seen as a route the drones would use.

Throaty coughs and growls lurked in the hedgerows. Charles warned the other men that long limbs were close. Private Jones took deep breaths as they moved along. He was originally excited about the mission, but it was now proving to be something he could never imagine. The creatures he had heard of were worse in the flesh than people spoke of.

Chapter 12

Fifteen minutes passed until they arrived at a thicket of trees. They had been advised by the corporal that on the other side lay a dry dock and small harbour. Drone soldiers were moving past, and for the first time since they landed, they saw riders of the north. These giant men and oversized horses looked very impressive. Tied together behind them were ten or more long limbs. Their stretched bodies, giant claws and human-like heads stood out. Private Jones was shocked by their teeth and ghastly-looking eyes.

Charles kept all six of them laying low. To be seen now would mean death.

The group of riders passed off down the track, taking with them their long limbs. Charles waited five minutes before getting the small group to move. Their next task was to sprint across an open field to get to a patch of scrubland; this would then give them cover to observe the dock and harbour they were about to attack. They left one at a time. Sergeant Butcher went first; seeing his silhouette move across the field and then slink down into the bushes and long grass made them all hold their breath. Captain Hayward said he would go last.

Captain Hayward watched young Private Jones race across the field. He had his rifle covering his run. Once he was across, Charles put his rifle over his shoulder and got ready to go, but something didn't feel right. Letting his hands slide down his body, he twisted his torso around. Eyes, yellow eyes, 10 feet or more away from where he was crouching.

The rifle was over his shoulder and his Adams revolver was sitting in its gun holster on his right-hand side. He thought about how a gunshot would bring the world down on them, but he also knew that whatever was in those bushes wasn't going to just go away. The next moment sent a chill down his spine – teeth; a jaw opened up revealing long canines, and its head started to emerge through the gorse bushes. It was a giant wolf; it snarled as it moved forward, saliva dripping from its mouth and the moonlight exposing its strange yellow eyes.

Strapped across Captain Hayward's back was a large knife. He had his sword, but there was not time to move for that. The creature now came closer, 12 metres, 10 metres, 8, 7, 6, 5, 4, *KAR-BOOM*. The wolf's head violently swung to the side as half its face exploded. Hair, teeth and segments of skin and bone shot onto the long grass surrounding it.

Standing in the shadows was Private Jones. His Lee-Metford rifle was smoking.

"I've never seen a wolf that big!"

The captain got to his feet.

"The creatures that now stalk Europe are a lot different than before."

"We must keep moving; noise will bring in the flesh-eaters."

Both soldiers moved across the open ground. Charles paused a second before entering the thicket. "Thank you." Private Jones nodded his head.

Sergeant Butcher had a concerned look on his face. He had started to go back when Private Jones did not come over. It turns out the young Marine had seen something in the corner of his eye that had made him wait in the middle of the field. Then the growls had drawn him in, and he couldn't believe his eyes at first. The wolf was maybe three times its usual size. The way the creature was lowering its body and almost crouching gave him an indication he was going to pounce.

The private could not directly see Captain Hayward, but he knew he would be a target. He thought about the flesh-eaters and how only head shots could kill them. Then he took a risk and shot the wolf in the head.

Bugles started to call out around them; the enemy were moving in.

A stroke of luck came the men's way as they moved from hedgerow to hedgerow. There, underneath a large oak, was a wagon and two drone soldiers. They had with them several tied-up civilians. The drones were busy cooking sausages and did not seem to focus on the bugle sounds. The captain looked at Sergeant Butcher and Corporal Heinz. Within a flash, they were over there and seized the moment whilst one of the drones relieved himself. Both drones were silently dispatched with. "Quickly, two of us must change into the drone soldier's uniforms." Captain Hayward dressed as one of them and Corporal Heinz the other. The corporal knew a bit of Russian and they hoped that would help if they were stopped.

The other four men climbed into the back of the wagon. There were sheets to hide under, accompanied with water barrels and other food items. The civilians were set free. None of them really knew what to do at first. Charles spoke in French to see if he got a response. One of them was a local farmer; he said the whole coast was full of monsters. Charles told them to make for Denmark if they could; there was apparently a camp there. They asked if they could come with them, but the captain said it was too dangerous. If they were caught with foreign soldiers, death would follow swiftly.

The local farmer said to the captain that he would lead the civilians to a safe house for the night, until things died down, and then they would take their chances. With that they darted off.

"Have your revolvers ready men." Captain Hayward then climbed next to Corporal Heinz. The fire was left burning, but the food had been given to the civilians. The Engineers with the explosives sat tight. The plan was now to get into the camp and sabotage it from within.

"We have around an hour before dawn, Captain."

"God willing we'll be on HMS *Orontes* by then."

The wagon trundled down a small lane towards the dry docks. Campfires were burning and there were drone soldiers scouting around the hill tops near to their position. Corporal Heinz brought the wagon to an abrupt halt; 12 metres away was a small field cannon. It was manned by six men. To the left-hand side of them was a priest commander, and to the right was a razor tooth tied to an ash tree. This giant beast was asleep, its colossal frame taking up a large area around the tree. Each claw stuck out from beneath its fur. The teeth in its mouth protruded out and looked jagged and sharp, hence the name razor tooth.

Captain Hayward held his breath. This was all about holding their nerve. Soon they would enter the hornets' nest.

A drone officer came over to the wagon and called it to a stop. He was a big man, with thickset shoulders, and hands the size of paddles. Luckily, he was on the side of Corporal Heinz.

"You're late," bellowed the officer.

"The whole area is crawling with British." The Corporal put on the best Russian accent he could.

"What are you bringing into the camp?" He started to move around the wagon, looking at the wheels and checking the canvas cover. The men inside started to feel the tension. One of the Marines next to Private Jones started to lift his body and Adams revolver; before he could move, a hand stopped him. Sergeant Butcher did not say a word, just held his hand on the soldier's arm.

As the officer made his way to the back, Corporal Heinz jumped out and came around the other side. "I might have something that will interest you." Thinking on his feet, the corporal reached in the back of the wagon and pulled out a bag. It was full of tobacco. "This was taken off a dead general in Austria." The officer looked at it, half interested and half not. "Give it here." Handing over the bag of tobacco, Corporal Heinz pulled down the canvas a bit at the back.

"These are South American leaves." He was very pleased.

The corporal now told him it was meant for a priest in the camp, but he believed the priest had since left to join the soldiers on the front. The discussion had worked a treat; all the officer wanted to do now was to go and smoke the tobacco. His ushered them in.

The wagon rolled past the guards and slowly into the camp. The camp was three times the size of the last one. Drones were moving everywhere. In pens were hundreds of flesh-eaters.

"You just saved our skins there," Captain Hayward said under his breath.

Just as they were leaving the checkpoint a voice rang out. "Your wagon wheel on the back left-hand side is slightly loose." It was the officer and he walked over to Captain Hayward's side. Corporal Heinz translated what was being shouted before the officer arrived. The captain then got down from his seat and looked at the wheel. The officer followed him. He stood over his shoulder talking. Captain Hayward did not say anything. He could not understand a word he was saying. "Are you listening to me, soldier?" The officer started to get irritated. Corporal Heinz jumped down and came around to them. "He's got a hearing problem. A shell in the battle of Reims." The officer did not look impressed. "They should have let him turn then," he said, walking away with a smirk on his face.

Both men climbed back into the wagon. Charles blew out his cheeks. "This is going to have to be a quick attack. They will soon figure out something isn't right." The corporal agreed. They steered the wagon down to the dry dock. There, sitting in the wooden runners, were ten landing boats. They all had sails and looked like they could carry a fair few soldiers or flesh-eaters. None of the vessels looked like they would be used to travel too far, but the British mainland would be an achievable target.

Charles directed the wagon to what looked like a storage area. There was a stable and haystacks, with only three noticeable drone soldiers working away. He told the corporal to distract the soldiers and he would move the wagon into a discreet position. Charles knew that they needed some more clothes or overcoats for the other British soldiers to be disguised in.

Corporal Heinz came over. "The drones have gone for a break; I said we would cover them."

"Great work, I've found some overcoats in the stables." Charles ushered the corporal to the back of the wagon. They passed the coats underneath the canvas sheet and told them to get changed quickly. Each man appeared wearing a long overcoat. It did the trick; helmets were left inside the wagon. The brief was to "set the explosives" and get out of there.

Private Jones was standing with the other Marine on guard by the wagon. They were told to look busy if they could. If spoken to, they would need to come up with a plan. Corporal Heinz had found out from the three drones that there were rumours some of the European prisoners had been half-infected and offered the chance to fight for Nazar. They would have to pass as British soldiers who had joined the enemy. No numbers were given of converts, and no concrete evidence, so caution was advised.

"We must leave within fifteen minutes, dawn is coming." Captain Hayward abruptly closed his pocket watch.

They did not have enough explosives for all ten ships, so they chose to blow up the ones in the middle and hope that would damage the outer vessels as well. Corporal Heinz was tasked with setting some charges around the harbour. They knew it may not destroy it all, but it would take time to mend.

Placing the explosives in the joints and areas that were supporting the boats was tricky. They didn't have too much time and once the fuses were lit they would all need to be on the move and get back to the wagon and leave. They had agreed on ten minutes before lighting the fuses.

Captain Hayward found a barrel of grease they were using to ease the runners underneath the boats. He thought it would help burn once the bombs had gone off.

Five minutes passed.

Three …

Two …

One …

He then lit the fuse which was connected to all the explosives. Charles knew he did not have much time now, and as he walked at a brisk speed to the stable, he heard a voice call out.

"They should have let you turn." Straight away he knew the tone of the voice, even if he did not know what he was saying. Charles carried on walking, but the officer followed him, talking away as they went.

A hand grabbed the captain's shoulder. He turned around to see the drone officer from the checkpoint standing there with a bottle of wine in his left hand. He looked drunk and was aggressively prodding the captain. It was only going to be seconds before the explosives went off. Reaching behind his back, the captain unsheathed his knife and in one fatal swoop brought it forward and into the officer's chest. Blood came out of his mouth and he fell forward, dropping his wine bottle in the process. His eyes had a moment of shock in them before closing.

Charles lowered him down, but as he did so the explosives went off. It shook the whole area. The noise deafened him, and debris slowly came down from the skies. Clang, clang, clang, a warning bell started to ring. The enemy were now pouring out of the tents, and cabins further up in the camp. Charles was a little dazed as he took a moment to adjust himself, and in doing so he did not notice the one job he had forgotten to do. The officer had changed quickly due to being half-infected. His left hand twitched and then his arm moved. His yellow eyes opened, and there was only one thing he wanted to do now and that was feed. Pulling himself around, with the knife still stuck in his chest, he managed to move up on top of Charles.

His strength shocked the captain; the flesh-eater tried to bite at his face and slowly lowered his snapping jaws towards his throat.

Charles could see drone soldiers coming his way with bayonets fixed, but this was the least of his worries, as the flesh-eater now reached millimetres from his nose. He was stuck; to wriggle more could allow the creature to get the telling bite, and the reality of the situation was compelling. He prepared his strength for a massive roll, but as he did so a bayonet came into the side of the flesh-eater's head. Standing over him was Private Jones.

"That's twice now, Jones," he quipped. The captain was helped up to his feet by the private.

Smoke was drifting across the camp from the burning boats and harbour. The initial outlook was good, maximum damage had been done. It was now about getting in the wagon and trying to escape.

All six of them made it back to the stables. Captain Hayward breathed a sigh of relief for that. He instructed them that they would try the same routine as they had done getting in, and four of the soldiers crept into the back of the wagon. Corporal Heinz sat again next to the captain. Drone soldiers were now swarming by the boats, trying to put out the fires. Then a sight they did not expect to see unravelled in front of them. French soldiers were being led down to the fires and used to help put out them out. They were prisoners from the invasion of Europe.

The men looked forlorn and tired. Many were malnourished and staggering, as if they were flesh-eaters.

Captain Hayward tried to look around at the enemy numbers and whether they could help them in any way. A quick snap of the reins and the horses jolted into action. The wagon rolled past the prisoners as they were being whipped and forced to extinguish the flames. Many were too tired to continuously pass water buckets in a chain that had been formed from a well. Those that fell over were shot or thrown to the long limbs.

Five of these large beasts had been brought down as extra incentive for the men to carry out the operation without fail. Corporal Heinz looked at the captain; it was a telling look of guilt. Their actions had caused for these retched souls to be mistreated in this way. Many of them would be suffering along the French coast and that would also include British soldiers.

The wheels kept on turning as they slowly approached the checkpoint. With all the commotion, no one had asked them why they were leaving. The guards now standing there were more focused on what was out in the darkness. A priest rode past with several giant riders of the north. A formidable enemy and someone Charles did not want to engage again in a hurry.

Both the wagon horses came to a halt at the checkpoint, and one of the horses snorted and shook its head. A guard, which had been focusing his attention outside the sandbanks, came down from his post.

"Why are you heading out when the whole coast is under threat?"

Corporal Heinz leant forward.

"We have supplies for other camps and must leave to help them." The corporal knew that they had loaded the wagon with enough items to carry this lie off.

The guard scratched his head. "I still don't get why you would go out now. Wait for an escort."

Captain Hayward started to reach inside his coat. His right thumb felt the Adams revolver handle and began to withdraw it from its holster. As he slowly got ready to shoot the guard if things turned ugly, Corporal Heinz stopped him. His conversation was getting quite animated. This was broken by a loud clap and boom. One of the fires had reached a small arms depot and it was now going off.

The guard seemed agitated by this; he lost his focus on them and waved them on. It was a lucky turn of events and Corporal Heinz sighed this time as they passed the cannon and checkpoint guards.

"Where should we head to, sir?"

Charles did not hesitate to instruct the corporal to make for the beach. It was time to head home after completing two successful missions.

"We will keep everyone in the back as it may help us pass more checkpoints."

They agreed to inform the other soldiers shortly of their plans. The track was quiet as they trundled along, and daybreak would soon be upon them. They stopped briefly to inform the others and then rode on for twenty minutes. Occasionally they could see movements in distant fields; each one was treated with caution. Whilst drone soldiers might be fooled, giant wolves, flesh-eaters or even bigger creatures would not be.

"Captain, stop the wagon." The corporal whispered this.

They came to a quiet standstill. Captain Hayward didn't say anything, just held the reins tight.

"They're moving this way." The corporal looked straight ahead.

Charles knew he had to think on his toes. "Go ahead and see how many. We might have to make a break for it."

The corporal grabbed his rifle and snuck out the side. As daylight broke, there had been a turn in their fortunes. Menacing dark clouds gathered over the coast and rain began to fall in earnest. The wind lashed at the covers on the wagon. Charles put his revolver next to him on the wooden bench.

Moments passed and Sergeant Butcher spoke through the canvas asking if they should disembark. Captain Hayward said they had to hold tight as Corporal Heinz scouted ahead.

Four minutes ticked by. Water ran from Captain Hayward's head and down his nose. He opened his mouth and had to spit out the water, such was the downpour now.
A patchwork of hedges broke the line of sight in front of him. The dark clouds kept visibility to a minimum and the rain made him blink if he looked straight ahead.

Then the bushes started to move to his right. He leaned over to grab his revolver, but a voice shouted in English not to move. It had a slight Austrian-Hungarian accent. Emerging in front of him was Corporal Heinz and dozens of British soldiers. Next to him was Major Sherborne. Following close behind was Captain Brewer and Captain Fairbrook. The officers made straight for Captain Hayward.

"Dammit man, the boats had to leave, we're in trouble now."

The major's helmet was covered in blood, his face bruised. He leant against the wagon as the other British soldiers formed an outer defensive perimeter. "Get that stinking uniform off." His breath reeked of alcohol.

"With all due respect, sir, we needed to disguise ourselves to escape our situation." Captain Hayward was firm. He then told his men to come out of the back of the wagon, in their British uniforms. He took himself down from the seat and both Charles and the corporal went to the back of the wagon to retrieve their uniforms. After changing, they gathered their equipment and rifles and joined the officers.

"We must move inland." Charles was insistent.

"Inland there are more of those bloody monstrosities." The major had a small map of France, and he asked for a candle to be lit inside the wagon. Then he asked Brewer, Fairbrook and Charles to join him.

His two captains looked a little forlorn. It was as if they had heard about the monsters in fairy tales, and today they finally met them. Major Sherborne was agitated and turned over a supply box, sending apples rolling across the wagon's wooden base and out of the back of it. He gave a quick description of how the action had unfolded in St Malo. The fighting had been ferocious and many men had died. He believed it had been worth it, though, as they had managed to destroy a dry dock and harbour.

There was a knock on the back of the wagon. "Flesh-eaters, sir," Private Jones said, whilst gasping for air, after running with the message from the guards on lookout. Major Sherborne did not answer, just kept on looking at the map.

"Tell the men to fix bayonets. We must try and make as little noise as possible." Charles took the situation by the scruff of the neck.

Reluctantly the major turned to Captain Hayward. "What do you suggest then?"

Charles brushed his stubble with his fingers. "We can head inland half a mile or so and then try and find a vessel to escape back to Great Britain on." Captain Fairbrook nodded his head. This was not appreciated by the major and Captain Brewer.

Gravely voices and lowly murmurs filled the air. "They're closing in" was a shout that rang out from a marine further ahead.

Major Sherborne did not seem to lose focus as the fighting began outside. He pondered over the map and brought the candle closer so that he could see where they should go. Captain Hayward drew his knife as the men sat inside the wagon.

"We should split the force," said the major, who looked happy with his suggestion. Captain Brewer and Fairbrook agreed but Captain Hayward did not. "Surely we stand a better chance if we stay together?"

The major began to close the map and blew out the candle.

"You wanted to go inland, then do it!"

Charles felt anger and frustration creep over him. "Alright, then we should move now."

As he lifted himself up, an arm grabbed him. "Don't get caught, we will not be waiting for anyone." The major had a stone-cold look on his face as he said this.

The new plan was to make it to a bay near Saint-Lunaire. Captain Hayward was to have the remaining Engineers and a couple of Marines.

Outside, more and more flesh-eaters were working their way through the hedges, which were fortuitously acting as a defence, but sheer numbers and weight could not stop these creatures from pushing through the hedgerows.

Sergeant Butcher was in front alongside Corporal Heinz. They had a good bayonet action going on, killing as many as they could. Two Marines further down the lane did not have as much protection, and once the flesh-eaters encircled them, screams and cries for help echoed around the position. The sergeant and corporal tried to fight their way to them, but the feeding frenzy had already started. Flesh and skin were being bitten into; everything was under attack. As the men began to be torn apart, Sergeant Butcher had one chance to kill both men. He did not miss. The gunshots rang out, which triggered the other men in precarious positions to start shooting as well.

Private Jones came alongside the captain. "I'm with you, sir." The captain nodded his head. "Get the men falling back. Tell Sergeant Butcher we have to leave before more of these things turn up."

They formed a line and began to unleash a volley of bullets. The noise was deafening, but it had the desired effect of thinning out the flesh-eaters. The major wasted no time after that and gathered his men and moved them off down the track. Captain Hayward rounded his men up and began to cut across the fields.

Chapter 13

"My lord, sorry to wake you on this stormy night, but we have been attacked along the coast." General Georgiy looked sheepish as he moved through the poorly lit tent. He came to a standstill when his feet touched something. Looking down, he saw the remains of a body. Half eaten and still fairly fresh.

"Darkness, General, darkness is all around us." The voice was rasping and gravely.

Nazar moved into the soft light being emitted from the lantern. His eyes were semi-closed. "What news do you bring me of the British?"

General Georgiy had aged in this campaign. His balding head was greyer and his beer belly more round. The weight of Nazar's expectations played on his mind, as he knew failure was a friend of death.

"My lord, we have been attacked nearly along the whole French coast; some reports have come in suggesting Holland as well."

He stood upright as he said this, as if to give off a more dominant stance. But Nazar moved in close to him; the carcass of the dead nurse squelched under his weight, crushing bones as he moved forward.

"Are they invading?"

The general felt sweat coming down his forehead. "We do not know yet, sire."

"You come into my tent, wake me with this news and yet have no answers?" Nazar's voice started to rise. The destroyer drone guards began to growl outside.

"Please forgive my lack of knowledge, sire." He lowered his head, fearing the worst.

Nazar gathered his robe and proceeded to move towards a cushioned bench. The wind howled outside, swirling and biting at the tent's poles. The corners needed to be fastened down again. Oksana was still asleep as the two men carried on the conversation. "Bring in the map of the coast." He wanted to view the points of attack and whether reinforcements were needed at key areas.

Nazar ordered the map to be placed on a table. Both were brought in by his personnel guards and placed in front of him. "Gather the other generals, Georgiy, we must prepare."

Within the hour, most of the senior officers had arrived. Explosions were going off in the distance and flashes of light illuminated the sky.

First to enter the tent was General Tarasov. Six-foot five and as broad as an ox, his beard was long and hair dark as the night. "My lord." The general bowed his head. "I have brought my regiment with me." He was told to stand and await the others.

The next general to arrive was Eltsina, a strong, powerful woman with a division of long limbs under her. She had been building her force to assist with the invasion of Great Britain. Her long, blonde hair added to her beauty, and even infected she still carried a sultry aura around her. As she entered the tent, she bowed to Nazar and then went and stood next to General Tarasov.

General Georgiy entered with four priests. They all bowed, but it was Alekseev, a priest from the high council, who came forward to speak.

"My lord, we believe it was a mission to sabotage our docks and ship-building capabilities," Alekseev said with confidence.

Nazar pondered over the map in front of him. As he did so, Oksana came from behind the silk curtain. Her eyes fixated on Eltsina. "Good evening, my high priestess." Eltsina was polite and lowered her head.

"Eltsina, since Europe has fallen, I have become your queen. Never forget this." Oksana did not like competition and a beautiful woman was a threat to her.

A young priest, who was amongst the four that entered earlier, saw his chance to speak to Nazar himself. "My lord, will this not delay our invasion?"

Nazar stopped reading the map. His eyes rolled, showing yellow in-between the pupil and outer eye. "It has hardly helped, has it?"

The silence that now filled the tent was deafening.

To compound this question, the young priest frantically thought of another one. "Your leprosy has gone, my lord?" He was shaking as he said it. "Some say it's the human flesh that you now consume, that's beaten the flesh-eating disease you had."

Nazar turned around to the young priest and smiled, before withdrawing a knife he had hidden in his robe and bringing it sharply across the priest's throat. For a split second it was as if nothing had happened. Then the blood began to gush from his cut jugular and his eyes filled with panic before he fell to the ground.

"Does anyone else have anything to say on the matter?" Nazar wiped his knife on the cloak of the dead priest. He then called for his destroyer drones to take the priest's body away and burn it.

The generals were now looking at each other. The three priests stayed quiet. It was only Oksana who slid in close to Nazar. She stood alongside him.

"My lord is tired; he is tired of your failings." She looked at Eltsina in particular.

Nazar ordered his generals to capture as many of these invaders as possible. He also wanted to know of his brother's army in Holland and whether they would be ready. Lev had not been seen for weeks. They were then dismissed.

General Tarasov spoke with General Georgiy as they left the tent and made their way to their escort. "He is becoming more dangerous day by day," Tarasov said, also commenting on his increased powers and how some priests were able to grow limbs to their bodies and become larger creatures at will. He wanted to know what was buried deep under the monastery in Russia. Was it the source of their power? Could there be a cure for this illness now inflicted upon them? General Georgiy stopped his colleague by putting an arm across his chest. "Be careful about what questions you ask, Tarasov. He may choose not to have a drone army one day." Tarasov nodded. "When the time is right we will talk more, but that time is not now." General Georgiy then left his side and made his way over to a carriage which was waiting with an armed guard.

General Tarasov looked back at the tent and then at the small fire to the side of it. He could make out the silhouette of a burning body. It was enough to send him on his way.

Chapter 14

"There is a farmhouse across the field. It looks deserted," said Corporal Heinz.

Captain Hayward had thirty men with him to escape France. Most were Engineers, whom Major Sherborne no longer saw as being as useful as the Marines. Private Jones was one of the Marines who had opted to stay with the captain.

The weather was still in their favour, as the dark clouds continued to suppress the morning light.

The group moved as one across the field. They were spread out in case of enemy fire. They approached a hedge outside a farmhouse with caution. The hedges along that part of France were a mixture of hawthorn and blackthorn, mixed in with beech and other bushes, and were very difficult to get through. Most had been added to the top of stone walls and grew from there. This gave the hedges a fair height, which was good for cover, but hard to break through.

The men fanned out alongside the hedge. Sergeant Butcher was at one end and Corporal Heinz at the other. Captain Hayward held the middle. He waved the men to go over the hedge, or in many cases through it. This was precarious, as they would be vulnerable should something be on the other side. Charles put his Lee-Metford rifle over his back and withdrew his revolver. Pushing through the shrubs, his eyes and ears looked and listened for anything that was not his men. A bird shot out in front of him, calling as it went. With his hand on the trigger, he released his grip and breathed.

Sliding down the other side, he found himself in a farmyard. It looked empty and lifeless, as if the owners had long gone. A cart still containing old hay lay overturned and the barn doors looked like they had been smashed open. There were no bullet marks in the buildings, so he deduced it had not been fought over. The other men joined him along the hedge line. Sergeant Butcher brought around the left flank and Corporal Heinz the right.

They gathered to the side of the house, with two lookouts posted either side. The farmhouse oak door was slightly ajar. Its stone walls and windows still looked intact. The plant pots to the side of the windows had dead flowers in them. A stony silence surrounded the whole property.

Sergeant Butcher came over. "Do you want me to go in, sir?"

There was a pause from Captain Hayward. "I'm not sure we should go in." He was still thinking as he said this. "Tap on the door gently." The men were ordered to spread themselves around the farm. Six of them waited outside the farmhouse entrance as Sergeant Butcher knocked on the door. "Remember, men, to use your bayonets if possible."

They waited for a second or two. Nothing! A Marine wanted to go inside and check out the building. Then, very slowly, a hand started to pull at the door. A shuffling, deep groaning voice could be heard coming from the other side. The door began to open, revealing a half-eaten man, with rotting flesh hanging off his body.

He could possibly have been the farmer, his eyes sunken and teeth chomping. His tongue came out, almost tasting the air.

"Let it come out," Captain Hayward told the Marines.

It began to come towards the men, and once it realised there was a meal to be had, its speed doubled. Private Jones was his intended victim. Stumbling down two large stone plinths, which had been used as steps at the front door, it quickly pulled itself up and moved towards the private.

This was as far as it got. Three bayonets slammed into the flesh-eater's head. It gargled a little before sighing and collapsing on the floor.

"Pull the door to, we will keep moving." Captain Hayward had changed his mind about going inside. He felt it was not the time or place to take risks.

The soldiers checked their weapons and began to move out. Corporal Heinz took point as they moved along the fields.

The rain and wind were coming down hard. Time was now against them, because the morning light would betray them. Charles gathered the men under two large oak trees. Its leaves had long gone, but it acted as a wind break. The branches still shook and twisted in the strong gusts. The fungus at the bottom of the tree looked impressive; its mass had spread around the base and looked to be making headway up the trunk. Charles looked at this disease, and thought about Europe and how it was now under a new ruler. Monsters now roamed these lands and maybe his family were still on these shores. So many questions he could not answer, but for now he wanted to get his men home.

Corporal Heinz appeared. "We're in luck." He had spotted a small dry dock with several vessels and only a handful of drone guards. There was a word of caution, because on the other side of the hill was a much larger encampment. The corporal added that he had not seen the major and his men.

At this point in time, no one knew whether the troop carrier ships were still off shore or whether they had already begun their journey back to the British mainland.

"We will take those vessels and set sail. If we're lucky, we'll meet up with a troop carrier." It was a risk, but Captain Hayward knew they had to do something before being found. The whole coast would be teeming with giant wolves and long limbs, and it would mean only one outcome then.

He split them into groups of five. An open farm field stood between them and a passage home. The animals that would have been in the field were either dead or had escaped during the evacuation of Europe.

A small fishermen's cottage lay at the bottom of the track down to the harbour. It was all about timing now. Even with the events unfolding along the coast, not all drone soldiers seemed to be on full alert. This was the time to strike.

The attack group spread out. Captain Hayward would lead the assault with his men against the fishermen's cottage and Sergeant Butcher would pick up stragglers. As far as they could tell, there were only two guards patrolling outside.

The Marines were tasked with taking them down. They moved swiftly using their knives to dispatch these unsuspecting victims. The bodies were dragged into the undergrowth.

"Wait for the grenades to go off, then we rush in." Charles knew that the noise would bring attention to their position, but it was about taking the men out and getting the boats and leaving.

A Marine knelt underneath a small cottage window, his back pressed against the cold stone wall. He had two grenades in each hand. Captain Hayward would strike a match and light both fuses. A third Engineer provided cover whilst he lit the match and then lit both fuses. The Marine waited until both were fizzing and then stood up and threw both grenades through the cottage window.

The men covered their ears in anticipation of the explosions that were coming. The house shook with each grenade. Charles lifted his revolver and led the three of them to the front door; the other two men in the attack group took the back entrance. Smoke escaped through the broken glass windows and damaged front door.

"Now!" Captain Hayward kicked the shattered door open. A wounded drone stumbled towards him; he did not hesitate in squeezing the trigger on his Adams revolver. The bullet hit the soldier in the chest. His next step was now weakened and his right foot hit a small table which was in the entrance. He fell forward, hitting the ground hard. Captain Hayward could not waste time and put a second bullet in his head. Stepping over the body, they moved into the house.

The two soldiers burst in from the back entrance. The scene that greeted them was destruction. Each grenade had made short work of the men inside. They had all been eating and drinking at the time and were taken by complete surprise. Some of the drones that were dead, but had their bodies mostly intact, started to change. Captain Hayward had spoken about the drones changing quicker as they were already infected.

He urged the men to walk around and check the dead soldiers. Several gunshots rang out as they finished off the would-be flesh-eaters.

A warm cauldron full of soup had miraculously survived the explosions. A Marine looked at the captain, who nodded it would be fine to taste. The soldier dipped his finger in for a moment and then brought it to his lips. His face lit up with delight as he tasted what they had been eating. It was also followed by a stooping of shoulders and a numb look on his face as he realised he would not be able to spend time eating it.

With a waving of his revolver, Captain Hayward moved the men out of the cottage. Sergeant Butcher said there had been no movement outside when the explosions went off. They filtered down to the dock as quickly as they could.

Two boats were moored, tied to the dock; both would be capable of taking a good number of soldiers to Great Britain. They were a mixture of sail and steam. Each boat had a rotating gun on the front and looked as if they were having armour plating put along the sides.

"Check the boats and prepare for the major and his men."
Charles wanted to give time for the major and his soldiers to have a chance of finding them.

Corporal Heinz left to scout over the hill, as the adjacent camp could hold a considerable force. It was thought that they would send a reconnaissance force to check out the noise. Private Jones reported back to Captain Hayward that flesh-eaters were coming across the fields about a mile away; he said they were numbering hundreds, if not a thousand souls. His face depicted the horror of this sight.

"It's a horde, that's what our Prussian comrades called them when they grouped together." Captain Hayward said this whilst taking his helmet off.

"Do we have any sighting of the major and his men?"

"No, sir," Private Jones answered.

Sergeant Butcher came over to them.

"Sergeant, take ten men and see what we can do to block the track down to the dock."
Charles's mind was racing with all the obstacles he now faced.

This was compounded further when Corporal Heinz returned, slightly out of breath and with sweat running down from his forehead. "They have British soldiers as prisoners close to the beach," he said.

"The major and his men?" Captain Hayward looked at the corporal.

"No, I think they're from the original task force."

"How can you be sure?" Captain Hayward asked.

"Their uniforms look worn and dirty, they've been there a while."

"Have scouts been sent out yet?" The captain wanted to plan for everything.

"Not yet, sir."

The men looked at each other and then waited on the captain's orders. With flesh-eaters closing in, and prisoners in the next valley, decisions had to be made.

"I have a plan. We must act now."

Chapter 15

Flesh-eaters were starting to appear in small numbers at the top of the hill. Sergeant Butcher told his men to roll over two carts and moved some corn sacks to act as a barricade. He then gave the order to hold their fire.

These creatures began to pick up speed with the smell of fresh meat. Some were dead drones that had come back, some included French, British and Prussian soldiers. Most were unfortunate civilians. There was no priest to guide them and they moved as a swarming mass.

Captain Hayward used the Marines he had with him to help with the boats. Most of them had sailing experience and were strong, hardy men. It would need a group effort to get the boats sailing out. His plan was simple. Start a diversion at their current location and draw the forces from the enemy camp in the adjacent bay over to them. They would then set sail and rescue as many of the prisoners as they could.

Things were going according to plan. Charles checked his pocket watch. Daylight was here; the murky wet morning was now breaking away and the sun was starting to show itself.

"Captain!"

Charles looked to the west as an Engineer ran over to him. "It's Major Sherborne. They're coming our way."

He thanked the soldier and told him to meet them by the sea path.

Sergeant Butcher looked over to Charles. The flesh-eaters were now upon his frontline.

"Take aim, men!" shouted the sergeant.

"FIRE!"

Baaabbaa boom. The 303. cartridges propelled out of the Lee-Metford rifles slamming into the oncoming flesh-eaters. They had been told to go for head shots, and the first volley was very effective. Ten flesh-eaters were flung back with the impact of the heavy round, sending skull and flesh pieces backwards from this walking army of death. This was only temporary, as their numbers were streaming forward. The sergeant gave the order to fire at will and fall back as they did so.

Charles could see the major arriving with his force. It was heavily depleted. It only took a few minutes for them to arrive at his position. Charles had his revolver in the air, waiting to help with the defensive line which was now falling back.

"Bloody well done, Captain." These were the first words to come out of Major Sherborne's mouth. His men looked exhausted and were carrying a few wounds. Captain Brewer and Fairbrook were bringing up the rear.

"We've lost a few men on route. Looks like your inland suggestion was the way to go after all." He said this while wearing a displeased expression.

There were around thirty-five to forty of them. It was not the time to discuss what had happened, as the flesh-eaters pushed through the barriers across from where they were standing.

Charles had checked that each vessel had a rowing boat on board and that they were of good size and could hold up to sixty men each. He did not have time to put forward his plan to the major, as they joined the line of soldiers. This enlarged unit began to lay down covering fire. The increased firepower had an immediate effect. The Lee-Metford bolt-action magazine rifles came into their own. Instead of re-loading after each shot, they could carry on firing at will. This sent down a wave of bullets into this hungry, encroaching horde.

Flesh-eaters were torn to pieces, losing limbs and huge chunks of skin and bones from their bodies. Blood was scattered over the track and the meadow grass beside it. "Fall back slowly, men." Captain Hayward took the initiative to begin the retreat. The major was reloading and firing his revolver as he retreated. He was a good shot and made sure his bullets were hitting the flesh-eaters in the head.

Corporal Heinz had taken five men and was on a small bank to the side of the dock. They began to lay down fire from a higher position. The impact of this heavy fire gave the retreating soldiers time to regroup. The flesh-eaters were still streaming forward, but not in sufficient numbers to break the line, and there was a larger group further back on the track. It would only be a matter of time before they reached them.

Captain Brewer stood alongside Captain Hayward. "You've got lucky here." He looked back behind him at the boats. Charles did not respond; instead, he ordered the first unit to board the boats and take up firing positions on board.

Three Marines who had been fighting to the side of a storage hut got cut off from the main group as the soldiers began to file onto the boats. Charles saw this and tapped Private Jones on the shoulder. "We must help them." As the captain said this, a hand came across his chest.

"There is no time; we must push onto the boats. You can't save them now." The major looked at Charles. Captain Brewer and Captain Fairbrook were at his side. The number of flesh-eaters was swelling and the soldiers broke from firing and filtered onto the boats. Whilst there was covering firing from the boats, it was not enough to stop the increasing flow of flesh-eaters.

Soon the three Marines were surrounded, fighting with every last ounce of strength they had, swinging bayonets and using their side arms until the bullets ran out. Corporal Heinz's men on the bank tried to lay down supportive fire, but they too had to leave their position. A vast number of flesh-eaters with the sharp, claw-like hands and teeth that could tear through clothes and skin were upon the three Marines. One of the three fell onto his knees as he was bitten multiple times. Screams of agony rang out. His two fellow comrades tried to help, but were overpowered. The feeding frenzy which followed was overwhelming. Arms and legs were bitten and flesh began to be torn off. Intestines were pulled out and internal organs scattered over the ground. Teeth that could snap through bones were upon them.

Cries for help and muffled pleas were lost as the creatures devoured their helpless victims.

"We could have saved those poor souls." Captain Hayward was losing his usual control.

"This is a war, man." The major took a second to breathe. "Men die."

The boats now had flesh-eaters staggering along the sides, their hands scraping against the wood. Supporting fire was focused on the Marines casting off the ropes; they quickly scrambled back on board after the vessels had been set free. Corporal Heinz and his men made it safely onto the same boat as Sergeant Butcher, Captain Hayward and Major Sherborne. Most of the Engineers were with Captain Hayward, and the other boat had the Marines with Captain Brewer and Fairbrook.

Sergeant Butcher had a blank face when he looked at the major. Charles could see his eyes focusing on the officer and his hand slowly moving towards his knife.

"This mission is not finished yet, sir." Charles spoke out as the boats began to leave the dock. The sails took them clean out with a soft breeze aiding their plight.

"What do you mean?" He looked puzzled.

"There are British prisoners in the next bay, and I intend to rescue as many as I can."
Captain Hayward leaned in closer to the major.

The major turned towards Captain Hayward. "I'm in charge here, Hayward, not you." He pushed past him to give out the orders to the rest of the men. As he did so, a hand came across his right arm, then his left arm. "What the hell are you doing?" His face was full of rage. "You'll swing for this."

"We have a duty to try and get some of the prisoners; you can stay on the boat and help out here." Charles was calm and to the point. "Take the major below and guard him." An Engineer looked at the captain. "Do not worry, soldier, you will not pay for my actions."

The ship was brought around to the next bay with the second one following. The plan was to use captured drone overcoats to disguise the men as they rowed into the shore and do a lightning raid; they scanned the beach using binoculars. The main tents for the drones were placed higher up on the hill. Enemy movements seemed to be soldiers moving inland, probably to investigate the opposite bay. There were guards on the beach and several lurking around the sand dunes, but their numbers were not too heavy. In one corner were four giant wolves and one razor tooth. Its huge frame was tied to a tree and was currently standing sniffing the air. The creature's distinctive teeth could be seen with the binoculars. They prodded out like tusks, and had an air of menace around them.

With no time to spare, the rowing boats were lowered. Captain Hayward and Corporal Heinz were going to land with five men each. Sergeant Butcher was left in charge. The other boat sailed further out to sea and dropped anchor a mile or so out. They must have been questioning the decision for the other boat to stop.

Rowing hard, the two smaller boats approached the beach. The guards did not seem to move forward; they continued to patrol up and down and amongst the sand dunes.

The pens in which the prisoners were being kept were closer to the sand dunes. One of these was full of British prisoners. Unknown to the captain was the fact that Private Brown, Heidi and Private Clegg were in these pens.

One soldier was left in each boat as they hit the beach. The soldiers climbed out into the cold water and followed the captain towards the pens. The problem was how far they could get without being stopped; Corporal Heinz could probably only get them so far with his Russian, but the daylight would start to give away their fresher faces, and their uniforms did not match fully the drone attire.

The sand compressed in with each step as the tide was going out. Captain Hayward had given instructions for the soldiers to have the rifles over their shoulders. He had also told them to have their revolvers ready. They had enough ammunition for a short raid, but should it turn into a gun battle, they would be in trouble.

Corporal Heinz led from the front.

They approached the first pen with caution. A soft breeze swept across the beach, the grass on the sand dunes blowing gently in this flurry of air. A guard came over to where they were standing; he looked at the soldiers now in front of him.

"Why are you landing on the beach and not coming along the tracks?" His eyes shifted around the different men. He looked down at their uniforms and then at their faces.

"Say nothing and you'll live." Corporal Heinz had one hand out in front of him in a calm manner.

"ALARM!" were his last words.

The corporal brought a dagger from behind his back into the guard's chest.

"Men, release as many as we can and get them to the boats!" shouted Captain Hayward.

The lock on the pen was smashed off with a rifle butt. Two Engineers moved into the pen, and the prisoners were a little taken aback with this sudden development. John woke Heidi by softly brushing her cheek with the corner of his hand; she was tired and weak, but looked up at him. "We're being rescued," he said. She smiled at John as he took her in his arms. The two Engineers helped them to their feet and moved the prisoners towards the pen gate. *Boom,* as a bullet rattled one of the wooden posts supporting the enclosure.

Captain Hayward told the other two soldiers with him to lay down covering fire. He ran over to another pen, and this time the prisoners were on their feet. There was a mixture of civilians, and French, Prussian and Austrian soldiers.

As John and Heidi moved along under fire, John saw Captain Hayward rushing around freeing men and women. He smiled and almost lost himself for a second as a tear rolled down his cheek. A bullet crashed into the ground, throwing up sand next to them, and it brought him back to his senses.

Corporal Heinz had seen more movement from the top of the hill. The forces up there were now in full swing. A clean shot hit one of the Engineers in the head. He fell back, with blood seeping out from under his helmet. A couple of British prisoners collapsed under fire as they moved; some could be helped, others were fatally wounded.

The two rowing boats were loaded swiftly with the weary prisoners. The soldiers guarding it looked at the captain, who ordered the rowing boats to set off.

The two ships at sea waited and watched on anxiously. Sergeant Butcher went quickly below deck to check on the major. As he did so, Captain Brewer had launched one of their rowing boats and landed with a small party of men on the sergeant's boat. The Engineers were caught off guard. Private Jones tried to raise the alarm, but was silenced by a revolver at his head.

Sergeant Butcher came up from below deck to see the ship had changed hands. Brewer had his revolver drawn and ordered him to surrender. The major was freed and he instantly came up to top deck. Drawing his sword, he put it to Sergeant Butcher's throat. "Should he not face a court martial, sir?" Brewer said, as all eyes were now on the major.

"I've just decided." He smiled. "Death."

He drew back his sword.

Sergeant Butcher looked him in the eye.

"Major, we have boats arriving starboard bow."

The prisoners from the beach helped pull the boats in close. This moment made the major hesitate. He then spat on the deck next to him and withdrew his sword from the sergeant's throat. "You might have escaped death today, but you'll swing once we're home." He said this to the sergeant as he walked over to where the rowing boats were now rubbing up against the side.

"Help these wretched souls onto the boat." The major made it look like he had ordered their rescue.

At the edge of the beach close to the sand dunes there were now four of them shooting at the drones on top of the hill. There was a third pen full of prisoners further inland, but they needed the boats to return to help the final escape.

Taking cover behind boxes and barrels stacked in the sand dunes, Captain Hayward and Corporal Heinz took shots at the enemy above.

"Once the boats start their return journey, we can free the final pen." Charles looked at the corporal as he said this. Bullets whizzed by and flung into the sand around them, sending small particles into the air. The crackle of wood splitting echoed around, as more and more bullets smashed into the temporary shields.

"Captain! Long limbs coming from the other bay," an Engineer shouted out, whilst pointing in their direction. Sure enough, pushing through the waves and partly in the wash, were a pack of long limbs. They were being led by a priest on horseback.

"Corporal, cover me. I will make a dash for the third pen now."

"Yes, Captain." Corporal Heinz took aim with his rifle and shot at any puff of smoke from the hillside. Ammunition was starting to run low and it was now or never to free the final pen.

Charles made his run in a zig-zag fashion. The enemy rained down fire upon this sprint. He threw himself behind any cover he could find. Sinking in the soft sand, he used a tuff of marram grass to hide his position. With a final push, he ran towards the pen; sand was jumping in front of him like small explosions.

The pen was being shot at before he even managed to get to it. The prisoners inside were trying to take cover the best they could but several had been hit. Their worried faces looked on at the captain as he smashed open the lock. They began to pour out, but for a moment were caught in no-man's land. Three were killed moving about in the open. Captain Hayward pointed towards the beach, but as he did so he could see a detachment of giant riders pouring along the sand dunes on the far end.

"Where are those boats?" he screamed out in desperation.

Some of the prisoners scattered and ran into the dunes, some of the European soldiers who had been in the pen crouched down the best they could. Drone soldiers began pressing through the dunes. Captain Hayward lay in the sand, pulling his Metford rifle into his shoulder, checking his sights and then breathing out. He squeezed the trigger, causing an advancing drone to collapse in a heap.

"We must fall back to the sea." He did not know whether they understood or not, but pointed that way. Charles led them the best he could from dune to dune. Corporal Heinz had killed three long limbs with head shots as they came in from the right. The two Engineers were doing the best they could with the soldiers on the hill and the approaching giant riders.

Huddled together around bullet-ridden barrels and boxes lay the group. There was no sign of movement in the sea. Charles thought about whether they could swim out and hopefully get picked up halfway, but too many of the prisoners looked sick or wounded.

It was the last stand.

"Check your ammo, men, and pick your shots," said Captain Hayward.

The major turned to the men on deck.

"Bring up the anchor, they are without hope now."

Private Jones came forward. "They are still fighting on the beach, we could come into the shallows and they could swim for it?"

Major Sherborne moved in close to the private. "You could be facing the gallows for the mutiny earlier." He then paused. "Take him with the other soldiers below deck."

Captain Brewer had brought more men from the second ship to help out with the prisoners and help sail the ship back to Great Britain.

Heidi and John were below deck resting. "I want to see if William and the others are on board." He gently rested her against a sack of grain and went up some steps to the top deck. He could not see Sergeant Butcher or any of the other men he knew from the fort in the Carpathian Mountains. His concerns were raised as a private was led past him with his hands tied. The Marines just told him to stand aside.

John searched the deck for an officer and saw Major Sherborne.

John saluted the officer. "Excuse me, sir, but we still have some men missing." John was looking a bit bedraggled, weak and pale. The major looked at him. "Captain Hayward betrayed his country; he tried to disobey my orders." He wiped his brow with a handkerchief. "The enemy will carry out the queen's duty for us." He then pushed past John.

"Sir, the captain just saved our lives." He said this with an honest look of concern on his face.

"What is it with you Engineers who fought with him in the Carpathian Mountains?" The major was looking a bit bemused.

"How did you know I was with him in that fort?" John asked, forgetting rank and etiquette for a moment.

"Because you're all so bloody loyal." He then turned and walked over to Captain Brewer. "Get this ship moving!" he growled. "They'll have artillery on us soon. And take that private and put him with the others." He paused for a second. "He'll swing for treason, too."

John was shocked and astonished with the major's command. He could do nothing as two Marines grabbed him by his arms and escorted him below deck to where they were keeping Sergeant Butcher and the other mutinous soldiers.

Both ships began to turn and head back for Great Britain, their sails picking up on the wind and lifting them up and along.

Captain Hayward and the others looked on in dismay. He scanned the horizon for possible escape routes, but this idea was lost in what he saw. Everywhere was now crawling with drone soldiers, priests and long limbs. The group circled together; some were wounded, some dying. Captain Hayward felt a tap on the shoulder. "Captain, it's Private Clegg, sir." The captain lost his train of thought for a second. "William? Is that you?" His face broke into a smile. "Yes, I wanted to say earlier, but it's been a bit hectic, sir." They both smiled.

Captain Hayward reached down and took out his revolver. He spun it round and handed the gun handle to him. He then ordered the other remaining soldiers to give their revolvers to the able men amongst the group. Corporal Heinz crawled over to Private Clegg and the captain. He managed to shake Private Clegg's hand, and said, "My God, it's good to see you, William." William nodded his head; he was weak and exhausted, but wanted to go out fighting.

The gunfire came to a sudden halt. The silence was painful as it swept along the beach and into hills and valleys beyond. The enemy began to advance at a slow speed from all angles. Their numbers now covered every escape route.

"If this is the end, men, let's make it a good one," Captain Hayward said, pushing forward the breech rifle bolt, slamming a .303 bullet into the chamber.

Striding through the wash on both sides were long limbs; they were also coming down from the hill and through the sand dunes. Their jaws open, teeth showing, they pushed on like an irrepressible flood. Charles and his men could not see any priests or drone soldiers, only these ungodly creatures.

The long limbs with their overstretched gangly bodies were now within shooting range for the rifles. "Fire at will, men," Captain Hayward calmly said. Four shots rang out and four long limbs collapsed with ruptured wounds. It did nothing to stop the advancing masses.

The wounded prisoners without weapons clenched their fists. Bayonets were handed over to those who could stand and fight. The beasts began to pick up speed; the soldiers began firing at will. Long limb after long limb came crashing to the ground, their bodies falling in an undignified way, blood spurting out of the heavy wounds inflicted by the .303 round.

Twenty metres, 15 metres, 10 metres, 5 metres …

They came from all angles. The soldiers did their best to stay as close to each other as possible, but these beasts were powerful. If they went on their hind legs, they would tower over a man at nearly twice his size. On four legs, they would be compared to the size of a polar bear, without its body mass. With razor-sharp claws and savage teeth, they burst in amongst the group. Biting, tearing and lashing out. It was a desperate fight.

Captain Hayward held his rifle out; as one long limb flung a British soldier to the ground and prepared to bite, the captain squeezed the trigger.

The creature recoiled in pain as the bullet twisted through its head and out the other side. Charles turned to see Corporal Heinz killing one long limb that had come at him through a pile of boxes. The beasts were too many in number and getting in each other's way as they clambered for the chance to kill and eat.

A wounded soldier was thrown in the air and grabbed by two long limbs as he fell to the ground. The screams were quickly muffled as he was bitten relentlessly. Chunks of flesh were devoured, after being torn from his body. Two of the prisoners next to him tried in vain to pull them off, but the attackers were joined by more of their kind. These two men fell victim to this unrelenting attack, suffering hideous wounds in the feeding frenzy that followed.

Corporal Heinz was still firing as much as he could. A head shot killed one beast to the left and then he spun around and rammed his hunting knife into the side of another as it tried to bite an Engineer who was reloading. Bullets were running low and it was becoming a frantic battle with men kicking, punching and using every last drop of energy against an attacking force that was hell-bent on killing and eating everything in its path. Charles felt in his ammo pouch that he was now down to his last magazine.

As he loaded this into the rifle, he was bashed into from the side; a claw swiped the rifle out of his arms and threw it into the sand below.

Charles reached for his knife and managed to stick it into the creature's side, slicing along its ribcage. It recoiled around as he did so and tried to bite at Charles's head.

Using his shoulder and all his weight, he pushed it back. A British soldier with a revolver then helped the situation by unloading a bullet in its head, but sadly Engineers were succumbing to the inevitable. Forming a small circle, they made their last stand. Knives drawn, rifles at the ready. Captain Hayward gave his rifle to a British soldier next to him who was holding a piece of broken wood. He then withdrew his sword. Captain Hayward's black helmet with small spike was knocked off in the last attack. His light blond hair was matted with sweat and blood. His red tunic was ripped and army webbing torn.

"This could be it, lads, die with pride." He paused, "You've given everything."

The long limbs surrounded them, pawing at the ground, letting out deep, throaty growls and snarling with their teeth. Others behind them could be heard feeding on the dead soldiers' carcasses, fighting amongst themselves for the bones that were left.

As the creatures around them began to steady themselves for the final attack, a horn was blown, the sound filling the air. At once the battlefield went eerily quiet. No growling, no feeding, nothing. The entire army of long limbs lowered their heads. Then they began to part; it was as if the sea was being split in two. It revealed an entourage of giant horses and priests riding them. They were flanked with destroyer drones.

This procession moved at a steady pace forward towards the small circle of British soldiers. Captain Hayward told his men to hold fire.

As clouds formed around the sun, only small rays of light were able to creep out. In this translucent light, a cloaked rider came forward. His frame was huge and his eyes glowed yellow in the darkness of his hood. The tip of a sword handle could be seen above his shoulders and the bottom of his sword was protruding to the right-hand side of his body. Every creature went silent, allowing the sound of waves crashing against the beach to fill the air. Seagulls circled patiently above, waiting to feed on what flesh was left seeping into the sand.

The man on the horse sat there for a moment and looked around. He then pushed back his hood. Long black hair flowed to his shoulders, his eyes were piercing and the daylight revealed a stern face. It was not until he smiled that they saw his teeth. Sharp and pointed. His tongue seemed to be able to come out further and taste the air, before slipping back in like a snake.

"You've fought well." Nazar's dark voice was in clear English. "But it was all in vain."

He brought his horse around; this larger than normal animal was covered in armour, its black mane was as dark as the night, and it also had no eyes.

Captain Hayward stood there in silence.

Nazar climbed down from his horse.

The captain was 6ft 1in, but Nazar must have been nearly 7ft. He towered over the men. His frame was not of a thin man, but a strong, powerful ox.

The British soldiers held their ground, as did the monsters that surrounded them. The sea breeze picked up a little, as the clouds floated over their heads at speed.

"Your attack on my ships has been successful, I hear?"

He undid his cloak to reveal two daggers and two revolvers. "Don't be shy, you can talk." As Nazar's words left his lips, Captain Hayward lunged forward and stopped with his sword in front of Nazar's throat.

"I like someone with risk in their soul." He smiled, revealing the teeth again.

"You will die like any man," Captain Hayward said in a calm voice.

Nazar looked at the captain. His yellow eyes seemed to grow brighter. He then pushed his own throat onto the blade. It cut into skin, sending blood down the sword and onto the captain's right hand.

"You can kill me, but there will be consequences."

Corporal Heinz looked at the captain as if to urge him to just do it.

Nazar paused.

"You kill me now and one million prisoners will be executed." His tongue came out of his mouth and licked around his teeth.

The captain reduced the pressure of the sword on Nazar's throat.

"Not so easy, is it, when their deaths will be on your head." A slight pause followed before his eyes lit up. "I suspect you have a family that could be under our protection." He smiled again, pulling back from the sword. "Otherwise you would have killed me. "I am the King of Europe now." He then raised his arms in the air with open hands. "The world will know my name … NAZAR!"

He looked to the skies. "Your name?"

"Captain Hayward," Charles replied.

Captain Hayward lowered his sword. It was the thought of Rebecca and the children being prisoners that stopped him. He wanted to plunge it into Nazar's throat, but was caught in two minds. Nazar's words had affected him.

The men around the captain looked tired; the fighting had been ferocious, but it had come down to that moment and they had now accepted their fate.

"Why have you killed so many civilians?" Captain Hayward had now pushed the sword into the sand.

"This is WAR. Has the British Empire not killed thousands?" He snarled to each side of the British soldiers and the long limbs began to move back slowly, creating space for Nazar to walk around this forlorn group.

"We used to preach about the virtues of life." He looked down at the sand. "Men are greedy; they lust for power and gold. They use religion for their own purposes." Nazar said this as his eyes focused on each man.

"Then if you despise that way of life, why imitate it?" Captain Hayward came out of the circle a step or two. "You are a Priest, after all?"

This brought a growl from deep inside Nazar's chest.

"Do not question morals with me." He clapped his hands; this signalled several destroyer drones to dismount.

"We have long stopped being priests. We worship a different messiah now."

Captain Hayward moved back into the circle.

"Mankind has many faults, and is far from perfect." Charles looked at his men, their red tunics torn and covered in blood. "But, you have chosen darkness over light."

"Ha, haa, aaaaaa. You will pray for darkness soon, Captain."

Nazar came close to Captain Hayward again. The destroyer drones circled the captain's men and waited on Nazar's command. Captain Hayward looked at Corporal Heinz; he had a disappointed look on his face. "Lay down your weapons, men." Charles was clear. The British soldiers took a moment or two to react, but then began to place the rifles and revolvers in the soft sand. These were picked up by the destroyer drones; knives and any other weapons they had were also laid down.

Nazar leaned into Charles's face. "Your pain is only just beginning." Captain Hayward looked down at the sand. In his mind's eye, he saw his garden in Sunninghill and Arthur and Emily playing in it. Their faces were happy and they were laughing with each other. He then saw Rebecca coming out of the house with a cool drink. His vision of that bliss began to fade. As his men were having their hands tied, he reached down to grab his sword, which was still in the sand.

Nazar had turned to the side as he watched the drones leading the prisoners away. This is when Captain Hayward struck. Moving his right hand forward, he pulled the sword out of the sand. Adjusting his feet, he lunged forward with the blade, pointing at Nazar's head. Nazar turned slightly, catching a quick glimpse of light flashing off the iron. That moment was enough for him to lower and twist his head. The sword's blade pushed through the soft skin around his jaw and travelled up the side of his face and out the other side.

The roar and snarl deafened all those around him. Nazar fell back with the sword still in his head. Captain Hayward pushed forward to try and finish the job. A destroyer drone swung his arm out to stop him. Captain Hayward brought his knee up into the drone's side and headbutted him in the face.

The creature went down, but the other drone next to him was already reacting. He threw out a kick and caught the captain in the side of his ribs. Charles flew into the sand.

Corporal Heinz had seen this action unravel as he was being led away; both his hands had not yet been tied. He let loose his unbuttoned tunic, revealing two blades that were strapped to his back over his shirt. Quickly withdrawing them, he sliced at the guards' throats next to him. They both fell to the ground holding their severed windpipes. The other British stood helpless with their hands tied.

Corporal Heinz continued to push forward, thrusting one knife into the heart of a destroyer drone that was coming straight at him. He did not stop and used his shoulder and body weight to come to the aid of the captain.

Nazar stood there, blood streaming from his wound. His body shook and his skin rippled. It was as if he was changing.

The sword had unfortunately missed his brain. Placing both hands on the grip and pommel, he began to ease out the sword from his head. Skin flapped as the blade came sliding out. Holding the sword in both hands, blood gushed over his fingers and along his arms. He looked down at the captain and then snapped the sword over his knee.

Corporal Heinz came to the side of Captain Hayward. Before they knew it, the captain and corporal took heavy blows to the back of their heads, which sent then flying onto a destroyer drone that was sprawled out on the ground.

Captain Hayward started to get up but the drone who had kicked him down took another swipe; Charles was quick to react and blocked his foot, causing him to lose his standing and come crashing to the ground. He let loose with five accurate punches, which knocked this beast back. He went to hit him again, but a hand grabbed the destroyer drone by the hair and literally flung him away like a rag doll. The creature almost squealed as he crashed into barrels behind Nazar.

Nazar came forward like a force of nature. His eyes were full of rage. Before Captain Hayward could move, Nazar stood over him and picked him up with one hand. He lifted the captain into the air. Nazar no longer seemed seven foot tall anymore, he was nearer to eight foot tall. His body mass had grown, and his face was more elongated. He brought the captain close to his face. Nazar opened his jaw, which could now dislocate to become wider, as if it was like a boa constrictor. The teeth were longer and more serrated.

"You have just made a huge mistake." Nazar's tongue licked at the blood on the side of his cheek as if he enjoyed it.
"I was going to have you shot like an officer, Captain." Nazar's eyes glowed a darker yellow.
"Now, you will suffer." He kept the captain in the air. He then ordered all the British soldiers on the beach to be nailed to crosses along the hilltop, next to the camp. He laughed in a devilish way to himself, before looking into the eyes of Captain Hayward again.

"You and your men will be hung, drawn and fed to the flesh-eaters." Nazar brought his fist into the side of Captain Hayward's head, knocking him unconscious.

He then slung the captain's lifeless body to the ground. Corporal Heinz was starting to come around when he was grabbed by two drones and dragged with the others along the beach towards the dunes and camp. Captain Hayward was thrown over a horse and led the same way.

Sand began to dance as heavy rain hit the beach hard. A dark storm quickly swept in from the sea, bringing thunderous waves along the coast.

Chapter 16

As Charles regained consciousness, he felt excruciating pain coming from his left wrist. Six drone soldiers were holding him down and one was taking a large nail and hammering it into his skin. They then repeated this on his right wrist. His legs had been bound together and tied to wood. It took five to ten minutes before he could focus; the rain was battering his face, which made it hard to see. When there was a brief respite, he could now see that he was nailed to a cross; to his left and right there were crosses for the other men who had tried to escape. Corporal Heinz was next to him on his immediate left and Private Clegg on his right.

Water was dripping off his nose and almost creeping into his mouth, occasionally causing him to spit it out. He tried to move his arms, but the two large nails sticking out of each of his wrist's held them tight. Wriggling his fingers showed him he still had feeling in his hands. The crosses were around nine foot off the ground.

"Corporal, Corporal!" Charles called out. His voice quivered a little in pain.

Corporal Heinz looked up and to his right. "I'm stuck, Captain." The corporal was also feeling the effects of being strung up on a cross.

Charles nodded his head. "I'm proud of you all."

The corporal smiled. "You were brave trying to kill him; I know your family must have been in the forefront of your mind."

"You're right, but there is no knowing if they're alive." Charles paused. "He is a monster and I took my chance." Another short pause followed. "Unfortunately, I failed."

"We did not fail. We gave Great Britain time." Corporal Heinz looked on solemnly.

As they spoke, Private Clegg joined in the conversation.

"If I die here, sir, I hope I will meet my family in the afterlife." William too was
sombre.

Captain Hayward looked to his right. "I'm sure you will, lad. We all will."

The conversation was broken with the heavy rain starting to ease. They could then see tents set further back. Not just hundreds, maybe thousands. In a cruel twist of misfortune, they had landed next to Nazar's main force, whilst trying to rescue the prisoners.

Drone guards were moving along the path by the crosses. They had giant wolves with them. This was followed by a patrol of destroyer guards with two long limbs. Nazar had no intention of letting these men escape. The cold sea air bit at any naked flesh; the gulls above could be heard. They were waiting for a moment to feast. Private Clegg said one of the prisoners at the end of the line of crosses had died and was now being visited by these feathered vultures from the skies. They were pecking at his open wounds.

Darkness was now creeping in.

Charles lost track of time as the evening wore on. He passed out many times and awoke periodically in pain.

"Charles, we miss you," Rebecca spoke in a soft voice.

He looked down to see her standing there, her long, blonde hair and beautiful, soft features.

"I miss you all, too."

Charles found it hard to know whether he was hallucinating or seeing her for real.

The clouds broke for a moment, allowing light to wash upon her face. She looked radiant, and her clothes sparkled in the light. It was as if she was going to the ball where they had first met.

"Don't give up, Charles."

The moon then disappeared behind the clouds.

A sudden jolt to his right hand brought him around. Croaking and squawking followed. It was a black-backed seagull. The blood flowing from his wrists had attracted this unwanted scavenger. The seagulls had become braver after the battles along the coast as Europe had fallen. There had been plenty of bodies to feast on and now they had become even more adventurous with the wounded.

He flicked out his fingers and let out a cry of anger; this was enough to make the bird take flight, but it quickly entered his mind that sleep would bring its own perils.

The vision of Rebecca in a strange way gave him hope. He then began to scour the hillside for guard movements. Charles racked his brain for ideas. This made him attempt to pull his wrists through the nails. The pain was so intense that several times he almost passed out.

"It's no use, Captain." Uttered a mirthful voice beneath him.

Standing below was a group of priests in cloaks. They had torches burning, with cinders flying off into the night from oil-coated branches.

Nazar then came forward. He had a bandage wrapped around his wound. Next to him was a tall elegant woman. She was also in a robe.

"Before you die tomorrow, I want you to suffer a little now," Nazar said.

He then clapped his hands and several destroyer drones began to take down two British Engineers who were nailed to the crosses at the far end of the line. Once they were free, they were dragged over to the bottom of Charles's cross.

"You thought by killing me it would stop." He laughed with his deep, menacing, disconcerting voice.

The soldiers were brought to their knees; they had their hands tied behind their backs.

"Let me introduce my queen." The woman undid her cloak, revealing an athletic body; her arms looked muscular, but her shape was still curvaceous and feminine. She was beautiful and dressed in a bohemian way; she had straps across her breasts, only covering her nipples.

The two soldiers who were kneeling were on the verge of death. Nazar stood over them and looked up at the captain.

"You see, power is a great thing, Captain." He snarled before drawing his knife and cutting the throat of one of the soldiers. The poor man twitched on the floor, as he bled to death from his wound.

"You don't have to do this, Nazar." The captain spoke in a calm voice. "Kill me now and let the others work as your prisoners."

Nazar wiped the blood from his blade onto his cloak.

"I could do that, but I won't."

He then spoke in Russian to one of the priests. They walked off into the darkness and came back with five flesh-eaters tied together. The soldier was turned around to face this shuffling group of death. His cries for mercy could be heard all along the hill top.

"Please Nazar, I beg of you. Spare him!!" Captain Hayward was now shouting at him.

Oksana stepped forward; she was handed a short sword in its sheath, and looking up at the captain she then kicked over the soldier. He fell on his back; he tried to turn and get up, but two priests held him down. She then withdrew the sword and balanced it on his stomach.

"You are too weak to beat us, Captain Hayward." She then brought the sword across the soldier's stomach, opening up a huge cut in his skin. The man cried out in pain and begged for mercy. Oksana gave the sword back to one of the priests and walked over to the flesh-eaters. They did not try to bite, instead just standing and looking at her.

Taking one of them by the arm, she dragged it over to where the wounded soldier lay.

"Your world is ending," she said. She then released the flesh-eater onto the man. He screamed out as it tore into his body. It was agonising to watch from the crosses. Charles felt rage and hate flowing through his veins. The priests, destroyer drones and Oksana turned and walked away, leaving Nazar standing there with a burning torch.

"You have done this by attacking me, Captain Hayward." He then lifted his torch into the air. "I hope it's hurting, I'll be back in an hour." With that, he disappeared into the darkness.

Charles had tears of anger rolling down his cheeks. He wanted to break free from the cross and kill as many of the enemy as possible at whatever the cost.

The other flesh-eaters had been released to feed on both bodies below, and their ripping and tearing sounds carried on the wind.

"I am ready to die, Captain. I have prayed to God that it is a quick death," Corporal Heinz spoke softly to Charles.

"I pray it is quick for us all."

Charles passed in and out consciousness. The flesh-eaters had been rounded up and taken back to their holding pens; the bits that were left of the dead men were being finished off by the gulls.

The wind chilled the men to the bone. They could hear screams and shouts in the distance. Chilling noises crept out of the bleakness and found refuge in the hanging soldiers' sub-consciousnesses.

Charles thought he was dreaming as he was brought around by a voice.

"Captain Hayward, part of me wants to let you die on the cross." Nazar paused and handed his burning torch to a priest next to him. There were only three of them this time. "Oksana sends her utmost apologies for not being here, but she is feeding on a prisoner." He let out a deep belly laugh.

He then spoke in Russian to the two priests, who began to take down Private Clegg. Captain Hayward did not wait this time.

"Are you the devil, Nazar?"

Nazar smiled. "No, but we do worship a different lord to you."

"It does show you whose messiah really is winning here." Nazar instructed the priests to leave Private Clegg nailed to the cross, but lay the wooden cross onto the ground.

"Let me fight you man to man, or you in front of your armies; if I win, you give orders for these men to be kept as prisoners." Charles felt frantic inside and wanted to avert any action that Nazar could take.

"Oh Captain. You haven't quite understood yet, but you will." Nazar opened his cloak and started to withdraw a hunting knife.

Private Clegg was speaking softly to himself. Nazar leaned in close to him. "Prayers to your god will not save you now."

He then took the blade and cut into the soldier's stomach. Private Clegg cried out in pain, but kept praying. This angered Nazar further, as he wanted more of a reaction.

Captain Hayward shouted at Nazar to stop this torture.

"I will kill you, Nazar."

Nazar looked up and smiled before biting into Private Clegg's stomach. He fed like a flesh-eater and teared and ripped into the soldier's internal organs.

During this savage attack, Captain Hayward pulled at his wrists. The nails had oversized heads on them and did not pull through the skin. Blood ran from his wound and fell down onto Nazar. This diverted his attention from his feeding. His eyes lit up at what had happened. "You know this soldier well?" Nazar was excited by this. William was barely hanging onto life.

"We survived from the Carpathian Mountains, and we will beat you in the end." Williams's last words brought a serious look from Nazar. It shocked him. He stood up, growling and snarling. He let out an animal roar.

Captain Hayward was half leaning forward, with arms almost behind him.

"Bring him down!" Nazar barked out his orders.

Charles was still devastated with the loss of Private Clegg. His eyes looked at the lifeless body of this young soldier, and he felt guilt that he could not stop this and that he did not manage to get him out of Europe the first time.

As soon as the captain was low enough, Nazar was snarling in his face.

"Where's the map, Captain Hayward?" His body size had grown and his face was elongated again.

With both of his hands, he grabbed the captain's head and pulled it up to make sure he looked at him. Charles gritted his teeth.

"Benedict, where is the boy and the map?" Nazar's eyes danced backwards and forwards as if trying to read Charles's soul.

Captain Hayward looked at him without saying another word. Nazar's response was to strike Charles across the face. Blood trickled down from his mouth.

"I'll ask you again. Where is the map?"

"What map?" Captain Hayward gave out a sharp response.

This aggravated Nazar further.

"Go and fetch me a spear. NOW!" One of the priests ran off to act on his command.

A few minutes later, the priest returned holding a spear with a bronze tip.

"It is not wise to try my patience." Nazar then took the spear from the priest standing next to him and walked over to Corporal Heinz's cross. He then brought the spear up to the corporal's stomach.

"Last time, where is Benedict and the map?"

Captain Hayward knew he had to choose his response carefully.

"Benedict, I believe, is in London. I did not travel from France with them." He said this while trying to pull himself back and his voice wavered. "I know nothing about a map."

Nazar took the end of the wooden spear and smashed it into the side of Charles's head.

"Doesn't feel good, does it?" Nazar smiled. He started to think either the captain was telling the truth about the map, or Benedict had not told them enough of its importance.

Blood started to run from the side of Captain Hayward's face. "Why not fight me like a man?" Charles spat out the blood that had trickled into his mouth from his head wound.

"There is no point fighting you, Captain." He lifted Charles's head up by placing the spear under his throat. "Because you are no match for me." He then let Charles's head fall down again.

"One last thing, Captain, I hope your corporal lasts through the night to see you hung, drawn and fed to the flesh-eaters." With that he walked over to Corporal Heinz and rammed the spear into his ribs. The corporal let out a yelp as the spear pierced his skin and went into his body.

Captain Hayward's eyes just looked at Nazar as he gave the spear back to one of the priests. He grimaced with pain, but kept eye contact with Nazar as he ordered the captain be stood upright again.

"Save your energy. You have a lot of suffering to do tomorrow." He turned and left for his tent. The priests put Captain Hayward's cross straight again. They kicked at the bottom of it and laughed. Private Clegg was left there unceremoniously in a heap. They would not be burying his body.

"Corporal, hold in there." Charles wanted to know how much damage the spear had done.

"I feel weak, but I'm still with you, Captain." Corporal Heinz's voice was wavering a little.

"Do not give up hope, Johann." Charles used his first name; he wanted to keep the corporal with him as long as he could. Without a miracle, the young Austrian would die on the cross.

Nazar entered General Georgiy's tent, which was placed right in the centre of the camp. The general was just about to tuck into a large cooked chicken.

"Feasting again, General?" Nazar pulled out a chair and sat himself next to the general.

"This is my first meal today, sire." He said this sheepishly, holding in his oversized waist.

Nazar put his hand on the table. It was still changing back from the incident by the crosses. His nails were like claws and he dragged them down the table, taking up small splinters of wood as he did so. "We have spies in Great Britain?"

"Yes, my lord, they are lying low awaiting our attack." General Georgiy was slightly relieved the subject had changed from his eating.

"I need them to find Benedict and kill him." Nazar stroked his beard.

The general then began to question if it would be wise to give away their position, thus raising concerns about what traitors they had in their own ranks. "If they find the map, then they will find the Monastery and possibly where the rock is?" He knocked the plate onto the floor with one quick sideswipe. "Find him and assassinate him."

Nazar then got up and began to leave the tent.

"Should we not send a division to the Monastery and castle?" General Georgiy asked this as he was picking up his chicken off the floor.

"Alert the orphanage and get them to send a force there." He stopped at the tent entrance. "I will need all my main forces for the invasion." Nazar then left into the night.

The general looked at the chicken, which now had bits of dirt and grass on it. He brushed it once and then began to eat.

After consuming his meal, he summoned in an officer and asked him to send messengers to the orphanage. It should be noted, he said, that this was a request from the new king of Europe and should not be delayed on. The officer commented it would take some time to get there, but none the less, he would send his best men.

Drone guards patrolling the hill top with long limbs stopped to let them feed on Private Clegg's body. His remains were dragged off by one of them into the long grass. Time passed with the winter breeze blowing strong from the sea. Captain Hayward was drained and tired, but suddenly felt a tap on his foot. It brought him out of his slumber, in which he had been saying a prayer; he expected this could be his time now.

"Are you still alive, Captain?"

Charles let his eyes fall on the people below. At first glimpse they looked like three drone soldiers; it was only after he refocused his vision that he could see there was a difference.

"Captain, it's Alexander Chamberlin."

Charles still did not say anything. He hoped he was not hallucinating and that this was really happening.

"Is that Private Chamberlin?" He was still cautious.

"Yes, sir, it's me." Alexander said he would tell him more, but they had little time now to speak. "I'm with some French guerrillas, we're here to rescue you." He told him there would be a diversion very soon and they would try and take down all the soldiers from the crosses.

A minute passed with nothing happening. Charles could hear Alexander speaking French with the men around him. Then a kaaaaboom shook the ground. It was followed by several more explosions. Out of the shadows came small groups of men dressed in dark clothes with their faces blacked out.

They moved quickly, taking the soldiers off the crosses. Captain Hayward said that Corporal Heinz had been injured and would need medical help. Charles was slowly lowered down and the nails carefully pulled out. Each group had a small lantern to work with, but were very conscious of giving away their position.

As the nails were eased out, Charles was given a soft cloth to bite on. The pain shot through his body, but the release as the last tip of the nail left his skin made him feel euphoric.

The British soldiers were then helped along and in some cases carried into the night. Lanterns were extinguished and darkness returned. "They will send an army up here soon; we must get to the woods." Alexander helped Corporal Heinz; he was struggling to walk and threw up as they moved.

The British and French guerrillas lay in a cluster of bushes and long grass; they saw a destroyer drone ride past on a razor tooth. He was oblivious to them being there, and he did not let the animal sniff the air as he pushed onto the hill top.

The plan was to get the men out of the camp and onto a boat to Great Britain. They could not go inland, as Nazar's armies were camped all around the area. Alexander said they had come from a coastal path which led to a smugglers cave, and from there they could access a small cove and a boat should be waiting. Captain Hayward spoke to Corporal Heinz and told him he would make it out alive. The corporal had been bleeding heavily out of his wound; they had wrapped a piece of cloth around the wound to help stem the blood flow. A French guerrilla soldier and Alexander were now on either side of him, helping him along.

The men moved across a small, open field containing dead, rotting animals. Their carcasses littered the ground, giving off a pungent aroma. Arriving at a hedgerow, they took a moment to rest. A bugle rang out, calling the drones to arms. A guerrilla came forward and spoke in English. He told them they would follow a small patchwork of hedgerows before coming to an escarpment and path. At the end of the path was a tunnel to a cave. With that, he rallied the group and led the way.

The sounds carrying in the wind were as if the land had awoken itself. Growls, groans, screams and shouts could be heard. Charles listened as they pushed alongside the hedge, pausing when the group heard something, or waiting whilst the French guerrillas swapped to help carry the wounded. All the British soldiers who had been on the crosses needed help walking.

A clap of thunder overhead made the men stop. They all crouched by the undergrowth; a flash of light in the distance signalled the start of a storm. Trees started to sway and a strong gust of wind blew over the hills and licked at the long grass around them. The commander of the guerrillas said they were not far from the entrance. He tried to get everyone ready to move as quickly as possible. Rain started to fall gently from the sky, at first like a fine mist, but soon it worsened in its severity.

The ground was a little sodden as they began to move at speed. The wounded men found it tougher, even if they were being carried or helped. Pushing through or over hedges was hard work. Bushes and leaves were dripping with water and hawthorn spikes pierced naked flesh whenever pressed upon.

There was a sigh of relief when they moved along the path and arrived at the entrance. Lightning lit up the sky around them and thunder clapped overhead.

Moving aside the hidden entrance door, they were shown inside. Most of the guerrillas were to assist them to the boat and then disappear to their hideout and continue to fight a resistance war as much as they could. Alexander Chamberlin was coming home with the British soldiers. He had asked if the French Resistance wanted to come with them, but they refused.

Nazar would be carrying out horrible repercussions for this. Skinning men and women alive had been his latest act for guerrilla attacks, but therein lay another problem – herds of flesh-eaters; some would be used in the invasion, while others wandered Europe in search of food. Alexander had survived out in the wild until he met up with the French Resistance, but he knew the problem was getting worse. If Nazar's soldiers didn't get you, then the flesh-eaters probably would.

Nazar did not concern himself with policing his new Europe too much; he knew that the demons that walked the lands would do it for him.

Chapter 17

The men worked their way through the tunnel entrance and followed it down some narrow steps which twisted left then right. The wind whistled up this passage and the waves could be heard crashing against the rocks.

Charles was being helped along with Corporal Heinz. They were tired and weak, but grateful to be alive. After about ten to fifteen minutes, they eventually made their way out of the tunnel and into a passageway leading to the cove. The rocks were moist and the air was damp. Captain Hayward had thought to himself that he would never leave these shores, let alone return to Great Britain. He had prepared himself for death; although the nature of what was planned for him was hard to comprehend, he had tried to come to terms with it and told himself at the time he would meet his family in the next life.

The soldiers came out onto a fairly large flat area. Several rowing boats were now waiting to take them out to a ship. This vessel would sail them to Great Britain. The soldiers thanked the French Resistance for all that they had done, which was in fact saving them from death. The wounded were loaded into the boats first and then the rest followed. The remaining French guerrillas shook hands with the men and then disappeared up the passageway and tunnel. They would only have a finite amount of time to get away from the area before it was overrun by the enemy.

Once full, the French sailors pushed off the rowing boats and headed for open sea. The sea smell filled Charles's nostrils. They rowed for a fair while in choppy waters. One of the French sailors spoke good English and said the British had been supplying the Resistance with weapons and clothes to help with the war effort.

There was a good-size fishing boat waiting for them. The weather was still stormy, but it had died down a little since it first swept in.

On board the wounded were taken below and the rest were led to a makeshift dining area. Charles knew that in Great Britain he faced an immediate threat from Major Sherborne. The corporal had suggested at the time that the major would not send the boats back for them, that they take their ship and go to Denmark and see if his family were hiding there. If they were, they could then sail to America and stay away from Great Britain. Charles had liked the plan, but pointed out it would be complicated.

The French coast started to disappear on the horizon. Captain Hayward reflected on the new leader of Europe and how dangerous he was becoming. He wished he had killed Nazar on the beach, and knew Great Britain would feel his wrath soon enough, if they did not find a way to stop this monster.

The journey was hard. The sea was unforgiving, and the men were tired and a little green when they sailed into Portsmouth. The sailors on board the ship had treated the wounds on the men with herbs and other ointments. The wrists on the soldiers had to be cleaned thoroughly and bandaged tight. Nazar had made sure the nails had been put through in such a way that the soldiers would not bleed to death too quickly. He had wanted them to be alive so that he could torture them in front of his armies the following day.

The French Resistance had raised a flag that had been given to them from the Royal Navy and struck a bell as they had been commanded. The fort batteries knew not to open fire on their vessel.

Passing the Isle of Wight, the men looked at the island. It was having defences built along its coast. Gun batteries were being placed facing out to sea, and earth and wood forts were being constructed at key sections along the island.

Travelling through the day from France and into the afternoon meant it was now dark. A smaller harbour was used by them; it allowed them not to get caught up in any Navy exercises. The Royal Navy had also started to patrol the coastline and would intercept any boat or ship that did not fly the British flag or sound out the bell signal to show they were friend not foe.

Captain Hayward had been with Corporal Heinz through most of the journey. Alexander had also been with them both. The corporal's condition was stable, but he was weak. He would need to be taken to a hospital once they landed.

Alexander told the captain that there were pockets of resistance left in Europe. Some in fairly large numbers. They had moved into the mountains and caves, or gone deep into the darkest forests. Some moved daily like Red Indians, camping in one area for a week or two before moving on. The main drone army forces were along the French, Dutch and Spanish coasts. The creatures were the things to hide from now in the new Europe. Flesh-eaters wandered around in large herds, which made them very dangerous if they managed to encircle you.

It seemed as if Nazar was not worried about this at the moment. His focus was on conquering the world, and then he would probably return to mop up resistance. Not much information had come out about Asia or Africa. The Empire had reported no major attacks so far on the parts they controlled. India had started to notice flesh-eaters in the north of the country. Not large numbers, but a flow as they sought food. Long limbs and razor tooths again had limited sighting.

The British forces in India had been drastically reduced mainly due to the war in Europe and the need to re-deploy them to Great Britain. This of course had given the tribes opposed to British rule in India a chance to rise up in some provinces. With that occurring regularly, their eyes were turned away from the small outbreaks of the flesh-eaters attacking villages. British intelligence had managed to get across that the virus would kill you once you were bitten and then that you would turn into one of these walking dead.

Charles updated Alexander on the exodus to America and how the wealthy were really the main beneficiaries of this withdrawal. He had also mentioned that he had not heard from Rebecca and the children, lowering his head as he spoke about this.

"Do not give up hope, Captain. Many of the catacomb survivors apparently made it to Denmark," Alexander said, putting his hand on Charles's shoulder.

"Thank you, Chamberlin." The men then heard the bell; they were nearing the harbour.

Chapter 18

Moving through dense undergrowth, Rebecca and the children were with a small group of survivors. They were all gathering wood for their camp, which was situated near Husum, in Denmark. Originally, they had made their way along the coast, passing through Belgium, Holland and Prussia. It had been a perilous journey, and they were fortunate to join another group heading the same way.

Arriving in Denmark, they had been directed by a Danish scout who was helping refugees evacuating mainland Europe. It had been late summer then; the flow had been regular. Many had made it across to Britain in the boats or ships leaving at that time. The enemy had not totally annexed the whole country, leaving areas unguarded. Nazar's military focus had been concentrated on the super powers – Prussia, France, Spain and the Nordic armies of Sweden, Norway and Finland. Denmark had put up a good fight, but the enemy slowly pushed up from Prussia, took the main cities and then receded again to reinforce Nazar's main attack on Reims and then Paris.

His orders were to keep small garrisons in the main cities and smaller units in strategic towns. Then the flow of flesh-eaters and other creatures would scavenge around on what was hiding out in the countryside.

Conditions were bearable, but as winter was coming, the group had been advised to travel further north and settle down in the larger forests; there was even talk of using one of the islands around Nykøbing.

Their daily routines had been to gather firewood and what food they could. The group was a mixture of Europeans. There were other British families that had come from France, others Prussia. Rebecca always kept the children within eyesight.

A Danish man called Hagen was leading the group. He was big – 6ft 5in – and as wide as a mule. His hair was blond and flowed over his shoulders, with an unkempt beard that initially drew awkward glances from the Victorians, but everybody soon realised this man was a fighter.

He had killed with his bare hands two giant wolves that had turned up one night at the camp. Not too much was known of his life before the war, or whether he had family. Some said they had been killed and burnt at his farm, but he never spoke about that or his past.

With an axe strapped to his back and a large hunting knife to his side, the children called him "the Viking". His English was good and he had a reasonable grasp of the German language. This helped him lead the group.

One of the British women with them had two children, a boy and a girl. They were of similar ages to Arthur and Emily. Florence was a woman with strong character; she had done her utmost to keep them alive during the invasion. She had been living with her husband and children in Prussia until the war had separated them. Florence was not sure if he was alive or not. With the fall of Prussia, she had joined the refugees, but was too late to take the last ships out of Denmark.

Some ships had tried to return to Denmark and rescue more people, but the drone soldiers had begun to have field batteries along the coast and harbours. It became impossible to escape and those that were left went into hiding. She was pleased to meet Rebecca and the children, as it made it easier for both of them.

Reports had reached the group about British attacks along the French coast. It created a buzz of excitement, as if the war could be turned if they landed a huge force and fought back this army of darkness. Sadly, it did not take long for the full picture to become apparent. The attacks were just focusing on docks and ports; their intention was to slow down Nazar's invasion plans. The euphoria evaporated on hearing this update. No one was coming to rescue them, and the only way they would get out was to find or build a boat and sail to Great Britain.

The hunter-gatherer group was on the outskirts of a small forest. Some were gathering wood, others catching rabbits and anything else worth eating. This small group had Rebecca and Florence looking after the children on the edge of the wood. They were gathering sticks and scrapping off silver birch bark for starting fires. They had two guards with them; both soldiers had rifles, but not too much ammunition. Hunting larger game was now carried out by bow and arrow. This was quieter and attracted less attention.

A rumour circulated around that four large deer had been killed. It meant they would be eating well tonight. Food played a huge part in the group's daily life and having a solid meal raised everyone's mood and spirits.

A teenage boy came over to the women and said that the hunters were taking the deer back to the camp. The children were welcome to come and see. Rebecca and Florence agreed they could look, once they were all back. They did not like being away from the main group, or too far from the camp. Hagen had made a spear for Rebecca as she had requested some sort of protection. Florence had declined and said that even though the Victorian etiquette had somewhat gone out of the window, she was not quite ready to go barbarian and carry a spear, although she did carry a small hunting knife in her pocket.

Rebecca began to bundle up the sticks and bark whilst Florence helped.

A scream rang out.

Coming across open grasslands were giant riders. They had a pack of long limbs with them. Rebecca dropped what she was doing and looked for the children. She knew they would be close, as that was the rule she had always given them. Her eyes searched the woodland all around them, then the bushes and grassland further afield. Her heart jumped into her mouth. With her mouth going dry and head spinning, she tried to work out where they had gone. The riders had not come across them yet, but the children were not in sight.

"The teenage boy!" she shouted out to Florence.

Rebecca grabbed the spear, which she had lent against a silver birch tree, and then set off with Florence in the direction they thought the scream had come from. Both women were nervous as they moved through the woodland. Checking over their shoulders, they could see the giant riders of the north turning their horses in their direction. They did not know the numbers of the enemy, or how long it would take them to get to their position.

Moving across open grassland, they came to a dip in the land. Below was a small stream gently meandering its way through the landscape. Clumps of heather and other small bushes scattered the immediate countryside.

Standing there, Rebecca could see the children running. They were with some of the hunters and the teenage boy, which gave her hope, but coming up behind them were four giant riders and two long limbs.

Sweating and out of breath, both women made their way in the direction of where the children were running. A fight had begun with two of the hunters and three of the giant riders. Sword and axe figured more than rifles and revolvers.

Whilst that was unfolding, Rebecca and Florence made a diagonal run for the children. They disappeared in front of them as they entered a large pine forest. Five to 6 metres in and one would be in darkness.

It took a couple of minutes for them to reach the forest glade; out of breath, and panting hard, they would have to enter the darkness. Screams and cries echoed around the woodlands. A fuzzy thud hit a scots pine next to Florence. The other group of riders was now firing on the women.

Rebecca took Florence's hand. "We must find the children."

A deep, croaky noise swept along the airways, and rang in the ears of the women. "Long limbs."

Rebecca held her spear tight and moved into the forest. Florence withdrew her knife. Pushing through the dead branches and dim light was difficult. It would take a while for their eyes to adjust to the darkness. A snap of a twig or branch sent a shiver down their spines, but the thought of the children being pursued by creatures that would eat them was unbearable.

Two barks and a growl signalled the long limbs had entered the forest.

"Stay close, Florence."

They could see an opening in the distance. It looked like a large pine had fallen over and taken with it some dead ones, creating a small opening for light to seep through. They were naturally drawn to this light.

The closer they got, the more worried they became.

Five metres away a crunching, slurping sound was coming from directly in front of them. As they moved within a few metres of the fallen tree, their eyes fell upon the hind legs of a long limb, crouching down feeding on a body. Its victim was covered in blood and lifeless. Florence brought her hand to her mouth, tears dropping silently to the ground. Rebecca felt like her heart had stopped there and then.

The creature carried on eating, tearing at flesh that did not come off easily. Rage engulfed Rebecca's body, and moving forward without thinking, she brought the spear back with both hands.

The long limb seemed to sense something was behind it and began to turn. At that point, the spear was plunged deep into its back, piercing skin and by chance its heart. It jolted as this action was carried out by Rebecca. Swinging around, it tried to bite at the spear that was stuck in its back. Falling to the side, as the extent of the injury took its toll, Rebecca seized on the opportunity; taking out her hunting knife, she quickly brought it to the creature's throat. Then, sliding the blade across its windpipe, she finished off what she had started. The long limb slumped to the side of her.

Florence rushed over to see who had been killed. Falling to her knees, she said it was the teenage boy from earlier. Both of them wiped away their tears. "We can bury him later, but we must find the children." Rebecca did not want to come across as harsh, but she knew they did not have long to find them.

More groans and coughing sounds could be heard. The long limbs would pick up on the scent of the dead beast and come to it.

Both women continued past the body and headed deeper into the wood. The snapping twigs and branches all around them increased the tensions. Rebecca had tried to remove the spear, but it had been stuck deep in the beast.

Then, a soft voice called out.

"Mummy."

Florence's eyes lit up. She tried to call back but her voice had dried up with nerves. After swallowing and clearing her throat, she tried again.

"Children, we're coming!"

Both women could see silhouettes of the children on the edge of the forest. "They must have gone in and then decided to find the others." Rebecca said this as they both moved towards them. Soon the two women were no longer walking at a fast pace, they were running. Their eyes had adjusted enough for them to dodge in and out of the trees. Their goal was now in sight. As they arrived, Emily ran to her mother. Florence's two children also came from behind a tree. It was then that Rebecca noticed three giant riders; they had dismounted and were coming their way.

A fourth giant rider was struggling with something in a cloth sack. Rebecca tried not to let her mind race off, but her heart said Arthur was in that sack.

Panic set in.

"Florence, keep Emily close to you."

She then began to move towards the giant riders. Rebecca could hear Florence's voice telling her not to, but it was all hazy as she moved forward with purpose.

The giant riders prepared themselves for an easy kill. Rebecca took out her knife; she looked at the men coming closer to her and then looked at the rider, who was attaching the sack to his horse.

A gravelly, croaky sound floated past Rebecca, and now to the side of Florence and the children was a long limb. Its gangly body was stooping forward and its claws and teeth were showing as it went in for the kill. She looked to the skies and prayed, but she was thinking, "Why now?"

This beast was suddenly stopped in its tracks; it screamed as an arrow was flung into the side of its right hind leg. Then another arrow entered its ribcage, and it fell to the ground in a heap. Emerging from the darkness was Hagen. He slowly walked forward, loading his last arrow onto its slit, then pulling back the bow, he let loose. It shot past Rebecca and into the throat of one of the giant riders. He looked puzzled for a moment; he then tried in vain to pull out the arrow before falling face down into the dirt.

The two remaining riders of the north looked at their dead comrade and then at each other. Both had axes drawn and they now had fire in their bellies. Without speaking, they charged at Hagen. Rebecca was merely a bystander for a moment.

With both riders running towards him, he stopped. Then as they got closer, he let his bow fall to the ground and put both hands on the pommel and grip of his sword. The riders of the north were in full charge as they came down upon him. Steadying his stance, he moved with lightning speed between them; his agility was that of a cat. Hagen's sword was brought around with deadly accuracy, cutting into the stomach of one of the giants and then severing the axe-wielding arm of the other.

The giant rider with the sliced stomach fell to his knees, while the other with the missing arm tried unsuccessfully to pick up the axe out of his severed hand. Both did not draw further breath as Hagen swung the sword again, cutting in half one of them and then ramming the sword through the heart of the other.

"Rebecca, where is Arthur?" Hagen asked in a stern voice.

Rebecca was still lost in her thoughts for a moment. She then screamed, "The rider, Hagen, he has him!"

The fourth rider was now mounted. He was joined by two other northern riders; they also had sacks, the contents of which were moving about.

Hagen swiftly took out the arrow from the dead giant and took aim. The giants were not turning to attack them, they were now fleeing. Pulling back on his bow, he let fly with this arrow. It struck one of the three riders, who fell backwards and off his horse. The other two did not stop to help him up; they grabbed his horse and proceeded to gallop off.

As this was unfolding, five hunters from the camp came out of the forest chasing a long limb; it had been hit by several arrows and was limping as it ran. A spear was thrown as they drew closer, but it struck its body and fell out. The second did hit the target; it was soon set upon as it tripped and fell.

Rebecca had already set off after the attackers, and Hagen followed her. She tried sprinting after the riders, but they turned their horses and began to gallop away. Two long limbs came bounding out of the forest and joined them as they made their way across the open grasslands.

Rebecca let out a scream. A deep, soulful groan followed. She began to cry, but as the tears hit the dirt beneath her feet, a gurgling and stuttered laugh could be heard. She wiped her eyes with her left arm. They looked in the direction of where the noise was coming from. The long grass was still with the lack of breeze, but there was a patch that swayed a little, moving erratically.

Rebecca got up and made a beeline for it. A large, twitching boot came into view. The closer she got, it helped her eyes focus upon a dying northern rider. He was the one that had been hit earlier by Hagen's arrow.

Hagen joined Rebecca by her side. She knelt over this giant of a man. His beard was long and his body odour emanated from him.

"You'll never see him again." The rider let the words roll off his tongue before coughing up more blood.

Rebecca was upset and angry; her next action was out of desperation. Raising her foot, she placed it on the dying man's wound.

"Where are they taking the children?" She started to place pressure on his skin.

He let out a cry; the pain was becoming unbearable.

"Kill me, please."

"First, tell me where they're taking the children." Rebecca applied more pressure.

The rider winced more, "They're taking them to the orphanage, some for slaves, others for flesh-eaters." His eyes looked for the final blow.

"To feed them to the flesh-eaters?" Rebecca's voice was full of concern.

"No, to become one." His eyes rolled and a bloody smirk appeared on his face.

Rebecca did not wait any longer and before he could say another word, her hunting knife pierced down into his heart. He breathed in, and then let out a few soft gasps, before one final sigh. She then sat back and cried, but it did not last long.

"We must go and find this orphanage," Rebecca said through the tears.

Hagen looked at her red, puffy eyes.

"You do realise we might not make it there?" His huge frame blocked out the winter's sun, casting a shadow on her face.

The hunting group came to join them as Hagen was helping Rebecca to her feet. Florence came over to Rebecca; her face was pale and her eyes full of tears. She knew that no words could help bring back Arthur. Emily paused before throwing herself into her mother's arms.

Both of them held each other close and Hugo the teddy bear slipped from Emily's hand. Rebecca eased her gently back so that she could look her directly in the face.

"I have to go after him, Emily," Rebecca said calmly.

Florence looked like she wanted to say something, but again stayed quiet.

"Florence will look after you, Emily, and I will return with Arthur."

She kissed her on the forehead. Hagen had spoken to one of the men in the hunting group and two of their horses were being prepared.

"Can you ride, Rebecca?" Hagen was clear with this. "I do not mean side-saddle."

Rebecca looked at him.

"I grew up on a farm." She then hugged Emily again and kissed her on both cheeks and the forehead. Hagen came forward and picked up Hugo. Emily had tears slowly appearing in the corner of her eyes.

"We must leave now, time is of the essence." Hagen held both reins of the horses now brought over to him.

"Mummy, please bring Arthur back, he will be worried now." Emily said this as she backed into Florence and brought Hugo to her face to use him to wipe her tears.

Rebecca felt a lump in her throat and her chest going tight, but knew she had to stay strong. "I will bring him back, my sweet child."

Hagen was given arrows and two rifles. He had a revolver attached to his belt alongside his knife. They then mounted their horses. "Do you know where the orphanage is?" Rebecca asked anxiously.

"I have heard of it," Hagen answered.

He said they should follow the giants' trail the best they could.

Rebecca was passed a rifle, which she took and put across her shoulder and back. She looked at Emily; her face looked older since this had all started, but still vulnerable. Rebecca blew her a kiss and then looked at Hagen.

He spoke briefly to his men, who would now lead the camp. He told them to move to the islands further north. With that, he kicked his horse, and both of them set off in the same direction as the giants had gone.

Chapter 19

Charles was with Corporal Heinz as they were being helped off the ship. A messenger had been sent to bring ambulance wagons to take the wounded to hospital. Corporal Heinz was stable but needed the care and attention of the medical staff. Private Chamberlin helped the corporal off and said he would go with him and Charles to the hospital.

The wagons arrived with three doctors and four nurses. There were also Mounted Military Police with a prison wagon. Charles knew instantly he would be arrested for the mutiny in France. Major Sherborne would be chomping at the bit to get at Captain Hayward.

Alexander slowly reached for his revolver, but Charles put his hand on his arm.

"Go with Johann to the hospital." He paused. "I might need you to take a message for me in the future." With that Charles smiled.

The military police did not draw their weapons; they just dismounted and came over to the captain. One of the officers in the group stepped forward. They were not interested in Alexander helping the wounded off the boat.

"Sir, I have a warrant for your arrest." The officer then showed the captain to a carriage that had bars. They would be taking him to the "Glass House", a military prison in Aldershot, given the name for its glass lantern roof.

Charles knew this establishment; it was a tough prison. The soldiers were treated more harshly than normal prison inmates. He had thought about what Corporal Heinz had said about going to Denmark and trying to see if his family was there. Part of him longed for that, but he also knew that he must get the information about Benedict to the high command and hopefully convince the officials that they should find Benedict's father's map and see if this could help save lives within the Empire. He included his family in that train of thought.

It was not the only reason he chose to go back; the other was his men who helped defy Major Sherborne. He had to protect them and make sure they would not die for his actions. For now, he sat on a cold wooden seat, with cast iron bars around him. The morning sharpness could be felt nipping at his fingers and ears. Charles's weapons had been confiscated and stored in a locked chest at the back of the wagon. Two military police officers sat in there with him.

"You're going to suffer before you swing." The officer leaned in when he said this and had quite a broad London accent.

"Watch yourself, soldier, I'm not in the mood for this." Charles felt tired after what he'd recently been through.

The Military Police officer smirked back. He looked over at his companion and smiled at him. He then tilted his head to the side and stuck his tongue out, which brought a smile from the other officer.

Charles's body had taken a battering after being strung up on a cross and then spending over half a day on choppy seas. He had passed out of consciousness a couple of times during the journey home, but tried to keep an eye on Corporal Heinz the best he could.

As the prison wagon trundled along, Charles thought about Nazar and his powerful presence. His mind thought about the darkness sweeping the lands and the fact that evil was now showing itself in many forms and guises.

Although the journey was not a comfortable one, Charles felt himself leaning into the corner of the wagon, and his eyes starting to go. His winter overcoat kept him warm enough, and the iron bars had a canvas covering over the top of them, which kept any rain or bad weather out. During the journey, the captain fell into a deep sleep, exhaustion and his wounds playing a part.

Hours passed.

"Wakey, Wakey!" The sound of a truncheon thumping against the bars brought Charles out of his slumber.

The two officers in the prison wagon grabbed him by the arms. Charles had not fully got his bearings back as he was unceremoniously dragged out of the wagon. He smashed his head against the top of the iron door on the wagon as they pulled him out. Sitting on the floor, Charles looked up; standing over him was a large, burly man.

"Nobody likes traitors." The man wiped his beard with the back of his hand. "Even if you're a captain, you'll be treated like the rest of the scum in here."

Charles smiled. It wasn't what the man was saying, it was the fact that only days ago he had met the enemy king who was now threatening the British Empire. It was all a bit surreal.

" I'll wipe that bloody smile off you face in a minute." The burly man turned and ordered the shackles to be brought forward. "Put those on the captain; that will show him."

The iron shackles were heavy and gave him excruciating pain due to the nails that had been put through his wrists. Charles was lifted to his feet and told to follow the guards into the prison. It was a daunting building, big and hostile. It housed around 165 inmates and was under construction to have that upgraded further.

Inside, he was told about the procedure of the prison and what was expected from him. As a captain, he would normally receive better quarters, but treason meant he would not be afforded such luxuries. They undid his shackles and then he was told to wash and they would check him over for diseases. All of this was done to break his spirit and make sure he would conform to the prison rules.

The burly man stood back and watched as a prison doctor carried out the checks. He was stripped naked, revealing his bruises and wounds. His wrists had been treated on the boat, but the bandages were taken off and the wounds re-examined. Charles winced in pain as his lacerations were checked and cleaned, before being re-bandaged. He felt lightheaded as he tried to dress himself in a prison grey uniform. He was then marched to his block. Standing outside the small single cell was the burly man, who stepped forward.

"He's going in the hole." This was a nickname given for a dark solitary confinement room.

The guards with him looked a little shocked. This was normally used for the aggressive offenders. Captain Hayward had only just arrived and was not in the best of shape after being on a cross, and now he was being put in the hole.

Charles braced himself as he bent down to squeeze in this confined space. His hands had been unshackled, but his legs weren't. The hole was barely big enough for him to stretch out and it was in complete darkness. The only light that came in was when they opened a small hatch for food and to take out the latrine bucket.

He lay there thinking about his family. His photo of them had been taken with his clothes. Their faces were ingrained into his mind, and the last time he saw them in Paris played over and over again. He tried to block out the look of sadness and panic as the flesh-eaters moved in, and focused instead on escaping.

Charles could see Arthur's smile and Emily bounding along carefree in the country lanes of Sunninghill. As these thoughts comforted him, he let his body relax and sink into the cold floor. Rebecca and her beautiful smile appeared in the forefront of his mind; it made him smile in the darkness and also gave him hope. He now had to think about staying alive and getting the information about Benedict to the high command. In the hole he lost track of time; food was served twice a day and the bucket emptied once in the morning and once at night. This was the only way of gauging time. The silence was deafening. Charles did not like small spaces, and found it hard to lie there in darkness. He could turn around, but it required a lot of effort and took energy out of his tired body. Relieving himself in the bucket was difficult; the smell in the hole was stale and unclean.

Occasionally at night he could hear squeaking and scurrying around. Rats had not ventured into his domain until the second night. On that night, he awoke and felt something biting at his sores on his ankles. The shackles had rubbed and broken skin and blood would have enticed them in.

He swung his arms around his feet and felt a large warm body underneath one blow. The high-pitched squeal told him he had hit one, but they disappeared before he could do more damage. They now began to visit him every night. He tried to sleep in the day, but his body clock was all over the place. He felt himself growing more and more tired as the days went on. The battle with the rats was draining; he thought about leaving food out, but then thought this would only encourage more. He tried to kill as many as he could in one go, but this only resulted in three being killed.

The food was a mixture of slop and stale bread. Charles tried to keep up with the days, mornings and evenings, but being confined in darkness and using the bucket was taking its toll.

On day four, Captain Hayward passed out and a fever took hold.

Chapter 20

"Grab him by the legs!" the burly man barked out his orders.

"He was only meant to be in here two stinking days!" He looked at the guards, who shrugged their shoulders.

"Sorry, sir, he's going to swing anyway," one of the guards replied.

"That's not the point; the major wants to speak to him before he swings," said the burly man.

There was a silence as the big man moaned a little under his breath, muttering to himself as if working out the solution to this problem.

"Take him to the prison hospital!" The burly man left to inform his superior officer of what had happened.

Charles was then hauled onto a cart, which was used to move the sick and wounded. They took him to the hospital prison wing. It was fairly empty; a few cases of dehydration and dysentery took up some of the beds. He was rolled to the corner of the long room; his bed had a view overlooking woodland and fields, but he was too weak to take in anything at that time. He was in and out of consciousness. The light hurt his eyes as he had been used to darkness.

Days passed as they nurtured him back to health. The doctor and nurses in the prison hospital wing were good. They did not carry the same malice as some of the other guards. Charles took this time to think of his next move. He had to get the message to the high command about Benedict's map in Austria.

The sores on his body were cleaned and his aching body slowly began to heal. The wounds from the cross had been treated well, and he had been fortunate that no infection had started whilst he was in the hole.

A week after coming out of the darkness, Charles was feeling much stronger. He enjoyed a cup of tea with one sugar and a read of a newspaper. As he sat up in bed drinking his tea, the door at the far end opened.

Charles's eyes fell upon Major Sherborne as he marched in flanked by officers at either side. He walked directly to the captain, without consulting the doctor in charge. Smiling and tweaking his moustache, he stood at the end of the bed. The major looked happy to have captured his nemesis.

"Good to see you again, Charles." He looked at the officers next to him. "God only knows how you managed to escape the enemy." Again, this seemed to amuse him. "Why you came back to hang, I don't quite understand." He said nothing for a moment or two. He then walked around to the side of Charles, where he leaned into his ear. "You will hang for mutiny, and I will watch you die."

Charles thought about telling him about the map, but knew it would not be actioned on until after his death, or maybe not at all. He had to play this situation with care.

The major wanted him dead for taking control in France, and during this time of war he could not be sure what sort of hearing he would receive. His father had some contacts in government, but many had fled already to America and even Rebecca's father was in America drumming up support for the influx of British nationals. He was a high-ranking officer who would have had a positive influence on Charles getting a fair hearing.

Major Sherborne then spoke to the doctor, who had now come over. He moved away from Charles's bed and conducted the conversation out of earshot. The officers with the major spoke amongst themselves.

All of the men returned to Charles's bed.

"It seems like you overstayed your welcome in the hole." The major looked pleased saying this.

"I have arranged for the court martial to be in two weeks. I do not want them feeling sympathy for you if you're looking sick."

"Major, you do realise I wanted to save lives?" Charles was calm.

"Dear man, you know how the army works." He rubbed his hands together. "If a senior officer gives you an order, you damn well obey it." His face crumpled up.

"You left them on the beach to die." Charles's voice was hoarse and dry.
"You're a coward, Major, I will state that," he continued, losing a little of his composure.

Major Sherborne stood there getting angry and flustered. "Nobody calls me a coward, least of all a traitor."

"Your day will come, Major." Charles said this after he cleared his throat.

This enraged the major, who withdrew his revolver and pointed it at Charles. He was shaking with anger. "I should shoot you in this bed."

The doctor and the officers around him looked on with concern; it took one of them to suggest this was not the time, nor place, for an execution, especially as he was sitting in a hospital bed. It would not look good for his career.

Charles sat there still, not trying to agitate the situation further. He had suspicions that the major was highly strung, but now he realised his alcoholic preferences were also affecting his judgement. He had smelt alcohol on his breath when he leant in, and noticed throughout the time he served him that the major had had a tendency to have a drink or two. It would probably not go against him, as many of the high command were heavy drinkers, but he could try and see if it could maybe be something he could use in the trial.

The major reluctantly lowered his revolver. "Looks like God is shining on you today." He slowly let the revolver slide back into its holster. "You've nearly used up all your nine lives, Captain Hayward."

Charles sat there this time, just looking at the men as they turned and left.

The doctor came over to him afterwards and asked if he was alright. He was shocked at the major's approach and sheer audacity in pulling out his revolver in a hospital. He said he would give evidence in his defence if needed. Charles thanked the doctor, but said it would be wasted words. In his mind, he knew there was only one way out of this situation.

***

A week passed before the prison governor paid him a visit. He had been moved to a normal cell. It was clean enough and the cell was about 12 feet long and 10 feet high. He had been kept separate from the other inmates, although he had asked the prisoner who brought his food whether there was a Sergeant Butcher in the Glass House. The answer had been "Yes".

During that week, he had been allowed to mingle with the other prisoners. Sergeant Butcher was chatting with some of the other soldiers from the ship. Their eyes lit up when Captain Hayward appeared in the yard.

He strolled over to them, walking unsteadily as the effects of the hole were still taking their toll on his body.

Sergeant Butcher held his hand out to shake Charles's hand. He shook it and patted him on the back. The other men came forward and shook his hand as well.

"Bloody good to see you, sir!" Sergeant Butcher boomed.

"Bloody good to see you, too, Sergeant!" Charles smiled as he looked at his soldiers. They had risked their lives for him, and now because of his actions also faced a court martial and possible execution. He had already made up his mind that he would take full responsibility and hoped that those deciding his fate would agree that his loyal men were just following his orders.

Sergeant Butcher brought the captain up to speed with the fact that they were taken to Aldershot and the Glass House prison as soon as they arrived back in Britain. Major Sherborne had wanted to carry out a quick trial with sentences that would carry the death penalty.

Lieutenant Colonel Adams had heard about the soldiers returning from France and the story of Charles and his men. He had spoken to several key figures in the army and they had been given time to await the return of Captain Hayward. It was decided that if the captain did not return, then the trial would go ahead after a certain amount of time. The major was not pleased with that, and argued that he had seen the enemy encircle Captain Hayward and his mutineers. This had raised eyebrows about why Captain Hayward had landed on the beach, for if he was taking over the ship, then why didn't he sail somewhere else?

The major just said he did not understand that himself.

The men had made their accusations about the major leaving prisoners behind on the beach. These had been quashed as desperate means to escape the gallows. Now that Captain Hayward was back, they knew the trial would begin; most expected they would be made an example of, but some hoped that the captain, who had prevailed on many occasions, may yet find a surprise solution.

***

The autumn sun bounced off the white walls and onto the metal frame of Captain Hayward's bed. Meeting his fellow soldiers had lifted his spirits and taken his mind off the gallows and thoughts of not seeing his family again. These thoughts were dark, and he tried not to let them overtake his plans to save lives by delivering the information he had. As he sat there reading a Bible, his breakfast arrived. It was a full English breakfast, and there was also a paper. The soldier who delivered it commented on how lucky the captain was for getting such a treat.

At first, he picked at the food, almost expecting it to be poisoned, but as the mouthfuls started, he couldn't stop himself eating all of it. There was even a hunk of bread to mop up the juices left over from the meat and eggs. He did so with relish. To finish this off, there was a pot of tea. He had had one cup with his breakfast and was just pouring a second when there was a tap on the prison cell's iron bars.

Charles looked up to see a short, stocky man standing there.

"Good morning, Captain," the man said.

He then entered the cell and sat on a chair that was pushed next to the captain's bed.

"Let me introduce myself, I am the governor of the prison."

Charles picked up one lump of sugar and dropped it into his tea; then he took a small teaspoon. He slowly stirred the tea clockwise whilst looking at the governor.

"I can't say that my initial welcome was anything I expected." Charles was referring to going in the hole.

The governor looked away and then back again.

"You're a traitor to this Empire, what did you expect?"

Captain Hayward lifted up his cup and sipped at his tea. "Some may say traitor, but saving lives, in my book, says otherwise."

"You disobeyed orders for your own self-gratification." The governor twisted in his seat as he said this.

"Why do I have the pleasure of this visit, sir?" Charles was to the point.

There was a pause.

"Your trial will start tomorrow." The governor got up after he said this.

"I hope you will not let my men go to the gallows for my actions." Charles was looking straight into the man's eyes.

"That's for the court to decide." He then turned around; as he was leaving, he mentioned that there was a soldier who had brought personal belongings from his quarters and a message from his family. He would be allowed to see the private in the afternoon. The governor then left the cell.

Charles hoped this was Private Alexander Chamberlin.

The day passed slowly as he sat reading. A prison guard came to his cell later in the afternoon to tell him that his visitor had arrived and was waiting to see him in the food hall. He was led to the food hall and, sitting at the end of a long table, was Alexander. The guard escorted Charles over to Alexander and told him he had five minutes.

Charles leaned forward and shook Alexander's hand. "Good to see you, Alexander." He shook his hand back and they both sat on a bench across from each other.

"Sorry to say this, sir, but you look rather ill," Alexander said.

"Yes, the treatment here is not quite like the Langham Hotel." Charles smiled.

Alexander put a bag on the table. He said it was from Lieutenant Adams. There were spare clothes inside and some extras for shaving and a toothbrush. All of these items had been checked and allowed in.

"Thank you for this, Alexander. I need you to get a message to the lieutenant colonel." Charles leaned in as he said this. He went on to explain that he had met the enemy king and that he was very interested in Benedict's map. They should put Benedict under guard and keep him safe. Charles believed the map could help them find the enemy monastery and castle in Russia.

He did not fully know what was at the monastery or castle, but he knew the enemy did not want the British Empire getting hold of that map. He had a plan formulating in his head, but he wanted Alexander to inform his brother-in-law of this map and for him to tell the high command. It would have to be quick, as the trial started tomorrow and Charles thought they would try and push this through quickly.

The men chatted for a few minutes more before the guard came over and kicked the table.

"Time's up, gentlemen."

They shook hands and Charles was returned to his cell. He felt relieved for the first time in a while that he might be able to get out of this mess and also take positive steps to help his men.

That night, when his head hit the pillow he fell into a gentle sleep.

Bang, bang, bang. "Wakey, Wakey, get out of bed."

The burly man was standing there with three prison guards.

"It's your trial today, sir." He said this sniggering a little, as if sir meant nothing.

Captain Hayward was enjoying his sleep and was wiping his eyes as two guards came in.

"Let me get changed and washed before we go," Charles said politely and calmly.

The burly man nodded to the other guard, who then entered the cell. Captain Hayward went to pick up his towel and toothbrush when a guard put a wooden baton over it. "Get your clothes on, Captain," said the guard.

Captain Hayward looked at the men.

"Weren't good enough to be in the real army, eh, lads?" Charles said this looking at the burly man.

The guard closest to him took offence to this and brought his baton up to Captain Hayward's throat. "Watch your tongue, traitor."

Charles stood looking at the guard. The baton was slowly lowered and Captain Hayward was allowed to dress himself. Whilst doing up his navy-blue shirt, he reached out for his toothbrush again. The guard who had earlier threatened him with the baton used it to strike the back of his hand. Charles moved backwards, holding his hand and letting out a groan.

The guard was laughing and looking at the other men around him. He did not see Captain Hayward coming forward with fist closed. The punch sent the guard flying into the wall, his head impacting hard before he fell like a rag doll to the ground. The two guards around him started to turn; Charles had already stolen a march on this and began to move in. He swung his elbow into the face of the second-nearest man, causing him to stumble back. As he did this, the guard's baton fell onto the bed. The third guard was now swinging his baton back, but brought it down as the captain moved to the side, thus leaving him open for a punch to his ribs and a knee to the right-hand side of his face. Blood spurted from his mouth and onto the white linen sheets.

The burly man was moving forward as this unfolded. He withdrew his baton, took it over his head and swung it at Charles's head. Charles had already moved around and picked up the other baton on the bed, blocking the burly man's strike. Charles then lashed out a kick, striking the standing leg of the large-framed chap. He stumbled back, dropping his baton.

"Strike me, Captain, that's what your type does." The burly man clenched his fists.

Charles waited a second or two. The emotions of the past few weeks had taken their toll on him, but he knew this was not the way forward. He lowered his baton. Two of the guards had pulled themselves up, slowly recovering from the blows. The third lay knocked out on the floor.

"Don't just look at him; get the shackles on his hands." The burly man said this whilst watching the captain intensively.

Both guards put the shackles on with an air of caution. Charles did not put up a struggle. Once they were on, the men stood back.

The burly man came forward and without saying another word threw a punch into Charles's stomach. He bent over as the pain winded him.

"Not so brave now, Captain." He smiled at the other two guards, who still looked on as if something would now happen to the burly man.

Charles raised his head and looked red and out of breath.

"Listen, lads, once we know when he's going to swing, he'll get a proper beating." The burly man knew they couldn't do it now, as there would be questions from the trial panel. Even if he was a traitor, it wouldn't look good if he had been beaten beforehand.

The guard who had been knocked out was left unceremoniously on the floor, as they led Captain Hayward out of the cell and along the gangway. Both the guards who were escorting the captain had blood dripping from their wounds. The burly man walked behind them as they made their way down a flight of stairs and onto the main courtyard. Standing waiting were the other Royal Engineers. Sergeant Butcher nodded to Captain Hayward, who nodded back.

They could see there had been a scrap but that the captain had come off better. The burly man shouted for the other guards to get them moving. The main food hall was going to house the trial. Three commissioned officers would be acting as the judge, jury and executioner. This was a field general court martial, and the outcome if all three officers agreed could be the death penalty.

The soldiers each had shackles on their wrists; the ankle chains had been removed. Charles was the first to enter the room. Sitting on the panel was Major Sherborne. He looked as pleased as punch to have finally got his man. There were some other officers sitting to the side of the main panel on a small collection of chairs. The accused had several benches to sit on and would be placed directly in front of the judges.

Charles sat at the front. His men sat next to him. Sergeant Butcher was sitting directly to his left.

"Had a bit of a scrap, sir." The sergeant said this with a wry smile on his face.

"They want us all to pay for my actions, Thomas." Charles had a look of concern on his face.

"We stood by you, Charles, because it was the right decision. We will die with you if need be." Sergeant Butcher had a resolute expression when he said this.

Charles's face filled with appreciation for his gallant men.

Once they were all seated, Colonel Montgomery began chairing the court martial. He was a tall man, with greying hair and an oversized moustache. His slender frame had been due to him fighting an illness. His fingers looked gangly and reminded Charles of long limbs.

"This time of war brings out certain characteristics in men." He coughed after saying this. He then looked at the accused.

"You are Royal Engineers." He paused for a moment. "You serve the British Empire and represent the greatest army in the world." Looking down at the table in front of him, he picked up a pair of reading glasses; after sitting them carefully on his nose, he began to read to himself from a piece of paper passed to him from Major Sherborne.

Major Sherborne was almost grinning as this summary was being carried out. His eyes focused on Captain Hayward.

The colonel continued, "On that fateful day, you let this Empire down, our queen, her loyal subjects and the British Army." He then began to go through the mission report and summarise what happened that night.

The accused sat in silence. Charles was aware that no one had asked for their side of the events whilst they had been imprisoned. The summary lasted nearly forty minutes. Major Sherborne was asked to give his side of the events. He stood and cleared his voice before giving evidence.

He spoke about his clear commands that they couldn't save the men on the beach and the fact that Captain Hayward was looking to climb up the ranks and saw this as an opportunity to gain some glory. The major was careful how he worded his evidence; he made sure that he came across as an officer who would do anything for his men. He said he was deeply shocked and saddened by the actions of Captain Hayward and his men and at no point in his military career had he seen such treachery in the lower ranks serving under him. In truth, he was convinced that this venture was wholly inspired by Captain Hayward and he should be held fully accountable.

Captain Hayward at that moment felt a little bit relieved to hear he was to be held fully accountable, but this feeling was short-lived. The major turned his eyes to the soldiers around Captain Hayward. "If we do not also make an example of those who served under him, we could well have anarchy on our hands in the future."

Charles stood up and shouted, "For God's sake, man, tell the truth!"

Colonel Montgomery stood up.

"There will be none of that in my courtroom."

He looked a little flustered.

Captain Hayward just looked at Major Sherborne, who stared back. The defence for the accused had sat in silence. The men had not even had a chance to speak to him. The lawyer was a military man; he had served ten years with the Royal Irish Fusiliers and seen some action in Africa. He was a short, bald man, with a well-kept beard.

"Sir, my defendant is just concerned about the charges levied against him and his men."

He got a sharp look from Montgomery and sat down.

The Engineers looked over pensively at their lawyer, realising he had no real say in this trial.

Captain Brewer was called as a witness; he was not cross-examined by the defendant's lawyer. Charles stood up and asked him to ask questions on their behalf. He was warned that if he spoke out again he would be sent to his cell and notified of the outcome.

Captain Brewer was asked by the panel for his account of what had happened that night, and he lied through his teeth. He smirked at Captain Hayward as he was allowed to re-join the other spectators to the side of the panel. Captain Fairbrook was next. He almost mirrored the account of the events told by Captain Brewer.

The bald lawyer just sat there; he never moved from his seat or said a word. Several more witnesses were called; some had not even been on the mission, but were allowed to give evidence declaring Captain Hayward and his men were like a bunch of looting pirates and were only interested in personal gains and cared nothing for the Empire.

Charles felt his blood starting to boil. Sergeant Butcher's calm exterior was also melting in this sea of lies. The session was broken for the men to be allowed to eat and deliberation was to follow after lunch.

The Engineers sat around two long tables, and they spoke of their disbelief in the lawyer that was representing them and how it felt like they were being railroaded into a guilty verdict. Charles spoke to the soldiers and said he would ask for leniency for them should a death penalty be passed, and he would swing for his commands on that day. They did not like hearing him say those words and they believed they had been through too much together to let him died now. Suggestions of a breakout were whispered around the tables. Some thought they could break free and get the senior officers and use them to gain their freedom and escape into the countryside.

Sergeant Butcher looked at the captain.

"I hear what you're saying, men, but they have trebled the guards around us."

The soldiers looked around, seeing the gangways swelling with military police armed with rifles and revolvers.

"They will not let this go lightly," Charles sighed.

As they sat there in silence for a moment, a small robin flew down and landed on the table. It pecked at the crumbs left on the table from the soldiers' lunch and was not put off by so many of them staring at him.

"My children always loved the robins that would come to our garden." As Captain Hayward said this to Sergeant Butcher, the burly man entered the room.

"Soldiers, it's time." He wiped away crumbs of food from his mouth as he said this. "Come on, move it."

The Engineers rose from their seats. They still had shackles on their ankles, which hindered any quick movement. Military police came down from the gangway and moved them along by force. They slowly filed back into the hall. The panel was already sitting down, looking through notes and documents.

Sergeant Butcher knocked the chair of their lawyer as he walked past. The bald man looked up and caught Sergeant Butcher's eyes. He quickly looked away.

Once they were all seated, the room fell silent. Captain Hayward looked around at the faces around him. He also noticed the heavy presence of soldiers in the room.

Colonel Montgomery stood up.

"Do you have anything further to add to these proceedings, Captain Rushmore?"

He shook his head indicating he didn't.

The accused started to murmur and mutter under their breath.

"After much deliberation, and no further questioning from the defence, we have come to a decision." Montgomery scratched his right cheek before continuing.
"We find the defendants guilty as charged." He cleared his throat. "They will be executed under Her Majesty's laws." He then handed over the paper to Major Sherborne.

"You will be hung from the gallows, first light, Friday morning." As the major said this, the Engineers, who had been sitting in shock, reacted.

Chairs were thrown at the senior officers, but the military police quickly rushed into the heat of the fight, using batons to quell the unrest. Sergeant Butcher and Captain Hayward tried to calm the Engineers. Once the situation was under control, Captain Hayward turned and looked in the direction of Major Sherborne.

"It's me who should hang, Major Sherborne, not my men." Charles's voice was clear and loud.

The room fell silent.

Colonel Montgomery began to lift his arm as if to speak, but Major Sherborne stepped forward. He had a cut on his left eyebrow where he must have been hit by a chair in the mêlée.

"You should hang, Captain Hayward, but I feel it will send a strong message to the rest of the army about mutiny; that is why everyone will go to the gallows."

Charles looked down.

"You know what is coming, and you will pay for your sins, maybe not in this life, but certainly in the next."

This drew a smile from Major Sherborne.

There was a tension in the room. No one dared move for a moment. As the stand-off cemented the moment, the doors towards the back of the room flung open. Walking through them came three officers. One of them was Lieutenant Colonel Adams. His demeanour was steely and determined. His face was clean shaven and his uniform freshly pressed. In his right hand was a piece of paper. Walking straight to the panel officers, he stopped when he reached Major Sherborne.

The discussion that followed started quietly, but then began to get heated.

Major Sherborne stood back and read the paper. "This cannot be true. I want this verified." He shook his head. "These men are traitors and tried to kill me on that boat." He started to share it with the other panel officers. His animated hand gestures and slapping of the paper got the defendants talking.

Captain Hayward looked at Sergeant Butcher. It took another five minutes of loud discussions before Lieutenant Colonel Adams addressed the defendants.

"Considering your actions and debt to the crown, there has been an offer put forward. We need your expertise to go back into Europe and find a map." He paused to clear his throat.

"We believe this map could have the location of the enemy monastery and castle in Russia." He carried on reading out the terms of the offer.

For those who decided not to go, the gallows would sadly still apply. The full mission details would be given and training undertaken at Aldershot barracks for those who chose to take this option.

Charles looked around at his men, who were smiling and looking at him. They nodded their heads in agreement. He then turned and stepped forward.

"It is unanimous, we all accept the mission."

Major Sherborne and the other two officers turned in disgust and stormed out of the room. They were followed by several of the officers who had given evidence. Lieutenant Colonel Adams came over to Charles and briefly shook his hand. "We will speak soon in Aldershot." He smiled and said, "Alex Chamberlin sends his regards and will meet us at the barracks." This made Charles breath in and smile as he breathed out. The men were unshackled and were led to gather their belongings.

The burly man was waiting outside the makeshift courtroom shaking his head. Charles approached him with Sergeant Butcher.

"If my uniform is not pressed and received in the highest-looking standard, then my sergeant will come and collect you and your men and return you to Aldershot." He paused. "You will then join us on our mission to Europe."

The burly man's face went pale and lifeless. "Yes, sir, we'll make sure it's perfect, sir."

Charles grunted at him and returned with Sergeant Butcher to be led out of the glasshouse with the other men.

Chapter 21

"Rebecca, we must rest here tonight," said Hagen.

They had stopped on a small hill overlooking rolling fields. There was a thicket of silver birch trees, with gauze bushes around them. It created a good barrier and shelter from a strong wind that had built up whilst they were riding.

The horses were tethered to a tree and both Rebecca and Hagen began to eat some bread and dried meat, which they had brought with them. Their conversation was a little dry as Rebecca thought about Arthur and Emily. She tried to stay positive and hoped that Charles was still alive. Her world had changed beyond recognition in the last year; it was now all about survival.

"We will do our best to find him and bring him back," Hagen said, then started to make up his bed using his saddle and blankets. "Get some rest, Rebecca."

The wind rustled the branches around them. Hagen took an axe to chop some gorse bushes to form a cover around them. He was aware of flesh-eaters and how they could just slowly walk up to them in the night and attack in the dark. Hagen made it clear to Rebecca that she should not leave the circle. Sleeping without a night watch was not what he wanted, but they would be setting off early and he prayed that nothing would come for them in the night.

"Thank you, Hagen, I would not get through this without you." She said this as she too brought her saddle close and two blankets to wrap around her. The moon was peeping out between the clouds. It made the wind carry a chill factor.

Soon she was in a deep sleep.

***

It wasn't the first twig snapping that woke her, it was the third. The horses started to stir and scrape at the ground with their hooves. Rebecca got up slowly; her bones ached after lying on the cold ground without a fire. Hagen was still sleeping as dawn was slowly approaching.

Something was moving outside their defensive circle. Its heavy breathing sound floated on a gentle breeze. She slowly bent down and withdrew her hunting knife from the side of her saddle. Rebecca thought about waking Hagen but was convinced she could investigate and deal with the situation herself.

Light bounced off the knife blade as she used it to push through the gorse bushes. She tightened her grip on the handle as her nerves were being tested. The breathing was coming from about 15 yards directly in front of her. A spread of trees and small bushes shielded the perpetrator of this noise from being seen.

Rebecca advanced one step at a time. Her heart started to pound, even her palms began to get sweaty. She had seen flesh-eaters before, but it had been a while since she had come face to face with one. Their camp in Denmark was fenced and they had guards who would go out and kill any build-up of flesh-eaters loitering around trying to get in. Now it was down to her; she knew only a head wound would kill them.

Pushing through the branches, she started to see the outline of the figure. It was tall and looked to be caught on something; its breathing was erratic and throaty. Rebecca thought it could be a woman but was not totally sure. Its flesh had been eaten and it had also started to decay. They did not know how long the flesh-eaters could survive, it was an unknown entity.

When the flesh-eater's eyes fell upon Rebecca, its arms and legs began to wriggle and twist harder. She could see what looked like an item of clothing snagged on a branch. As she got closer, it raised its arms.

Snap ... a branch broke under pressure from this creature trying to pull itself forward. Then the clothing started to tear. It was almost free.

Rebecca quickly moved around the back of the flesh-eater as it tried to turn and grab her. With that, she plunged the knife into its head. There was an "arghhhhh" sound before its body went limp and crumpled to the ground. Rebecca wiped the blade on the victim's torn clothes. As she turned around, she saw that another flesh-eater had come up behind her. The shock made her drop the knife; she then fell back onto the body of the creature she had just killed. This new flesh-eater was smaller and looked like an old man; his mouth was snapping and went straight for her legs. Rebecca lashed out to try and stop the beast from attaching its arms onto her.

He was strong – they seemed to possess different levels of strength – and she lashed around kicking and punching, but she could not stop him grabbing her left leg. To compound her sheer panic, another flesh-eater started to appear from her other side.

She was about to scream, when a whoosh of air caught her in mid-breath. A head rolled down to her left-hand side, its eyes still moving frantically. An axe then crashed through skin and bone on the arm that was holding her leg. Two further strikes brought the axe down on the attacking flesh-eater's head, splitting it down the middle. A tongue and eye slid down onto Rebecca's leg. She looked up at the figure standing over her, its features hidden in this world of night and day.

"I told you not to leave the circle, Rebecca." Hagen's voice was soft but firm.

She rolled the butchered flesh-eater's body away from her and stood up.
"I'm sorry, I should have listened, but this is the new world now, and I must be able to fight them." She looked him in the eyes as she said this.

"Ok, but your training will start on this journey." He turned and made his way to the horses.

She followed behind him, and replied, "I already know how to fire a revolver and rifle, but using a knife and sword would help."

"Then I'll teach you that." He checked over the animals and fortunately they were unscathed.

They both started to pack their gear up and take the saddles back to the horses. Dawn broke with a wonderful sunrise. Hagen dug a small hole and made a fire; he had some fresh meat with him from a rabbit he had snared the day before. His culinary skills were good and he even had seasoning with him. Rebecca remarked on how in Victorian England they had been fortunate enough to have a cook to prepare their food. She had been very hands on as a child and enjoyed helping to cook when she was younger.

As a teenager, she had been more rebellious than the other Victorian girls; the etiquette had been very strict and uptight. She wanted to be more involved in the world and not just sit and embroider or be with the women all day.

Hagen said his existence was different as he had grown up on a farm and knew how to look after himself. His family had been dispersed in the war and now he was trying to keep alive the people around him.

"The British Empire will need every man, woman and child to stop Nazar's army of darkness."

Rebecca sat back on a log. She was handed cooked rabbit meat in bread. "I fear for my country and the people in it."

Hagen sat down across from her. "Sadly, this is the new world, and only God can help us now." He then began to bite into his meat sandwich.

After they had eaten, they set off. Their destination was Kiel. The orphanage had been set up outside the town, and was being used to turn some children into flesh-eaters, others into workers and future drone soldiers.

The giant riders were tasked with patrolling Northern Europe and bringing in stragglers who they found along the way. Nazar was not too concerned about the small pockets of survivors who were scattered across Europe. If they started to carry out guerrilla attacks, then he would send units after them.

Depending on the number of casualties it took to take a country, he would then reflect on the level of destruction it would receive afterwards. He knew his forces needed replenishing. Flesh-eaters and long limbs could not win this war on their own. They needed soldiers who could take orders. The drone army was the driving force behind his success.

The weather was not being kind to the riders. A soft breeze had brought in a light rain, which had made visibility difficult. Hagen was caught in two minds, whether to ride straight to Kiel or try and find the northern riders before they got to the orphanage. The horse hairs matted together as Rebecca looked at her shoes as she rode along. Water was running down her legs and off the end of the shoes. She was tired from riding so much in the saddle; she would normally ride when she visited her family, but now this was an intense reintroduction.

The following night, they found an old deserted shack; some of its wooden beams looked loose and it had a worn feel to the place. Hagen said it was perfect. The horses could be tethered inside and it meant the whole building could be made secure. Before sleeping, he showed Rebecca some basic sword and knife moves. He was impressed at how well she took to handling the weapons. They both slept well that evening.

At sunrise they set off again. They rode quietly at times, not talking for hours on end. Long limbs were spotted on the second day moving around a small brook. They were feasting on deer which they must have rounded up and then hunted down in a pack. Rebecca thought about Arthur, his cute smile and his sense of humour; he was growing into a fine young man. He wanted to be a doctor or in some sort of job where he could help people. Arthur viewed the military as something that kept his father away from him and in recent times had taken his father possibly forever.

She also saw in her mind him playing with Emily, his first steps and his first words. "Mummy" was proudly blurted out. She allowed tears to roll down her cheeks as her memories flooded back. It did inspire her to press on and she asked Hagen how much further they had to travel. He told her that they were close and should stop soon to review a crude map he had of the area.

Sliding off his saddle, they stopped by a large pine tree.

"We're close, Rebecca." He pulled out a small piece of paper. It was a basic map, but it gave them the idea of where they were and more importantly how close they were to the orphanage.

As he looked through the map, Rebecca's hand touched his. She then slowly turned her head.

They both stood looking at the horizon. The long grass swayed in the autumn breeze, and the sky was lit up by the midday sun. Their eyes transfixed on what was moving through it – the rumours were true. Children, hundreds of them, but there was a difference with these young souls. They were all infected, and were now flesh-eaters.

"Hagen, we must find Arthur soon." Rebecca looked worried.

"There should be a holding pen, before they decide the child's fate."

Rebecca looked one more time at the child flesh-eaters slowly walking through the grass towards them. They were still children, but their eyes expressed another soul within them. No love or joy was left now, just hunger.

Hagen mounted his horse and waited for Rebecca to do the same. He then kicked his horse on and they galloped off down a small farm track, hoping to find the pen before Arthur's fate was decided.

Chapter 22

Arthur was thrown out of the sack by the giant riders, landing in a muddy puddle. The loose soil softened the blow, but it still hurt. He looked up at his captors. One of them moved towards him. This man had a long, unkempt beard and smelt of sewage. Arthur's eyes followed this stocky, hairy man as he grabbed his foot and dragged him towards a makeshift pen. He tried to gain his bearings as he was pulled along through the soil and grass. The pen only came into sight once he was lying across from it.

"Get up, you little maggot," the stocky giant said.

Arthur gingerly got to his feet. Wiping mud from his eyes, he looked at the pen. It was full of young children. Most looked like they were around his age, but there were some younger ones clinging to others; all of them looked hungry and scared. Arthur felt a shove in his back as he was pushed from behind and into the pen.

He fell to his knees, crashing into the wet soil below. It felt cold; no one moved whilst the giant riders hung around. Screams and crying filled the air, mixed in with different sounds which travelled on the wind. The riders turned and left towards a small outbuilding and a run-down farmhouse next to it.

Arthur got to his feet. Looking down at his muddy knees, he felt a little lost. The other children stayed still for a while, as if they were scared sheep in a pen, clinging together for support. Then out of the bodies came a large lad, maybe a year or two older than Arthur. He was quite broad and did not have a friendly face. Arthur just looked at him as two more boys and one girl came towards him.

The leader of this pack moved in front of Arthur.

"You look British." He smiled and then spoke French to the other children with him. They had heard the giant riders speak English to Arthur. This young lad's English was quite good considering his age; there was an accent attached to it, but Arthur understood.

"You'll not last long here, boy. This is a dark cupboard for children." He turned and smiled at the others. As this was unfolding, several men and women had arrived behind the pen. There were two drone soldiers with them. Arthur was still just standing there, watching it all with his hands tucked in his pockets. He had thought about his mother and sister, and even his dad briefly, but that had all been lost a little with fear and hunger.

An old woman with keys came forward and undid the pen. She then spoke in several languages, asking them to come out. They slowly shuffled past Arthur, who was a little confused and in shock. The older boy who spoke to him earlier nudged him in the back, causing him to fall forward. Arthur looked around angrily, but saw that this gang were laughing at him as they filed out.

A hand came out of the crowd of children. "Quickly, get up, or you're not getting up at all."

Arthur reached out for the hand. He was then pulled up. He had not thought about girls before, but there in front of him was a tall, cute, blonde-haired girl. Her English had an accent to it, but it wasn't French. She could see him looking at her.

"Keep moving towards the orphanage. We do not want to be out here after dark."

Arthur knew about flesh-eaters, but this place had a new kind of menace sweeping around it.

"Thank you for helping me," Arthur said shyly.

The girl looked at him. "They will decide our fates tomorrow."

Arthur continued to follow everyone else; he wondered what she could mean. A building began to come into sight, it was grey and tatty. He looked down at his shoes; the mud had built up on them, and they had made him grow in height by an inch. The downside was the weight of them had doubled.

Their small group was joined by four other pens of children. The children all looked tired and lost. The boy who had pushed Arthur down kept his friends close; he looked like he knew the sequence of events and was biding time.

They were marched to the front gates of the orphanage. Arthur looked at the building; it was much larger than he had expected and looked like it had newer parts added on the sides. There were also wooden cabins running in rows along the back walls. These walls were over thirty feet in height and gave the feeling of turning the whole site into a prison.

A loud, screechy voice sounded out behind the wall. It was followed by silence. Then a horse's head and body slowly revealed itself by the gate. Sitting upon this horse was a priestess. She had long, black hair and a pointed nose. She shouted at the children to line up.

"My name is Isabella." She smiled, showing off her sharpened teeth. "Follow my orders or you will be killed." She spoke in French. The older woman who had opened the pen to put Arthur in then translated into several languages. Arthur stood there completely still; he did not want to catch the priestess' eye. She rode her horse around the children. The animal had armour attached to his saddle and head piece, with spikes coming from it. Several more drone soldiers started to filter out from behind the wall and they were followed by a collection of what looked like slaves. The slaves were carrying rope and sticks.

"I will now choose one child." She smiled and then dismounted. "Do not fear, this child will be well looked after." The children's eyes looked panicked. The priestess began to walk along the line of children. Arthur prayed inside his head that she did not pick him. She held out her hand and extended her index finger, letting it touch the children's heads as she moved along the line. Arthur tried not to look as she slowly worked her way along. He could not help but count the children from him, five, four, three, two, one, and then the finger touched his head. He felt like he was going to cry; she looked into his eyes and soul, but her hand rested there only a second before moving on to the next head.

She then stopped. It was a small, round boy with brown hair and green eyes. He did begin to cry. She brought him into her chest. He was speaking to her in French and she spoke back. The priestess seemed to comfort him, and as far as Arthur could see she meant well, but her long nails on her hand began to dig into his head causing the boy to look at her with worried eyes. Two slaves that were standing behind her came forward and took the child by his arms; he looked at the rest of the children, not really knowing what to expect. He was then ushered away.

No tears, no cries, just a look of despair.

Arthur's eyes followed the boy as he disappeared into another building.

"Right, we will meet him later." She said it in French again and it was translated by the old woman.

The children were then herded through the gate. Arthur looked up, noticing the iron cross on the gate had been turned upside down. He did not look for long, and just followed the other children into the orphanage building.

The interior was dark, with paint coming off the walls. The air felt damp and carried with it a stale smell. They were filtered through into a large dining area. It had long wooden tables with benches either side of these tables. At the top lay another table. An order was given out for them to sit, but not at the top table. "You will all soon be fed, my children."

The girl who spoke to him in the pen took his arm and led him to a bench. She sat down next to him and told him to be quiet for now, but she would tell him more later. They all sat in silence as guards walked around them. The children did not make a sound and the atmosphere was tense. Some of the slaves disappeared off through a side door. The priestess sat at the top table, looking at the children. She was brought food first; it was a feast of roast chicken and fresh bread, and there was also cheese and fruit. Arthur's stomach rumbled. He had not eaten like that for months. The camp only had basic food, but he still longed to be back there.

She wasted no time ripping into the chicken; bones were crunched and torn apart. Arthur watched the sharp nails gripping and clawing at the food like an animal. Her eyes briefly looked in his direction, causing him to look down.

"Do not make eye contact with her," the girl said.

"I don't understand, why are we here? What do they want?" Arthur wanted answers.

She was about to tell him when their food was brought in. It was roast chicken as well and batons of fresh French baguettes. It was followed by cheese and fruit and other items. There was almost a little cheer as this happened. Once the food was set down on the tables, they were told to wait.

The priestess stood up. "This is what I give you, now eat." She clapped her hands and the feast began.

Arthur could not contain his hunger and grabbed a chicken leg. The girl took a chicken breast and bread. The feeding frenzy lasted a while. Every morsel was cleaned off the plates.

Slowly, a small murmur of noise crept across the hall. The food was having an effect on the children's wellbeing. They felt more alive and even began to laugh a little. Isabella sat there, her eyes rolling over the children sitting having fun. She let her long tongue slide out of her mouth and wrapped it around each of her fingers one at a time, cleaning them as she went along. The children were unaware of this, blissfully enjoying a full stomach. But there was one keen observer. Arthur saw her tongue and it sent a shiver down his spine. He did not like the set-up here, and could not understand why they would be so nice to the children of their enemies.

"Don't keep looking at her, or you'll go the same way as the other boy," the girl said softly.

"Look, I don't even know your name?"

"It's Anna, and yours?"

"It's Arthur."

"Look, Anna, I don't understand." Arthur was frustrated by not knowing why he was here.

Anna looked around. "I can't tell you here, but I have been here once before and escaped." She had tears starting to well up in her eyes. She started to tell him the orphanage was not how it looked and they should trust no one. Anna's explanation was cut short. Slaves started to clear empty plates, and the children were told to stand. Isabella was then joined by the old woman and several drone soldiers. She asked the children to follow her to the courtyard.

Walking through dark corridors and hearing the odd scream brought the children down from their excitement of having eaten well. They started to cluster closer together. The courtyard itself was larger than Arthur imagined. It was a deceptively large building. The children were again told to line up and await orders.

Anna stood next to Arthur. Another short lad joined them; he instantly introduced himself as Samuel. "I'm scared, I don't like the priestess," he said.

Anna told him to be quiet or he would attract attention to them.

The priestess spoke with the old woman and then two of the slaves.

"Children, this is where we sort you out to become heroes for our new nation."

Isabella then started to walk down the line. She paused to check children's teeth and physiques. Speaking in Russian to the old woman, she proclaimed she only wanted the strong children to become drone soldiers.

After walking up and down several times, they walked to the front.

"I will now put you into two groups." She licked her lips, letting her long tongue come out and then go back in. "Workers and drone soldiers." She smiled, showing off her sharp teeth. The children started to shuffle their feet as fear crept in. Arthur turned and looked at Anna. She had a worried look on her face, and before they could even whisper to each other, Isabella clapped her hands. Two slaves opened a large oak door leading into the courtyard.

Nothing happened for a moment or two, and then emerging from the darkness came the round boy from earlier. He was no longer the same; his eyes had no life in them. The boy's skin was pale and his mouth hung open. Tied around his neck was a long piece of rope which was quickly grabbed by one of the slaves. As soon as the boy saw the children, he began to move faster towards them. He started to snap and groan to get at fresh meat.

Some of the children panicked and began to run to the other doors in the courtyard. They were all locked. Isabella stepped forward.

"Children, you must not be scared." She took over holding the rope from the slave.
"But I do have a word of caution for you." She smiled to the children. "Some of the children have tried to escape our home here." She looked at the slaves, who scurried off and brought two young children back with them. Their hands had been tied and their feet chained together.

The boy and girl who had been brought to the courtyard started to shake. Arthur looked anxiously at Anna. She had tears rolling down her cheek. "What's happening?" Arthur whispered. His heart was racing as he watched Isabella walk around the children. The infected boy was snapping and pulling on the rope, trying to get at the boy and girl.

"I want you to learn a lesson today." She then released the flesh-eater boy.

He was onto the poor souls within a second. They did not have a chance and his endless desire for food was temporarily satisfied. The screams could still be heard as Arthur covered his ears. Anna looked at the ground.

The rope holding the flesh-eater boy was picked up again. He was left eating whilst Isabella studied her captive audience. Their young faces showed fear beyond control. Most had seen the horrors of the war, but not in this manner. Isabella kicked the flesh-eater boy and pulled him away from eating. She then began to walk him around the children. They all huddled together as the flesh-eater boy lashed out, trying to get his next meal.

As she made her way around the courtyard, Philippe, the boy who had pushed Arthur, stumbled over his feet as the flesh-eater child drew closer. Another boy in the group tried to help him up as the creature closed in. Philippe took his hand and threw him in the direction of the flesh-eater. The boy rolled into its path, but it took a lot of effort to stop the creature from biting the child. Isabella called over to a slave who was standing by one of the doors. She then looked at the flesh-eater boy. The slave did not wait and rushed over to take him off her. The child who was nearly eaten lay there crying.

"You, boy, the one who threw this child on the floor?" Isabella was snarling.

Philippe began to physically shake.

"Come forward, and let me see you." Isabella stood upright and moved like a serpent eyeing its prey.

With tears starting to roll down his cheek, he stepped towards Isabella. "Good, come closer." She beckoned the boy forward.

Then she brought him into her arms and gave him a long embrace. The other children stood in silence. "You are the future." She brushed his hair back. The child that had been crying on the floor slowly got to his feet. He looked at Isabella and Philippe and quickly scurried back to the main bulk of children.

Raising her voice, she said, "If you want to be part of the new world, then you must be ready to fight for it." She then pushed Philippe forward.

"He will be a future general." She then told him to stand in one corner of the courtyard. The boy who had nearly been bitten was told to go to the other corner. Isabella then began to work her way through the children. Workers and drones, she wanted to make sure the strong children would be hand-picked for Nazar's future army. He knew his plans to take over the world would need soldiers; flesh-eaters and long limbs would not be enough, and even with all the other beasts he had, he still needed an army. Some of the drone children would be altered into destroyer drones within time, but for now, Isabella's orders were to build them up and train them.

The drone children would work as slaves and then be used throughout the world to service his empire. Those who did not make the grade or tried to run would be either fed to the flesh-eaters or made into flesh-eaters.

Arthur shook as Isabella came close; she looked him up and down, checking his teeth and bone structure. "You could turn out to be a very good drone soldier, boy, but for now, a worker will do." Anna was also checked up and down. The strong girls had been used as drone soldiers or cavalry.

Anna breathed a sigh of relief as she was selected to join the workers. Arthur tried not to show his joy, as he thought Isabella would separate them. Slowly but surely, the two groups were decided. The children were then ordered to follow the selected guides to their new quarters.

The future drone soldier children would be housed indoors; their accommodation was clean and fresh. Isabella wanted the new army to have better conditions than the workers.
The workers would be housed in long, wooden huts. Boys and girls would have to share them together. The huts were not in the best of condition.

Arthur was shocked at what he saw as they made their way through the orphanage and out to a walled area behind the main house. He could not believe how many huts there were. He also saw in the distance a fenced area; the wooden stakes had enough room for arms to come through. These arms were moving erratically, clawing at thin air at times. Straight away he realised where the children flesh-eater pens were.

Their guide stood outside their hut. He was then joined by four teenage children. They would be in charge of keeping the children in check and teaching them their new roles. A tall teenage lad called Robert stepped forward.

"Do as we say, and I will try and keep you alive." Robert looked at the children as he said this. They had a teenage girl translating his words into other languages. He spoke for a while, telling them to wash and then rest. Tomorrow they would be learning how to plough and make weapons. Nazar knew he needed weapons and food for his armies.

Anna came with Arthur as they were led into a washing area. It was metal baths filled with soapy water. The children did not like the lack of privacy. Anna undressed and began to wash; Arthur looked away as she did so. He had seen children and adults washing before, but he was a Victorian and manners had been drummed into him. Anna was quick to remark that unless he washed now, they could be prone to getting lice. That was enough for Arthur to strip and undress. He washed as quickly as he could and took the new clothes that had been given to them.

They were all now dressed in grey. Anna had secured them a bunk bed together, and she allowed him to take the top bunk. Samuel had been helped as well by Anna; she got him a bunk bed next to theirs. The teenagers patrolled the rooms of the wooden huts to make sure no children were still up or in the toilets. Then the candles and lanterns were blown out. Robert and the teenagers would sleep at either end of the wooden huts. They would also be punished for any of the children trying to escape their hut.

Anna told Arthur to stay awake and she would tell him more. Arthur waited; he felt so tired and to stay awake he had to fight every natural instinct in his body to sleep.

"Arthur, are you awake?"

"Yes, Anna, just."

"I have been here before." Anna said this as quietly as she could. She went on to tell Arthur that she had been taken from a camp five months ago, but managed to escape. She had shorter hair at the time and they did not recognise her this time around; she was also with a group of children who had not been caught before. This played into her hands as they were all fresh faces.

She paused for a moment. Arthur sensed that something was wrong. "Are you ok?"

"They never made it, the other children." She sobbed a little. Arthur said how sorry he was and understood it must be hard. She took a moment to find her breath and then slowly continued. "We were lined up as before, Isabella had just arrived to the orphanage and was about to become in charge, and she wanted to flex her power. She selected them the same way as the poor boy the other day. They were not infected like him, but they were told to fight a large group of flesh-eater children. They never had a chance." Anna said she had got lucky by not being selected.

"We have to plan an escape, Arthur." She stood up from her bunk. "If we do not, then we will perish here."

Chapter 23

Hagen brought his binoculars up to his eyes. He was lying in a small patch of grass, on elevated ground. Slowly scouring the buildings in front of him, he realised the orphanage was much larger than he originally thought. It had long, wooden huts stretching back as far as the eye could see. Then there were the pens. He guessed this was where the children flesh-eaters were being kept. Rebecca waited patiently next to him.

Nazar had seen an opportunity to use this as a training camp for his future armies. He had already started to set up other orphanages around Europe and was looking to keep his forces well stocked over the years.

Hagen turned to her and placed his binoculars on the grass next to him.

"It looks like the size of the orphanage has trebled, Rebecca." Hagen paused. He then handed her the binoculars. "Look at the wooden huts and pens." She took the binoculars off him. Letting her hands tighten on the grip, she studied the orphanage.

"How can we find him in this?" Her voice was soft and almost broken with emotion. "Do not give up hope." Hagen told her they must find a place to camp first and then discuss options.

Rebecca struggled to leave the hill. Her maternal instinct was to go down to the orphanage and rescue her son. Hagen felt her anxiety and helped her along with a gradual pull on her arm. She looked at him with worried eyes, but his stare back was firm. "You cannot save him by just riding in there." Hagen led her to the horses. "When we go in there, it will be under the cover of darkness." Mounting his horse, he waited for Rebecca to mount hers. They then slowly made their way to denser forest.

Hagen found a glade which had been opened up by several trees falling over, causing a clearing as the trees rotted down. There was a small bit of grass for the horses to graze on and even ground for them to build shelter. Hagen said that they would cook early before the sun went down and save some of the meat for later in the evening.

Rebecca gathered wood from the forest and some berries for them to eat. As the food was cooked, Hagen checked around the area. He looked for flesh-eaters and long limbs roaming in the woods. For now, it seemed the flesh-eater children were being kept in the pens. He took time to explain his plan as they sat down to eat. Rebecca listened intently; she wanted to act, but knew she had to bide her time and listen to how Hagen wanted to get them in there.

He said they should monitor the orphanage over the next few days. The new intake would be sorted; Hagen was surprised by how Nazar was now using the children he had captured. Nazar had shown long-term planning now; he wanted to build and stock his armies for the future. Rebecca asked if he thought this gave Arthur more of a chance. He believed the emphasis had changed slightly from building a flesh-eater army of children. This could be because it was large enough or he was advised to have more soldiers.

It was decided they would take it in turns for the night watch and go out early in the morning to scout closer to the orphanage.

The ground ivy near Rebecca's saddle and blankets made a good mattress. She was tired and fighting a constant battle within her head about leaving Emily with Florence. She trusted Florence, but knew of the dangers of this new world. As Hagen took the first watch, she thought about her family being separated from each other. She prayed they were not scared or in pain.

Letting her eyes close felt soothing. Hours passed and Hagen took most of the watch; he knew Rebecca had been tired and wanted her to sleep well. When she awoke, she insisted he sleep on a bit in the morning. He begrudgingly obliged.

Breakfast was short and sparse.

"We need to see if they will take some of the new children out of the orphanage to gather wood or other supplies."

Rebecca listened and sipped out of a water canister.

"What about the other children with Arthur?" Her face gave away what she was thinking but she felt she had to ask.

"We will not be able to save them all." Hagen looked sorry for his remark, but they were only two and the orphanage had plenty of drone soldiers.

They finished up breakfast and covered the equipment they could leave in their temporary camp. Before they set off, Hagen showed Rebecca some more sword moves. He wanted her to get used to swinging the sword and hitting in to soft wood. He was impressed at how useful she was with a sword.

Keeping within young ash trees helped give them excellent cover. Moving in and out of the young trees kept them camouflaged. Hagen was happy with the lack of wild enemy creatures. They had not seen any long limbs or flesh-eaters. He wondered if Nazar had started to gather in as many as he could to prepare for an assault on Great Britain. It was speculation, but it would account for the creatures' low numbers.

Using the binoculars, he studied the orphanage from a closer range. He saw hundreds of children in black uniforms training over an assault course. They were being made to carry bags and each other. Some had rifles and were drilling with them. Hagen looked at the vast pens with poor soulless children wandering around inside them. He felt sadness in his heart and hoped that Arthur was not in there. Rebecca took a turn to look for her son. She saw the children training and the pens. She could not see anyone else, but as she started to take the binoculars from her eyes, a hut door opened. This was followed by several more long hut doors opening. Children began to emerge from them. They were not in black uniforms; theirs were grey and dishevelled.

She did not see Arthur, but this sight of other children gave her hope. These children were not chosen to fight; they had been chosen to do something else.

Hagen took her around the whole orphanage perimeter. They looked for weaknesses in the outer fence. The main wall around the orphanage building was thick and patrolled along the top. The guardhouses had several drones sleeping in them. Hagen believed they had not been attacked here and felt no immediate threat.

He felt the side of his horse, running his hand down its soft mane. It stirred a little, making Hagen and Rebecca suspicious. They looked around and saw nothing. A breaking branch snapped through a cluster of thick hawthorn trees. A field maple tree blocked their line of sight. "Move into the open, Rebecca."

Rebecca looked at him. She then steered her horse to the open grassland. They were fairly close to the camp and she was conscious of being seen. Hagen backed his horse into the open grassland.

Nothing.

Hagen stood his ground, letting his hands fall to his sides. The branches started to snap in a steady fashion. Something large was now coming towards them. Leaves started to rustle directly in front of them. A giant wolf started to emerge out of the foliage, its eyes transfixed on Hagen. It had saliva dripping from his mouth, and its teeth were showing. Its fur was standing up. Rebecca reached for her revolver. Hagen told her to not move.

The growl came before the beast charged.

It covered the ground between them quickly. Hagen turned his horse to face the wolf directly. As the beast jumped, the horse reared up, and the weight of the wolf knocked the horse back, but it kept its feet. The wolf steadied itself and then swirled around. A deep throaty growl vibrated the airwaves around them. It then charged again, and Hagen's right arm reached back and let his hand grip the handle of his axe. He then brought this slicing through the air. As the wolf jumped up to sink its teeth into his leg, the axe came into the side of its neck. The blade cut through the fur and skin like a warm knife cutting through butter. Its head instantly fell to the side, the bone crushing on impact. Blood burst out of the wound, causing the animal to yelp with pain and fall to the ground.

Hagen brought his horse around and slid off it with ease. The wolf whose head was half hanging off was pawing at the ground around it and breathing heavily. Blood soaked into the soil beneath it. Hagen did not prolong the creature's agony; he brought the axe up and then down on its head. The beast's tongue rolled out the side of its mouth.

Rebecca came over to Hagen and asked, "Will there be more?" He looked at her and shrugged his shoulders.

"We have to drag the body into the undergrowth," Hagen said as he grabbed the creature's hind legs.

Rebecca dismounted and helped Hagen take a leg. The wolf was heavy; his bone structure was twice the size of its normal kind. They took the body into dense heather and scrub. Covering it with leaf litter and soil, they remounted and left.

"We now have a lead on the snatched children." Rebecca sounded positive as she rode with Hagen. "He must be with the children they are grooming to become slaves."

Hagen looked at her.

"You may be right, but we must locate him soon. The longer we're out here, the more chance we'll be seen."

They rode back to their camp, stopping for the horses to drink at a small brook along the way. Throughout the day, they carried on making short trips to study the surrounding outbuildings and fence line. The wall looked impregnable and would take some climbing to get over it.

Whilst they sat eating, Hagen said that once they knew which wooden hut Arthur was in, they could then start a diversion. They spoke about the giant riders returning with a fresh bunch of children, but there was no timeline to go by. Hagen said they would go out one more time before dusk. Rebecca liked his determination, but told him they could wait until tomorrow. He said it was worth one more look.

Moving through the woods and to the side of the grasslands, they went to a well-trusted viewing point. At first, Rebecca thought it was deer grazing in the small bushes at the side of oak woodland. It was only on second glance that she saw they were not deer, but children. She called Hagen over to check whether they were infected or not. The light was fading, but he was able to confirm it was children in grey clothes. There was a small collection of drone soldiers with them, and the rest of the adults must have been slaves.

They were making their way back to the orphanage carrying wood, bags of berries and dead rabbits. Rebecca asked for the binoculars; she studied the young faces as they closed in on the main gate. A gulp of air and a slight high-pitched noise gave warning to Hagen that Arthur was alive. She began to turn towards her horse, but felt an arm across her shoulder. "We will catch them tomorrow. They're too close to the gate now." Hagen was calm. Rebecca watched as she saw them disappear inside the main walls. Her heart sank for a while, but she smiled as she watched them make their way back to their camp. She knew now that he was alive.

Chapter 24

"Arthur, we must make a new plan to escape." Anna said this quietly as she stacked wood to the side of the barn. As they worked away, Philippe walked past with six of the youth drones. Arthur did not see him at first as he was trying to stack the wood properly, but he did feel a foot in the back of his calf muscle. The pain made him spin around and push away the foot which was pressing against his leg.

"You're going to suffer, English boy." Philippe said this laughing and then pointed to the pens. "I'm going to put you in there soon." There was evil in his eyes and his words excited the boy and girl drone soldiers that were with him. He had taken to his new role very well.

He then stepped forward and kicked Arthur in the side. The blow winded Arthur, who held his side as he went down into the soil. Anna shouted at Philippe to stop and called him a monster. This just brought laughter from the others.

A girl drone stepped forward and slapped Anna around the face; again, there was a flutter of giggles and excitement from the new recruits.

Philippe wanted more and began a run up to kick Arthur again. Anna tried to move to stop him but was blocked by the girl drone. Arthur sensed Philippe's actions and as he moved forward rolled to the side, causing Philippe to kick at thin air and fall over. Arthur wasted no time and as Philippe turned, he came into his side, pushing him down. He grabbed a sharp stick that was by the side of the woodpile and pressed it into Philippe's throat. He did not push it all the way in, just enough for Philippe to stay still and look anxious. The group of drone soldier children looked unsure what to do. Anna pushed the girl away from her.

"You're making a big mistake, boy!" Philippe said loudly, but his voice was wavering. "I'm now a junior officer in Nazar's army." Arthur looked around. "You're one of many, Philippe. They can replace you, like they can replace me." He paused, before continuing, "There are thousands of children in this camp." A tense stand-off followed. Arthur knew that if he released Philippe, then he would give the order for Anna and him to be killed. The problem was where could they go?

"Release the officer, slave!" A drone soldier on horseback rode over.

Isabella was riding with her advisers nearby and also came over to see what the commotion was. The drone on horseback withdrew his revolver and was now pointing it at Arthur. Isabella dismounted and walked over to the children.

"What is going on here? Mutiny will be severely punished." She moved slowly towards them.

"I was doing my job when he attacked me." Arthur felt his nerves kick in as she approached.

"Is this right, Philippe?"

"He was not doing his job properly," Philippe blurted out.

Isabella looked at Anna and then at Arthur.

"Let him go now and you will live," Isabella said harshly.

Arthur looked at Anna; she looked as if she thought he should obey the priestess. He relinquished his grip on Philippe, allowing him to get up. Philippe then looked around. He reached to his side, unsheathing his hunting knife which had been concealed by his overcoat. "You will pay for this, maggot."

Arthur braced himself.

"Stop, Philippe! This is not the time or place." Isabella came between them both; her hand took the chin of Arthur. He could see her sharp nails and the tiny bits of soil underneath the tips of them. "This boy and girl will be given a last warning. If they fail to listen, then you can kill them."

"Maybe you two should join the drone army." She looked at Arthur and Anna, then snarled at Philippe. "You need more training, boy," she said, slapping Philippe across the face and piercing his skin with one of her nails. Blood trickled down his neck and onto his uniform.

Philippe reluctantly joined his fellow drone recruits and they continued on their way. He looked back at Arthur, who was still pretty much frozen to the spot. Isabella had remounted and was continuing to observe the rest of the orphanage.

Anna took Arthur's hand and moved him from the ground he was stuck to. He felt his sore ribs as he moved and winced a little with every step.

"Thank you, Anna, but Philippe will have it in for us now." She looked at Arthur as he said this, knowing that he spoke the truth.

"We have to plan tonight; we may only get one chance to escape." Anna's eyes lit up a little and she knew this painful experience to Arthur would in fact aid her quest for them to attempt an escape.

"Samuel will also come with us; it will mean we can carry more food and water." She was getting excited by the sheer thought of it.

"Anna, they have horses, and soldiers. How can we escape from them?" Arthur stopped walking and looked at her.

"Arthur, I've escaped before and I'll do it again, with or without you." She looked upset with him for not being so positive, but Arthur felt his side as they were led to an open area to eat. There were no tables here, just logs to be used as seating. The bowls of soup brought to them was no longer the feast they had enjoyed a while back; this was more like gruel. Thick, pasty, flavourless and hard to swallow. Arthur began to sit down next to Anna, but he struggled to lower himself down, so she helped ease him down. "Thank you, Anna, we can talk more about your plan tonight."

That night the wind picked up and brought with it a cold chill. Hagen was pragmatic and told Rebecca to come closer to him. "Our body warmth will keep us alive."

They had checked around the area and put rope around their camp. It would not stop attackers, but it would warn them. Hagen had also built a wooden shelter; he had also roped together a door. It was not ideal, but it would give them a chance should flesh-eaters arrive. Because of tiredness, it was essential they both got a good night's sleep.

Hagen awoke to soft raindrops running off the shelter. The air was cold and had dampness to it now. He looked out to check on the horses. They were both standing and looked calm and happy. Hagen then looked around the local vicinity; he could not see anything, no flesh-eaters or wolves.

"Rebecca, it's time to get up." He then started to get his things.

Rebecca was wrapped up like a ball. She looked very happy and content; her mind knew she had to get up, but her body wanted to rest.

Hagen looked at his Webley Revolver, pushing the barrel forward and checking the bullets in the cylinder. He closed it back up and returned to gather his things. Their breakfast had been sparse, but they hoped this was the day to perform a rescue mission for Arthur. Hagen made sure to double-check all straps and saddles on the horses. He told Rebecca to make sure everything was secure in her saddlebags. She checked her own firearm. Everything seemed to work fine, and she followed instructions from Hagen about what to look for.

The light rain drifted across the open grasslands. The horses pushed on, their hooves sinking into the soft soil, which was now being softened by the rain. The field maples started to look empty without their leaves, like lost souls in a sea of green. Rebecca and Hagen took up a position where they could monitor the comings and goings of the camp.

Hagen discussed about how they should approach the situation; he said they might have to take on several of the guards and kill them if necessary.

"What about the other children?" Rebecca had raised this before, but it troubled her. "Do we just leave them?"

Hagen said nothing. Instead, he took out his binoculars and scanned the outer perimeter. Rebecca did not question him further; she took out her rifle and walked over to a fallen tree. The branches had long since rotted away, leaving the main trunk covered in moss. She bent down, bringing the butt of her rifle into her shoulder. Rebecca then looked down the sight. She panned along the outer wall of the orphanage and then the wooden fence around the pens and long huts.

Her eyes lit up when she saw movement from one of the wooden huts. Lowering the rifle, she looked over at Hagen. For once he showed some emotion and smiled. "We must be ready soon."

Chapter 25

Anna had told Arthur about her plan. She said their best chance was to use this opportunity whilst they were out in the forests gathering wood. It involved them running in different directions near the pine forest to the east. Samuel was included in this plan as well. He had told them he could not last in this orphanage, or wherever they would be sent afterwards.

The morning started with a thick, gooey porridge. The worker children had been told that they would be fetching wood in the forest that morning. Anna was sent to fill up the water canisters, whilst Samuel and Arthur loaded stale bread into wooden boxes. The drone soldiers with them were not so focused on the children. The older teenagers were more vigilant. Their position and privileges centred a lot on the worker children staying in line and quotas being met.

The weather had dampened spirits and left most of the children dragging their feet as they went about doing their chores. Isabella had seen this as she carried out her morning patrol of the orphanage on horseback. She did not like this attitude, and steered her horse towards them. Her entourage followed.

"What is this?"

She took her horse amongst the children. An older teenage came forward and lowered his head.

"My priestess, what is wrong?" The lad who had been in charge of Arthur's hut spoke softly. She did not take well to this. She led the horse into the young man, pushing him backwards slowly.

"Please, I don't understand."

"You will do." Isabella then got the horse to rear up, causing the young teenager to fall over.

"Take him to the pens and feed him to my special children." She let her tongue roll around her lips and then snapped it back in.

The teenage boy began to scream and pleaded for his life as two drone soldiers dragged him off. His cries echoed around the camp. There was silence for a minute or two, before the screams became more intense. Some children began to cry; this only seemed to excite Isabella more, she looked at their small faces and let out a hideous laugh.

"Now, whip those children who are not working hard enough." She turned her horse to face a young teenage girl who had been second in command.

"You are now in charge, fail me and face the consequences." Isabella then looked over in the direction of the nearest pen. Bits of flesh, arms and legs were being devoured by ever-hungry flesh-eater children.

Arthur picked up his speed, as did Samuel. They looked at each other and both knew escaping was the only choice.

When the supply wagon was full and two more empty wagons were ready, they set off. Arthur walked with Anna and Samuel. They occasionally looked at each other, only in glances, but they were telling glances. Isabella took up a position on a small mount, at the edge of the camp wall. She looked like an empress sitting on her horse, watching her slaves going off to forage.

Luckily, she did not increase the amount of guards. Three mounted drone soldiers rode with them. The teenage girl, who had been given command of the slave children, was anxious not to suffer the fate of her former leader. His carcass was visible as they walked past the child flesh-eater pen he was thrown into. Arthur allowed himself one quick glance and saw scattered bones and the odd child chewing on the last remains of flesh.

There were some adult slaves walking with them. They had whips and large batons. Even though they were slaves, they had built up some privileges under their new rulers and would follow Isabella's instructions to the letter.

Rebecca and Hagen watched from the forests. They could now see the troop of children being escorted out of the orphanage. Hagen looked at the number of soldiers with them and the wagons. He saw that one had a canvas cover over it and the others were empty. He then deduced that they would be collecting food or wood. Hagen passed the binoculars to Rebecca. She scanned the line of children. A smile erupted on her face; Hagen saw this and knew she had found her son.

"We will track them for a while." He then pointed in the direction of the large pine forest to the east. "Then pick our moment to strike."

Hagen thought they would be heading there for supplies. Both Rebecca and Hagen checked over their weapons again. Rebecca felt her heart racing; she had waited a while for a chance to save her son and now it was close.

They followed them for around thirty minutes, but stayed at a good distance so as not to be seen. The next hour, the children and the slaves worked on collecting wood and catching rabbits and other animals. Hagen saw a slave bringing back a deer he had killed in the woods. The drones did not seem too concerned that this slave had a bow and arrow, which raised the question as to how loyal they now were to their new masters.

Hagen and Rebecca watched them from a distance. Their plan was to strike whilst they were out gathering wood, hopefully grabbing Arthur and using the forest to escape capture.

***

The children did not talk as they set about carrying out their chores. Arthur was walking with Anna and Samuel. They stayed in the glade next to the large pine forest. Anna only spoke when she was bending down to pick up wood, and Arthur and Samuel did the same. They had agreed to spread themselves out along the forest edge and prepare to go within ten minutes. This would involve them counting to themselves. After that, they would run into the forest and hopefully meet up at some point. There was a chance they might not all make it, but each of them had agreed it was their only choice.

Each of them counted under their breaths as they bundled sticks together, then, after looking around, all three made a dash for it. They were well spaced and did not draw attention to themselves at first. The first alarm that went up was a teenage slave seeing what was happening. This alerted a drone solider, who took aim with his rifle and squeezed the trigger.

Bang.

A bullet whizzed past Arthur and smacked into a rotten log next to his left leg. He did not stop running, though; the drone took aim again but he was now amongst the trees. Calling out to the teenage girl who was now in charge, the drone told her to send a messenger to Isabella to let her know that children were escaping.

Rebecca and Hagen had not expected this. They had been biding their time, waiting for the right opportunity. They were about to mount their horses, when Hagen grabbed Rebecca's reins. The gunshot had drawn in a patrol of mounted drones. They were maybe ten or more. Rebecca's face was now white with fear for Arthur.

"They'll kill him if they catch him."

Hagen looked at the mounted drones galloping into the woods.

"I will get into the orphanage and cause a diversion."

Rebecca had tears rolling down her cheeks. "You would risk your life for him?"

Hagen nodded his head and rode off at speed.

Rebecca tried to keep her distance; she could see the original three drones had joined in the hunt. The senior slaves had rounded the other children together and began to take them back to the orphanage.

Screams and shouting made Rebecca lean over on her horse and throw up. Her nerves were now hanging by a thread; she reached into one of the saddle side pouches. Hagen had packed some whisky. She had lost a lot of her Victorian ladylike ways since the war, and now without thinking undid the cap and took a swig, then screwed it back on and slid it back in the pouch. She wiped her mouth and felt the handle of the sword attached to her side. The alcohol had helped steady the ship.

Kicking her horse gently, she entered the large pine forest. There was shouting and shots fired in the darkness of the forest. Rebecca kicked on and took the horse in and out of the pine trees. The light burst through the treetop canopies where some trees had fallen.

Rebecca saw flashes of movement in the distance. Then a scream and shout in English. It sounded like Arthur. She charged the horse further into the darkness, but it was the sound that was deceiving her now. It had moved around and was heading away from the forest. Moving the horse by pulling back on the reins and turning its head, she ploughed along another route.

Breaking back into the open glade, her heart sank. Riding off in the distance was a group of drones; they had children tied over the front of the saddles. Rebecca could not see if it was Arthur or not, but they had three. She deduced that because all of the drones were returning with the captured children who had tried to escape.

Not wasting anymore time, she set off after the drones. They were moving at a good speed, which meant Rebecca had to work hard to keep up. She tried to work out in her head what she could do. Her mind focused on Hagen creating a diversion back at the orphanage.

The time disappeared quickly, as did the distance. Soon the outbuilding and orphanage started to come into sight. This was not the only thing that caught her eye; further inside the camp, a fire had broken out. She knew Hagen was behind it, but it worked well. As the riders rode through the gates, they took the children to the long wooden huts. Then several riders shot off in the direction of the fire. This left three drone soldiers with the escapees.

Rebecca was able to come through the gate unseen. A bell was ringing and this sent everyone into a frenzy overdrive. Buckets of water were being fetched and carried towards the flames. She slowly rode her horse towards the children. Arthur had blood running down his forehead and onto his face. He looked determined and brave. Rebecca could see a girl and boy being held alongside Arthur; they looked dazed and unsure.

The drone who had hold of Anna was the first to see Rebecca; he stood still as the bullet penetrated his head. It was as if he was shocked to see someone coming into the orphanage and did not believe his eyes.

He fell backwards, releasing his grip on the girl. The other two turned to see what had happened and the drone that was holding Arthur recoiled as the back of his head left his body. Arthur stood still.

The drone holding Samuel flung him to the ground and reached for his revolver. It was in vain and Rebecca squeezed the trigger on her Adams revolver. The first bullet hit him in the chest, the second in the neck. He fell forward into the dirt and grass in front of him. Rebecca rode alongside and put one more in his head.

A squeal followed the last gunshot.

Arthur looked up with a smile that only a child could have for his loving mother. In the distance, the burning barn created a smokescreen, its thick black and grey smoke drifting across the open ground within the orphanage and keeping Rebecca and the children hidden for the time being. Sadly, this was short-lived. A raking cackle laugh pierced through the smoke. Rebecca looked around to see figures emerging through it.

Isabella's horse was first to stick its head out, its dark mane and sharp eyes staring directly at Rebecca. Isabella was sitting on the horse with a cape wrapped around her shoulders. To her side was a sword.

"These children belong to me," she spoke in broken English, as if she knew Arthur was related to this woman.

Fanning out behind her were four mounted drone soldiers. They all had their swords drawn. Isabella held her right hand out as if to tell them to wait until her command. She then rode on within a couple of feet of Rebecca. Her long black hair lifted up in the soft breeze.

"You must be here for these children? Maybe the boy?" Her eyes looked at Arthur; his face was full of fear and anguish, and this was enough to tell her that her suspicions were correct.

"So, this is your son." Isabella said this in a harsh tone, with a wry smile written across her face. "Before he gets fed to the flesh-eaters, he can watch his mother suffer."

Rebecca kept her eyes on Isabella and the drones. Her heart was beating hard, but she knew she had to stay alive long enough for Arthur to escape.

"Run, Arthur, run like the wind!" she screamed at him.

Isabella's horse pushed forward into Rebecca's and the priestess swung her sword at her midriff. The swing was badly timed and missed, thus allowing Rebecca to turn the horse and draw her sword. Arthur shouted at Samuel and Anna to run, and he started to move himself, but was caught in two minds as his mother fought.

The clanging of swords hitting each other filled the air. The drone soldiers sat poised, ready to intervene. Rebecca tried to bring her horse around to help him but was sliced in the back by Isabella. She yelped in pain, and brushed the tip of the sword away.

Arthur did not see Philippe and two of the children drones grabbing Anna and Samuel. When he did turn around, it was too late. Philippe landed a punch on his jaw, knocking him to the ground. The shock of the impact sent him flying backwards, and pain erupted in his jaw and nose. He looked up with dazed eyes to see a larger boy standing over him.

Philippe laughed and said, "Your mother is going to suffer the same fate." Whilst he said this, Arthur could see Isabella fighting Rebecca in the distance; the horses were thundering into each other and the clanging of blades excited Philippe more.

Philippe then called over to another drone child soldier to bring Samuel over. Samuel kicked and fought as hard as he could, but this boy was three or four years older and twice as strong. He was thrown at the feet of Philippe. Arthur tried to stand, but was kicked hard in the ribs.

"Nazar's armies will rule the world." Philippe revelled in his position of power. He had the other boy pick up Samuel and hold him tight; he then withdrew his knife, which was tucked into his belt. "Arthur, your friend will be first." As soon as he said this, he plunged the knife into Samuel's stomach. Samuel's mouth opened and sucked in air as the blade sunk deeper into his skin and intestines. He let out a cry of desperation as blood poured from the wound.

"Please Philippe, please let him live," Arthur begged him. Philippe just smiled.

Anna was trying to free herself, but another member of Philippe's group had joined them. There were now three young drone trainee soldiers, and two were holding Anna.

"Take him to the pens." Philippe then turned to Arthur, and said, "No, wait," as he reached for his belt. His hand brushed over a small revolver that was tucked into his trousers. He pulled it out and walked over to Samuel, whose eyes fell upon Arthur's. He could see fear in them, and sadness.

The sound of the revolver going off and Samuel falling lifelessly to the ground made Arthur lose his breath. Behind them, the battle between Rebecca and Isabella raged on. Arthur did not even hear Anna screaming, his eyes slowly drifting down to Samuel.

"Take them both to the pens," ordered Philippe.

Arthur's body had lost some of its strength seeing Samuel being executed. Anna was still fighting hard, but could not overpower the two drone children.

Rebecca was tiring; she had fought incredibly well, but her brief training was exposing her to Isabella's craft and guile with a sword. In effect, she was being toyed with. During a moment of holding the swords against each other, Rebecca was knocked off her horse. Isabella laughed.

"You're no match for me, your world is coming to an end." She then looked in the direction of Arthur. "You will soon be able to hear your son scream as he is fed to the flesh-eaters." Then the cackling laughter returned.

Rebecca gingerly got to her feet; her sword was lying 3 metres away.

Isabella sat on the horse, raising her sword. She was enjoying watching Rebecca struggling. She could see Philippe taking Arthur and Anna to the pens. This just excited her more; she had not wanted to kill Rebecca quickly, it had to be drawn out for her enjoyment, but that time was coming to an end. Isabella wanted to see Arthur and Anna being fed to the flesh-eaters. Her horse scraped its front left hoof into the dirt. Then it began to come forward, picking up its pace with each step.

Through the acrid smoke, sunlight crept towards Rebecca, warmth of the light brushed against her face and for a short moment she saw back to her family home. Arthur and Emily were playing in the garden and Charles was bringing her a glass of wine. She smiled, then with blood seeping out of her wounds, she lurched forward to grab the sword. Isabella was bearing down on her now with speed.

With a sidestep she brought the sword hard down across the horse's front legs. It had an instant effect, causing the creature to buckle and fall forward awkwardly, slamming hard into the ground. Isabella crashed into the mud below. Her horse struggled to get up, causing her eyes to water and then fill with anger. She placed her sword through its head, killing it instantly.

"You will now suffer for that," Isabella vowed, before screaming at the guards to come and support her. The drones began to kick their horses on.

Arthur was being held up as Philippe made him watch Anna struggle as they prepared to throw her in first. "I want to see your face as she's eaten alive."

Anna stopped struggling and looked to the skies as the gate to the pen was being opened. That moment was broken as a battle cry rang out. Hagen cut through the smoke, bellowing out his war cry. The drones that had just begun to advance forward now had to adjust their horses' movement. Hagen was already bearing down on one of the drones who was furthest to his right, his axe claiming a chunk of his shoulder and severing the man's left arm from just above the elbow. Blood pumped out of the open wound, causing the rider to fall. Hagen was already across to the second drone who tried to reach for his revolver, and in a flash, a glint of metal sent the man's head tumbling.

As Hagen pushed on to the other two, they charged him with swords in the air.

Isabella was taken aback by this sudden attack; her usual air of confidence was broken and it was now or never to kill Rebecca and escape to gather reinforcements. She came at Rebecca with fury, and both of their swords clashed heavily together. Isabella swung high, but Rebecca saw this coming and ducked at the right moment. Isabella countered her manoeuvre by bringing her right knee into Rebecca's shoulder. This caused her to go down on one knee. "Ha, Victorians are so weak," she taunted.

Isabella followed this up with a heavy blow which took the sword out of Rebecca's hands. "Time is slipping away. You've fought well, but must die." With that she brought her sword up in the air. She had not calculated on Rebecca having a knife strapped across her back. Whilst Isabella spoke, Rebecca had unsheathed it, and as the sword went back, she thrust it forward into Isabella's chest. The priestess coughed as the blade sunk in. Blood started to pour from her mouth. Rebecca stood and pushed the blade in further. She brought the priestess closer using her cloak for leverage. "The war is not won yet." She then let her fall to her knees. Isabella's dark, radiant hair lost its glow, as the life drained out of her.

Rebecca did not wait; she immediately grabbed her sword. She wanted to help Arthur and needed to move quickly.

Philippe had not seen the demise of the priestess; he was watching Anna being dragged into the pen. Arthur glanced at the priestess kneeling down. Without a second thought, he grappled Philippe, who had been careless, allowing his revolver to be unfastened in his belt. Philippe was twice as strong as Arthur, laughing as he threw him to the ground and kicked him in the shoulder. "Let the flesh-eaters eat her now."

"Philippe." Arthur stood up. He had the boy's revolver in his hands.

Philippe's eyes dropped, and in that moment he stopped being a leader of children and became the 14-year-old boy again.

"Please, I'm sorry," he said, whilst secretly reaching behind his back to grab his knife.

"Arthur!" Anna screamed out as she fought off one of the flesh-eaters; the rest of the infected children now smelt fresh meat and moved in.

BANG!

Arthur shot Philippe in his left thigh. The boy squealed in pain. Arthur then shot him in the other leg. Anna seized on the moment; while the three drone children stood staring at Philippe lying on the floor, Anna grabbed the nearest boy who had not shut the pen gate and pushed him back. He fell against the pine wood and onto the soil beneath. He was not able to raise himself. A child flesh-eater was quickly on top of him; he pushed the flesh-eater back, but was abruptly joined by three more. The other drone children tried to help him, barging past Anna in a desperate attempt to free his body. The trouble was that the flesh-eaters in the pen were amassing by the gate and were spilling out.

Anna ran to Arthur, who was standing over Philippe. "Come Arthur, we must go." Rebecca was coming towards them both.

"You will now pay for Samuel's life, Philippe," Arthur said. Behind them, the screams of the other drone children panicked Philippe, as the flesh-eaters tore into their victim's skin and bones. Arthur did not listen to his pleas for mercy. He did look around once as they set off to meet Rebecca. He saw Philippe clawing at the ground the best he could with two flesh-eater children closing in. The screams of the first bites let him know they had caught him.

Rebecca swept both children into her arms and hugged them. She had tears rolling down her cheeks. "Come, we must help Hagen."

Hagen had killed one of the two men he was fighting with a savage head cut. The other drone looked around and ran. It was not the time to chase him down, so Hagen gathered his horse and rode over to Rebecca and the children. The flesh-eaters were pouring out of the pen. The alarm was being raised, but the fire had caused panic. With other wood huts opening, many of the children saw the chance to flee; the older teenagers took their chance, too.

"What about all the children?" Rebecca asked whilst holding Arthur and Anna.

"I have killed the guards at the gates." He paused, looked down and told Rebecca they must chance it. "There are too many drone soldiers here, we must leave."

Rebecca looked around; hundreds of the children were being led out by the adult slaves. Some were taking wagons, while others were fighting with drone soldiers. Hagen looked over at the flesh-eater children, who were now heading their way.

"Mount up, Rebecca. I'll take Anna on my horse." Hagen lifted the young girl up as if she weighed nothing. Arthur jumped onto the back of his mother's saddle. She felt him squeeze into her tight. The feeling was euphoric.

Outside the orphanage, adult slaves and children were leaving in a column. They had wagons and food. The drone soldier children were being amassed on the other side of the orphanage, but the keys to the armoury iron cage were being kept by Isabella, her body now left lifeless in the dirt. This had meant that the drone soldiers had held off due to their lack of firepower and knowledge on the number of attackers. Hagen knew it would only be a matter of time before they realised they would have the upper hand should they access the armoury. The other problem was that the drone soldiers had the armoury cache in a temporary wooden hut, next to the burning barn.

He saw the desperation on the children's faces and emptiness in the adult ones. "Tell them they must move quickly." He spoke to a man who understood German; Hagen spoke several languages and, in this war, it had served him well. This worn-out group of human beings began to pick up their pace. Rebecca looked at him; she knew it was a risk, but it was one they had to take.

Not everyone had made it with them; some had scattered and run into the large pine forest to the east. Others had wanted to go their own way. Rebecca looked back as the fire had spread to the wooden huts and armoury hut. The explosions shook the ground and made the children cower as they walked.

"Do you think we can make it, Hagen?" Rebecca said as the orphanage burnt.

"We have a chance." Hagen moved his horse next to Rebecca's.

He went on to explain his thoughts about the drone soldiers controlling the flesh-eater children. They were half-affected, so the flesh-eaters would not attack them. The young drone trainee children had not been half-affected yet, so they were at risk. All of this played into their hands.

Rebecca wanted to hug Arthur more, so she told him to hold her tight as they rode. He told her about his experiences and how badly he missed her and Emily. He added his father Charles after a minute or two. He said he did not want to give up hope of seeing his father one day. He said he had seen some terrible things and felt heartbroken for losing his friend Samuel. Rebecca spoke about how war took innocent lives and was an awful thing. He said he even felt bad for shooting Philippe in the legs, knowing that he would get eaten. Rebecca found it hard to tell him he had done wrong, because he had saved his own life and Anna's. She said he had done what he had to do to survive.

She spoke with Arthur for hours until they stopped to make camp for the evening. Anna had come over to speak to Arthur. She thanked him for saving her and gave him a hug; he blushed, and walked with her to have some soup.

Chapter 26

"Captain Hayward," the officer said, tucking his gloves into his coat.

The captain turned around.

"We've found the men you requested."

Captain Holfer stepped into the room; he was followed by Captain Müller. Charles's face lit up.

"Captain Müller, so good to see you again." Charles shook his hand.

"Likewise," said Captain Müller.

He then shook Captain Holfer's hand. The officer had short, blond hair and was clean-shaven. He looked like he'd worked on a farm previously, as he was stocky and broad-shouldered.

Captain Holfer explained that he had been sent from Colonel Kiesl to help them. The colonel had wanted to join them, but his rank and new orders meant he was better served putting together an Austrian detachment to help the British Empire. Captain Holfer had served under the colonel and was regarded as a trusted soldier by him. He had faced the enemy in Europe, and was fully aware what they were capable of.

Captain Hayward was standing beside a table. Spread out on it was a large map of Europe. He began to relay the plan, and it involved them going back to Europe. Benedict had been found and was under guard for his own protection. He had volunteered to help find the map in his father's house.

Captain Hayward was going to lead twenty of his own men, and be accompanied by Major Sherborne, who would also have twenty of his own men with him. He explained the situation to the captains, but they made it quite clear that many knew what had happened to him and his men in the courtroom and suggested that it would not have been allowed to happen without an attempt to free them should they have gone ahead with the decision to execute. Captain Hayward thanked them again; he knew he had the right men around him to get this job done.

Once they had found the map, they would head out of the former Austrian-Hungarian Empire and head for the sea, and from there they would sail to Siberia. Benedict had said the enemy castle and monastery were in the mountains there. Rumours of a burning star, that fell from the sky hundreds of years ago, were thrown around. No one really knew what was at the castle or monastery, or how Nazar had started this whole war off with the creatures he now controlled.

Captain Hayward said they would be using the latest rifles, machine guns and grenades. They would be heavily outnumbered, so operating away from the enemies' prying eyes would be essential. He told his officers that he did not trust Major Sherborne or his Marines, but for now they would have to work with them. Both groups were scheduled to undertake four months of training and planning. This was partly to get them fully ready, and also to miss the winter. Nazar was coming, but exactly when was not known. He could possibly launch a winter offensive, but the Channel crossing could be awkward and with the British Navy patrolling, it would not be ideal. The high command predicted a summer invasion.

The captain spent three hours briefing his officers, and then let them leave to relax and wait for supper. Sergeant Butcher had been contacted regarding Alexander Chamberlin joining them on the mission.

Once Captain Hayward heard he wanted to join them, a dispatch was sent immediately. He knew Chamberlin had survived longer than most in a hostile environment; he was also an expert sniper and could teach them a thing or two about marksmanship.

Captain Hayward had met Private John Brown and Heidi, and both of them had expressed their desire to help him with his future plans. Charles thanked them for their loyal support, but believed they would be better suited to serve under Lieutenant Colonel Adams, who was now going to be in charge of Fort Cumberland in Portsmouth. Charles had not told them about the mission to Europe. This wasn't because he did not trust them; those who served under him, he trusted with his own life. It was more for their own safety. As the long nights were drawing in, news of sabotage and espionage spread around the country. If John and Heidi were overheard talking about Benedict's map and Serbia, it would endanger them and all those travelling with Charles.

John and Heidi had suffered in the prisoner camp on the beach. They needed time to rehabilitate and help prepare the defences. The British Empire had to be focused on getting ready for the largest land invasion since the Norman Conquest came to Britain.

Corporal Heinz joined Sergeant Butcher and Captain Hayward in his command office. The news was in that Dr Brown would be travelling with them. This was something Charles was very grateful for. Corporal Heinz and Sergeant Butcher were experienced soldiers, with some good medical knowledge, but having a doctor was a great asset. Captain Holfer and Captain Müller each had a corporal with them. Charles knew in times of conflict, and with this sort of mission, that your right-hand man had to be chosen wisely. He had chosen two, Sergeant Butcher and Corporal Heinz. Corporal Heinz was well on his way to recovery. It could be a month to six weeks until he was allowed to exercise fully, but they had time. He would attend the briefings and weapon training.

The remaining eleven men who made up the twenty on Captain Hayward's side were all Royal Engineers. Some had been with Captain Hayward during the retreat from the Carpathian Mountains, while others were soldiers who had fought in France and wanted to do their best for the Empire.

Later on in the evening, Charles was alone, looking at a map of Europe. His eyes pondered over Reims and then Denmark. He had heard of survivor camps in Denmark, but there were many stories floating around. He let his finger hover over Europe; he had not been given total control of the operation. Charles still had to convince the man who wanted him dead that his plan was the right one. Only time would tell how this would pan out between them. One thing was for sure and that was that Captain Hayward would not let Major Sherborne jeopardise his men again.

Christmas came around quickly; Charles did not go back to Sunninghill or the family home. He was spending Christmas with Rebecca's brother James. Charles had received news from America that both his and Rebecca's parents were doing well and were working on planning a life for them in America should they require so. They had not given up on Rebecca, Arthur and Emily, and told Charles to also think positively.

James was a strong character, but by Victorian standards he let his emotions out over a whisky during the Yuletide period. His wife and children had been packed up and sent to America, and he missed them. He did not want to talk about it in front of Charles, especially as Charles did not know whether his family were still alive or not. This did affect James, as he worried about his sister and his niece and nephew, but this only truly came out when he'd drunk a bottle of single malt whisky.

"I dread spending time away from them," James said, whilst gulping back his whisky a little too eagerly. "I'm sorry, Arthur, I should choose my timing." He was referring to Rebecca, Arthur and Emily still being missing.

"I know you care, it's ok to talk about Emma and the children, James." Charles knew he was worried and that he might not see his family again. He did well to listen to his brother-in-law and hold onto his own fears and worries.

The conversation turned towards Europe. James had heard that Queen Victoria had summoned the men to meet her before departing on this mission. The importance of what needed to be done had not gone unnoticed further up the hierarchy. Spies had reported the massive build-up of tents and camps along the French and Spanish coast. It was even reported to reach up to Holland.

James spoke about his command at Fort Cumberland and how he would look after Charles's men that weren't going to Europe with him. He added that he was to receive a detachment of Bengal rifles to Fort Cumberland. The British Empire was reinforcing her shores with foreign regiments. The Raj had some excellent fighting units and would be needed should a land invasion happen.

They did not know the number of ships Nazar had, but were still confident of pushing back a land invasion by destroying their navy.

James thought that the British Navy would stop any large armada, but appreciated that Nazar had a force unseen before in the modern world.

Charles agreed on the British Navy being one of the strongest in the world, but he had seen the largest European army ever assembled destroyed in battle. Nazar's forces were too strong for this modern force. His main weapon had been the flesh-eaters and long limbs, but there were also the giant wolves and riders of the north. Stopping this army had not been successful so far, but Charles hoped to change that.

That night, James was helped up the stairs to his bedroom by Charles and the butler. It had been a hard Christmas without their families; good food and long walks helped pass the time, and discussing how to defend the British Empire was a needed distraction.

Chapter 27

January was cold. A soft layer of snow fell halfway through the month; this delayed some of the training exercises. As the weeks passed, the weather improved; spring was starting to push its way through.

Charles met his men on the parade square. The officers were to the side of the privates. Captain Holfer and Captain Müller would fall under Charles's command even though they shared the same rank. The talk of promotion for Charles had been quashed due to the Major Sherborne incident. They had granted Charles full control of his men and to be the leader of this mission in Europe. Major Sherborne had presumed he would be given overall command due to his rank. This had been a moot point for the major; he had wanted to oversee all operations, but had been restricted from doing so due to his lack of time spent in the European theatre of war. It was also noted that his combat experience with this new enemy was behind that of Captain Hayward and his officers, and that this could be quintessential for their mission to find the enemy base.

The soldiers stood there whilst the winter's sun fell slowly behind the now bare deciduous trees. Their parade uniforms glistened as light reflected off polished buckles and boots. Charles felt honoured to be out there; most of these men had served him proud since the war began and he owed them an immeasurable debt of gratitude.

He was happy that the soldiers who had been with him in the court martial and who were not going on the mission would be serving under his brother-in-law, Lieutenant James Adams.

Charles took his time during the inspection. As they rolled through the months, there would be less time for formal parades; it would now be about training to be ready to fight in a small group and to be as covert as possible.

The weekend was the first time they were planning on using the new ten-round, box-magazine Lee–Metford rifle. A brand-new Maxim machine gun that had just been commissioned and fast-tracked through was ready for the men to practise with. Grenades had been worked on, but their format was still roughly the same. They would come in useful for house-to-house fighting and other enemy situations that needed them.

The new Enfield revolver was being trialled with them as well; each man would be equipped as the need for firepower per individual was great. Captain Hayward was keen on reliability and accuracy. He knew that they had to move stealthily through Europe where possible, but should the situation arise where they required strong firepower, then they would be ready.

Chapter 28

Major Sherborne and Captain Hayward's officers would be called into a meeting to go over the finer points of the mission. Once they had located the map, then it was about finding the enemy monastery and castle. The rumours regarding the monastery and what had been buried there for hundreds of years was unconfirmed. Some said it was just local old wives' tales, but since the start of the war, with the beasts which Nazar had at his disposal, these rumours had begun to be taken more seriously.

Benedict would be present at the meeting; he had first-hand knowledge of where his family cottage was and information from his father on what he had seen there.

Arriving at the Hawley Lake, the men disembarked from their wagons. Captain Hayward and the other officers were on horseback. They would all be staying a week, and camping outside. There would be soldiers from the Queen's Royal Regiment taking part in the training exercise. Their role was to look for the major's and captain's men.

Captain Müller joined Charles as they surveyed the training ground.

"This could be invaluable training when we head back over there," Jurgen said. His English had improved since he had been staying in Great Britain.

"I think you're right, Captain. We must succeed." Charles took out his binoculars and scanned the countryside.

It was not possible to see far, as a mixture of silver birch trees and gorse swallowed up the landscape. Pine trees and scrubby bushes were also mixed in the environment with heather playing a big part in the ground cover. Before the men were debriefed, there was time to set up the soup kitchen and serve up warm food.

The warm food took the chill off the morning and was a welcome relief from travelling.

There was a firing range prepared and two Maxim guns to trial. They also had new uniforms to use. These were khaki in colour and had been trialled in Africa. The idea of having uniforms which would make it harder for the enemy to see them was very important to this mission.

After the men had eaten, they changed into their new uniforms. A broad selection of sizes had been taken with them. They also had support from a detachment of Royal Army Ordnance Corps. They would not be alongside them during the exercise, but had set up a HQ to refer back to. This training was now going to be part of a schedule with a week-on-and-week-off rotation. They would train at the barracks, predominately using the rifle range, but also practising bayonet attacks and hand-to-hand combat.

Once the men were kitted out in their new combat dress, they were each given a Lee-Metford rifle which had a ten-round magazine box. They also had a Lee-Enfield revolver each. The next part of the day was spent in the rifle range. The men enjoyed firing the Lee— Metford; having ten rounds meant they could keep their aim and keep firing.

Private Chamberlin and Corporal Heinz assisted with the shooting practise. They both had a keen eye for a target and the men were impressed with how accurate they were. The target practise went on until early afternoon and before dinner they were shown the two Maxim guns which had been assembled. They saw in the field in front of them that there were around fifty stuffed scarecrow figures. The main trunks of their bodies were filled with sand.

Captain Hayward stood close to Sergeant Butcher as they all gathered around one of the Maxim guns. A soldier from the Grenadier Guards sat behind the machine gun to operate it. It could fire around 600 rounds per minute, and was more reliable than the Gatling gun. It could recoil and eject each spent cartridge, before inserting another. One man could fire the machine gun, but it was best suited to have a small team. A re-loader and a spotter increased its effectiveness and helped to carry it.

Silence fell around the men. Then the Grenadier Guard squeezed the trigger and the machine gun began to open up. The effect was devastating, cutting through the scarecrows and ripping them to pieces. The soldiers' eyes widened at what they had seen; it was much more deadly than the Gatling gun, and less manually operated. The rate of fire and reliability seemed improved as well.

Once the gun had finished firing, they went to inspect the damage. Captain Holfer remarked on how this would help them with their mission. All of them agreed it was a very useful part of their kit. The rest of the day was spent firing, dismantling and rebuilding the Maxim gun. Everyone in the squad had to be able to fire it and look after it. By the evening, several campfires were roaring away. Chicken and pig roasted away, and there was a broth to go with it and some ale to wash it all down.

The soldiers sang and laughed. Captain Hayward even found himself tapping away as one of the men took out a fiddle and Sergeant Butcher recycled some Cornish songs. Charles thought it was good for them to enjoy themselves. They would be leaving the main camp tomorrow to begin their cat and mouse game with the Queen's Royal Regiment, but for now it was time to drink and sing.

***

The soft dawn bird call was interrupted by a piercing bugle call. The men were awoken and began to fall in. Breakfast was served and after that they were told to pack their kit and get ready to ride. They would be on horseback, and if seen were expected then to out-think and out-manoeuvre the Queen's Royal Regiment.

Captain Hayward had been told that Major Sherborne and his men were training near the Forest of Dean. They would be meeting up in a couple of weeks to brief the mission to all the men. Then it would only be six weeks until they left.

All of them had been practising riding on horseback. Some were better than others, but they had time to get fully competent. The twenty men were riding in small groups of five. Captain Hayward had Sergeant Butcher and Corporal Heinz with him. Corporal Heinz was making a good recovery. He was not back to full fitness and would not be spending the whole week with them, but they still wanted him to get a feel for the group. Private Chamberlin and one more private made up the captain's five.

The groups were all in sight of each other, but it helped to hide their numbers. The mission for the week was to find and take the flag of a pre-set-up camp. It would be lightly guarded this time.

Later that afternoon, it all went very smoothly; Captain Holfer found the location and rode close to it before dismounting and tying up the horses. He took his corporal and two Engineers to capture the camp. The Queen's Royal Regiment was told not to put up a physical fight, but could point their rifles in the fake enemies' direction. All parties had no ammunition for this training.

The main idea for Captain Hayward's men was to evade being seen or caught. Nazar's numbers were great in Europe, but many pinned their hopes on there being less forces the further inland they went. Flesh-eaters would follow for a while, but they could be outrun on horseback; even long limbs only had a short sprint speed. Drone cavalry and riders of the north presented a real problem, even a collection of priests. They had only met the destroyer drones in France, and they believed their numbers were small and mainly restricted to guarding high-ranking priests or the queen and Nazar himself.

The next couple of days were spent doing some reconnaissance of a mock-up village. They were expecting to go in there and find a map in the main manor house. This went quite smoothly; a couple of scuffles broke out as the soldiers jostled for position. Corporal Heinz was not involved for the remaining days. He was given more time to recuperate.

Special care was taken with the round bombs they were throwing; the grenades were not ideal, but did the job. They used them around the village in training and had models inside to represent the enemy. All the men had been practising with a sword. It was a decision taken that they would all have one on the mission. Captain Hayward was happy with how it was all coming together.

The following weeks went well, and no major injuries occurred. They were due some hand-to-hand training at Box Hill, before having a full debrief. Major Sherborne would be there with his men. There was also the matter of meeting Queen Victoria.

Chapter 29

That day came with a blink of an eye. Captain Hayward's men were meeting her first and then it would be the turn of Major Sherborne and his men.

However, she was not residing in Buckingham Palace, but was staying in Windsor Castle. This was fine with Charles as he had liked visiting Windsor with his family and walking alongside the River Thames. The men travelled to Windsor by train. The weather had been drizzly at first but cleared to allow the sun to break through between the clouds.

The Coldstream Guards regiment were barracked at the castle and looked very impressive in their bearskin helmets. There were extra patrols marching around the castle and police to handle the increased refugees who were being housed in Windsor Great Park. The government had finally allowed many of Europe's former soldiers to enlist into the British Army. They would be working with their former officers where possible, to get new regiments together. The army had been very keen for this to happen long before the approaching summer. It had only given them a few months to train with their soldiers and adapt them to British military ideas.

Rifles, cannons and machine guns had been fast-tracked into production; however, the politicians had fought over food and other health concerns because so many refugees were arriving from Europe and there was also the risk of plagues sweeping through Great Britain. All of this made them halve military production and focus on the sick and needy.

Some politicians wanted the Empire to strike up a deal with Nazar. They knew that if this war continued, then the country would suffer greatly, as they could not cope with the number of people living without accommodation. Cholera, diphtheria and consumption were some of the main diseases threatening to spread. Some believed the government had already sent envoys to Nazar and that he had sent their heads back in a basket.

Charles knew that Queen Victoria had worn black since Prince Albert had passed away in 1861. She had become quite a recluse after this, and behind closed doors had even been called 'the widow of Windsor'.

As they waited to enter her throne room, Charles looked at his men. They were all in their parade uniforms and looking very smart. Captain Müller and Kiesl had British uniforms on and carried them well. Sergeant Butcher leaned in and said if only his mother and father could have seen him now.

Charles looked at the magnificent pictures and the sheer scale and grandeur of the rooms. He felt honoured and humble to be part of the British Empire.

Corporal Heinz looked over and nodded to Charles. Two officers and the Queen's Counsel came through the throne doors.

"The queen will now see you gentlemen."

Breathing in, and swallowing once to get saliva into his mouth, Captain Hayward entered the room with his fellow soldiers. There sitting on her throne was Queen Victoria, dressed in black. She had two attendants standing next to her and Field Marshal Douglas Horatio Carrington. Charles knew they would now take it in turns to receive a special engraved sword and an emblem to attach to their khaki uniforms in 'Royal service of Queen Victoria'.

She looked him in the eye as he came forward and bowed; he then looked up at her. "Good luck, Captain," she said, with a strong, determined voice.

Chapter 30

Nazar sat on a large wooden throne overlooking the sea. Draped around his shoulders and legs was a bearskin, this once fearsome creature reduced to nothing more than an animal pelt. He watched a black-backed gull swoop down on a half-eaten prisoner and peck at his decaying flesh.

General Eltsina slowly made her way towards him. Standing 10 yards back from Nazar were four destroyer drones. They were also in winter pelts, as the weather was particularly cold that day.

"State your business, general," said the captain of the destroyer drones.

"I'm here to tell the Emperor some news." She said this with a stern voice. He then told her to wait where she was, before turning around and making his way over to Nazar. A short conversation followed before she was allowed to go over to him.

"Your highness." She lowered her head and waited to be spoken to.

"General Eltsina, the nights are drawing lighter and the time to invade will soon be here." He brought over his bearskin across his chest as he gazed out over the English Channel.

She did not know whether to take that as a signal for her to speak to him or wait. The words balanced on the tip of her tongue. She knew the news about the orphanage would not be taken well. A feeling of nervousness started to creep over her.

"Is this about the orphanage, Eltsina?" His voice was dark and he growled out the words.

"Yes, my lord." Her voice clearly wavered as she spoke.

"Come closer, look into my eyes." He beckoned her towards him. She reluctantly took steps in the direction of the throne. Standing a metre away, he signalled for her to come closer again. She leant in.

Before she could move, his left arm grabbed her by her side. "Look into my eyes."

She was scared but did what he said. "Tell me what happened."

She explained about the attack, and Isabella being killed. She told him they believed it to be bandits and thought it carried no real threat.

Nazar turned his head left to right. He said these attacks were becoming more common and wanted the patrols around the orphanages to be doubled. Executions of those caught attacking the new Empire would be severe. After speaking about that, he let his hands run up the sides of the female general. She felt uncomfortable, but dared not move. Nazar then leaned in and kissed her on the lips; his longer tongue wrapped around her face and slid back in. He then began to feel her breasts. She shook her head, but a growl from him made her stop.

"Come with me to my tent." The Destroyer drones escorted them to the tent entrance.

"What about the queen, your highness?" It was Eltsina's last throw of the dice.

"She is in Spain with the northern riders, now undress."

She had to take her clothes off outside the tent. The grunts of excitement as she stripped naked before walking in were quickly silenced by a snarl and Nazar baring his teeth. The guards left to patrol around the tent within seconds.

An hour passed until Eltsina walked tentatively out of the tent; she was naked, with blood oozing out of a cut lip. Bending down to pick up her clothes, one of the destroyer drones came close to her. "You'd better not tell Oksana what you've done." He smiled as he said this.

General Eltsina dressed herself and wiped the blood away from her mouth. "Return to your post, soldier, or you'll be dealt with severely," she said in a harsh tone. The destroyer drone looked a little shocked that she could have that much fight in her. He did not say another word and disappeared off on patrol. She then went over to her horse, which was tied to a tree, mounted it and rode off to join her soldiers in the camp.

Nazar lay on his bed, almost submerged in different pelts and animal skins. He had nail marks on his back and arms. Soft veils surrounded his sleeping quarters. "Was she what you wanted, my king?" Oksana brushed through the veils as she said this.

Nazar looked at her. "No, she is not my queen."

Oksana unclipped her robe and let it fall to the ground. She then climbed into bed with Nazar. The guards outside could hear laughter and growls as the two made passionate love.

The sergeant Destroyer drone kept his men from talking and looking backwards. He told them to just look forward and guard.

Later in the afternoon, General Georgiy was summoned to the main tent. Nazar and Oksana were both sitting on wooden thrones which had animal fur draped over them. Two large church candles burned brightly either side of them.

"General," Nazar said in a light voice.

The general was concerned why Nazar seemed to be in a good mood. He had heard of what had happened with Eltsina and hoped Nazar was not going to have him executed for what happened at the orphanage in Prussia.

"My lord, I take it you are well." The general stood in front of them both.

"Soon we will be launching the attack," said Nazar. He then brought a goblet of wine to his mouth and drunk it in one tipping motion.

He went on to talk about how he wanted his navy to draw out the British Navy to the Celtic Sea and give them a battle that would last days. Whilst this was unfolding, he would then launch the biggest invasion the British Empire had ever seen. He planned to land his drone soldiers and beasts all along the south coast and around into Norfolk.

The general asked about the soldiers landing on the beach and what sort of defences the British had made. Nazar nodded his head, before replying, "We have spies working for us, General." He told the general that the first wave would be flesh-eaters, the premise being to get them into reasonably shallow water in wooden cages. The cage gates would be opened, and then rowing boats would drag slaves with open wounds and dripping blood in front of them. Nazar was pleased with his plan. "It has already been trialled here in France." He smiled to himself.

"My lord, sorry for asking such simple questions. Are you saying they will follow the wounded slaves onto the beach?" The general opened his hands as he said this.

"Have I not just said it has been tested?" His tone was growing darker.

He explained that each boat would carry young priests to help guide the destroyer drones and long limbs to pull the slaves onto the beach. "Once we land hundreds of thousands of our flesh-eaters, they will walk towards the enemy lines." He clapped his hands for more wine as he got excited. A slave girl came in with a jug and refilled his goblet.

Oksana looked at the girl and smiled at Nazar, but he shook his head a little as if to indicate not now.

"They will soak up machine fire, rifle fire and cannon fire." He drunk out of the goblet again, letting wine spill down the side of his mouth. "Then we will land the long limbs and drone soldiers."

General Georgiy looked impressed. "What about the razor tooths, riders of the north and even the wolves?"

"Once we have a foothold along the coast, we will land the cavalry and creatures that have speed." Nazar smiled. "We will then race behind enemy lines and it will be the beginning of the end." Nazar knew that his force was unmatched, and if the British Navy was kept busy, he stood a very good chance.

Nazar and the general studied the maps of Great Britain. Nazar had decided that the attack would happen in June.

"They have many churches in the British Empire," he said, moving small-scale ships across his map. "They will need a god to save them."

The general nodded his head. Oksana let out a raucous laugh and moved from her throne to stand by Nazar.

"General, we will debrief all of the senior officers next month." Nazar turned to him. "Find the bandits who attacked the Prussian orphanage and kill them."

Chapter 31

Captain Hayward was happy with how the training had gone at Hawley Lake. Time had passed quickly and they were meeting Major Sherborne and his men at Box Hill to go over the mission in full. An enormous tent had been erected and it would house all the men who would be undertaking this mission.

A huge map was hung at the top end of the tent. It showed the planned route to the former Austrian-Hungarian Empire and the route into Russia. The men were gathered in and three senior officers from the high command began to relay the planned operation.

Major Sherborne looked over at Captain Hayward as they all filed in. The two groups were split from each other and took turns to give each other the evil eye. There would be no love lost between them. Major Sherborne would have primed his men about how un-British this particular set of Royal Engineers were; even if it was pure lies, he did not care.

The men sat for two hours. They asked Captain Hayward to talk through the Austrian-Hungarian operation. Major Sherborne snorted at his two captains, shaking his head as if he were all-knowing. He wanted to show his disdain for this mission. Charles made sure he was clear about how they were going to land in Italy and sail up the Tagliamento River. They would have four vessels, two ships and two boats. They would sail the smaller boats up the Tagliamento River and use the two larger ships for supply. It would not take them all the way, but would get them into Italy and onto the borders of Austria, where they would work their way on horseback. Benedict would help guide them once they were in the former Austro-Hungarian Empire. The map was in his father's house; he believed it to be either in the attic or cellar.

Once the map was located, they would plan the next part of the mission. There would be enough explosives to destroy a castle. There was only speculation on what was at the monastery and fort in Russia. The rumours of a rock falling from the sky thousands of years ago were so far unproven. The generals had kept an open mind and insured them they were well equipped to be away for a very long time if need be.

Major Sherborne clapped sarcastically when Charles finished speaking. Charles looked at him straight in the eye and said nothing.

The senior officers stated the mission was set for May. It was only a few weeks away, but the men were ready. Charles was going to have his men housed at Fort Cumberland. Major Sherborne was staying near the Forest of Dean. Both men would have their own ship and smaller boat to carry out the next part of the mission.

As they were walking out, the major stood by the door.

"Captain Hayward, you will fail, and when you do, I will be judge, jury and executioner." He said this with a sickly smile on his face.

"Just have your men ready, Major." He then paused as Sergeant Butcher and Corporal Heinz joined him. "There will be nowhere to run this time."

The major went red with anger and stormed past him.

***

The morning of the mission was glorious. The air was fresh and the gulls were in full voice. Captain Hayward looked out of his quarters; he took in a deep breath of sea air and then went for breakfast in the officer's mess. His brother-in-law was sitting reading *The Times* newspaper.

"Good morning, Charles," he said with an honest ring to his voice. "I believe you will succeed in your mission, but beware of the major."

Charles sat down next to him and was offered a cooked breakfast and a pot of tea. The orderly then went off to prepare the breakfast. Charles sat looking around the room. There was only one other officer in the corner; he was drinking tea and writing notes. James said he felt that the invasion was not that far off. He had prepared the fort and Box Hill the best he could. There were still defensive works going on around the whole country, but the main issue lay in where Nazar would attack and how they should cope if he landed.

Both men had discussed the British Navy's power, but Charles had pointed out that the sheer size of the enemy force was unmatched and would cause any army a huge problem. The British government had been pressed to ask for assistance from America, but the political powers made it difficult to pass that through, with money being a major sticking point.

The men spoke at length about different scenarios as they had breakfast, but time was now pointing towards Charles leaving. He stood up and shook James's hand and in an un-Victorian way brought his left arm around his shoulder. "Take care, James, remember to shoot the flesh-eaters in the head."

James had a troubled look on his face; he too expected Nazar to land on British soil, the big question would be if they could fight them back.

"I will see you off from Portsmouth, Charles."

"Thank you, James." Charles then left to join his men as the ships were being loaded.

Sergeant Butcher and Corporal Heinz were busy checking lists and watching the cargo being loaded on. The two main troop carrier ships were HMS *Orontes* and HMS *Jumma*. They had used them in the raids on France and Charles was happy to use them again. Major Sherborne was in HMS *Jumma*. They had two smaller boats which they would use to sail down the rivers on. Both of these were steam-powered. The ships had enough storage to give this mission the best possible chance.

Captain Müller and Captain Holfer were talking to the other Engineer soldiers. All of them were now dressed in khaki uniforms. Each man had his Lee-Metford rifle with the new ten-round magazine box, a Lee-Enfield revolver, and the commissioned sword from Queen Victoria. The emblems had been sewn onto their sleeves and read in Latin, '*fortes fortuna iuvat*' – fortune favours the brave.
Charles had seen Major Sherborne leading his men to HMS *Jumma* and hoped that would be all he would see of him for now.

Benedict arrived; he had grown a little since Charles had first met him. He was with Doctor Brown and shook his hand as he went onto the ship. "Welcome, Benedict." He was shown to his quarters. Benedict had been at the Box Hill debrief and was up to speed with the plans.

Charles had had a late arrival to join his mission. He would be serving under him and was recommended by James. His name was Private William Green. He was fluent in Russian and had spent some time working in Siberia several years ago. Charles had a few multilingual soldiers, as he knew this would help them in Europe. The smaller boats they were taking would be carrying the Nazar colours, and flags to use when they started to sail up the rivers in enemy territories. They had acquired drone soldier uniforms from when they were behind enemy lines, and other useful information to help them through the occupied countries.

The soldiers were helping check over the cargo and loading things into their quarters. Most of the men had been chosen because they did not have wives or families. It was not uncommon to remain unmarried, as wives were not always allowed to live in the barracks.

The sun was shining, but there was a strong wind making the sea a little choppy. Charles hoped this would quieten down to give them a good journey. He took five minutes to look into his room. It was a fair size and had a porthole looking out over the sea. The ships and boats had a small crew. They would have men to operate a mounted cannon and several maxim machine-gun crews. Charles looked into the mirror next to his cabin toilet and sink. He had a few grey hairs on his beard coming through, which made him look twice. He believed the stress of the situation had brought them out, but he was not too bothered. Charles longed to see his family, to hug his children and hold his wife close; they were in his prayers every night. He had not given up hope of them being alive. As he pondered that thought, a knock on the door broke the silence.

"Captain Hayward. Lieutenant Colonel Adams is asking after you, sir." The soldier was standing outside and saluted him as he left his room.

"Thank you, Private." He saluted him back and left to go up onto the top deck. James was waiting for him. He was in his smart red tunic and wearing a black helmet topped by a spike.

"Charles." He smiled and shook his hand.

He wished him well and told him to come back alive. Charles could not express his concern for James; he felt they would not hold the enemy back should they get a foothold, but wanted those thoughts to stay hidden in the back of his mind. He hoped that if the country did fall, he would get out to America, but he was a soldier and his duty was to serve the Empire. He told him to fight well and vowed they would meet again. James could see the look in his eye, that hinted that there was a wave of darkness coming that no one could fully understand unless they had seen it with their own eyes.

By early afternoon, the ships were ready to sail. There was no big send-off as this was to be a secret operation. Charles felt in good shape; he had looked Nazar in the eyes and knew what the world faced if they did not stop him. If Major Sherborne had been able to execute him and his men, he would not have been able to talk to the high command about their nemesis. They were fascinated to hear about his stature and mindset. Many of the British papers had run stories on him being the devil himself, and it was hard to argue with that. The dead were coming back to life; there were an array of different monsters that now followed this leader to war. He was Emperor of Europe, and was now coming for one of the greatest empires known to man.

Charles stood on top deck; his eyes looked at the English coast and the Isle of Wight as it slowly disappeared over the horizon. He was joined by Captain Holfer. "We're on our way then?" the Austrian asked calmly.

Charles nodded his head. "I hope to see my homeland again soon." He knew this was a sentiment shared by all of the foreign soldiers now serving with the British and all of the refugees who wanted to return home.

"What do you think they found in that rock that fell from the sky?" Captain Holfer was to the point.

Charles scratched his beard, and replied, "I'm not really sure, but whatever it is, it's given them a force to take over the world."

"Do you think we can blow it up and stop the source?" The Austrian stood looking at him.

"Possibly, or at least bury it, giving us time to think of our next move." Charles had been given a lot of explosives on the main ships. These were to be used for whatever purpose deemed necessary. He was not sure what the rock was, or whether they could even find it, but for now the first part of the mission was to locate the map. That would help them find the monastery and fort. From there, they could then decide what their next move should be.

Major Sherborne's ship and boat were sailing alongside Captain Hayward's. He had wanted to undertake the whole mission himself, but had come up against strong opposition. Rumours had begun to circulate that he did leave British soldiers on the beach, and it was Captain Hayward who was trying to help them. With the country being at war and with an invasion pending, it was not seen as a pressing concern to start a full-on investigation into what had happened in France.

Major Sherborne had already spoken to Captain Fairbrook and Captain Brewer about Charles and his men not making it back from Russia. He saw this as a major opportunity to come back as a hero, take a huge reward and to maybe even be knighted. He was secretly shocked at what he had seen in France. The dead walking and trying to eat the living, and the other creatures that he believed could only have come from fairy tales. This was cast to the back of his mind, as for now they had to find the map. He would swallow his pride and make sure Captain Hayward trusted him.

The journey would take around seven to ten days, depending on the weather. They had a small escort to meet them off the Bay of Biscay. Again, it was not enough to draw attention, as Nazar knew that the British Navy was patrolling the seas around her coast and monitoring his actions.

The weather was kind to them, and the seas relatively smooth. The men enjoyed watching a pod of dolphins following them for a short while, jumping in and out of the water with such grace and elegance.

The days were passed checking equipment, looking over maps, and discussing stories of women and previous battles. They had a day of rain and stormy weather, which kept the men below deck. A few of them felt seasick, but this passed as the weather improved the following day.

No enemy ships were sighted.

Charles spoke with Doctor Brown on whether he had heard anything more about the flesh-eaters' sickness and whether it could be cured. He unfortunately had no news. Corporal Heinz joined Charles and Sergeant Butcher for a cup of tea.

"It feels strange that it's so quiet." Corporal Heinz said this as he sipped his tea. Sergeant Butcher waded in with the comment that he liked the weather being good and the fact there had been no sightings of the enemy.

"We have to be mindful of Major Sherborne." Charles looked up at the picture hanging in his room. It was of the battle of Trafalgar. "They will not let us return to Great Britain alive."

"Would he be that foolish to attack us?" Sergeant Butcher looked at Charles as he said this.

"Maybe not straight away, he wants us to help find the map and possibly destroy the rock." He sighed. "I am not sure when he will try something, but he will at some point."

The men agreed they would be ready.

***

Steady as she goes was a call that rang out, as they slowly slipped through the Strait of Gibraltar at night. Nazar had a small garrison at the fort there, but was not patrolling the seas around it. If they had gone during the day, then things could have been different. They had heard of outbreaks of flesh-eaters in Africa, but not of Drone soldiers. The British forces in South Africa had been fighting the Zulus, but with the outbreak of war in Europe, they had withdrawn the majority of the forces. The Boers were dealing with the walking dead for now.

The ships sailed slowly past Morocco, Algiers and Tunisia. They wanted to stay away from mainland Europe as best they could. Malta had originally been chosen as a stopping point, but again nothing was known of who controlled it.

The weather was warm as they steered further into the Mediterranean Sea. The next part of the journey was to sail up through the Ionian Sea and finally into the Adriatic Sea. From there, they would work their way to set anchor off from Lignano Sabbiadoro. The smaller boats they had with them also had specially designed landing craft. It was stored at the back of the boat and was made so that they could lower into the sea, and the soldiers would then sail it to an unoccupied beach.

The plan was to set them down and then sail back. They did not want to be seen and were trying to keep the mission away from Nazar's spies.

They finally arrived at their destination. All of the ships and boats were now flying Nazar's flags and colours. It was a symbol of a priest riding a horse, followed by a demon. They disembarked into landing crafts. Some of the soldiers in each craft spoke Russian and the men manning them were dressed in drone clothing. The general of Nazar's troops in the area would realise that Nazar was now recruiting other men and women from Europe to join his army, but the majority of his foot soldiers were still Russian. This was to be the British troops' cover. Captain Hayward and his men set off.

Major Sherborne and his landing craft were creeping in as well. The landing spot had been decided in advance. It was early evening, but the visibility was still good; a soft, warm breeze swept over them as they pushed along. Both groups had an Italian soldier guide, and Major Sherborne had been given one of Captain Holfer's Austrian soldiers to help him and his group through the former Austro-Hungarian Empire when they arrived there.

Crouching down, Charles looked at the faces of his men, some anxious to get on dry land, others focused on what lay ahead. Water splashed over the side as they moved along. All of them were in their khaki uniforms apart from the crew manning the small vessels. The horses were cordoned in by rope and had several crew keeping them calm.

Charles pulled in his Lee-Metford rifle to his chest. He looked down at the magazine box and nodded to himself; it had proved invaluable in the recent mission to France. Each man had a sword strapped across his back, which wasn't really orthodox, but it meant they could crouch down and be more flexible. They had their revolvers and ammunition pouches attached to their belts, and further equipment in packs, which were strapped to the horses for now. The idea would be to land and not carry too much should they come under fire. Each man could carry more items, once they had established a beachhead.

The closer they got to the shoreline, they had spotters checking the surrounding slopes and hills. No one spoke, unless they were given an order to do something. Gulls screaked above, as the beach came closer.

A nod from a seaman meant that they were coming into shallow water. The men held their rifles tight as they awaited the front of the craft to be lowered. It felt like a lifetime as the front ramp came down. As soon as it was lowered enough, the men darted out of the vessel. Major Sherborne and his Marines landed 100 metres away. They carried out the same drill. The beach was not too long, and the part where they had chosen to land backed onto woodlands.

Once the men had established it was safe, they brought out the horses. Captain Fairbrook rode over to them.

"Captain Hayward. We have secured our end of the beach." He was civil and to the point.

Charles acknowledged him and proclaimed their side had also been secured. Benedict had been trained to shoot and worked on his riding skills. He was to assist with finding the map, but every man on the mission had to be able to help fight, should that be needed.

Mounting his horse, Charles led his group into the woods; he briefly looked around to see the landing crafts leave. They would have to return to the ships. Both the ships and the boats would have to sail out to the Mediterranean. The mission time given was around four to six weeks to find the map, and return to the landing crafts. They would then sail to Russia to find the monastery and fort.

He knew now they were on their own.

With the extra additions, both squads had twenty-four men each. Charles split his men into two groups. Captain Müller and Captain Holfer were in charge of the second group. They hung back about 500 yards as the group set off. Major Sherborne had done the same with his group. This just helped with making it more difficult to see them. Major Sherborne's group was spread 500 yards to the right of Captain Hayward's squad.

The warm weather was appreciated by the men as they moved along through the scrubby woodland. Charles noticed the silence again, the same feel he had when they first left the fort in the Carpathian Mountains. There were birds and rabbits hopping around, but it was as if nature had taught these creatures to be extra quiet now.

Riding on horseback meant they could travel at a good speed. Corporal Heinz led from the front with Private Chamberlin. Both had good vision and a sense for danger.

After riding for five hours, they chose to rest in a clearing next to a small brook. Guards were posted at the four corners around them. The officers scanned the maps of the local area.

"Captain Hayward." Major Sherborne had a look of a man who had just been kicked between the legs. He was not best pleased to speak to Charles, but knew he had no other choice.

"Major." Charles was courteous.

"We might as well go over the route together?" The major was bringing out his map from his binocular pouch.

Captain Brewer and Captain Fairbrook walked over to join the major. The rest of the men set up several small stoves buried in the ground. It was dark now, and only the moonlight lit up the countryside.

A tent was quickly erected so that they could study the map under cover. The material used was of thicker fabric, so it did not let light out. It had been specially designed to be used in the evenings for the officers and men to check their location under candlelight.

They were following the Tagliamento River as a guide to get them closer to the Austro-Hungarian border. The first part of the river had sandbanks, which meant they could not take one of the smaller boats up it, but it did get wider the further up they went. If there was a steamboat they could acquire, this would save a lot of time.

Their Italian guide joined them in the tent as the men looked at the map; he told them he knew of a good place to camp for the evening. It was just outside the village of Spilimbergo. They would break now for thirty minutes or more and then set off again. A few flesh-eaters had been spotted along the way, but they had been in the distance and were of no trouble to the group. The soldiers had been told not to engage them unless they were a direct threat.

The major looked up and down the route and made remarks about crossing through the mountains. He said it would be a hard slog, but knew there was no other route. Charles kept his cool and just went through the correct procedures to do with the mission. He did not trust Major Sherborne, but for now he needed his men and support.

After the break, they packed up quickly and carried on further up the river. The night air was cooler since the sun had gone down; it also carried howls and strange noises. The Marines looked more concerned; some had been with the major in the recent French raids, but they hadn't stayed long enough in enemy territory to experience this new world. There were things out there now that just wanted to kill and eat. Soldiers now almost had to sleep with one eye open and it was unnerving for them.

Passing a farmhouse, a light drew looks from the men. Charles had instructed his officers to keep going and not be drawn into buildings as they did not know who was occupying them. Rumours had circulated in Victorian Britain of many of the Europeans left behind starting to collaborate with Nazar. Most did not have a choice, although some were doing so for money and power. This could mean turning in a group of foreign soldiers for a pot of gold, or even land with a title.

Nazar had appreciated the fact that he did not need to kill everyone; human beings would sell him their own souls for the right price.

Chapter 32

"Excuse me, sir, any news on the captain and the mission?" Private Brown asked quietly, so as to not draw too much attention.

"Nothing yet; I believe we will not hear from them until they've found the map and are back on the ships." Lieutenant Colonel Adams knew he could trust any of Charles's men; they had already shown their loyalty in battle and at the trial.

Private Brown thanked the lieutenant colonel for allowing Heidi to serve as a nurse at the fort. He had told them that they must keep their relationship above board whilst on duty and not kiss, cuddle or show too much emotion in front of the other troops. He did allow them to share a room at Fort Cumberland. Their room was well situated away from the main barracks. The Victorian army did allow some wives to live with the soldiers at the barracks and changes were slowly coming into the army. In general, though, there were still tough rules around this, and if you were a private or held a lower rank then your options were more limited.

John was not on guard in the evenings that week. He returned to his room and waited for Heidi; both had eaten some supper in the army kitchen hall earlier and now they were only interested in one thing. She spoke German to him as she slowly undressed from her nurse's uniform. Sliding her hand onto her blouse, she winked cheekily at John; he was like a dog on heat and could not keep his eyes off her.

Heidi was a beautiful, blonde Austrian girl and had a body which would be excellent to paint; she had curves in all the right places.

She started to undress John from his red army tunic. His bronze buttons unclipped with each twist of her fingers. She then lowered her head between his legs and teased him. John shouted out with delight, and the evening passed well for this young couple. They momentarily were able to put the prison camp behind them and be young and free again.

Heidi looked at John as they lay side by side. She held his hand and brushed his cheek. "I love you, Private John Brown."

His smile beamed from one side of his mouth to the other. "I love you too, Heidi."

They fell asleep in each other's arms.

Chapter 33

Captain Hayward and his men packed up their blankets and kit quickly in the morning. The evening had passed without incident. There had been rumblings in the bushes and trees around them, but no flesh-eaters emerged or attacked.

Charles spoke to Doctor Brown about whether he thought the flesh-eaters would eventually just rot away? The doctor had said not enough was known of these creatures.

The groups dispersed, with Major Sherborne taking his Marines and guides with him. Charles knew they had to commandeer a boat to sail them up the Tagliamento River and save time. They had been informed back in Great Britain that this had been used as a trade route on the larger parts of the river, where the sandbanks would have no effect on the boats.

The horses stirred up a little dust as they moved through the dry dirt paths next to the river. Charles hung back to see the impact the dust would make on their position. If it was minor, then scouts would probably just think it was a herd of livestock moving by the river, or flesh-eaters on mass. He looked to the clouds as if almost to pray for some rain. They rode until early afternoon, and did not stop for food or water.

Corporal Heinz rode down the line at a good speed. He stopped by Captain Hayward.

"Captain, we found some boats," said the corporal, who also revealed that Private Chamberlin had stayed close to the mini harbour and was monitoring the situation. He instructed the corporal to update the major and lead the groups to a safe vantage point.

The Engineers and the Marines fanned out before they reached the small harbour. Their khaki uniforms helped conceal them more than their former red tunics. Binoculars were being used by the officers to scan the landscape for movement. They could see there were maybe five to six drone soldiers wandering around, and a couple standing on guard chatting. The rest of the people were fishermen or slaves who manned the boat.

Charles spoke to the other captains and Sergeant Butcher. The men crouched in the long grass and bushes on the edge of the harbour.

"We'll take two groups of seven men and come around their flanks." Charles said this as the major came over.

"We should do a full-on attack, to get this over with as soon as possible." The major was taking off his leather gloves as he said this.

"With all due respect, Major, if we can get away without having to fire our weapons, then it will help us draw less attention." Charles was polite, but firm.

"Very well, Captain, let my Marines take the right flank under Captain Brewer." He nodded to his captain to come over.

This was one of the reasons Captain Hayward had asked for the major and his men not to come on the mission. He felt their presence would be awkward when carrying out raids exactly like the one that was about to happen.

Charles was going to lead the Engineer unit. Captain Brewer got his men to take off surplus kit and just take their weapons with them. Swords were across their backs and revolvers attached to their belts. Rifles were readied with bayonets.

Charles spoke to Captain Brewer about keeping the noise down to a minimum where possible when they took the harbour. With that, there was a simple nod of heads and he moved his men to the right flank, scurrying over open ground and into pockets of woodland. The Marines were using any dips or uneven ground to crouch in.

Captain Hayward then brought his men around the left flank. They had open grassland to negotiate, before getting close to some disused cowsheds. He had a couple of men covering them as five of them burst from the long grass towards the cowsheds. The sun had lit up the blue sky. Charles crouched by the wall, holding his rifle upright and leaning against the corner before taking a quick survey.

Soon, though, the cold stones in the cowshed wall gave some relief from this warm sun; it would creep around to heat them up as well. His men pressed against the wall, and they looked sharp and ready. The two soldiers who had been covering them had now joined them. One of these was Sergeant Butcher.

"Sergeant, take two men and search the buildings by the roadside." Charles was now going to take on the two guards who were chatting and then the guardhouse. Captain Brewer was coming around the right flank.

Charles drew out his hunting knife, and he leaned his rifle up against the wall. Another Engineer did the same thing; he still had his sword across his back and his revolver on his belt. The other two soldiers with them attached their bayonets. Charles looked again around the corner and saw the two guards had stopped to sit and eat some bread. This was the moment they were waiting for.

"On the count of three."

"One …"

"Two …"

A thunderous gunshot shook the ground. Charles and his four men had just left the corner of the cowshed; caught in no-man's-land as the guards threw down the bread and grabbed their rifles, one of them turned to see the four British Engineers moving towards them and let out a cry. The soldier next to Charles squeezed his trigger, and a .303 round blew the drone soldier backwards and off the wall he had been sitting on. The other drones who had been moving supplies had started to run to the guardhouse to get their rifles.

Several more gunshots rang out; they were coming from the right-hand flank. Charles did not have a clear view on what was occurring. Bullets started to zip through the air as they hit the deck hard. "Get to the wall." He pushed his hunting knife back into its sheaf and unclipped the revolver holder pulling out the Enfield in one quick action.

Gunshots started to vibrate their way around the buildings. A piece of brick exploded next to Captain Hayward's shoulder, as a bullet slammed into it. "Keep down men," he called out.

More bullets hit the wall. Further down the lane was the guardhouse; some of the soldiers had now started shooting from that.

"We're pinned down, Captain," A private said as he desperately looked around for better cover.

One of the drone soldiers made a dash to get to the outbuilding across from their position; he would then have a great vantage point to shoot at Charles and his men. Before he could get there, a sniper took out the drone's legs; the bullet ripped through his left kneecap and into his right leg. The screaming and yelping did not last long as another bullet smacked into his head.

Covering fire from behind meant that they had a moment to pick themselves up and get into a small outbuilding. It had farm equipment stacked to one side, and some broken glass windows to the front. The men quickly began to fire out of these, laying down a constant barrage on the guardhouse. The ten-round box magazine meant that they could keep firing and not spend so much time reloading.

The drones who had been outside took cover behind walls and wagons; some of them did not have weapons and stayed low. Captain Brewer had already moved his men nearer to the guardhouse. He waited outside before lighting a grenade and throwing it through the window. The explosion shook the ground, causing dust to fall off the old beams above.

Charles used this time to come out of the outbuilding and move down the side of it. Sergeant Butcher and his two men were in another outbuilding laying down covering fire. Charles had one soldier with him as they scampered across open ground. Bullets whizzed by as they ran. They both sprinted up to the harbour house and around the corner into a drone soldier who was reloading. The drone used the butt of his rifle to knock the private with Charles down to the ground, and as he went to finish him with his bayonet, Charles pulled out his revolver and squeezed the trigger, shooting the man in the chest. He wasted no time and shot him again in the head. He knew all drones were infected and would come back if the brain was not destroyed.

The Marines were now sweeping through the small lanes. The guardhouse was on fire and a couple of burning drones came out and were shot as they did so.

Major Sherborne had ridden to the boats and secured the area. Sergeant Butcher rounded up the workers and boat crews as they searched each building. There did not seem to be any more drone soldiers there. They believed the commander was killed inside the guardhouse.

There was a quick discussion on what to do with the workers. They were not slaves and worked for Nazar. Charles was not sure of the relationship they had with their new masters. They did not look as off colour as the drone soldiers, but had to be dealt with none the less. Charles's plan was to secure them in one of the outbuildings. He knew they would break out, but it would give them time to sail up the river and then continue their journey after that.

The soldiers collected together the civilians and checked over the steamboats. The crews on the boats did not put up a fight and came willingly to join the others. The Italian soldiers questioned them as to why they had joined Nazar's forces and the answer was simple – adapt or die. Nazar had executed hundreds of thousands of people, but had also come round to the idea of using some for slaves and others to control and work with him. He was offering some noble families that joined him the chance for local power and the spoils of war. Most had not taken up the offer, but a few were persuaded.

Major Sherborne rode over whilst Captain Hayward and his officers were speaking.

"Bloody lucky us Marines were here." He sat up straight and looked very smug.

He then went on to talk about having the prisoners executed. "Just line them up and we'll do the rest." He cleared his throat. "It's a war, after all."

"You're right, Major, it is a war, but Nazar will only gain more followers if we start killing Europeans." Charles was firm.

"They're hardly Europeans now, look at them." He pointed to the civilians being led into an outbuilding. "They're not slaves, they're workers."

"I have made my decision, Major." Captain Hayward instructed the doors to be locked.

Benedict and Doctor Brown walked towards the captain. They were both carrying rifles. "We're ready to board the boat now, sir." Dr Brown was helping out with everything he could. Benedict was the same, but was not allowed to be at the front of the group or to be involved in skirmishes unless it was inevitable.

Major Sherborne rode off. He was not best pleased. He spoke to Captain Fairbrook and ordered that the last soldier on the boat should be a Marine. That Marine should start a small fire inside the outbuilding adjacent to the ones the prisoners were in. He said they would not have time to turn back and the filthy animals would get what they deserved.

The ship was loaded with horses and their supplies. It was not too dissimilar to the boat they had used before when fleeing Europe through the Austro-Hungarian Empire. They were going to retain some of the original crew and were offered freedom at the end of it.

Once the steam had built up and the last Marine had helped set off, the boat got under way. Flesh-eaters had been drawn to the gunfire – not many, but it was a sight to observe as they filtered through the fields and woods and into the small harbour.

The order had gone out for the soldiers on top deck to dress as drone soldiers. The Nazar flag was already flying.

Captain Müller watched on top deck with Captain Hayward. "Just like old times." He said this with a wry smile. "This time, though, we're heading into the darkness, not away from it." Captain Müller did have point. He thought aloud about how the civilians could work with the flesh-eaters. They would surely have to keep them apart or they would become food for them, he pondered. Charles wondered if this would aid Nazar in his oppressive regime. People would be told to keep within forts or fenced areas. This way Nazar would control them by fear of the unknown.

They spoke for a while until Captain Holfer joined them to point out buildings burning in the harbour. Charles took out his binoculars but the river was starting to bend around and small, scrubby trees were growing up alongside the banks, blocking his view.

Charles asked his officers to study maps below deck regarding going through the Italian mountains and into Austro-Hungary. He then made a beeline towards Major Sherborne's quarters. There was a guard outside; the Marine stopped him as he approached.

"Sorry, Captain. The major is having a meeting with his officers." The soldier brought his rifle across his body.

"Tell the major I have a question regarding the harbour." Charles stood there.

The Marine waited a second, then he saw Sergeant Butcher arrive behind the captain with another Engineer.

"Sir, I can't let you knock if there is going to be trouble. Do I have your word there will not be any?"

"You have my word, Marine." Charles was allowed to knock.

He was beckoned in. The major was there with Captain Fairbrook and Brewer. They were drinking whisky and had a collection of wine which they had found on board.

"Captain, join us." He looked very relaxed sitting in a red leather chair. "They've looked after this room; I'd thought they would destroy everything." He then brought his glass to his lips and knocked back its contents.

"Major, did you give the order for the buildings to be burnt with the people inside?"

There was a silence.

"It was necessary for the mission, Captain." He paused to refill his glass. "They're the enemy, and if you let them live, they will bring the enemy soldiers after us."

Charles held his anger in for a moment, while he tried to compose himself. "They were civilians surviving in this hellhole of a new world." He knew he could not stay in the room without doing something he regretted. "If we're not careful, we'll end up being just as bad as the enemy." He then turned and left the room, striding past the Marine on guard outside.

He went up on deck and stood in the fresh breeze for a while. He then went and sat in a corner which was not too exposed. Charles took that moment to take out a picture of Rebecca and the kids. It seemed to take him back to the time when he saw them briefly in Paris; their worried faces and panicked eyes were lingering in his mind.

His moment of solitude was broken when Corporal Heinz came up the steps from below and asked to speak with him. Charles asked for the corporal to sit with him on the bench.

"Captain, is everything ok?"

Charles looked around. "The major killed the civilians back at the harbour."

Corporal Heinz looked shocked and angry. "It does not surprise me; he left us to die on the beach." He then looked around himself. "I do not trust them, Captain, they will betray us before this mission is over."

Charles nodded his head. "I know, but for now we need numbers." He then went on to say an old warrior saying: "Keep your friends close, but your enemies closer."

The corporal agreed. They spoke for five minutes before going below deck. All of the soldiers ate well and slept well as the boat gently moved along. The channel they went along was man-made. Its riverbeds were shallow and gravelly, which meant there was not much deep water. The local governor of the area had been requested to find a way for the steamboats to use the river, and he had then requested for a channel to be dug out. This would normally take some time, but they had brought in many of the slaves from the local area and used them to dig. They did not care if they died on the job; those that did were fed to the flesh-eaters. The new channel did not pass as far as they would have liked, but it meant they could rest a while whilst travelling and cover some ground.

It was the Marines' night to stand guard over the crew and to make sure they did not attempt mutiny whilst they slept. Not all of them were needed and half were sent to rest. The evening was relatively quiet, apart from the new sounds that now floated on the wind in Europe, the odd scream or growl.

Charles locked his door. He put his revolver by his bed and let himself fall into a deep sleep.

There was a thunderous bump against the boat. Then a bell started to ring in the wheelhouse, and this was followed by an explosion. A cry of pain filled the small corridors. Charles was putting on his trousers when a third explosion shook his cabin violently. The humming in his ears caused him to stagger from side to side.

He got himself dressed and put on his belt. Charles grabbed his revolver and clipped it to his holster. Smoke started to drift under his door. There was another loud bang; this time it was not on the boat, but coming from the nearby bank. He checked his watch – it was five-fifteen. Dawn had broken, but it was still a little dark.

The next sounds to come from the steamboat were sharp metal twangs. This was followed by aggressive, *dink, dink, dinks*. Charles knew they were under attack, but this confirmed that bullets were now hitting the side of the boat.

He grabbed his rifle and sword and left his room; the smoke was quite thick in the corridor and the ship was starting to tilt. Gunfire was being returned from above deck. Charles looked up and saw soldiers rushing to the top deck. Corporal Heinz came along the corridor.

"Are you ok, sir?"

"All good, Corporal, and you and the lads?" Charles asked anxiously.

Corporal Heinz said the engine room crew had been killed and that it was on fire. The wheelhouse was also burning after being hit. They had lost two Marines from the explosion as well. The artillery piece had stopped firing and the quick assessment was that they were bringing up more shells.

Sergeant Butcher had taken a boat with eight men and gone over to the other side. They had a fixed bearing on the cannon, which was firing at them, and were making a beeline for it. The gunfire from the bank had been sporadic, giving some indication that this was not a large force that the British were encountering.

Private Chamberlin had got himself placed in between three wooden boxes and grain sacks. Charles came up top, and crouched as he tried to get an idea of where the enemy fire was coming from. The soldiers on deck pointed over to a small cottage and a patch of trees next to it. There were horses tied together further back.

Private Chamberlin breathed in, waited and picked his target. A flash of a body moved from the cottage to the woods. He did not make it all the way, *boom*, as the figure in the distance fell onto his knees and then to the ground. Before Charles could take aim, Private Chamberlin had hit another drone crouching on the riverbank.

This was followed by shouting and an explosion further up the river. Charles hoped Sergeant Butcher and his men were safe. Captain Brewer came over to his position. "Have you seen the major, Captain?"

"No, I woke to us being hit." He then pointed to below deck. "Check below deck again, and see to the horses."

The enemy gunfire from the bank was less intense now. Captain Holfer had gone to the front of the boat and scanned the area with his binoculars. He reported back that there was maybe two to three drone cavalry left on that side.

As he spoke, Private Green, the soldier that had joined them late to this mission, squeezed his Lee-Metford trigger. A drone fell from behind the tree and rolled down the bank into the water. "I got one," the young soldier shouted out.

"We need to get everyone off this boat. Gunfire would have attracted a lot of unwanted attention," Charles said. The men on the top deck could see Sergeant Butcher and his men sweeping through the cottage and woods next to it. Private Chamberlin monitored them from his position. He looked at two figures moving through the woods; the darker uniforms gave them away as drone soldiers. This was all he needed. Two loud shots from the boat brought the figures to a halt. Sergeant Butcher and his men checked the bodies and looked around the area. Whilst this was unfolding, Major Sherborne arrived next to Captain Hayward. He looked shell-shocked and dazed.

"What's happening?"

"Major, we've been tracked by a cavalry unit, who had a small field gun." Charles paused and wiped his brow. He looked at the major, "It could have been the taking of the harbour. Or the fire that followed."

The major gave him a look of distain upon hearing those comments. "We need to get off this boat," he said.

Charles had given an order to Captain Müller to check on Benedict and keep him safe. Doctor Brown was still with him; they were a little shaken, but unhurt. The boat was sinking, so they had to unload. They had been fortunate as the boat had been steered closer to the bank.

Captain Fairbrook reported back that ten horses had been killed in the blast. This meant they would be left short. There were horses on the other side, but some had been set free by the drones during the skirmish.

Charles could not think about that at that moment; they had to get everyone off the boat. The crew had been killed along with the two Marines. The other injuries suffered by the soldiers had been minor. The horses started to be winched into the water; they had ropes around their back and barrel, which helped soldiers to pull them towards the bank. As this was unfolding, noises of snarls and groans were heard from behind the bushes on the bank, causing concern. Those noises were a prelude to the figures, who started to come through the foliage wearing dishevelled clothes.

"Flesh-eaters!" Rang out from the soldiers on the bank.

Captain Hayward told the soldiers on top deck to cover the soldiers on the bank. The gunshots began again.

A large, male flesh-eater, who had stumbled through the foliage first, was hit straight between the eyes. He fell forward in one motion, sliding down the gravel bank, but two more flesh-eaters started to come through the bushes. An older woman and a teenage girl. They were hit a couple of times before headshots finished them off.

Charles tried to gather his thoughts.

"Captain Müller, take five men and see how many more are being drawn in," said Charles, before then speaking to the major, who was looking at his map. The major looked up briefly, but was lost in his own world. His officers joined him at his side, as if they were planning their own mission or focusing purely on their own survival.

Whilst this unfolded, a soldier came up from below deck; he was breathing heavily and stammered his words out. "Captain, the engine room is flooding and the livestock will be lost if we do not get them out now."

Charles knew they could not waste any more time if this mission was to succeed. "All hands on deck," he shouted. "Get me a report on the artillery piece and whether the other bank is secure."

The boat became a hub of activity. Soldiers were rushing around trying to get the essential supplies and livestock off the sinking boat.

Sergeant Butcher had rowed back through the channel with two of his men. He had a rope lowered down to him. Once on board, he reported to Captain Hayward. He composed himself before proclaiming the far side bank clear. He also added that they had managed to get some information out of a dying drone soldier. "There had been a small detachment in a local village, when a worker had run to them and told them what happened at the harbour." Sergeant Butcher said this with apprehension.

Charles knew killing the workers would never help this war. He had to hide his disgust and his inner urge to take action on the major. It was neither the time nor the place to start an internal battle.

Horses were being lowered over the edge at a good rate. The boat's rowing boats were filled with ammunition, rifles, explosives, machine guns and the men's equipment. The next thirty minutes flew by; Charles was happy with how the men were rising to the challenge. However, this moment of joy was short-lived.

A scout who had gone out with Captain Müller returned at full speed.

"They're coming, hundreds if not thousands!" the soldier shouted from his horse, as if anxious to get back to help his other scouts. Charles lowered himself over the side and swam over to the bank and rider.

"Are they drone soldiers?" Charles said.

"No, sir, flesh-eaters, but they're not adults. They're children." The soldiers around the scout looked at each other. The Engineers had seen flesh-eater children before, but never en masse.
Charles knew Nazar would use whatever was needed to win this war.

Why he had infected children he did not really understand. He thought it might be the lack of will by mankind to deal with infected children, or something completely out of their understanding. Flesh-eaters had only been studied for a short while in London.

Charles returned to the boat and was hauled back up." Double the guard on Benedict!" Charles barked out his orders, before then turning to face the scout from the top deck. "We'll send a unit with a Maxim machine gun, tell Captain Müller not to take any risks."

"Major Sherborne, send four of your Marines with a Maxim gun," said Charles, then he turned to speak to Sergeant Butcher.

"Captain, I have already lost two men; sending four more will not stop thousands." He folded his map whilst he did this.

Charles turned to face him. "I am in charge of this mission. Are you disobeying me, Major?" There was a silence.

"Remember your rank, man; you're an officer of Queen Victoria's army and one that should have swung for treason." The major lowered his hand towards his revolver.

"If you disobey my orders now, we will see who will swing." He also began to lower his right hand towards his own revolver.

Smoke drifted across the boat, and the soldiers around the two men slowly stopped unloading, whilst the two officers stood staring at each other.

"Captain, our men have come back from the other bank. The enemy are closing in, giant riders of the north; they may have long limbs with them." Charles turned to face the soldier who stood there after delivering this news. "We have brought four horses with us, sir. We will be six short."

The major was still looking at the captain, but his eyes caught those of Private Chamberlin and Captain Holfer. Both were carrying their rifles, and looking menacingly at him.

"Captain Fairbrook, tell Sergeant Edwards to take three men and a Maxim gun, and to assist Captain Müller."

"This is not over, Captain." The major pushed past him with hatred in his eyes.

Charles did not have time to think about what to do with the major for now. His main concern was getting everything they needed off the boat.

Ten minutes passed before a bullet snapped into a wooden joist on the old steamboat. Splinters fell to the ground from the impact. Muzzle flashes let them know the riders of the north had arrived.

The boat shielded them as the remaining men were ordered off it. Charles heard a *rat-a-tat-tat*. The Maxim machine gun had started to fire.

He moved up over the edge of the riverbank and through a pocket of trees. Then he clambered down a bank to the other side. The men were waiting.

"Those without horses, double up, we will find more." Charles looked over to Major Sherborne; all of his Marines were mounted.

Corporal Heinz came forward with Captain Hayward's horse. "We must get to Captain Müller and the Marines."

The Royal Engineers without horses mounted up with a comrade. They then followed the captain as he rode to support Captain Müller.

The sight that greeted them as they got to the top of a hill, where the machine-gun fire was coming from, was breathtaking. It was a sea of flesh-eater children. They were not seeming to be led by priests; it was just a large horde. The sheer numbers had started to enclose the group; even on the hill where the other soldiers were was starting to get encircled.

Captain Hayward quickly spoke to the sergeant and corporal. Major Sherborne came forward on his horse. He was shocked at what he was seeing, which reflected in his voice, which had become faster and lighter. "I can get Benedict into Austria; we will meet you at the village of Villach."

Charles was reluctant to give up Benedict, but the situation was becoming perilous; the boy had to be taken to safety. They had to get the map and complete the mission.

"Major, take two of my men with you. You'd better be waiting for us."

With that, the Marines leaving told the remaining soldiers to keep the escape route clear. Captain Holfer was given command of the hill. Charles then rode down to a fence, where Captain Müller and his men had set up the machine gun and two shooting points.

"Captain, mount up." The flesh-eater children were closing in on the machine gun even with it firing away.

"Captain, we can't leave the Maxim gun."

The groans and snarls became amplified as soon as the machine gun stopped firing.

"We must leave."

Captain Müller's soldiers broke down the Maxim gun and quickly packed it the best they could. They did not have enough time to gather all the ammunition. It was a frantic effort.

Charles pulled out his revolver and started to shoot at the flesh-eaters; the soldiers with him did the same. The gunfire from the hill grew louder.

Captain Müller shouted out the order for his men to mount up. As he did so, the first wave of children hit the wall, soon starting to put pressure on it. As this was unfolding, he managed to mount his horse. The eyes of the children made Charles shake his head in pity; their only desire now was for food. The skin of some of them was hanging off, while others looked as if their nails had grown and their teeth had sharpened. Many of them had tatty, ripped clothes, while others were not too dishevelled.

As soon as Captain Müller and his men were mounted, they followed Charles to the top of the hill. It was a chaotic scene as the flesh-eaters were coming up the front and side of the hill.

"Bugler, sound the retreat!" Charles had wanted to keep the noise level down, but after the firefight and with the enemy already knowing they were there, it was better not to lose any more men.

They pushed on at speed, shooting from the saddle and using their swords when flesh-eaters came close as they tried to escape. Corporal Heinz was riding with one of the Italian soldier guides; he took the group along a small road and then up into the hills. He did not want to follow the river too close as he feared this would now be guarded by drone soldiers.

They rode non-stop for three hours; Charles had hoped to catch up with the major, but nothing could be seen of him yet. They approached a disused barn with caution; it was scouted out first for inhabitants and then cleared for someone to stop and rest. They had been lucky with supplies, as hardly anything they needed had had to be left on the boat. The main concern now was how the enemy would react. They did not think it would be too obvious that they were heading to the former Austro-Hungarian Empire, and the khaki uniforms did not give away a British force. They hoped that they would be seen as bandits from the hills, although the Maxim machine gun could be an issue.

Some tea was prepared over a fire and the captain found a crossbeam, that had fallen in from the old barn roof, to lay his map across. On the outskirts of the town of Villach was the chosen meeting point of Major Sherborne's. Staying more towards the mountains to the west, they would not venture near the town. The next several days would be spent navigating the Italian mountains and getting into Austria safely.

Whilst Captain Hayward spoke to his officers, guards were posted around the makeshift camp. It was discussed that they would probably send a small search party for the major's group, but it was not decided if this would get to Nazar or not. Fortune had shone on them as no priest had witnessed their escape or attack on the harbour.

If this had been the case, then they might have been more inclined to send news to the more senior officers about the attack. Now it might be left to the corporals and sergeants to make that call. They hoped this would be the case.

The decision was given to spend the night in the barn and run-down outbuildings. It gave them shelter and a good defensive point. Guards were posted around the four corners of the camp and the horses were left saddled in a large wooden barn. The men took their backpacks and blankets to sleep on; Charles wanted to make sure that they could escape with ease if necessary. Some pots and pans were used to cook up a hearty supper.

The Maxim machine gun was set up in a small, empty cowshed. The Engineers had knocked out the windows, which gave them a good line of vision and meant they could cover the back of the farm buildings from attack. Wagons and other equipment were used to create a good, strong perimeter.

"Captain, we're set for the evening, come and have some rabbit stew," said Sergeant Butcher.

Captain Hayward was walking around the camp. "Thank you, Sergeant, but just before we turn in, please get some of the men to take down these young sapling trees." He pointed to the grey elms and black pines; there wasn't an extensive area to clear, but it was enough to let an attack group get closer than they should.

Charles then walked along a deer track, which led off deep into a pine forest. He stopped short of going in; the soft breeze picked up in branches and caused them to rustle a little. The forest stood firm, like a wall into another world. Charles knew they would either have to pass through this, or around it. The Italian guide said he could find a way. Whatever way it was, it was not to be tackled tonight.

He turned and left for the safety of the camp.

Chapter 34

"My generals and priests we are gathered today to continue the war."
Nazar was dressed totally in black. His hair and beard had been
trimmed, a dark cloak covered his light, black armour, his sword was
strapped to his side, and standing next to him was his warrior queen
Oksana. She was looking powerful and also dressed for war, but this
did not detract from her beauty. Many of the priests and generals were
in awe of her long, flowing hair and athletic figure, but knew all too
well that if they stared for too long, they would lose their eyes.

"My one wish would have been to have my two sons witness
this coming of the new age." He walked around, looking at those who
had gathered. "But this is not their time, it is our time." He stopped by
a glass of wine, which had been half-drunk. His audience's eyes were
captivated with their leader's presence and demeanour. Then in one
swoop he took his sword out and smashed it down onto the glass and
table underneath. The glass shattered and the wooden table split with
the force of the strike.

His long tongue rolled out and licked around his lips. "Our
warships are already sailing to meet the British Navy in the Atlantic."
He withdrew his sword from the split table as he said this. His senior
generals Georgiy, Tarasov and Eltsina stood still as he walked around
them. The high priest of the council Alekseev looked down as if not to
catch his eye.

"Is there anyone who is not ready for this battle?" The wind
blew hard on the sides of the large tent; its drapes whistled up and
skipped around as if alive. No one spoke; he then sheathed his sword
back into his scabbard.

"Good, then we are all ready."

He clapped his hands and wine and food were brought in for
everyone. The mood in the room lightened and the officers and priests
began to drink and eat. Thirty minutes passed, and then out of nowhere
the destroyer drones covered all exits.

Nazar laughed as if excited about what was coming.

Three slaves were brought in. They were tied together and had
their hands bound. The audience looked at them and then at Nazar.
Oksana let out a high-pitch laugh which hurt the ears of the generals
near her. The priests were much more excited than the generals. The
slaves were told to kneel.

Nazar then beckoned his queen to come forward. She was presented with an axe from a destroyer drone nearest to her. She did not wait to ask what to do and brought the axe down on one of the slave's necks. Blood shot up in the air like from a fountain; she moved forward and let her body take some of the falling blood, covering her from head to toe in red liquid. The other two slaves screamed for mercy.

Nazar walked around the room and saw General Tarasov wince a little with this action.

"You will kill the other two." He then smiled at the general and gave him the axe.

General Tarasov looked at the body, which was now no longer spurting up so much blood. He also saw the fear in the eyes of the slaves.

He said nothing, and in two quick actions beheaded both of them. He then passed back the axe.

Nazar laughed and then kissed his blood-soaked queen. "You are a good general, there is hope for you."

He then ordered that everyone in the room must drink the blood of the slaves for the battle to be won over the British Empire. As his captive audience awkwardly drank blood from Nazar's victims, his dark, rasping voice boomed out his demands for the coming days. They would set sail late in the week and whilst the British Navy destroyed his fake armada, he would land the real one from Norfolk to Cornwall. "They have never seen an army like this before, or fought an enemy like us."

With this, he clapped his hands again. Nervous eyes looked around the room, but this time no slaves were brought in. Four Destroyer drones came in with a long, wooden table. They set the table down in an area which was clear and then left the tent. Nazar came over to the table; he had picked up a long, rolled-up paper, which he then began to unfurl. It was a map of Europe; he called his followers in close to have a look.

Nazar then went over his plans in more detail for the invasion. He had ordered this information to be given to the other officers on the day of the invasion and the senior priests were to do the same to the other priests.

Later on in the day, as dusk fell, Nazar looked out over the sea. The flames of the oil-soaked branches burned along the clifftop. Oksana joined him by his side.

"Soon you will destroy the British Empire." She let her right hand stroke over his neck and down his right shoulder.

"Yes, my queen, we will rule it together and our children will become kings and queens of the world."

Chapter 35

"Cold morning, sir," the private said to Lieutenant Colonel James as he walked along Southsea Beach.

The beach had wooden stakes dug deep into the sand. A detachment of the 24th was guarding that part of Southsea; they did not have the standard blue helmet topped with a spike. They were still in their colonial dress with white helmet. Many had been recalled from the pending war with the Zulus and there had not been time to re-issue new uniforms. The government's efforts in recent months had focused on weapons and regrouping the European forces that had come over during the fall of Europe.

Sandbags had been built up along the seafront and earth mounds used as further fortifications. The Royal Artillery had gun emplacements with several eighteen-pounders and rotating long-range heavy artillery. There were also new defences built for the Maxim machine guns. They had built up the sandbags at the sides and given the top a protected wooden roof. The civilians had nicknamed them pillboxes. Through this hole the machine-gun crew could fire from side to side, with protection from gunfire and shells to a certain degree.

Lieutenant Colonel Adams thought about Charles as he strolled along. He smiled to himself, thinking about the amount of whisky drunk over the Christmas period and how he missed normal day-to-day life with his family.

The gentle sound of waves breaking on the beach put James at ease. He was taking this time to survey the defences before returning to Fort Cumberland, which was only a ten-minute walk away.

The sun started to rise slowly in the sky, chasing along the beach and awakening everything in its path. James could hear distant thunderclaps, but he could see no menacing storm on the horizon. As he faced out to sea, his eyes fell upon tiny dots. They were everywhere on the horizon, like a sea of ants spreading out as far as the eye could see. At first, he stood there, watching a little in awe of this spectacle. He rubbed his eyes again and then gasped. Turning in a frantic way, he almost lost his footing in the sand as he raced back to the soldier who was patrolling along the earth mound. The man was now having a cup of tea with his fellow private.

"I need a pair of bloody binoculars quickly, lads." James had forgotten all protocol and was almost shaking.

"I'll have a look, sir; I believe the sergeant had a pair in the hut." The soldier rushed off and came back with a pair. "Here you go, sir." He passed them over.

James stood up on the highest part of the earth mound. There was an eerie silence.

"My God, they're coming."

***

Half an hour passed as the ships came closer into view. Then the shelling started. The Isle of Wight was under heavy bombardment. She returned fire, but it was as if a sea of shells were raining down upon her.

Lieutenant Colonel Adams had sent messages out about the forthcoming invasion. He did not know of the scale of this attack which was unfolding from Norfolk all the way down to Cornwall.

The 24th filed into the trenches dug along Southsea Beach. All along the coast, soldiers were being scrambled to the front. The noise was deafening; a constant pounding of artillery shook the very ground they stood on. Gunpowder filled the air, almost burning the nostrils of those who breathed it in. Lieutenant Colonel Adams was watching from Fort Cumberland. He had ordered most of his men underground during the heavy shelling. The exploding shells ripped up sand from the beach and flung it hundreds of feet into the air.

Some of the shells were landing a little further inland; clumps of soil and grass would fly up into the air after each explosion. Smoke drifted across the land with a watery mist from the bombardment. Church bells rang out, warning of the impending invasion.

James scoured the horizon with his binoculars. He could see the muzzle flashes lighting up the sky from the ships. The soldiers were keeping their heads down and below ground. The sheer scale of this attack sent butterflies to Lieutenant Colonel Adams' stomach. He had not seen a gathering of ships like this before in his life. The British Navy did not have this many ships.

Some of the ships had tried to set sail from the British ports but had been either destroyed or had retreated back. The sea battle over the Atlantic Ocean was still being fought. Nazar had sacrificed so many ships there, but he did not care. He knew the British would destroy his fake armada, but they would not be able to return in time for the land invasion.

On the Isle of Wight there were houses and villages burning, as they were closer to the bombardment. It had also been used as a quarantine site for recent European arrivals to be vetted for bites from flesh-eaters. These wretched souls had little to no cover as the shells tore into their refugee camps, obliterating tents and store sheds with ease. Sheer panic had sent many of the refugees at the far side of the island to Cowes. There were no ships available to leave upon and be saved by during this attack, meaning many huddled together in the woods and buildings to try to escape this furious onslaught.

The shelling lasted thirty minutes. When the attack stopped, the British guns opened up; some had been destroyed while others sprang into action. They had some success with the targets being so plentiful; plumes of smoke and fire would come out of direct hits, and large explosions erupted everywhere. The enemy did not return fire, rather they waited.

Telegrams were being sent by Morse code around the country. This meant news could be sent of the enemy positions at greater speed than through a normal horseback rider.

James called the bugler to sound the call to arms. He had Royal Engineers and Marines stationed in the fort. He also had some of his men stationed on Box Hill. He prayed they would not be pushed back that far.

Great Britain was now seeing a flurry of activity. Thousands of men were being scrambled into makeshift fighting units. Those that were not in the regular army would be given pitchforks, axes or iron bars. Basically, anything that could be used as a weapon. Parliament was called into session to discuss the pending invasion. Some politicians had already left their properties on the news of Nazar's ships being sighted off the south coast and were now trying to find a vessel to take them to America.

The refugees had started to panic, as they did not see a way out of Great Britain. Some started to set off for Scotland and Wales, while others began to riot. The British police were heavily outnumbered and could not control all of the camps. In some cases, they abandoned them to their own fate.

Not all of the camps were in disorder. Some had more foreign soldiers who had finally been allowed to regroup and reform their previous regiments the best they could. These camps were more structured and even had help from their units to build a better infrastructure within them. The Prussians had a good size force and were being directed to help secure the east coast.

The high command was looking over maps in Aldershot. Messages and dispatches were being sent constantly via riders. James walked around his men. The Royal Engineers from Charles's regiment stood by with their rifles, waiting for further orders. The Marines had started to filter out around the fort; they were all taken aback by what their eyes were seeing. The tiny black dots filled every part of the sea; even with plumes of smoke showing, direct hits of enemy ships were not enough to get excited about.

The British heavy artillery kept on firing. More shells had been requested from the armories around Portsmouth. The orderlies were bringing ammunition boxes and opening them in the trenches; they did not want there to be unnecessary delays once the enemy boats landed.

Lieutenant Colonel Adams scanned the horizon again; he looked at the enemy ships and then saw the first opening of an attack. They were pushing onto the Isle of Wight. The artillery on the east side of the island started to open up. The soldiers looked on as the boats vanished out of sight. Messages started to flood into the command centre in the fort. The Isle of Wight was now under full attack. The pounding of heavy guns was soon followed by machine-gun fire and rifle fire.

The soldiers looked at each other, some with anxious faces, and others who were in deep reflection about the poor souls now fighting for their very lives on the island.

The sea batteries on the far side of the island ceased fire. Private Brown went to the lieutenant colonel with a telegram. "For you, sir," he said.

"Thank you, Private Brown."

To the High command:

They are landing on the beaches. Their numbers are unforgiving. We will hold them off as long as we can, before making a final stand at the town of Newport.

God have mercy upon our souls.

General Harold Grisham

Isle of Wight

The lieutenant colonel stood there in silence for a moment.

"Sir, boats are coming."

The gunfire on the island was non-stop. James walked to the edge of the fort and took up his binoculars again. He scanned the wash of the boats; there were thousands of small boats with ropes dragging things behind them. There was no real second wave coming behind the first. James wondered what the ropes were dragging, but he had no real idea. After five minutes, the British artillery targeted the incoming boats. Huge bursts of water shot up as the shells slammed into the sea. If a boat was hit, the explosion would send thousands of tiny bits of wood and metal into the air.

Another five minutes brought the enemy closer into range. These boats were steam-powered and seemed to be carrying drone soldiers within them. James could see the odd priest at the bow of the boat.

A further five minutes brought them closer to the beaches. Lieutenant Colonel James checked his revolver. His right hand was twitching slightly. To relieve this, he held his right hand with his left for a second or two, and then took two deep breaths before moving on the battlements.

"Bugler, sound at the ready."

The soldiers had been told not to fire until the enemy were in range. The field artillery were preparing to unleash directly upon the landing soldiers.

As the boats came into shallower waters, they did something that took all of the officers by surprise. The boats stopped. The field artillery took this as a sign from God and opened fire on the sitting targets.

Lieutenant Colonel Adams was joined by Captain Pritchard. He had known James before and had recently returned from Africa.

"Colonel, why the hell are they waiting?" The captain was perplexed by this manoeuvre.

"I do not know, Captain, but I hope our artillery will give them what they deserve now."

The British guns then fired into this armada of boats. Bits of flesh and wood were scattered into the air as shells found their targets.

The ropes behind the boats had worked loose. James looked through his binoculars at the drone soldiers at the back of the boats working away. This was happening on every boat. Then this was followed by hundreds of men jumping into the water. The British soldiers were told to hold fire until they reached the beach.

A slight crosswind blew the smoke from the burning boat carcasses across the front of Fort Cumberland. James had to wait for it to clear before he could see the white helmets of the 24th Regiment of Foot. They were still holding fast and waiting in their trenches. The enemy had not landed on British soil yet.

The first swimmer to come out of the sea was not carrying a rifle; he was bleeding and staggering slightly. There was not time to evaluate much further as a sniper shot the man straight in the chest. Different bugler calls then sounded out along the coast. As these men slowly emerged from the water, the soldiers took aim and fired at them from their trenches. The machine guns and cannons held fire.

Lieutenant Colonel Adams scanned Southsea Beach. He saw the men that were coming out of the sea starting to hold their hands in the air. The Lee-Metford.303 rounds continued to rake havoc on the desperate souls coming out of the water. Some of the men seemed to wait in the water, looking anxious and confused. None of them were armed. The officers quickly sent dispatches along the trenches, telling the soldiers to hold fire.

The calls went up for the soldiers to cease fire.

The smell of gunpowder wafted around on the gentle breeze. The heavy artillery took a moment to hold fire. The men in the water stayed still; the ones alive on the beach curled up or lay there. This was short-lived.

Emerging out of the water came the dead – thousands of flesh-eaters. Lieutenant Colonel Adams now understood what the ropes had been pulling at the back of the landing craft. There must have been some sort of cages full of flesh-eaters, and then the wounded slaves had been sent first to help draw in the ever-hungry beasts. It had worked, because now thousands of flesh-eaters started to swarm the beach. At first, their victims were the slaves who were almost too tired and weary to fight off these insatiable, ravenous beasts.

The soldiers were almost too much in shock before the orders were given to open fire. This time the pillboxes opened up with the Maxim guns. The *rat-a-tat-tat* of this iron lady of death buoyed their spirits. The flesh-eaters knew no fear and walked to the British lines. The soldiers had been told about shooting towards the head when it came to flesh-eaters.

The chunks of wet flesh flew left, right and centre and the bullets carved their way into the advancing victims.

Lieutenant Colonel Adams searched further out to sea through his binoculars, and it was as he had suspected. The second wave was now coming. The boats which had taken the flesh-eaters in to shore now started to head back to the ships. This would then allow space for the landing crafts. These boats looked different to the others; James could see that they had a wider front and there seemed to be drones crammed inside them.

The flesh-eaters were being torn to shreds by the British soldiers, and the machine guns were making easy work of this cumbersome attacking foe. They did not have the same numbers to back them up as they had in the battle of Reims, but James suspected the flesh-eaters were there to absorb bullets.

There were flesh-eaters around the bottom of fort, but again the soldiers were picking them off from above.

Before the second wave hit, Nazar's ships offshore started opening fire again. Some of the 24th on Southsea Beach had come out of their trenches to get a better aim at the oncoming flesh-eaters. These men were affected most as the shells landed around them. Bits of red tunic and white helmets were splattered into the soil and surrounding sandbags, from where they had been crouching. Screams and shouts were muffled by explosions. This barrage kept on even as the landing crafts came into the shallows.

Captain Pritchard was moving around the battlements. He was trying to keep the men calm. A shell landed within the fort, sending stones and dust into the air, and another shell clipped into the east side of the wall, killing three Marines.

"Colonel, we have six wounded men from the south battlements, shall I send in the reinforcements?"

Lieutenant Colonel Adams was still crouching as the shells exploded around them.

"Not yet, Captain, wait until the enemy's second wave lands." James did not want more men killed unnecessarily by shells.

Three minutes passed as shell after shell pounded into British soil. The air was thick with dust and debris, and smoke from the exploded shells. When the shells stopped landing, James quickly looked over the battlements.

"Bugler, sound the call to arms." He looked at the coastline as far as he could see. It was unrecognisable, covered in shell holes and debris. Buildings were alight and bodies were strewn across the beaches. The Isle of Wight had smoke coming from the south-west of the island, as they fought house to house for every inch of it.

The 24th had lost a few men, who had been out of the trenches when the shells landed. They were regrouping when the landing crafts arrived.

The British heavy artillery and light field artillery started to open fire as the crafts came in closer. Each shell that hit its target sent a sprawling mass of wood and flesh into the air. The British soldiers knew they were loaded with enemy soldiers.

The flesh-eaters had been almost totally wiped out in the first wave. This had meant that ammunition had been requested to the frontline. Telegrams had gone out along the whole coast regarding this issue. Something that Nazar had hoped for.

When the landing crafts hit the beach, the fronts of the vessels came down. There inside were rows of drone soldiers, and mixed in at the back were long limbs. Not every landing craft had priests with them, most had sergeants and corporals. Lieutenant Colonel Adams scanned the Southsea Beach as they landed. He could also see them coming onto the beach at the front of the fort.

The cannons at the fort were firing away at the landing crafts, but the machine guns and soldiers were waiting until the enemy left their vessels. Once they touched the sand, or shallow waters, and the front went down, there was a massive roar. It was carried on the wind as if they were landing all around the country. James did not wait any longer and gave the order to fire at will.

The machine guns readied for the first sight of the enemy soldiers. Then they opened fire, and those that were still crammed inside the landing crafts were cut to pieces within seconds. The shouts and screams were drowned out in amongst the gunfire and explosions. It was a slaughter; the field guns fired shells into the opening fronts, again causing carnage. The sea was turning red with the blood of the dead drone soldiers; if they had not been shot in the head then they started to come back as flesh-eaters.

This was swallowing up precious ammunition. Lieutenant Colonel Adams had his rifle and was shooting at dead drones that were coming back to life. The British casualties had been low; the main cause of death had come from the shelling. The enemy could not form a beach head. The second wave of crafts began to leave; some were stranded burning, or sinking slowly. Bodies were now piling up all along the beach. Some of the drones and long limbs that had made it close to the trenches were eventually shot.

Captain Pritchard updated James with a status report. As they discussed the enemy's second attack, five severe explosions came from Ryde on the Isle of Wight. Boats were trying to leave, but the enemy soldiers were now landing on that side.

The Isle of Wight had fallen.

There was not time to discuss all of this, because a third wave was now coming in. The machine guns were warm and low on ammunition. Lieutenant Colonel Adams had sent telegrams explaining that they had gone through more ammunition than they first thought and would probably need more reinforcements.

The third wave came in fast. They were landing a little more in the shallows as well as near the beach. Some of the drone soldiers were trying to wheel off small field cannons from the landing crafts along the beach.

All of the machine guns hadn't really had time to cool, and were instantly thrown back into action. The *rat-a-tat-tat* was a haunting sound. It peppered the oncoming enemy soldiers, bullets thumping into flesh and tearing out the other side. The British soldiers in the fort shot from the battlements, picking their targets and temporarily stopping the inevitable advance.

The third wave was encountering the same problems as the others; the machine guns and field cannons finding their targets and the soldiers doing the rest. This was until a call went out that two of the machine guns were jamming. They were basically overheating, and to make matters worse, a messenger brought news that the pillboxes along Southsea Beach were running out of ammunition.

This was the foothold the enemy needed. They started using sunken boats as cover; some of them worked very hard to get the field guns into a firing position. Whilst this was going on, the fourth wave was now in full swing. Lieutenant Colonel Adams told his officers to focus fire on the soldiers with the field guns. He warned Captain Pritchard to be ready for the fourth wave.

They were bringing up rockets and grenades to throw over the wall whilst the battle raged on. The fourth wave landed under less fire. The heavy artillery was still firing and was still having good success due to the amount of boats and landing craft in the water, but sadly this was a mere drop in the ocean to the number out there. Nazar had gone for a numbers game and he expected to lose thousands of men. He did not care.

The fourth wave was making headway up Southsea Beach and was also getting closer to the base of the fort. The enemy return of fire was now taking its toll on the Marines and Engineers. Two men who were leaning over next to Lieutenant Colonel Adams were hit, one in the shoulder and the other in the chest.

"Orderlies, men down," James bellowed out.

His sergeant reported a fifth wave was now coming in.

"Bring up the reserves to the wall." James knew they were now in trouble. A couple of the pillboxes manned by the 24th started to fire again. The machine guns had a devastating effect, but they did not stay in action long enough. The enemy began to use their small field cannons and scored a direct hit on one of the pillboxes. The machine gun and its crew were torn to bits.

James took aim and squeezed the trigger, killing a drone with a clean head shot. The man was stopped in his tracks as the heavy round almost took his head off. He pulled back the bolt again and shot another drone soldier running for cover.

The fifth wave contained more long limbs; they scampered at speed off the landing crafts, moving towards the British lines.

Southsea Beach was now being swamped. Waves six and seven were coming in, and they sensed an opening. The long limbs were amongst the 24th, hand-to-hand combat was raging, bayonets and grenades were in full swing. They fought gallantly and managed to push back the creatures, but the small field cannons started to take out the pillboxes, which had stopped firing. The heavy artillery began to land shells on the frontline. Some signals were not getting back correctly.

Lieutenant Colonel Adams was helpless to do anything; he did not have enough reinforcements himself, but he knew too well, once the beaches fell, that the forts could become obsolete.

Thinking on his feet, James got his best riflemen to lay down covering fire for the 24th. He hoped they would use this opportunity to retreat. They never did; each man stood side by side, fighting to the death on the very soil they stood on. The sheer numbers and their overpowering strength were now in Nazar's favour.

The west side of the fort had sieging ladders laid against it. Private Brown was over there with some of the Engineers.

"Private Thompson, keep the left side clear, we must have an escape route." Even though Private Brown was only a young soldier, he had now seen a lot of action in Europe and was not shocked by the creatures now swarming around the fort. There were others like him who had served under Captain Hayward, or had seen action at the battle of Reims. This was now a time for cool heads.

The field cannons on the fort were still firing onto the beach and oncoming landing craft. It was an almost fruitless task with the amount now swamping in. Each hit did send drones and long limbs hurtling in the air. Screams and cries of the wounded could be heard all along the coast.

Telegrams were being sent to Lieutenant Colonel Adams at a constant pace. The news they had all feared did not arrive until late afternoon. The fort was now creaking; enemy cannons had found a foothold around the beach area and were shelling the fort itself; the drones were being supported by riders of the north, their size and presence helping them push forward with the heavy weaponry; and Nazar was also bringing machine guns to the battlefield; he did not have many, but used wisely they could turn a battle.

James picked up the latest telegram. He crouched down to read it.

Norfolk is close to falling. Hunstanton is in enemy hands and Norwich is being heavily shelled and attacked. They said the warrior queen had landed with thousands of the enemy cavalry, wolves, bears with two heads and razor tooths. She was also gathering long limbs. James knew they would now try and push their advantage with speed. She was their mobile arm and with such a large force, it threatened to cut the North and South of Britain off from each other.

James checked his clock. Captain Pritchard was fighting over on the battlements to the far side.

A corporal came running over; he had lost his helmet and his red tunic was ripped. "They're over the west walls, sir."

"Send the reserve unit to the yard and use the last Maxim gun there." James had prepared a small reserve unit should the fort fall and with a machine gun they could buy some time.

As James reloaded his Enfield revolver, a soldier next to him fell with a chest wound. The drones were now coming up the walls; his men were out of grenades and ammunition was running low. He withdrew his sword and waited for the first drone to stick his head above the battlements. It did not take long before three came up at once; James jumped forward, slashing at two, the sword slicing deep into their facial skin. The other he shot in the neck with his revolver. It was now frantic; the Marines around him had been injured or were fighting for their lives, and the bugler boy was using a pike to jab at drones coming up the side of a buttress.

The corporal in the yard had ten men with him. All Marines, "Put up a bloody good fight, lads." He shouted. They had sandbags and placed the machine gun in the middle. The main gates had gone and the sight that greeted them was thousands of flesh-eaters and long limbs coming at them, with drone soldiers following close behind.

The soldiers opened fire, the first volley ripping into the oncoming masses. The machine gun then started to open fire. It was a killing machine; swathes of flesh-eaters fell on the bodies in front of them, and long limbs had their legs smashed as they pressed forward. Then there was a loud click, "We're out of ammunition." The gunner yelled.

In the seconds that followed, the flesh-eaters surged ahead into the men. The corporal was fighting from the front with his bayonet. "For the Empire!" was his last cry as he swung like a madman with the masses all around him.

Lieutenant Colonel Adams could see the yard had fallen. Long limbs were now coming at them on the battlements. Private Brown arrived next to him with two other Engineers.

"The fort has fallen, sir," he said in a solemn voice.

"Dear God, have mercy on our souls." James crouched down for a second. Captain Pritchard had six men in front of him laying down volley fire on the creatures, as they swept towards them. It was short-lived as a shell burst to the side of his men, killing three of them, and taking a leg off another. Captain Pritchard tried to gather himself; he looked over to the colonel and signalled for them to retreat and save themselves. James reluctantly nodded his head. "Sound the retreat."

The bugler boy brought the bugle to his lips and belted out the call.

"Private Brown, we still have the wounded and nurses in the stronghold. We need to get them out of there and through the tunnel." He was ordered to take the bugler boy with him.

John was relieved, as he knew Heidi was with the doctors and nurses. Moving the wounded was going to be hard. He rushed off, bayoneting a flesh-eater en route and using his rifle butt to smash another back.

The order to retreat had just left the lips of the lieutenant colonel, but as he turned around, a long limb had Captain Pritchard by the neck, and it shook him like a rag doll. Another came in and grabbed him in the midriff. James let out an involuntary shout, and moved to go forward to help, but was grabbed by a burly Engineer next to him.

"They're coming from behind us, sir. We must secure the stronghold doors." They turned and left at speed. James allowed himself one sorrowful glance at the captain and the men around him.

The fort was now teeming with flesh-eaters and long limbs. Drone soldiers started taking up positions higher up on the battlement walls and were firing at the men and women in the compounds built into the earthworks.

The eyes of James and the two Engineers fell wide open as a wave of monsters came towards them. They squeezed through the stronghold doors and managed to close them tight as hands and claws tried in vain to grab them. "Grab the iron bars and secure this entrance" The lieutenant colonel and the other Engineers used all their strength to stop the doors from being pushed open. Once the bars were slid across, this allowed them a little more time. Candles lit the way through the dark rooms. Two Marines nervously rushed to greet them. The men could tell they were pleased it was British soldiers and not the enemy.

The temperature was a lot cooler in the bunker rooms; they had been built to withstand heavy shelling and had thick walls. John was already with the army surgeons telling them they had to evacuate. Heidi was helping an injured soldier stand up. She looked over at John and he could see her breathe a sigh of relief that he was still alive.

Lieutenant Colonel Adams joined the men and told two guards outside the makeshift medical wing to go and help support the others. He then went on to the surgeons.

"Gentlemen, we need to move the wounded now," he said. He looked at John and another Engineer who was with him.

"Colonel, sadly we cannot take them, most of them are bedbound now." The surgeon pointed over to the wounded as he said this. James could see the blood-soaked soldiers, bandages already saturated. The ceiling shook overhead as a shell landed directly above them; it caused dust to fall from the roof. The candles flickered a little. The noise of the flesh-eaters and long limbs digging and scratching at the doors or windows of the fort buildings was soul-destroying.

James paced up and down for a moment. He just did not know how to get everyone out safely.

"Colonel, take the wounded who can walk, and I will stay and surrender to the victors." The surgeon was sincere; he must have known deep down that it was a death sentence.

James knew his question had now been answered. He begrudgingly nodded his head, and gave the order for the walking wounded to use the escape tunnel and be evacuated straight away. Heidi helped an injured soldier to his feet. John and the other Engineer did the same. Two other surgeons agreed to stay with three orderlies. Each of them was given revolvers. They carried on tending to the wounded.

The door was slowly being battered away at the front entrance. The drone soldiers had not tried to destroy it, and were following orders from their officers and priests to press on. Two priests were in charge of the fort now and they were letting the creatures do the work for them.

Lieutenant Colonel Adams shook the surgeons and orderlies' hands and turned to join the others leaving down the tunnel. He wiped a tear from his cheek in the darkness. Victorian etiquette was to be strong at all times, but the sheer gallantry and bravery shown by these men touched him in his heart.

James caught up with John, who was leading the group through the darkness with a lantern.

"John, we must get to Box Hill and get the heavy artillery raining down shells on these devilish creatures." James was full of anger and hate. His country was now being invaded and they had gained a foothold.

Chapter 36

It was a warm evening and Captain Hayward fell into a light sleep. He was not due to take guard until 4 a.m. The disused farm outbuildings had been secured the best they could be. Some time passed before a clap of thunder awoke the captain; there was enough light from the moon to allow him to check the time, and he saw that it was 3.45 a.m. This meant that it was nearly time for him to take his shift. He wiped his eyes, and slowly got up and stretched. Sergeant Butcher was asleep next to his rifle. Corporal Heinz came over with a coffee.

"Morning, Captain."

"Morning, Corporal.

A ghastly snarling groan came from the woods behind the outbuildings; before the captain could take his mug of coffee, he heard a cry of pain.

"Flesh-eaters at the rear of the farm."

Charles reached down and grabbed his rifle. He then followed Corporal Heinz to an overturned wagon, which had slightly rotten sides. Thousands of eyes reflected back at them; they were coming their way en masse. Bullets started to pierce through the old wooden sides, as they unfortunately offered little protection.

Captain Hayward gave out the order to get the men moving. Bringing the rifle up to its sights, he began to fire. The first shot took down a flesh-eater; he could not miss as there were so many, although the sight of children who had turned played on his conscience. They were soon leaning against the wagon. Corporal Heinz used his body weight to help stop the wooden frame from being pushed back. Suddenly, the Maxim gun started to open fire. Swathes of flesh-eaters started to fall; the groans did not stop as the bullets rained down pain upon them.

Some of the priests had sent riders of the north into the camp. These big, burly men were now fighting the soldiers, who were trying to gather their belongings. Two soldiers were killed whilst trying to defend the horses. One was chopped in half by a northern rider and the other felled by an axe.

Sergeant Butcher was awake and grabbed his rifle, and as a northern rider brushed past, he ducked to avoid the swing of an axe, and retaliated with a bayonet in the attacker's leg and through into the man's horse. The animal reared up, knocking the man off the horse, and he fell to the ground in a heavy heap. Looking slightly dazed, he tried to get to his feet, but his recovery was short-lived, as the sergeant ran the bayonet into his heart and out again. He then turned and started to help the other soldiers get mounted up.

Captain Hayward and Corporal Heinz moved towards where the machine gun was firing. Captain Müller was there with his second in command. They were still firing at the masses as they tried to get forward. A bullet smacked into the wall in front of Captain Müller, flinging a chunk of stone into his shoulder, which knocked him back. Whilst he was temporarily incapacitated, his second in command quickly took over. He then gathered himself and started to help load ammunition into the machine gun.

More riders of the north were now seen coming along the track leading to the old buildings.

"Leave, Captain, we will fight on here." Captain Müller carried on loading for his no. 2.

Charles shook his head. "We can all make it if we leave now."

Charles then leaned against the wall with the sergeant and used a whole magazine box's worth of ammunition shooting at the enemy, picking them off as they rode along the track.

A private rushed in behind them and shouted, "They're coming from the right flank, sir!"

"We must leave now; it doesn't need to end this way," said Charles, feeling that he could not leave anyone behind.

Captain Müller turned to him. "You must leave, we will be the diversion. It is your only chance."

He then moved over towards them, crouching as he went. "Send a message to my family that I love them and always will." He quickly reached out his hand to shake hands with the captain and the sergeant. Instead, they pulled him in to embrace him. "May God have mercy on you, my friend."

Captain Hayward turned; he could not look back and found it hard keeping his emotions under control. Both the sergeant and the captain moved out, creeping as they went. Private Green was shooting outside of the dilapidated barn. He was down on one knee, crouching as he shot.

"Follow us, soldier." Captain Hayward pointed towards the sergeant, who had two Engineers with him firing from their saddles; they had horses next to them. Corporal Heinz and Captain Hayward used their swords as flesh-eaters started to swarm in. The machine gun started up again behind them; it was keeping the main group of flesh-eater children from totally overrunning the camp.

There was no time to wait as the men mounted their horses; Charles shook his head in frustration. The flesh-eaters were streaming into the building now. Most of the soldiers had mounted up; those that hadn't were already dead and were being ripped to pieces for their flesh.

They could hear the gunfire for a mile or so as they galloped away. Then it suddenly stopped; the soldiers looked at each other as they rode, knowing it meant that was the final moment for Captain Müller and his no. 2.

The Italian soldier who was their guide had survived. He led them along mountain paths and through valleys. They did not stop for a rest. Charles sent Corporal Heinz ahead. Captain Holfer rode with him.

"We lost five men in that attack," Charles said, sorrowful in his tone.

"You could not control that attack, Captain." Holfer was to the point. "Captain Müller sacrificed himself for us and the mission."

Charles rode on with the Austrian captain. His kind words did help Charles focus again, but he knew deep down inside that he felt responsible for all his men.

Private Alexander Chamberlin was also riding ahead as a scout. His sniper skills would be invaluable on this mission. Their group had been reduced and that could have serious implications.

They rode all day and into the night. With the border to the former Austro-Hungarian Empire in sight, there was a feeling of progress. It wasn't a physical line to cross as such, but a mental one. The marker was the village of Hohenthurn; it was in the distance, but it gave them a focal point. They would not enter the village; there probably wasn't an enemy presence, but the small harbor had revealed that civilians were doing what they had to do to survive, even if that meant collaborating.

They would rather err on the side of caution. All efforts were now directed towards meeting up with Major Sherborne outside Villach. Charles wanted to get Benedict under his command again.

Before they could continue, the horses and the men needed to rest. Food was limited; the attack had meant that some men had lost supplies. They would have to replenish at some point. The horses were taken to the middle of a small clearing. The soldiers on guard were given binoculars to scan for long limbs, herds of flesh-eaters and anything that could cause them a danger at quick notice.

Some dried meat and biscuits were passed around. Water was in good supply, and was given to the animals. Charles knew that they had enough to get them to the outskirts of Ternberg. Corporal Heinz was now leading them through Austria. Captain Holfer and his sergeant, a tall man with black hair, spoke to Corporal Heinz in German. The khaki uniforms had fared well; it had given them that extra cover from enemy scouts or civilian eyes. Sadly, it could not hide them from the flesh-eaters or other creatures who relied on smell.

"It's late, Captain. What do you advise?" Sergeant Butcher asked.

"We'll press on; we will still have light from the moon tonight." Charles knew it had been a clear day and anticipated it being a clear night sky.

They mounted up and continued down the mountain paths. The occasional lone flesh-eater was seen wandering around, but no drone soldiers or civilians. They had discussed the priests leading the attack at the disused farm outbuildings, but they did not think it would cause a mass search. The khaki uniforms would hopefully lead them to think this was just resistance fighters, but nothing could be taken for granted.

They rode late into the evening. Charles sent out scouts to look for the major or signs of him. They were a good distance away from Villach, but hoped he would also have men looking out for them.

When the scouts returned, they reported no sightings at all. Charles was concerned; his first thought was that they had been captured, which could prematurely end the mission. Without Benedict's map, they would never find the monastery or fort in Russia. He then began to let his mind stray further; could Major Sherborne have pressed on to the house without them?

They would have to bed down for the night. Using bill hooks and axes, they made a thicket defence on the flat top of an escarpment, either side having steep banks. There would be patrols throughout the evening. Charles did not want to take any chances.

The night passed quickly; there were only a couple of sightings of flesh-eaters, but none of them got wind of the soldiers. All of them were up early in the morning and the scouts were sent off to search again.

They rode closer to Villach; the sight of drone cavalry riding with priests, patrolling the outskirts, stopped them from going any further. Charles had to make a decision. They knew the village where the house they were looking for was, but it would be impossible to find the right house without Benedict. He decided they would press on; his hunch was that Major Sherborne would now go alone, find the house with Benedict, and possibly kill him once he had the map. This would also mean the end for Doctor Brown and the Engineers with them.

Half a day passed; the weather was warmer now as they entered into the month of June. Riding through the mountains made sure that it was not as hot as the lowlands, but warm enough to be comfortable. The landscape was awe-inspiring, with snowcapped mountain tops and sweeping valleys below. He thought about what would happen to Europe, now it was not controlled by the European people. Nazar was leaning towards his own feudal system, but it would be a harsh regime of punishment and death. He would turn people against each other; he had enough soldiers and beasts to spread chaos across the world unless he was stopped.

Warm rays of sun bounced off Charles's brass buckles, and off his kitbags attached to the horse. He thought about Emily and Arthur, and prayed that they were still alive. He thought about his wife Rebecca and how he missed her soft lips and touch. Charles had flashes of memories as he rode along the mountain paths. A few summers back, there had been a large family gathering in Devon. They stayed in a small seaside village and enjoyed the beautiful beaches for a week. Charles could see his children playing on the beach and himself and Rebecca taking a naked swim in the moonlight. She was very un-Victorian at times, and this was part of her appeal.

He did not let his mind wonder too far into the darker places, the places where you see things that you do not like.

"Captain, I think I have a lead." Corporal Heinz was slightly out of breath, but he had a positive look on his face.

"Excellent work, Corporal, we'll pick up the pace now." They doubled their speed, and Corporal Heinz said he had found several smoldering fires and some British food wrappings.

He deduced they had only left several hours ago. It was a good feeling; Captain Hayward now had hope flowing through his veins. They would have to approach the major with caution, and due to the timing he was more or less certain that they had not been waiting for the captain and his men.

The rest of the day, they carried on riding at a good pace, stopping for lunch and to let the horses drink water when they found a stream.

Then, as the night drew in, the scouts caught sight of the major's men. They had stopped for the evening and were making a camp.

Charles spoke to his senior officers and men. He suggested that this could be a tricky situation. He wanted all of his soldiers to know that Major Sherborne could be up to something. Due care and attention was needed.

It was decided that they would camp close by and enter the major's camp early morning. This way there would be no risk of them not being identified. That evening, Charles ordered the night watch to keep an eye on the other camp. He did not want them leaving in the darkness. Charles did not sleep particularly well, as the thought of being so close to Benedict was playing on his mind.

They had an early breakfast and then sent two riders with a British flag and a white flag towards Major Sherborne and his men. Captain Holfer said he would go; Charles had originally said it should be him, but the captain persuaded Charles it would be better to see their reaction to him first. They were in dangerous territories now, far away from the coast and lacking any serious firepower or support. They did not want to get into a fight with the Marines, as it would draw attention to them.

None the less, Charles had his best snipers set up in the undergrowth. Soldiers were posted for flesh-eaters and enemy scouts. Then he watched with his binoculars, waiting and hoping it would go smoothly. The message being sent with Captain Holfer was one they understood; the mission came first and they also knew why they must not wait around.

Captain Holfer rode in slowly. A Marine had already spotted them coming and the captain felt he was being watched under the barrel of many rifles.

"Stop there, and declare who you are?" a voice said from a cluster of bushes.

"Captain Holfer, serving under Captain Hayward and the Royal Engineers and in service of Her Majesty the Queen." The captain was calm and relaxed.

Their horses swatted away at flies as they stood still, awaiting confirmation.

"Come into the camp." Again, the voice was faceless.

The men rode forward, lowering the flags as they entered the camp. The further they went in, more British soldiers emerged. Captain Brewer came over to them and saluted them.

Once they had dismounted, Major Sherborne appeared carrying a mug of tea.

"Are you the only ones who made it?" He was straight to the point.

"No, Major, more of us made it, we're the advanced party." Captain Holfer saluted the major, who begrudgingly accepted it.

"I'm surprised you made it past that herd of flesh-eater children; there seemed to be thousands of them." He began to drink his tea.

Captain Holfer told them about being attacked in a disused farm, and how Captain Müller had given his life for them to escape. The major seemed to express a disappointment at them losing an officer, but he also had a look of a man who had hoped they would all have perished in the attack.

"Well, bring them in; we must press on to Ternberg."

Captain Holfer looked around; the other soldiers seemed to be relaxed and started to continue with their morning chores. The soldier with Captain Holfer rode out in the open field and signalled for the rest to follow.

Charles was concerned, but had to trust his officers. They needed to stay close to Benedict. He spoke with his men and told them to be ready with their swords and Enfield revolvers. Should the situation turn, they had to get to Benedict and get him out.

One train of thought was to let the major continue to the house, retrieve the map and return to the ships in the Mediterranean. That way, none of his men would be put at risk and there should not be friction from the major, as he would take the credit. The problem lay with the fact that the major could decide it was too risky and not complete the mission. The fact he had pressed on alone had surprised Charles.

The soldiers moved across the open space, the long meadow grass folding over and leaving a path made by the horse's hooves as they headed towards the Marines' camp. Charles led from the front. He did not know whether the major had decided on letting them come in or had stopped them in their tracks. As the seconds passed, Charles rode into the thicket of bushes and trees. To his left was a machine gun with crew around it. To his right were Marines with rifles lowered. For now, it would seem the major wanted them alive.

Charles rode all the way in until he saw Captain Holfer. The captain was drinking tea and seemed relaxed. The soldiers behind Charles came to a halt once he raised his right hand.

Major Sherborne walked over. "So, you're still alive. They do say a cat has nine lives."

Charles was still sitting in his saddle. "It's good we've been able to catch up with you, we'll stand a better chance together." Charles knew he had to play it cautiously.

The major gave the order for Doctor Brown and Benedict to be brought out to greet the captain. The atmosphere was tense and felt a bit unnatural. The Marines were still going about their tasks, packing up and readying the horses to leave.

Walking through the trees came Benedict and the doctor. They looked fine, but were being escorted with Marines either side of them.

Charles dismounted as the men came over to them. He walked over to them and shook their hands. "Good to see you, gentlemen." Charles made sure he did not create a situation that could jeopardise all of them.

The major let them talk briefly and then said Charles should have something to eat and let his men rest a while. He suggested they should look at the route ahead and discuss tactics. The major was coming across as very polite and friendly. Charles did not trust his approach.

The two men sat down amongst the bushes that had been made into a thick defence hedge around where the major was sleeping.

"This looks secure, Major." Charles wanted to come across as affable.

"I'll be honest with you, Captain, this Europe is nothing like I've seen before; the creatures, and the fear of death, is with you every second of the day out here." He poured himself another cup of tea as he spoke. Charles was then offered a cup as well.

Charles sat back and slowly sipped at his warm tea; there was even sugar to add to it.

The major looked a bit more erratic now Charles could study him at close quarters. His movements and speech were all over the place. He was forgetting his words and seemed very concerned about how fresh the sugar was.

"You're right, Major; this is not a safe place anymore. We have sadly lost men on this mission and maybe we should stay together from here on in?"

The major finished his tea and poured himself another. Then he added four large spoonful's of sugar. His eyes narrowed, as if he was an old witch, figuring out if a plan was being made against her or not. "I hope you have put that nasty business in England behind us."

"Of course, Major, our focus is finding that map, getting to the enemy monastery and fort, and doing as much damage as we can."

He sat back a bit, half believing Charles, half not believing him. Then he produced a map, and both men looked at the route suggested by the Austrian soldiers amongst them.

It involved steering clear of the main towns and villages. They did not know what sort of messages had been sent about their arrival in Europe. If Nazar got wind of Benedict, he would more than likely ask his commanders in France to locate and kill their group. They had to presume something would be sent and that meant getting the map from the house before the mountains were teeming with drone soldiers or worse.

As they packed up to leave, Major Sherborne said Charles's men could ride in front and he would bring up the rear. He suggested Benedict should continue to ride under his command. Charles did not like this suggestion, but knew this would be a sticking point. The two Engineers who had been sent with the major would still be with him and the doctor. Captain Hayward offered to send Private Chamberlin. He said that he was a very good shot.

"Yes, fine, but wasn't he the failed Marine?" The major spluttered this out as he took a bite of dried meat.

"No, it was more like a disagreement with the establishment." He paused. "He could be the difference between life and death out here." Charles did not want to discuss the merits or failings of his men.

They browsed over the maps once more and then the major called for one of his guards to roll up the map and pack it away. Two hours passed while Charles and his men fed and rested. The odd flesh-eater was caught and quietly dispatched with.

Charles spoke with Private Alexander and Corporal Heinz before walking to his horse. He also passed Captain Fairbrook and Captain Brewer saddling up; they gave him a smug look and then mounted their horses.

"Good luck out there, Captain." Captain Brewer looked him in the eyes when he said this.

Charles did not say anything back; he just kept on walking. The two groups merged together, with Captain Hayward's men taking the lead. They rode at a steady pace, with Alexander shadowing Corporal Heinz. The mountain paths were dry and the dust drifted down the slopes. They tried to stay out of the open and stick to the wooded areas or pine forests. Grazing on a hillside was a herd of cattle; they did not seem too alarmed to be coming into contact with the mounted soldiers.

Corporal Heinz was concerned about this and wondered if they had shepherds to monitor and protect them. He sent a message back to pick up the speed. Charles hung back to keep an eye on the forests as they rode past. Sergeant Butcher joined him by his side. The major and his captains looked at him as they rode past.

They let the soldiers almost go out of sight and then followed on. The cows had moved on along the hillside.

"What do you think, Captain?"

"I'm thinking there must be priests here." Charles was adamant.

Sergeant Butcher asked why. Charles said that the cows would have been attacked by flesh-eaters at some point by now since Europe fell, but they were fairly calm and did not scatter, meaning they had not been threatened by the creatures. He was sure that they were now protecting livestock and this could put them in danger.

"We must be careful; we do not know how many forces Nazar has put in the former Austro-Hungarian Empire." He reached into his right pocket and pulled out his watch. "It's coming up to three o'clock, we really need to press on to where we're going."

The two officers rode after the rest of them.

The next two days were spent moving through the mountains at a steady pace. They tried to use the woods and forests where possible. There had not been a large force following them, and whilst they saw the occasional civilian and drone cavalry, it was relatively quiet. There were flesh-eaters and long limbs to be wary of. Benedict did not go out of sight; he was guarded at all times. Major Sherborne had put four of his Marines close to him.

They were closing in on Ternberg, the home of Benedict. The young lad then wanted to lead the way. He was allowed to ride at the front, but had soldiers around him. His face lit up on seeing familiar landmarks; as they crossed fields and passed through woods he seemed to urge his horse on more. He was told to slow down and take his time. The party stopped a fair distance from the village, and several scouts were sent in all directions. Within twenty minutes, they had all returned with the news that the village was no more. It had been burnt to the ground; in fact, all the farms and cottages close by had been destroyed. In the centre of the town was a pile of bones. Benedict could not listen to the descriptions coming back. He knew those people. He was aware what was happening across Europe, but it came home to him when it was his own village.

Captain Hayward sat on his horse, and he and all of the men felt deflated. They had travelled all this way, only for Nazar to have gotten there first. It also raised concerns about how he knew which village it was. Could he have spies in the British government?

Benedict did not want to give up. He told them to follow him to his former house. The men fanned out. Benedict was allowed to lead the way with Corporal Heinz; it took them ten minutes to get to his cottage. It was also burnt to the ground. Benedict circled with his horse; the outbuildings from their small farm were also destroyed.

"Maybe he didn't leave it in the cottage. Maybe he moved it?" This had the men sit up in their saddles.

"Quickly, boy, where could it be?" Major Sherborne was growing anxious.

"There is a dried up well, he could have hidden it there." Benedict told them to follow him.

He had thought his father had hidden it in the house, but felt he could have moved it when the war started to come their way. Benedict took them through a small coppiced area and scrabbled around for the top of the well. The soldiers dismounted to help out. Sergeant Butcher pointed out a storm was coming. The clouds had started to gather menacingly overhead, then the sky lit up in the distance.

"Captain, I've found it!" Benedict stood by a small stump.

He was helped to pull back the overgrown grass and weeds, which revealed a makeshift wooden cover. They used their bayonets to help lift it. There underneath was a piece of iron running from one side of the well to the other. It had a rope attached to it. "Pull it up, boy," Major Sherborne said anxiously.

Benedict was helped by two Marines. The rope scuffed as it brushed against the side of the well. Coming out of the darkness was a bucket. Once it had come to the top, the two Marines grabbed it. Captain Hayward asked them to hand it over; they paused and looked at Major Sherborne. He nodded.

Benedict looked inside the bucket; his eyes were drawn towards a box. Undoing a small silver catch, he opened it up. There were several bits of paper with writing on it and a folded map. He opened the map and looked at it briefly. Benedict then began to read the bits of paper which were with the map. One of them was a letter from his father, and as he read it, tears rolled slowly down his cheeks. Major Sherborne did not have the patience to wait. He snatched the map out of Benedict's hand and studied it with the eye of a jeweller checking over a diamond.

"This map could save the Empire," said the major, who seemed very pleased.

The dark clouds had now surrounded them above, and the wind was starting to pick up. The major put the map in his pocket.

"What are you doing, Major, I'm in charge of this mission." Charles was annoyed that the major had done this.

"You were, Captain Hayward, but now we have the map." He turned and looked at his officers.

Charles turned around to see Sergeant Butcher and Captain Holfer being led over with their hands held up. "What is the point of this now, Major?" The two Marines to Charles's side had their rifles pointed at him.

This moment was broken with a Marine scout riding over to them at speed. "Sir, three razor tooths are heading our way."

The major turned to the captain. "It's about the future, I want to be successful in Britain and I'll need money. Queen Victoria will reward me for this, it could turn the war."

Charles's men had been gathered together. The Marines had them under the watchful eye of a Maxim machine gun.

Private Chamberlin and Corporal Heinz had not returned yet. Charles suggested they would be stronger if they stuck together, and he was sincere about this. The major was not interested. He then pulled out his revolver.

Charles lowered his hand towards his revolver, but realised he had already handed it over.

"Please give me the opportunity to shoot you, Charles," the major smirked.

Charles just looked at him.

"Don't worry, there's no point killing you now. I need you to fight off what's coming."

The roars echoed through the trees. The major had sent out a scout to find an enemy force in order to lure them back to eliminate Captain Hayward and his men.

"You're a bloody fool, man. The next time we meet will be our last." Charles's hands started to clench.

"No need for the dramatics, we're taking your horses and tying the rifles over there." The major signed for the rifles to be tied to a tree. He also put the swords and revolvers there. "You'll be dead, or flesh-eaters before you know it." He turned and led his horse to join the other Marines. Captain Brewer rode past, and said, "You were always going to pay for your crimes, Captain."

They then kicked on and disappeared through the trees.

"Sergeant Butcher, get the rifles!" Charles screamed out.

They still had their backpacks and small supplies, but were now limited to ammunition for the rifles and revolvers. There was one key weapon left behind, the Maxim gun. It had one belt of bullets and was quickly manned by three Royal Engineers.

The remaining men sprinted over to help the sergeant cut the rope and free the weapons. The major wanted it to look like they had been ambushed, and not left to die without weapons. He did not know whether the British Empire would take back Europe soon, but he did not want any civilians or rebels finding the bodies killed while unarmed, in case news of it got back to Great Britain.

Benedict and Doctor Brown were given a rifle each. Charles told the machine-gun crew to be ready for what was coming. The old, burnt-out cottage and out buildings offered some protection. The stones were brittle from the fire, but this meant the men could hide behind something.

"Fix bayonets!" As the order was bellowed out, riders of the north appeared on the left flank. There were around twelve of them; leading from the front were two priests. Captain Holfer and his second in command joined the machine-gun crew.

Corporal Heinz and Private Chamberlin came running over to Captain Hayward. "Sir, 300 or more flesh-eaters coming our way."

"Damn this godforsaken land." Charles wiped the dust away from his eyes and unsheathed his sword. With his revolver in his left hand and his sword in his right, he prepared for the onslaught. Coming at speed, the first razor tooth creature burst through the undergrowth. Its mouth open as it roared, showing off its long, sharp teeth. The second followed quickly behind, with the third gaining ground. Coming from all angles were the riders of the north. They let out a war cry as they burst onto the battlefield. Amongst them were the two priests, swords drawn and black clothes trailing in the air as they moved with speed.

"Fire at will!" Charles barked out the order.

The machine gun started to open fire on the two charging razor tooths, its bullets of death crunching and ripping into the creatures' fur. Blood gushed from their open wounds but they kept on coming, 200 yards, 100 yards, 50 yards, and as they approached, the men manning the machine gun shot at the giant animals' legs, which started to go. The first slumped forward, losing momentum, collapsing into a heap and sliding along the dry soil; the second almost clipped the first razor tooth, causing it to turn sideways and roll and bounce on the ground, before coming to an undignified stop.

The Maxim gun tore into their bodies and caused internal damage and death. The third creature was now being peppered. As the gun unleashed its devastating fire, a rider of the north came from the side of the gun crew, swinging an axe, which he struck into the man reloading. He cried out in pain as the axe cracked into his back and came out through his stomach.

Captain Holfer turned to shoot the rider, but was knocked over by the large horse he was riding. Private Chamberlin had climbed onto the burnt-out shell of the cottage; it still had one wall, which was raised, and also had burnt joists sticking out of it. From there he intended to rain down terror on the attackers.

Captain Hayward and a small group were scattered in one of the outbuildings. "We must deal with these cavalry before the flesh-eaters come. We will not stand a chance otherwise. Sergeant Butcher and Corporal Heinz leaned into the walls, and as a rider of the north came at them with a lance, they took aim, a thunderous shot hitting him in the ribcage; blood spurted out of his mouth. He slumped forward, and Corporal Heinz squeezed his trigger; his bullet struck into the rider's left shoulder, knocking him off the horse. He fell to the ground like a rag doll falling off a bed.

Sergeant Butcher looked at Corporal Heinz. "Good work, lad." This moment of joy was short-lived. A priest with three riders of the north jumped into the outbuilding; the priest had a revolver and pulled the trigger. The Engineer next to Charles fell forward, clenching his lower back.

Captain Hayward swung at him with his sword, Slashing the priest on the leg and causing him to slip from his horse. The giant riders came at the men. Corporal Heinz thrust his sword at one of the giants, who knocked it back with his own sword.

The man had a large scar running from the top left of his forehead down to his cheek. He laughed at Corporal Heinz, as if he was no contest for him; he then swung his sword down towards the corporal's head. The corporal was ready and blocked the blow; it was a heavy hit, causing him to move down with the force. But as he rose up, he used his speed and agility to kick the leg of the giant man and then bring the sword around to his stomach, cutting it open and releasing his intestines. The man looked down at his wound and then back at the corporal. He did not get a chance to say anything else as the sword was struck through his throat and out again.

Charles was grappling with the priest on the ground; both of them had their knives drawn and it was a case of brute strength and willpower. The priest headbutted Charles in the mouth, causing blood to gush from a cut lip. He then quickly sliced Charles's knife-wielding arm, causing the captain to drop his weapon. The priest began to shake, as if he was changing. Captain Hayward remembered the shape changer in the old manor house, on the retreat from the Carpathian Mountains. That creature had been a devil to kill. He looked around for his rifle; the Engineers around him were involved in hand-to-hand combat with riders of the north. One of his men was hit with an axe to his left arm and lost it in a flash. He was then beheaded with a second blow. The priest began to grow – his veins stood out, and his nails began to change into claws. His mouth started to stretch and become elongated.

Charles reached down for his rifle, but as he turned, a hand punched him in the chest, causing him to fly backwards into the charred wall. With blood dripping from his lip, and slightly out of breath, he looked up. Standing over him was the second priest. He was smiling, a content smile. He did not bring up his sword to finish Charles off; he looked over his shoulder, waiting for the transformation of the other priest.

When that priest stood up, he was twice the size of the giant men of the north. He barely resembled a man now. How they were able to change like this Charles did not know, but he feared the worst.

As this beast of man and flesh started to more forward, something caught its eye. Charles braced himself.

Bits of flesh and skin landed on Charles's cheeks; a clean headshot into its skull ended the demon in his tracks. The other priest started to raise his sword, but was struck in the chest; he lost his breath as the bullet shattered his left lung. Charles reached down and followed up swiftly with his rifle and bayonet, stabbing the priest in the forehead.

Sergeant Butcher was helping Corporal Heinz finish off one of the riders of the north. They used their bayonets and rifle butts and for a second lost themselves in the heat of the battle. The other two riders of the north took flight after seeing the killing of their commander and his second in command.

The remaining razor tooth was a wounded animal; it was circling the machine-gun crew. A rider of the north came back on another charge. Captain Holfer took aim with his Lee-Metford rifle and pulled the trigger. He hit the rider in the cheek, taking teeth and skull with the bullet. The captain went down on one knee, pulled back the bolt and took aim again; his second shot smacked into the horse's neck, sending it tumbling to the ground. He did not take another shot and instead focused on the razor tooth with the remaining men.

The creature clawed at the ground as it stood directly in front of them, sending up a small dust cloud. Its eyes a deep crimson red, its open wounds leaked blood. The snarl it gave showed its dark brown gums and jagged teeth.

Captain Holfer stood in the firing position. "Let him come at us, then aim between his eyes."

The soldiers stood next to him, their Lee-Metford bayonets catching the light from the sun. The razor tooth reared up onto its hind legs, and when it came down it charged. It picked up speed with each step. As the distance between them and the beast shortened, the first volley was unleashed. The bullets struck into the animal's shoulders and one went into its right eye. It let out a yelp as the impact crunched through soft and hard tissue.

"Make your shots count." The creature was now within striking distance; the men had reloaded and took aim again.

Boom!!

The four rifles sounded in unison. The large .303 rounds all hit the beast's head. The effect was conclusive, killing the razor tooth in its tracks. It fell and crumpled in a heap, 5 yards on from where he was hit.

The last remaining riders of the north were now turning and fleeing. Private Chamberlin was picking them off at will. His expert shot was unforgiving. Captain Hayward moved from the ruins. "We must move quickly," he said. He looked around and re-sheathed his sword. "Collect the wounded."

They now totalled sixteen men, including the doctor and Benedict. The supplies were loaded into the backpacks and all items that could be carried or stuffed into pouches were done so. They had several men with minor wounds and the doctor gave them a quick field dressing. This unfolded as the first wave of flesh-eaters arrived; they were a mixture of adults and children. Each flesh-eater was in a different state of decay; some looked like they had turned recently, others maybe months previously.

Charles asked Captain Holfer to take six men and lay down covering fire as they prepared to leave. The slow shuffle and groaning was deceptive; these creatures were killing machines and would be more feared than any other predictor on the planet. They were relentless, never sleeping, never resting and always hungry. They were the perfect killing machine.

As the gunfire erupted in front of the men, Benedict came forward and said he knew of an old fort in the mountains not too far from where they were. The fort had stables and he believed they would have a small detachment of drone soldiers there, and more importantly, horses.

Captain Hayward said it was imperative that they get to their ship before it set sail. He hoped and prayed the major would tell the other ship to give Charles and his men some time to make the situation look normal. Benedict had written down everything he could remember from his father's note and the map. It would maybe give them a chance of catching Major Sherborne.

The soldiers used bayonets on the most advanced flesh-eaters, and then started to fall back. There were too many to engage with in combat. Captain Hayward asked Benedict to accompany Corporal Heinz at the front and lead the way. The pace was quick; fortune had shone on the wounded, as most were bearing light wounds and could move at speed. Charles had envisaged having to make a stretcher and carry some of the men out. It would have been a big task.

They pushed through bushes and crossed open grassland. The flesh-eaters had fallen behind and this allowed the men to go at a steady pace. Sergeant Butcher was bringing up the rear. He stroked his beard as he moved along. He was accompanied by Private Green; he was wondering now whether he should have stayed in Africa and faced the Zulus, although that operation had been curtailed in the end as Queen Victoria's soldiers had been needed to reinforce the army in France, which in turn lost the majority of the British forces at the battle of Reims.

"Quick question, Sergeant." The private was aware that Sergeant Butcher did not look like he was in the mood for speaking.

"What, Private Green/"

"Is it true about what they said about Captain Hayward at Aldershot?" He was a little sheepish when he asked this.

"What have they been saying at Aldershot, lad?" Sergeant Butcher was straight to the point.

"Well, sir, that he left men for dead and turned his back on his country. I just wanted to ask someone who has been fighting with him."

Sergeant Butcher stopped in his tracks and turned to face the young private. "Listen, lad, you have a very little chance of surviving this war and the small chance you have is leading us from the front." He said this controlling his emotions and then turned and carried on moving, always checking behind them as they went.

"Sorry for asking, Sergeant." Private Green continued to check for the enemy as the men closed in on the hills and mountains.

They had been moving for five hours or more. Benedict had taken them on a direct route which had seen them climb up rocky escarpments and steep ground. It now meant they were closing in on the old fort.

The main packs and supplies were taken off and covered with heather and long grass. Corporal Heinz checked around the fort; it was a reasonable size and bore the scars of the damage from the war in Europe. There were impact craters from artillery shells and slight damage to the north-facing wall. This was something they were going to exploit. Charles split the men into two groups; Captain Holfer had one, and Charles had the other. They watched the fort for thirty minutes; in that time they only saw two guards wandering around.

Charles would attack from the front, and Captain Holfer would come over the north wall. Private Chamberlin would hold back; he was tasked with getting to a high point within the fort and then assisting from there. His sniper skills were not matched by anyone in the unit. Charles secured his sword and revolver; he had his rifle in his hands and went forward on his stomach. The other soldiers started to push forward. The only two men staying behind were Doctor Brown and young Benedict. The latter had insisted he was ready to fight, but he was still needed for his map knowledge.

Captain Holfer moved from tree to tree. One of the Engineers had been entrusted with a rope from the beginning of their mission. He kept that with him and prepared to use it to help scale the wall. A metal hook had also been taken with them for this task. Due to the damage previously inflicted on the wall from a shell, the men would not have to climb too far.

The evening sun was starting to sink beneath the mountains; its orange glow was like a dragon's breath, lighting up the sky one last time, before slipping into the darkness.
Corporal Heinz gave out the call for the attack to commence; an owl sound was the chosen signal.

Charles and his men crawled to be near the wall. Then they sprinted over to the main gate. Captain Holfer's unit threw the rope and hook several times before catching onto something. The first soldier to go up and over on the north wall was not seen. Charles had Sergeant Butcher knock hard on the front gate. A well-fed drone soldier came to the gate and peered through a wooden hatch. "Who's there?" he asked.

"Stop screwing around." This was said in Austrian, but Corporal Heinz translated it to English for the captain. Charles knew that men would join Nazar's cause to save their lives; this was how he had boosted his army so quickly. Once infected, the drone soldier would fight for his new master or be left to turn into a flesh-eater.

They waited outside the gate a moment or two before knocking again. This time, the drone soldier opened a small door, which was within the main gate. He stepped outside without thinking, and before he could realise what was happening, he had a bayonet rammed into his side and was thrown to the ground.

Charles gave the nod and they began to rush through. Captain Holfer and his men were now all on the battlements and making their way around the fort. A Drone guard was leaning against the wall smoking a pipe; he was shocked to see soldiers coming at him and took a while to react, and when he did reach for his rifle, it was too late. An Engineer lunged his bayonet into the drone soldier, who fell effortlessly over the side of the wall. The noise of the body falling down the side brought a drone out of one of the tower doors. He saw Captain Hayward and drew his sword. He then came forward at the officer. Charles had drawn his, too, and the two men swung a heavy blow at each other, their blades clashing together making a sharp hissing sound. They then exchanged a series of swipes and blows; each man was blocking the other's attack. The drone rolled his shoulders, and said something in Russian. Charles just responded with, "Surrender and live!"

The soldier smiled and came at him again; he thrust hard at the heart of Charles, but could not find the angle to follow through. Charles knocked the blade to the side of his left shoulder. This left the drone unguarded; it was his only mistake, but it was a fatal one. Captain Hayward stuck his sword through the chest of the soldier. His eyes looked at Charles and then down at the sword sticking into his chest. He muttered something else in Russian, then in English said, "The head." Charles knew then that the man knew he would change. He withdrew the sword quickly and struck the man's head to finish him off.

The rest of the Engineers were now overrunning the fort. Some gunshots were heard, but the enemy had been caught totally off guard. They had been preparing a feast and were not geared up for an assault.

A couple of them had surrendered and were locked in a holding room. Charles was making his way through the fort, whilst Sergeant Butcher and another Engineer were checking rooms behind him. Charles came across a room which had a finer crafted door. He put his hand on the door handle and turned it quickly. His eyes fell upon a drone officer frantically writing a message. There was a crow sitting in a cage next to his desk. The officer looked up, his eyes met Charles's, and they both looked at the crow, the letter, and then to the desk. Sitting on a pile of papers was a revolver.

"You don't have to do anything stupid," said Charles. He did not know if the man understood English, but wanted to give him a chance.

The man replied something in Russian and reached for the revolver. Charles had already undone the clip on his Enfield and pulled it out at the same time as the man grabbed the gun. Charles squeezed the trigger, unleashing a raucous sound, followed by the officer recoiling backwards with blood coming out of his chest. Captain Hayward then walked around the side and shot the man in the head. He could take no chances; drone soldiers that were infected would come back as flesh-eaters.

Sergeant Butcher came rushing in; he had his revolver drawn and sword in the other hand. "Captain, are you alright?"

Charles was looking at the note. He knew Benedict could understand a little Russian like Corporal Heinz could. He told the Engineer to take it to them and read what the officer was writing. Charles then walked with Sergeant Butcher around the rest of the fort. There were some long limbs locked in the dungeons, they were going wild and hissing and snarling at the British soldiers. "Keep the men away from here," Charles said. He thought about shooting these foul beasts, but decided on saving ammo.

He made his way to the kitchen and banquet hall and told his soldiers to feed whilst they could. There was enough food to feed twice as many men as they had.

Corporal Heinz joined them in the hall and reported that there were also enough horses for them to use for escape.

Sergeant Butcher came over to Charles as he sat on a long, wooden bench tucking into some food.

"Do you think we'll catch the major?"

"I hope so, Thomas, I really do." He said they would rest for an hour and then set off. The gunfire could bring in unwanted guests. The flesh-eaters would be drawn to the noise, and if there were enemy scouts in the area, then they would also be alerted.

Chapter 37

Private Brown was helping unload shells to the artillery pieces near the armoury at Box Hill. Telegrams were coming in that the British forces along the South Downs were putting up a gallant effort in holding back waves of enemy soldiers. The 24th Regiment of foot was one of the regiments involved in stopping the enemy advance.

They had heavy artillery along the South Downs which was causing severe casualties to Nazar's forces as it advanced. Nazar had countered this by sending thousands of flesh-eaters at the batteries.

The government had held an emergency meeting in London. Many of the Cabinet had already fled, and those that were left were secretly planning to leave in the evening.

Lieutenant Colonel Adams in the observation point took his binoculars from his second in command, an officer named Captain Henry Bromton. As his skin touched against the cold metal, he saw a sight that made him look twice. The sea had been full of Nazar's ships whilst they were in Portsmouth. Now the countryside was full of his soldiers and creatures. He panned from left to right and saw figures moving towards them in their thousands. Smoke was rising all across the horizon; gunfire and cannon could be heard in the distance. The heavy artillery was not firing yet from Box Hill or along the rolling hills there. They would have to wait until the enemy was in range. James knew they were the last line of defence before London.

The European armies that had been assembled out of the refugees from Europe had been brought up to the hills. They were filing into the trenches, along with the British forces. The white helmets of the soldiers withdrawn from Africa stood out; there were also Bengal Lancers and an attachment of West India Regiment rifles bedded in near James's Engineers.

Captain Bromton had left the observation tower and was speaking to the men moving shells and other ammunition. A Swedish infantry regiment was going through rifle drills. They had an English officer with them who had lived in Sweden and could translate orders, plus the Swedish soldiers had also had a crash course in English. They had been given English uniforms, which were a little crude but helped identify them as British soldiers. They had taken badges of their previous regiments from their old Swedish uniforms, which gave them a sense of belonging.

Stakes had been dug into the hills along Box Hill and beyond, making it look very menacing to any advancing force. The problem was that this force was not normal; the flesh-eaters and creatures did not know what damage these spikes could do, and they did not care. Their minds were set on flesh and the British Army was on the menu.

James put his binoculars down; he was slightly in awe of the enemy advancement. The sheer numbers and movement of this colossal force was emerging, and something that caught his imagination. He did not linger too long on this, though, as it would soon be time to meet with the Royal Artillery commander and prepare for the battle.

As he left the observation post, a soft breeze rippled the British flag flying at the top of it. Its colours were strong and vibrant; they had a sense of unity in them. James felt proud and honored to fight for his country and people.

The lieutenant colonel went to his tent before going to the frontline. He looked at the belongings he had taken from his house and the pictures of his wife and children. There was also a picture of Charles, Rebecca and their children. He smiled and wondered if he would ever see them all again. This train of thought was interrupted as a bugler blew a call to arms on his trumpet. The soldiers started lining up from the field barracks and tents. The call sounded out all along the hills. Commanders spoke to their officers and men. This was the last line of defence before London.

The heavy artillery started to open fire. Captain Bromton arrived and was waiting outside the colonel's quarters.

"Captain." James nodded his head to the officer as he said this. "So, the battle has begun."

The captain told him the commanding officer wanted to see him before he went to the armoury at Box Hill. Any buildings along the hills had been fortified; even small cottages now had machine guns in them and sandbags at the windows. James walked past several of these houses as he made his way to the HQ. The thunderous sounds shook the ground. Shells were already being moved along makeshift rail lines which would have normally been used for mining, and now carried a very dangerous cargo on their tracks. He looked at the leaves on the trees; they were now in full leaf. The birds had left due to the noise and maybe other pending engagements. James felt nature knew what was coming and tried to save as much of itself as it could.

Outside the HQ, there were several guards and two machine guns behind sandbags with their crews. The headquarters had been built into the hillside and was similar to the armoury which James was in charge of. He saluted the soldiers as he walked into the building. He was escorted through a maze of dimly lit corridors. The air was a little dank and thick. Voices could be heard the closer he got to the main operations room; inside there was a whole spread of different regimental commanders. The field marshal was in there reading telegrams and speaking to his aide.

James stopped and saluted. The other officers were now too busy moving around small models on maps. This was to help them predict the current situation facing the British Army and her allies. Nazar's forces were represented by small grey blocks. James's heart sank a little as the grey blocks spread across most of the maps. They were at least not underestimated.

The field marshal stopped talking to his aide and came over to James. He was a man in his fifties; he had looked after himself and was not a heavy drinker or smoker. He had acquired the position after the fall of Reims and the death of the previous field marshal. His hair was dark brown, but had specks of grey appearing. He also had a slight limp, some said due to a bullet he received in India.

"Thank you for coming, Colonel." He placed out his hand and shook James's in return.

"Time is against us, sir, but we need to make sure we hold them off as long as possible," the field marshal said. James picked up on the fact that the field marshal had not said stop them all together. The marshal paused for a moment.

"The enemy has landed in Norfolk and is sweeping round with cavalry and a various arrangement of creatures I believed only existed in Hans Christian Andersen fairy tales."

His head turned to the map and then slowly towards the lieutenant colonel. He sighed, and said, "We're the last line of defence for London."

The rumblings of the heavy guns firing shook the bunker they were in. The thing that stood out for James was the resignation and almost acceptance of defeat by the field marshal. The moment continued whilst the field marshal stood looking blankly at the lieutenant colonel, before James said, "We will do our best, sir, to hold them back."

The lieutenant colonel was shown the defensive plans again by the field marshal's aide. He was told to hold the ammunition depot at Box Hill as long as he could. His shells would be crucial in helping control the battle.

After the briefing, James looked back once at the frantic war room, and then turned and left the room, moving through the dimly lit corridors and out the front of the bunker.

Soldiers were busy carrying supplies and ammunition to the frontline. James wasted no time in getting back to his soldiers. Captain Bromton took the lieutenant colonel to the observation post by the artillery. The Royal Artillery commander was busy giving out orders, whilst his cannons thundered away.

James took his binoculars and scanned the fields and villages in the distance; plumes of smoke covered vast areas of land. This in a way acted as a veil and was a concern for the British forces on the hills. The enemy was taking heavy losses, but was still moving forward. Priests were leading large herds of flesh-eaters, flanked by long limbs.

A division of razor tooths mixed in with bears with two heads were being ushered forward. There were cavalry units, but they were not concentrated. The main bulk of the force was drone soldiers. Nazar was eager to take London and he believed going through the hills would give him his prize.

The soldiers in the trenches along the hillside crouched and waited; the enemy were still tiny dots at the moment. Some of the enlisted soldiers were young, possibly in their early teens; many had been called up to help fight the invaders. The foreign forces had been dispersed over the British Isles, but many knew they could have been utilised earlier.

Captain Bromton pointed out that Nazar's army was bringing up artillery. They had tried to use the railway lines, but the Royal Engineers had destroyed a lot of the tracks as they retreated.

The dots were starting to grow larger. Captain Bromton returned to the fort on Box Hill. He was making sure that the shells were being taken to the cannons at a regular rate. James was going along the front trenches. He wanted to wish the men well. He joined the Swedish lines; they were of Viking stock and he was glad that they were fighting with the British. They would need every man, women and child to stop this horde of darkness.

The Royal Sussex Regiment of Foot was dug in around Box Hill fort. The Hampshire Regiment was to the side by the small railway tracks. Several machine-gun posts had been set up there. Lieutenant Colonel Adams had his Engineers around him at the armoury fort.

As he spoke to his two sergeants, a shell landed in the woods behind them. The enemy had begun getting their heavy artillery firing. The explosion shook the ground around them; the smoke from the shell drifted across the flora and fauna and surrounded the men like a soft mist.

The rifles started to open up on the lower trenches. The sounds of the oncoming creatures and army carried in the wind and could be heard by every man and woman in the hills. James almost found himself unable to take the steps up to the observation tower. As he eventually moved up the wooden steps, another shell whooshed over his head and landed in a field further back. Once he arrived at the top, he reached for his binoculars and stopped. He could see without them that the mass of figures was now swarming up the hills all around them, and now directly in front of Box Hill.

Chapter 38

Nazar scanned the hills whilst sitting on his horse. His officers rode alongside him, along with several priests. General Tarasov kicked his horse on and joined Nazar's side.

"My lord, we will lose a lot of men attacking them head-on."

Nazar looked at him with a blank face. "And?"

"Would it not be better to let our queen sweep around with her forces?" The general was steady with his words.

Nazar looked at him again as if to imply he should choose his words wisely.

"The battle is now; the war is now." He pulled back on his horse's reins, bringing it to a halt. "If you are not capable of taking those hills, then say so." Nazar's eyes narrowed, and he continued, "If you fail, pray you will be one of the fallen men." He then kicked on his horse, leaving the general sitting there as the others rode past him.

Nazar moved into a small village back from Box Hill, which had been attacked hours earlier. It was still burning from the fighting which had taken place there, and there were dead British and drone soldiers littered on the roads and fields.

Shells were still landing around the village, sending swathes of soil and debris hurtling into the air. Nazar was not fazed; he wanted to watch his forces take the hills. His reinforcements moved constantly to the frontline; it was as if they were never-ending.

His horse was taken to a shelter in a courtyard by the side of a cottage. He walked towards a small embankment which had a hedge running along the top of it, and there he was joined by his officers and priests. Nazar smiled and moved around from side to side; he was enjoying the atmosphere of battle and he liked the screams and noise which surrounded him.

"Bring me wine, bring me wine!" Nazar was fully engrossed.

Wine was brought to him in a goblet; he grabbed it off the soldier who was carrying it to him and began to drink, pressing the tip of the goblet to his lips and letting wine flow uncontrolled over his mouth and chin.

"Now for the spoils of war." He clapped his hands.

Four women were dragged from behind the cottage, where they had been held. They were all distressed and crying. Nazar let his long tongue roll out of his mouth and down the sides. He then looked at two of the priests with him.

"Take them inside the cottage." He moved quickly over the open ground and entered the building; the women were kicking and screaming as they were taken inside. Groans and cries rung out of the building, and some of the whimpering which had followed died down. The officers outside stayed still, most amongst them smiled, but some looked worried.

Nazar emerged with his top off. He was carrying an arm in his left hand. The men outside looked at blood dripping from it and could see it had been newly ripped off its victim. "Spoils of war," he snorted, as he went to drink more wine.

Chapter 39

James was inside the armoury helping load shells; his tunic was off and his sleeves were rolled up. The men were hot and tired and could not really keep up with the demand for shells; they were working flat out.

"Sergeant Smith, keep the lines of communication coming down to us here," Lieutenant Colonel Adams said; he wanted to know what was happening up top regularly. Twenty minutes passed before news came that the enemy were now pushing up the slopes.

The lieutenant colonel grabbed his tunic and put it on. He then took his sword and revolver, and moved quickly through the candlelit rooms. Sergeant Smith followed behind him. They both picked up a rifle and fixed bayonets onto them. The noise hit them as they left the underground fort. It was a constant sound of battle; it filled every crevice, every dark space, it reverberated off trees and sunk into the long grass that swayed in the gentle breeze.

Moving from the fort, they entered the battle trenches. Sergeant Smith followed the lieutenant colonel as they passed wounded men being moved to the medical tents. The Royal Sussex Regiment of Foot was engaged in heavy fighting at the front. The Swedish line infantry had repelled two waves of flesh-eaters, but were now struggling to contain long limbs and drones, who were breaking into their trenches. Private Brown was helping lay explosives around an artillery piece that had been damaged. It could not be moved, so the next step was to render it unusable.

He saw the lieutenant colonel and went to salute him but was told to carry on his good work. Three more Engineers joined them and followed the lieutenant colonel. His destination was the heavy artillery. As James flew around a corner, a large claw swung past his face. Standing above a wooden gangway was a long limb, saliva dripping from its mouth and teeth showing as it widened its jaws. James reacted quickly and brought the rifle up and into its shoulder, and he squeezed the trigger automatically without thinking. The bullet clipped the beast's left limb, causing it to reel back, and the soldiers behind him had now taken aim. Four bullets thumped into the long limb's body, causing it to fall forward onto the wooden gangway above. It crunched into the timber, sending dust and soil onto the men below. The weight of the creature then caused the timber to split and it followed the long limb into the dirt below.

"Keep moving, men, we must reach the artillery." James led them forward.

Bullets whizzed over the top of them as they moved along the trenches. Empty ammo boxes lay strewn on the ground, followed by wounded or dead soldiers. The taste of dust and gunpowder lingered in the mouth. As they moved forward, there were wooden steps leading up onto the bank, where the cannons were situated. The firing point was raised and was heavily protected with sandbags and earth mounds, wooden stakes jutting out of the ground around it. The cannons had stopped firing and the Royal Artillery was frantically trying to limber them up and take them to another firing point away from the frontline.

Lieutenant Colonel Adams looked around as the battle raged on. He could see lines of enemy soldiers breaking on the defences like waves on a beach. The British machine guns were firing and cutting through the thick lines, but therein lay the problem – once they could no longer maintain that level of fire, it was down to the soldiers and their rifles. Packed together side by side, their red tunics gleamed in the soft sun.

The lieutenant colonel told the soldiers with him to assist the Royal Artillery with the limbering up of the heavy artillery. Small shells were exploding around the British lines. James glanced over again at the enemy forces fighting with the British and Allied soldiers. The Swedish infantry were putting up a brave fight, but they had been swamped with long limbs and flesh-eaters. Screams of men being ripped apart and devoured swept across the battlefield. Even the bravest could not hide their fear or dislike for the enemy.

The British forces were fighting for every field, every stone and every blade of grass that made up this extraordinary country. Men who had served together for years were now dying side by side.

The cannons began to be pulled free by the horses and the Royal Artillery commander came over and quickly thanked the lieutenant colonel and his men. Captain Bromton appeared at the bottom of the steps.

"Colonel, the headquarters have fallen."

The Hampshire Regiment was starting to fall back and laying down covering fire as it did so. James told Sergeant Smith to round up the Engineers and fall back to the fort. Captain Bromton stood by the lieutenant colonel's side; the other men left empty battery positions and joined the maze of trenches.

"What now, sir?" Captain Bromton could see the Royal Sussex Regiment of Foot fighting hand to hand.

"It all seems such a shame." He lowered the butt of his rifle to the soil beneath him.

Captain Bromton stood next to him and looked on. The enemy were still pressing up the hills and their reinforcements could be seen coming from miles away. Their numbers were unsurpassable.

"Ok, Captain, let's join the others at the fort." James had needed a moment to take it all in. The fighting unfolding around them was savage. Some of the officers had no choice but to form small circles as the enemy came from all sides. They were swarming over the trenches like ants invading an alien nest.

The two officers moved at speed through the trench system. There were five Hampshire soldiers setting up a Maxim gun; this would help cover the retreat. Within seconds of them passing it, the crackle of the bullets flying through the machine gun could be heard.

The enemy was on their coat-tails as they raced through the winding alleys. Gunfire carried along on the airways as they moved. Heavy artillery shells started to land along the frontlines. The order must have been given to slow the assault. The British forces were mixed in with the enemy, but it was only a matter of time before the front was totally overrun.

Lieutenant Colonel Adams raced across open ground with Captain Bromton following him. Both men had their Lee-Metford rifles close. British soldiers were moving around them and heading towards the woods and forests at the top of the hill. Some reserves were stationed in these woods and would act as a counter-attack. As the two men looked around, the sight of four long limbs coming out of the trenches after them was enough to put an extra yard of pace into their stride. James stopped.

"Keep running, Henry!" Captain Bromton shouted, looking at James. His eyes saw it was not a time to repeat his suggestion.

The lieutenant colonel crouched onto one knee. Bringing his rifle up onto his shoulder, he pulled back the bolt and then looked down the sights. He had to choose a target quickly out of the four long limbs that were racing towards him. Their claws and open mouths were unsettling and the speed they were coming at James was striking.

Bang!

The first creature in the group collapsed to the ground, falling over its front legs and twisting in the air. The yards were now falling away. He pulled back the bolt, and sent another bullet into the chamber. Looking down the sights, he chose a long limb that was running closely to the one next to it.

Bang!

This long limb fell and caused another one to tumble, but the fourth was upon him. He steadied himself with his bayonet. As he looked up and braced himself for impact, a whoosh of air passed by. Lancers dashed past, and he saw a flash of blue uniform and a white helmet. The long limb that had been about to pounce found itself getting a lance in its side. The creature spun in agony and tried to claw it out. A second Lancer came in and finished the job. They then hunted down the long limb, which had taken a tumble when the creature next to it was shot.

James stood up; an officer on horseback came up alongside him.

"Not the time to be in the open, Colonel."

James sighed and smiled softly. "No, you're right." He then pushed the Lee-Metford rifle over his shoulder and started to move across the open field towards the fort. He was escorted by the Lancer officer.

Lieutenant Colonel Adams rushed past the machine-gun posts which flanked the armoury fort. The crews were bracing themselves for the advance. The 16th Lancers filed in behind, and James thanked them for saving his life; the officer in charge of the Lancers acknowledged that with a stern look. It was the look of a man who had lost everything, and now would die fighting for the cause.

Captain Bromton was glad to see the lieutenant colonel.

"Did you send in the cavalry?" James looked at him as though he shouldn't have, but inside he was relieved.

Barely a minute passed before the machine guns started to open fire. James was helping the Engineers set the charges in the rooms, which had leftover ammunition and shells. They had done well to shift as much as three quarters of it to the battle front and towards London. Many had hoped the enemy would fail on taking the hills, but their sacrifice of hundreds of thousands of drones, creatures and anything else that came at the British lines was proving more than enough for them to win this objective.

"They're still coming and we've lost one of the Maxim guns, Colonel."

Private Brown was moving a medical box to a wagon, where several nurses currently were. Heidi was one of them. She looked on anxiously. They had experienced escaping the horde in Europe and more recently in Portsmouth. Now it was knocking on the doors of Box Hill.

"Private Brown, ask the bugler to sound the retreat. Go with the nurses and make sure they get to British lines."

"Yes, sir." Private Brown rushed around the corner. The bugler was currently firing out through a gap in one of the fort walls. Flesh-eaters had started to bash against iron doors and the very walls themselves. Destroyer drones had been used as shock troops against the fortified positions along the coast and inland. Nazar had seen the need for more specialist soldiers breaking the enemy strongholds. These soldiers had the power of several men, and were dangerous fighters.

The bugler managed to sound the retreat but was then hit with a bullet to his left shoulder. Private Brown tried to help him up, but was knocked back by an explosion outside the wall. He gingerly got to his feet; the wall was now under pressure from the build-up of flesh-eaters. John took his rifle as the wall broke, and the creatures almost fell in amongst the rubble. As this was unfolding, three destroyer drones had taken up firing positions on top of the fort. They began to shoot at the soldiers rushing about below.

Captain Bromton took six Engineers and moved to the front of the fort. The flesh-eaters were clambering to get at the wounded bugler, who was crawling away the best he could. Private Brown was using his bayonet to kills as many of the flesh-eaters as he could.

"First row fire, second row reload!" Captain Bromton barked out the orders as he moved his unit forward.

Sergeant Smith took three men to deal with the destroyer drones on the fort roof. They crept around the side of the fort as the smoke drifted through the trees and across the fields. The front units on the hillside of the forts were starting to be overrun. Royal Sussex Regiment of Foot were fighting a desperate rearguard fight, and long limbs were battering into the fortifications all around them. The defences on top of the fort had been breached. A large razor tooth was attacking several soldiers and a small artillery piece. It was backed up by drone soldiers.

Sergeant Smith took his men to a small mound. They waited for a swirl of smoke to pass them by before taking aim at the destroyer drones on the side of the fort. The first round of bullets sped through the air and into their unsuspecting victims, killing one of them and wounding the other. The remaining destroyer drone quickly moved down, and unbeknownst to Sergeant Smith, he had been preparing to throw a grenade onto the soldiers below; this now came their way. It bounced once on the dry grass on top of the fort bunker and then exploded amongst Sergeant Smith's men. The impact was devastating. One of the soldiers lost his legs in the blast and two others were badly wounded. The destroyer drone took his chance to finish the job and came at the sergeant, who was still recovering from the blast.

As the drone came at the sergeant, he reached for his rifle. This was instantly kicked away. The destroyer drone's teeth were on full show as he snarled at his victim below. Sergeant Smith lashed out with a fearsome kick to the side of the drone's leg, sending him stumbling. The sergeant got to his feet to lay another blow, but the drone had already scrambled up as well. They both stood toe to toe. Sergeant Smith was no small man, 6ft 2in at best, but the destroyer drone stood at about 6ft 7in. He was a beast with claws and teeth.

Sergeant Smith came forward, throwing punches to the ribs and face of the creature. The power of the punches forced the beast back. Blood started to run from the drone soldier's nose. As it wiped away the blood from his face, it then let out a roar. Bearing its open mouth and with claws spread out, it came at the sergeant. He tried to brace for impact, but the sheer power of this half-animal, half-man was too much and sent him flying backwards. The destroyer drone bit down into his shoulder, causing him to let out a screech of pain. He was picked up and spun around; there was not much he could do.

Sergeant Smith was on his side; the destroyer drone saw the opportunity to kick him in the ribs, and stopped and laughed. He then picked up a rifle as if to finish off the sergeant with the utt of the weapon.

Lying there, Smith looked around; the sounds of battle surrounded them. The sun shone over the English oaks, and he was ready.

The destroyer drone brought the rifle high above his head. He had not seen the wounded British soldier behind him stagger to his feet. He had his bayonet in his hand and lurched forward, thrusting it into the neck of this giant soldier. The drone let out a yelp of its own and turned to grab the wounded soldier. They grappled for several steps before both falling over the edge. Sergeant Smith had pulled himself up and grabbed his rifle. He looked over the edge; both of them lay there at the bottom, motionless.

He then checked the other two soldiers, finding that both were dead. Hurriedly, he made his way down to the fort entrance. Captain Bromton was with his men, who were still firing at the fast-approaching flesh-eaters. Private Brown saw Sergeant Smith gingerly making his way towards the main doors, and went over to help take him away from the front.

"No point going inside, Sergeant, we've set it to blow." Private Brown assisted him towards Heidi and the other nurses. A soldier who helped load the sergeant on the back of the wagon told them they had to leave. Private Brown looked around; long limbs were now coming over the top of the fort. Drone soldiers were along the edge of the forest and taking shots at them. Heidi called over to him to move on. He swung his rifle over his shoulder and got on the back of the wagon.

Captain Bromton was reinforced by seven more Royal Engineers. Lieutenant Colonel Adams was pinned down with a small force to the side of the fort. They were exchanging fire with the enemy, and the lieutenant colonel wanted to get all of the men out. A shell landed close to the fort entrance, damaging bricks and sandbags on impact. The drone forces had overrun the defences directly in front of the fort and were now focusing their efforts on this compound. A Maxim gun was wheeled out by a small unit of Swedish line infantry; they had retreated to the fort, but now found that this was under siege.

James was concerned that they were being trapped. The bugler had sounded the retreat, but the fighting had not allowed the British forces to fall back en masse. James was aware of the wounded and some units retreating to the second defensive lines, but he had wanted to get more soldiers out.

The long limbs poured into the fort. Captain Bromton tried to get his men to fall back, but the long limbs came around the back. He drew his sword and placed his rifle over his back. Then, in the other hand, he held his Enfield revolver. He shot at flesh-eaters as they stumbled towards them. Head shots caused them to fall down to the ground like a tree being felled with an axe; these creatures were once human, but now had distorted faces and an insatiable lust for flesh.

Captain Bromton's men formed a small circle; they were being attacked from all sides. Lieutenant Colonel Adams tried to rally his men, but several were shot as they left their positions. A second push allowed them to leave a defensive line of sandbags. He then got them together, their red tunics and blue trousers distinctive of the Victorian British Empire and standing out in the midday sun. They lined up with their rifles and tried to push forward. Flesh-eaters had begun to cut them off from the captain; using bayonets, they tried in vain to reach him, but were forced back. Rifle fire was cutting into their ranks from the advancing drones.

James used his sword as he swung at the creatures in front of him. Slicing off hands and arms, they still poured forward. A soldier next to him was hit in the head, and blood poured out of his white helmet as he fell lifeless to the ground. Another soldier to the right of James was dragged into the mass of flesh-eaters, and his screams were drowned out in the noise of battle. He was being eaten alive, as were many on the battlefield. Lieutenant Colonel Adams and his men were being pushed back. There was a slight mound before open ground and then woodlands. He knew it would involve a dash for it if they were going to make it.

Captain Bromton was now surrounded. His men huddled in their small circle, fighting away flesh-eaters and drone soldiers. The long limbs pushed through the enemy ranks, their size enabling their advantage. When they came across the ever-decreasing small circle led by Captain Bromton, a surge brought them into biting distance. Now it was a case of the captain trying to hold firm; he brought his sword into the first oncoming long limb, driving it through its head. The second swipe slashed at a giant claw as it swung out at him. He used his revolver as flesh-eaters joined in the attack, shooting two in the chest and one in the head, but as he brought his revolver down, a long limb sunk its teeth into his back. The pain caused him to try and shake it off, but the beast was too strong for that.

The men around him were now being either shot or bayoneted by drone soldiers, leaving flesh-eaters to seize their chance and start feeding where they could. Several priests were now amongst the attack. Nazar had not committed too many to the main battle, and whilst he valued no life, he did value priests over drone soldiers and officers.

Lieutenant Colonel Adams could see the small circle disappear as the enemy closed in. Captain Bromton had fallen out of sight and was now being torn to shreds by long limbs. They snarled at the flesh-eaters, who tried to push forward, but were held back by the priests. Any survivors were executed on the spot. Nazar wanted senior officers where possible.

He had received some offers of support already from London and other places within the British mainland. These wealthy families wanted to preserve what they had and were willing to sacrifice nearly everything to keep that. Maps of British strongpoints, and military numbers, were just some of the things traded. Nazar in return would give those who helped him special privileges in his new kingdom. This had worked well in Europe and was brutally carried out. Those who did not toe the line in Europe, were either fed to the flesh-eaters, or worse.

Lieutenant Colonel Adams signalled for the soldiers around him to make a dash for the defences to the south of them. The enemy was swarming around the fort. Two severely injured Hampshire soldiers said they would light the fuses to the remaining shells once the fort had fallen. James knew this was their best chance to get some distance between the frontline and the enemy. With his handful of men, he began to fall back, firing as they retreated. The enemy was more concerned for the time being on the fort's prizes. Five destroyer drones now worked on taking off the iron gates guarding the entrance.

Whilst this unfolded, a priest lined up a detachment of drones. To the other side, he ordered an officer to get the long limbs and flesh-eaters ready to press on. Lieutenant Colonel Adams could see how the enemy was lining up for a charge. He knew they would not withstand a full-on attack and gave the order for his men to make a rapid retreat.

The soldiers turned and started to run. Shells were still flying over them in both directions; some were landing in front of them, others landing close by. The whole horizon behind them was a scene of the enemy preparing to charge. The languid flesh-eaters moved up the side, and pockets of long limbs came to the front. The priest in command had some cavalry around him, with two junior priests tagging along. Drone soldiers had lined up and were now attaching bayonets. Captain Beaulieu was the officer in charge of this detachment of drones. He had come over to Nazar's side after Europe had fallen. He was eager to impress; having not been able to work his way up the ranks in the French army, he now saw this as his chance.

The retreating British did not need to see that they were coming, the roar was deafening. Lieutenant Colonel Adams and his men were making good ground, but the enemy was closing in. They could see field artillery and soldiers behind sandbags. This was part of the second defence of Box Hill.

The cavalry hooves galloped over parched grass. James felt his heart flutter as his helmet strap rubbed against his chin. The heavy .303 rounds for the Metford rifle rattled around in his ammunition pouch. James afforded himself one quick glance over his shoulder, but it was not a good idea. The enemy cavalry were almost upon them. As the British soldiers ran, a bugle sounded out. It was the sound of a charge. Coming from both sides of the battlefield were British Lancers. At the front was the commander, who had saved James's life. The sheer number of British 16th Lancers was amazing; they charged en masse, catching the enemy unprepared as they bore down on the survivors from the fort.

The clash was thunderous, and the British Lancers cut through the enemy in droves. The enemy priest was knocked off his horse and was killed by the captain of the Lancers; they continued to push into the drone soldier ranks, cutting them down as they charged forward. The flesh-eaters were mowed down and the long limbs were picked off. This attack was enough to cause Captain Beaulieu to signal the retreat; as his men fell back, they pushed back onto those reinforcing them. The British artillery seized this moment and rained down terror on their close-knit ranks.

The 16th Lancers did take casualties; it was inevitable on such a large battlefield. Once the momentum had gone out of the attack, and the shells were landing amongst them, they rallied by their bugler to the British lines. Whilst this had unfolded, Lieutenant Colonel Adams and his men had fallen back to the second defence.

There was a quick round-up of his force and then he was met by the commanding officer of the second defence. He had orders for Lieutenant Colonel Adams and his men to go to Windsor Castle and help evacuate the royal family. He was to escort as many of the wounded as they could to Windsor. Private Brown was relieved to see so many of them had made it, and the fact they were now moving away from the front for the time being.

Chapter 40

Captain Hayward cleaned his binoculars one more time before searching for their vessel. They had made great time riding from the small fort they had captured, to the coast in Italy. Charles knew they would have a chance of catching up with the major if they could get back to their ship.

"Corporal, I've found it." Charles ordered Corporal Heinz to scout the boat and make sure it was still in friendly hands. He was to scout the shore with a three-man unit.

They would take the horses as the mission was still to get to the source of Nazar's power. Benedict was with Doctor Brown and two Engineers. He was no longer the boy who had joined them back in Austria at the Benedictine Abbey in Melk; the war had aged him. Corporal Heinz gave the signal for the all clear. Fortune had favoured them as they arrived at the boat; the sailors said they were preparing to leave. Major Sherborne had said two days, and then they were to return to Great Britain.

The horses and the soldiers were quickly loaded onto the boat. Captain Holfer checked all the men were on safely and reported that back to Captain Hayward. They quickly joined the ship that was moored out in the Mediterranean. The captain of the ship said that if Nazar had not been planning an invasion of Great Britain, there would have been more ships in these waters. He wasted no more time, raised the anchor and departed for Russia. As they set sail, Charles spared a thought for those who did not make it back from this mission. Captain Müller was one of them. Charles spoke to his men and then asked the officers to reconvene at his quarters in two hours.

The men quickly settled down to wash and then eat. Weapons were stored away, and would be cleaned and readied for action later that evening. Captain Hayward cleared a side table in his cabin and laid down the maps and charts they had for the next part of the mission. His food was brought to him along with some fresh water. The first thing he did was pour himself a large glass of water. Then, picking up the glass, he brought it to his lips and let the cool liquid roll down his dry throat; it quickly needed refilling and he drunk once more. After that he was ready to eat.

When the other officers joined him in his quarters, Benedict was with them. He said he was ready to give as much information as he could remember. Captain Hayward had not spoken to the ship's captain about Major Sherborne. He wanted to plan their next move first, but he knew at some point the question would have to be approached as there was only one course they were set on now and that was confrontation with the major and his men.

Benedict looked at the maps long and hard; he studied the Russian coastline and was cautious not to just guess. He asked for some time, as he wanted to be as accurate as he could. Charles told him to take the maps and get some rest; they would reconvene in the morning.

The light bounced off metal rails on the ship's deck. The Engineers were busy cleaning equipment and getting ready for the next part of the mission. Breakfast was enjoyed by all. The chef had some cured meat, to which he added some fresh bread. The smell of baking bread drifted around the ship; it was a homely smell, something the soldiers took in. Many had moments of small reflection, maybe about their families or whether they'd ever see home again.

The British Army had been galvanised during this impending invasion. Those who had not fled across the Atlantic would be involved in a fight to the end.

The visibility was good, and they were making steady progress. "Strange not to see any enemy vessels, Captain." Charles was to the point.

The ship's captain looked over with a telling face. "The invasion must have begun." His words were plain, but the implications were clear – Great Britain and the Empire were fighting for her existence.

"We must double the efforts then; whilst we cannot help with the invasion, we can help to hit the enemy at their source." Charles thanked the ship's captain and left to join the officers and Benedict on top deck.

They were in good spirits after a night's sleep and a hearty breakfast. As the men drank tea, Benedict looked eager to talk. "I think I have found our location, Captain."

His eyes danced as he spoke. He then described their route. They would enter Russia along the Pechora River; this had been a trade route for hundreds of years, and from there they would follow the river down until they reached the Usa River. This would be the route they would take to the Vorkuta River. The town they would be looking for was Vorkuta.

There in the foothills of the Ural Mountains was meant to be the fort and monastery. Benedict had said his father had spoken to a trader, who claimed the monastery was built on something which had come from the skies many centuries before. The mission was to try and find the source and eliminate it if possible or to deny them access.

Benedict spent time relaying anything he could think of that his father had told him over the years. Captain Hayward led the applause for Benedict's information. He patted him on the back and then turned to his officers.

"Gentlemen, Major Sherborne is ahead of us, he will be trying to destroy the monastery and what lies beneath." Charles was clear that the mission was to take care of Nazar's source of power, but if Major Sherborne became a problem, he would have to be dealt with. After the debrief, the soldiers went back to preparing for the next stage of the mission.

The days passed, and a summer storm slowed them down with a short, hard burst. They made up ground as they sailed past Spain and Africa, but moving through the Strait of Gibraltar they had their nervous moments; however, the captain of HMS *Orontes* was experienced. He was a wily old chap, and loved the seafaring way; his ilk were now invaluable to the British Empire.

Sailing between the French and British coasts was eerie; the weather had been kind, as a light fog hung just off the English Channel. There was not total silence, as distant explosions could be heard. The soldiers all gathered on top deck and leant against the rails. They stood quietly and listened to the faint noise in the background. Every man's face was glum and showed concern. Captain Holfer patted his hand on the shoulder of Captain Hayward as a sign of support. The battles were raging on as they spent the next day passing along the English Channel; many held private hopes of the war being won on British soil, whilst others worried it was being lost as they sailed on their mission.

The rumbles lessened as they sailed off the Prussian coast, and from there they would head up past Norway and around to Russia. The weather was fair for the journey thus far; on stormy waters, the soldiers hunkered down below. Unless you were a hardened sailor, this was a hard time.

Days passed until they started to cut through the Norwegian Sea, before moving into the Barents Sea. Following the coastline, they would look for the entrance to the Pechora River, and then navigate down through it. They had taken some Russian sailors with them on both ships; this would save them valuable time to help find the location of Nazar's monastery.

Days were rolling past until they came to where the river's mouth met the sea. HMS *Jumna* was moored. They could see that the boat she had been helping direct for this mission was gone. This meant that Major Sherborne was already on his way. Charles knew the mission was more important than his personnel conflict with Major Sherborne; he had briefed his officers and men as such. They had to try and complete the mission the best they could and not jeopardise it over the major and his men.

They did not waste too much time loading into the boat to travel to Vorkuta. Weapons had been cleaned and supplies readied. The caption of HMS *Orontes* spoke to Captain Hayward and said he would make contact with the other ship and check on their status. Charles had told him what the major had done, but he had also pointed out the major would have told another story to the other captain, so it would not be worth pursuing an aggressive course of action as the major had already left.

The energy now was to be channeled into what lay ahead. This was not like going back into Europe; this was now going into the lion's den. Whilst Nazar might not be in residence, his evil and power were.

***

There was no special defence system at the mouth of the river. Maybe this was because it attracted no attention to what lay ahead, or Nazar no longer feared a man-made army could trouble him.

They passed along it at a good speed; just like the rest of Europe, the lands had a different feel about them now. The air often carried a deathly stench; it was as if the trees held the secrets of what happened here and the demonic energy was trapped around them. There was wildlife, but it went about its business in a more cautious way. They had only travelled a couple of miles or so down the river when they saw their first herd of flesh-eaters, maybe a thousand or more, lumbering along, looking for flesh to feed on. Even if the soldiers were used to seeing these beasts, their presence still drew the attention of their eyes. En masse, this force was almost unstoppable; Charles and Captain Holfer spoke about what would happen if they did manage to defeat Nazar, how long it might take to rid the world of this force. The likely answer was always shown on their concerned faces.

The river was long, and without the Russian sailors it would have taken longer to navigate. They dressed on top deck with captured drone soldiers' uniforms and flew Nazar's flag. This was his territory and they hoped to get lucky as they sailed along it. The villages were marked on their maps and this would mean extra care was needed when passing them by. The boat was loaded with supplies to help it look as inconspicuous as possible. If stopped, they would explain the supplies were for Vorkuta, and hope this was enough to allow them on.

As the days rolled by, the boat was stopped along the way. Each time was as tense as the next. Some of the drones were bored, and wanted to question anyone who was coming through, while others wanted to hear of the war and how the new Empire was doing. Fortune sometimes did favour the brave, as none of them took time to search the whole boat. The Russian sailors who they had with them did the majority of the speaking, and Corporal Heinz could help out as his Russian was good enough. Captain Hayward and the rest of the soldiers waited below anxiously, each time praying it all went smoothly.

August was slipping away as a month; the weather was becoming colder. They knew this mission only had legs for a short period of time before bad weather could ruin everything. They estimated a week to get there and a week to get out. A lot wasn't known on the level of communication Nazar had at his disposal. Telegrams would hinder the escape as they could warn ahead after the attack. Mooring the boat a good distance from the town would helper lessen the association with the attackers coming from the river.

Moving down the Usa River and then on down the Vorkuta River, the tension on the boat rose. Most of the men became a little twitchy; stories of flayed humans or being eaten alive was enough to test any man's resolve, but they were now so far behind enemy lines that everything was going to come down to the mission going to plan.

"The town of Vorkuta is coming into sight, Captain," said Corporal Heinz, his eyes alive, half glad to be there, half worried about what lay ahead.

The mooring inlet chosen for the boat shielded it from sight. It would allow them to unload their horses and explosives. A skeleton crew would remain on board to help defend the vessel the best they could. The rest of the soldiers would again ride on horseback, dressed as drone soldiers and prisoners.

They expected there to be a high priest or commander overseeing the town and looking after Nazar's prize asset.

They had made sure that they arrived early morning so as not to draw too much attention. There were other boats around, but most of those were moored in the harbour. Strangely enough, there was no sign of Major Sherborne's boat, and they hoped this was a good sign and that it had not been captured.

A soft breeze tilted down the tops of the pine trees near them, a strong smell of rotten flesh carried in the air. There were also sounds of an industrial factory working away. Captain Hayward took out his pocket watch and flicked it open quickly; there inside was a picture of his family. It made him smile before he closed it down again and slid it back in his pocket.

Corporal Heinz would lead the way along with two Russian soldiers. They had been hand-picked to help with the language and customs. Nazar's army was picking up other nationals as it conquered the world, but many suspected they had not made their way back to the headquarters of his Empire.

Pushing through scrubby undergrowth, they came to a muddy track; it had a battered sign saying "Vorkuta". Captain Hayward looked at Captain Holfer; they both nodded without saying anything and spurred on their horses.

The growling sounds did not come at first, or even the groans; they came more as the men neared the gates of the town. The woods and fields around the town had not been covered with flesh-eaters or long limbs. In fact, they had seen very little enemy life at all. What they could see was the burning torches outside the main gates and along the town walls. The track was a little more solid and less muddy, the closer they got to the gate. There were things hanging all along the outer walls; the soldiers could not quite make out what they were, not until they arrived in front of the gates.

They were people, some in various stages of decomposition, others still barely alive. Some were flesh-eaters, scratching around having come back from the dead. They had been hung up by their shoulders, slowly causing the weight of their bodies to pull down on those joints and cause an agonising death.

The Royal Engineers, aided by their allies, waited outside the main gate. Nothing happened; there were just the shrieks and groans surrounding them. Corporal Heinz rode forward and knocked on the gate hard, but there was still nothing. Charles wondered if it was a trap and felt for the revolver attached to his belt.

Then a creaking, scratching noise confronted them as the gates began to open.

Standing in front of them were four giant men. They were maybe twice the size of the riders of the north, and looked twice as formidable. Their heads looked slightly squashed and were almost hairless. The men were all similar looking, but not all identical. The British and Allied soldiers sat on their horses, a little in awe of what was in front of them. No one said a word.

"State your reason for being here, drones?" a booming voice bellowed out of the giant who was standing at the back of the four. He started to move forward, showing that he was even bigger than the rest. Only the Russian-speaking men could understand, and the rest of the group watched on anxiously.

"This gate hasn't been used for months." He walked up to the Russian soldiers who were sitting on horses at the front. They both began to squirm a little in their saddles. This giant man came alongside them as they sat there; he then lowered his huge head close to the soldier on the right. "Uhhh," stated the beast of a man.

"We have brought prisoners from Europe," said Corporal Heinz, as he rode over to the giant who had been asking the questions.

"Why here? The prisons here are for our special guests!" He said this and laughed, prompting the other three giants to laugh as well.

Corporal Heinz had to think on his toes. "They were caught trying to locate maps of this area." This instantly had an effect. The giant leader turned and walked over to the Royal Engineers, who were sitting there wondering what was unfolding. Each step he took sent a tremor along the ground.

"Trying to steal from us, were you?" He said this in English.

The soldiers said nothing; they just sat there in their saddles. The giant leaned into the nearest Engineer to him. "You must be scared, has the cat caught your tongue?"

He then put his large hand on the man's shoulder, and gripping him tight, he lifted him out of the saddle, looking at the other giants as he did so. Captain Hayward kicked on his horse, moving it slowly forward.

"I'm in charge here, not this man." Charles could feel the tension amongst the group.

"Are you, Captain? Are you indeed?" Letting his hand open, the soldier fell back into his saddle. The giant wiped his brow before walking over to the captain. He stood in front of Charles and his horse. Then, without further notice, he swung his giant hand, knocking the horse across the neck and sending it and Captain Hayward onto the track below. The animal struggled to get on its legs and Captain Hayward just lay there for a moment or two. Sergeant Butcher felt for his sword, but saw Captain Holfer bring his hand out to the side, as if to say hold fire.

Charles gingerly got to his feet. His horse's reins were caught by Corporal Heinz as he stopped it from galloping off. Now standing in front of Captain Hayward was the giant. Charles looked up at this never-ending body. He instantly thought of David and Goliath, and tried to work out his next move.

"Do you feel like a captain now?" He let out a bellowing laugh, which finished with him snorting out of his nose and then coughing.

"I'm Captain Charles Hayward of the Royal Engineers, serving Her Majesty Queen Victoria and the British Empire," he said, as he straightened himself up.

The giant's shoulders dropped, as if he was getting ready to strike. His face crumpled up, taking offence at Captain Hayward not cowering at his sheer presence. The truth was Charles was still dazed and did not really comprehend fully what was going on. This moment was broken abruptly by three loud horn blasts. The other giants began to turn. Speaking in Russian, they called over to their leader, who responded angrily, before turning back to the captain again.

"I will come and see you suffering soon enough, Captain. You'll beg for death, just like the others." He then swung his head around and spoke in Russian to Corporal Heinz and the other Russian soldiers, telling them to take the prisoners to the work sheds near the large stone barn.

Charles slowly got onto his horse; Sergeant Butcher rode alongside him, and steadied his horse as he did so. "Are you alright, Captain?"

Charles looked around and smiled. "I think so."

Corporal Heinz rode to the British soldiers and kept up the illusion of them being prisoners. "Follow me, you lazy dogs, move or die where your stand."

Several drone soldiers appeared at the gate as the giants disappeared off down another track. As the soldiers on horseback moved through this formidable entrance, they were greeted with a bleak landscape – the trees looked sick, and the soil barren. Long, stone sheds with chimneys burning filled the area in front of them. To the far right, on top of a hill, were large iron cages, and inside them silhouettes of things moving around caught the eye. It was unnerving. The sounds that swept along on the wind were a mixture of groans, growls, screams and shouting.

Charles sank into his saddle; he felt that if there was a hell, they surely must have found it. They moved slowly along a well-trodden track. A small drone contingent escorted them for a while, before breaking off to return to the wall. The lack of attention to who they were was probably down to a couple of things, one being, without Benedict having knowledge of this place via his father, where would one start to look in Russia? The other was who would be bold enough or stupid enough to ride into the lion's den? Charles prayed they would get their chance to have an effect on this war in some way.

As they approached the prisoner sheds, more drone soldiers began to filter outside. Three large kegs sat across from what looked like a guardhouse; the drone soldiers were all in a boisterous mood and some were carrying pint glasses.

"Move the prisoners to the empty shed on the left," a drone sergeant said.

Captain Hayward and his men had concealed their weapons in their kitbags. They were shown inside the shed by one of the drone soldiers from the camp and Corporal Heinz followed in behind. There was a small log burner in the corner, and farm sacks lying strewn around on the floor. The air in there was musty, and the little heat from the burner did not fill the room. Charles had seen there were hundreds of these sheds; he could only guess to how many poor souls were being used as slaves. It tormented him that they could not try and free these people, but their numbers were so few and they had to try and stop some of Nazar's power if they could.

Corporal Heinz was chatting to the drone soldier; he started to laugh and patted the corporal on the shoulder. The two Russian soldiers who were with the Allies stood next to him and joined in. The British soldiers gathered what they could to make themselves comfortable on the floor. Their kitbags had been stored away near the guardhouse and, fortunately, had still not been searched.

It took around thirty minutes before the drone soldier left. Corporal Heinz then came over to the captain.

"Sorry that took so long. He has been told that you and the rest of the British will be presented to the high priest tomorrow evening." The corporal almost shook his head as he said this.

"Thank you, Corporal, I guess we're not going to get any warm soup tonight." Half joking, half being serious, he was joined by Sergeant Butcher. Captain Holfer also came over to the men. "We will not have long to plan this out, gentlemen, but my suggestion is we set the charges after meeting the high priest tomorrow evening."

The men pondered the captain's plan; he was right to suggest attacking as soon as possible, because they did not know if they would be split up or, even worse, tortured. Charles had seen the flayed bodies as they came to the sheds. This was Nazar's home and the evil that resided here was the worst he had ever seen. Sergeant Butcher added that whilst they were being presented to the high priest, maybe Corporal Heinz could get an idea of where the rock was that fell from the sky. The two Russian soldiers were to stay with the British soldiers to help escort them back to their shed afterwards.

As the men spoke, the ground began to shake, then a deep, gravelly roar vibrated around the wooden hut.

Each man moved quickly to the small windows which were dotted along the wooden shed. On the right-hand side stood something different; its legs were thick and its skin leathery. It was different to the razor tooth, but shared its sharp teeth. It stood taller than a house and had a head that was similar to a long limb. Sitting on top of this giant beast was in fact a giant. The creature and its rider did not stay too long and continued to move on. The rider had a huge lantern, which helped light up the night sky, and in his other hand was an axe. Its blade was the size of half a man. The men could see in the distance more of these lanterns. The giants patrolled the walls and camp at night. Charles knew then that they would need a miracle to get out.

Clang, clang, clang, clang.

"Get up, you useless dogs." The drone soldier who had entered the shed had broken English, but it wasn't hard to understand what he wanted the British soldiers to do. He kicked at any sack that was near to him. Groans of pain filled the shed. Corporal Heinz and the two Allied Russian soldiers had spent the night in a barn rather than share with the other drones in the guardhouse.

He swung his foot at a sack near the door and seemed to get it stuck. His face crumpled up as he got frustrated by this. As he pulled it out, he fell backwards. This made his helmet drop down over his eyes. When he readjusted it, he found a figure standing over him. Sergeant Butcher looked at him with steely eyes; the drone soldier was shocked at this resistance. He snapped his head around to look at Corporal Heinz and the two Russian soldiers. It took them a moment to realise what was unfolding; they soon came to the drone soldier's aid and pushed back the sergeant to make it look convincing.

The drone soldier stormed out and said something to the corporal as he left.

"He wants you all to be ready for some hard labour," said the corporal, who looked on apologetically, but Captain Hayward was already telling him there was nothing he could do. The captain went around checking on the men, making sure they were ready for what lay ahead. The sounds of machines grinding outside were new; they had not heard this the previous day. The rest of the sounds were familiar, groans and growls, screams and grizzly snarls.

The khaki uniforms meant the soldiers did not stand out as much as they would have done if they had been wearing the red tunics. Leaving the musty shed, they lined up outside; the summer sun was not as strong now as the autumn closed in. The Engineers with their allies lined up in a proud, smart line. The captain of the drone guards came out to them.

"So, this is what is left of the great British Empire army?" He spoke good English. Pausing to flick some dirt off his left boot, he continued, "You do realise your country, what is left of it, is crumbling as we speak." He had a smug smile on his face. "I always found the British so arrogant with their Empire, as if it was they who invented everything." He stopped and looked at Captain Hayward.

"Now, you can see how quickly things can turn around in life." He was smiling to himself. "You will probably die here, in our leader's capital. Fitting, don't you think?"

"You will never be free in Nazar's world, Captain." Charles spoke to him directly.

"What do you Victorians know about being free; you have thousands of people living in poverty and a social class system that failed." The officer was angry with Charles's comments.

"You seem as if you need to be educated in the world, how can you let this madness guide you?" said Charles.

"I have studied in Europe, and I've been to London. I saw the problems; just because we can now see real monsters in the world, does not mean they weren't already there."

Charles sighed. "Will you raise a family into this? What hope do you have for your children?"

The captain flicked out his right hand; this made the drone guard start to come forward. Behind them, several wagons were ordered to come closer.

"There is a new world order coming; we will all have to adapt or die." He then began to walk away, stopping for one final remark. "Enjoy moving the logs today, and tonight you'll meet the high priest."

Charles and the soldiers were rounded up and put in the back of the wagons. They kept their calm as they sat on the small, wooden slat seats. All of them looked around at the busy landscape. The Ural Mountains towered over everything in the background, but it was more the size of the camp which seemed to shock most. The sheds rolled into the distance, and across from them were large, industrial-size buildings with smoke pouring out the chimneys. It looked like Nazar had set up factories and was in the process of using his slave army to supply more equipment and weapons.

Dominating this backdrop was the fort and inside that was the monastery.

Captain Hayward looked around at the anxious faces of his men. They were also taking in being so close to the enemy, and yet still in control, as long as Corporal Heinz and the two Russian soldiers were not found out.

The wagons began to move through the camp, the wheels jumping awkwardly with each rock or uneven part on the road, and as it slowly trundled along, Charles looked at the bodies of men and women lying at the side of the road. Some were being fed on by dogs, others by flesh-eaters on chains. He couldn't really understand the brutality or the sheer waste of human life by these monsters, but he had met Nazar face to face and looked into his dark eyes. This was a leader who would stop at nothing to gain control of the world. His armies were now made up of so many different beasts, it was as if the devil himself walked this very earth. Many soldiers had spoken of his armies being unstoppable and how the war was already lost. In a way, they were right – Europe's most modern army could not hold back what Nazar had, and with the flesh-eaters always able to add to their legions, it became an even greater task.

Thirty minutes passed and they were still within the camp walls; they now understood the scale of this fortress and the amount of people trapped here. The gates came into sight, and behind them they could see the treetops. They had been told their day would be spent logging and then in the evening they would meet the high priest. Before they could leave, a procession of prisoners was marched past. They all looked completely worn out and tired. Hardly any of them managed to even look up at the wagons, as if it was now too much of a waste of energy, which should be saved for work. Once they had passed out of the gate, the wagons followed.

While passing by the gates, they saw that two men had been strapped against two crossed stakes; they had been flayed and were barely alive. The sight was shocking for all to see and sent out a clear message – if you try to escape, you will be punished. The British soldiers shook their heads in disbelief at what they had seen.

The work being carried out in the woods was back-breaking. Using axes, they were expected to clear a marked area of woodland or be disciplined for not doing so. Sergeant Butcher was a burly man; he had spent years working on farms before joining the army. He took to this task like a possessed soul. Every one of his swings with the axe set the standard for the other soldiers there. Charles looked at him in awe; he was a solid character and in this uncertain time he was glad he was with him. Doctor Brown was still with Benedict; he had kept his head down and worked with the men. Private Alexander Chamberlin was always surveying the typography of the land. He had survived longer than most in hostile territory and was a great asset to have in this environment.

The drone guards drank beer and watched on. Some walked around shouting orders, but as a whole, they were more interested in relaxing. The Engineers were efficient and finished their selected area in good time. The drones did not seem to care at this point, and allowed them to cook a meal over a log fire. The food that had been supplied was old vegetables; some of it had small creatures crawling around in it. The cook did the best he could picking out what was edible. Then he brought out some seasoning, which he had concealed inside his tunic. Charles smiled at his slyness and was grateful for it. The soup was then left to stew for a while.

The soldiers continued to load the wagons, which had been brought up to them, then after an hour or so the cook called them in. Whilst the soup was not the best they had ever had, it certainly satisfied them. The general feeling was of gratitude to him for making something out of nothing. They had barely finished eating when the orders were barked for them to return to the camp, and as they climbed back into the wagons, hundreds of drone soldiers marched past. They were followed by long limbs, which had been tied together and led by a razor tooth. This beast was ridden by a destroyer drone; he smirked at the defeated soldiers. At the end of this procession was drone cavalry; their horses were black and had polished tacking, with pristine saddles. Sergeant Butcher leaned over to Captain Hayward and whispered on whether this could be the "house guard". The captain slowly nodded.

The route back was slow; they had to stop for herds of sheep and cattle being moved around. This was why the flesh-eaters were chained up. Captain Holfer had discussed before how he could not understand how Nazar would stop this army of dead killing everything in its path. Most of the drones were infected, but there were signs of others not being given the illness, meaning they too might be susceptible to being attacked by the flesh-eaters. It was a question he pondered to himself; he could not really understand the logic to it. Charles had pointed out that maybe Nazar would not care once he ruled over it all.

When they arrived back at their sheds, six giants were standing there. The one that had had a run-in with Captain Hayward came forward.

"Wash now and get ready to meet the high priest." His voice bellowed out from his powerful lungs. Several cold troughs of water awaited the weary British soldiers to wash in.

The soldiers were allowed a small piece of soap each and were constantly watched by the giants. Whilst this unfolded, a unit of around thirty destroyer drones joined them. Charles looked at Corporal Heinz, Sergeant Butcher and Captain Holfer. It was a concerned look; this whole camp was a hornet's nest and it was hard to visualise how they would accomplish their mission with so many enemy soldiers and beasts here.

After washing, they were then ordered to wash their clothes in preparation for meeting the high priest. Standing wet and tired, the next order was to put them to dry in a heating shed. This had four burning fires and was used in the winter to dry the drone soldiers' uniforms. The drone officer who had spoken to Captain Hayward the previous day was there.

"Do not get used to having clean uniforms, this is the first and last time for that." He said this in an assured way. "Soon you will wish you never ended up here at Vorkuta."
Charles looked at him, but said nothing. He knew he was pushing for a response.

Whilst the men waited, Corporal Heinz brought them pelts to cover them; the officer asked why he had helped them. Corporal Heinz responded saying he thought it was better that they were able to work a while, before becoming ill and being useless for Nazar's Empire. The officer was not totally convinced, but for now, he let it be.

They waited an hour or so; the uniforms had not fully dried, but they felt cleaner after a day's hard work. The sun slowly sank behind the mountains, and as it began to drop, the lanterns and torches were lit. The camp burst into a strange world of flickering light.

A priest arrived on horseback; he had the hood on his cloak over his face and sword attached to his back.

"The high priest will now see our enemy soldiers."

The drone officer mounted his horse and got the British soldiers to march behind him. They were flanked by destroyer drones riding horses and two giants riding on what the British had nicknamed "Lagorians". It was a name from one of the soldier's childhood past. An oversized dog lived close to his cottage on a farm; this beast always scared the soldier when he was a child, and his sister had nicknamed it a Lagorian beast. She had come across this name from their grandfather telling them fairy tales, about a giant monster who lived in a forest and ate naughty children.

As the soldiers marched, these giant creatures looked over at them, occasionally snarling or showing their teeth. Further back behind the group were thirty drone soldiers. Corporal Heinz walked with the two Russians, anxious and wanting to be up with Captain Hayward and his men.

The road started to rise as they walked towards the fort on the hill. The monastery was situated in the fort at the back. It was built into the hill. Captain Hayward spoke briefly to Sergeant Butcher and Captain Holfer; he asked them to look for anything that could help them later on in the evening. The large, wooden doors began to come into sight. "Stay calm, men, we will soon be entering the enemy headquarters."

As they came to the gate, four large cauldrons sat burning oil on each side of it. They lit up the front of the entrance, revealing gargoyles etched into the wooden planks. It was a chilling sight; an air of menace surrounded them. Being so much higher up, they could see over the whole camp; it stretched for miles, consisting of buildings and sheds. The lanterns and torches gave an idea of the sheer scale of the place.

The officer dismounted from his horse and walked towards the entrance. There next to the right-hand side of the gate was a large rope; he gripped his hands tightly around it, and pulled down hard.

A dark, dull tone rang out.

A small window opened and eyes peered out of it. Nothing was said.

Then a creaking, scraping sound came from the entrance – the two large, wooden doors sprung into life and started to open. The drone officer just stood there in silence.

Once the doors were fully open, six destroyer drones marched out. A priest followed them out; he was very tall and gangly. Charles thought it could have almost been a long limb, but he was human. His robes swept along the floor and he spoke quietly to the drone officer. After that, he moved along to the British prisoners, and he stared at each man. His eyes were larger than normal; they resembled fish eyes; his teeth were yellow and sharp.

He stopped by Captain Hayward.

"Ummmm, I recognise you." He raised his thin arms and then his long, boney fingers touched the captain's chin, turning it to get a better look.

"Yes, oh yes." He stood inches away from his face. Charles could feel his breath on his neck.

"Do I know you, Priest?" Charles asked in a soft tone.

The priest laughed a little to himself. "Maybe, maybe not." He paused. "I'm not the high priest, so don't get too excited."

He then went on to explain how he had seen the captain around the fort in the Carpathian Mountains; he was watching them before his wolves attacked. It was making him smile more as he started to move around Charles. "You fought hard over those days; it was an indication of what was to come in Europe." He now stood in front of Captain Hayward, this time a metre or so away. "But the outcome was the same – you lost."

His arrogant manner was picked up by everyone standing there. Captain Holfer was thinking something else as well. He wondered in the back of his mind if they somehow made long limbs out of this priest? It sent a shiver down his spine; he couldn't understand the science behind it, but he thought something was very familiar.

After the priest had postured for five minutes, he waved everyone forward.

The first thing to hit the soldiers as they moved inside the courtyard was the strong smell. The air was pungent; one of them whispered it smelt like lead. The next thing to hit them was the soft whimpering. It was hard to locate where it was coming from; the courtyard was expansive, with stables and other buildings. This sound seemed to creep out of every dark corner, or from behind every stack of hay.

Tied to several posts near the gate were long limbs; they did not seem to stir when the British were marched past. Their heads just followed the men as they moved; their body language was of a beast that had been beaten to obey. Everything about the fort felt oppressive, the windows were shaped in a certain way like eyes staring at you. There were crosses which had been turned upside down, and rotting corpses hanging in metal cages.

The destroyer drones now accompanied the soldiers on either side as they were marched through the fort. Captain Hayward knew his twenty men had to have a large slice of luck to get through this mission in one piece.

The gangly priest ordered them to stop. Directly in front of them was another gate; this time it had thick, iron portcullis blocking their path. They stood there and waited, then one of the giants walked forward to the wall at the side of the portcullis. He reached up, and built into the wall there was a small bell. He pulled on the rope dangling from the bottom of it. It was a soft sound, but it was enough to get the gate moving up. Charles shook his head, as if to ask himself, *"How are we going to get into the monastery tonight?"* It was so secure. As they moved forward, he looked around, searching for something which could help them later.

The second courtyard was smaller; it had buildings around it, possibly barracks. The other main difference was the large, stone tower at the back of the fort. Behind this, higher up on the hill, was the monastery. It was impressively lit up; torches burnt from its walls and light shone out of glass windows from a centrepiece tower.

Two cannons sat outside the stone tower in the second courtyard. Next to these were two giants. Both of them were wearing armour and carrying swords that appeared "larger than life". Charles could see the anguish on the faces of his men. Even Sergeant Butcher looked concerned at what may lie ahead.

The priest took the group to the stone tower; he then told the giants to wait there whilst they entered the monastery. The only soldiers that were allowed to follow with them were the officer and the destroyer drones. Moving through the portcullis, he led them into a tunnel; it went on for 20 metres or more. At the other end was another raised portcullis. Torchlight lit up stone steps leading up to the monastery, and sitting at the side of the steps were two chained razor tooths. Again, they were subdued; Private Green, who was at the back of the group, saw a possible reason.

Bloody limbs were scattered at their paws, and other bones lay strewn around. He hoped they would not suffer the same fate. "Do not try anything stupid as we enter the monastery," the gangly priest muttered. "We have ways of making you die here that you would have never dreamed possible," he said, as they were led up the steps.

The steps were fairly steep, and took time to climb; at the top there was a plateau, which bordered the fortified monastery. The doors into the monastery were guarded by two massive wolves. Sergeant Butcher remarked to Captain Hayward that this place was very well protected. The gangly priest looked around as he heard them talk. The wolves growled as they moved through two open wooden gates.

Inside, lit torches were fixed to metal poles around the yard. It was no longer a place for worshipping a holy god. There were markings on the stone pillars which helped to hold up the various building corners. No crosses hung, just the flags of Nazar and other demon-worship items.

The men did not stop there long; they were ushered into a large banquet hall. The tables had been moved to the back and sides of the room. At the front stood two large chairs and two small ones. There was a priest sitting on a large chair, the light obscuring his face. Four destroyer drones pushed them into the centre of the room. A large chandelier hung over the top of them, with what seemed like thousands of candles burning away on it. All around, eyes watched them, and flashes of teeth were revealed as mouths opened and shut.

Then there was total silence.

The British soldiers stood there waiting for someone to speak.

"So, I meet the enemies of my king?" The figure on the large chair came forward and out of the shadows. He walked over to the British soldiers. He was not as tall as the other priests, he was old and did not have the strange discolouration in his eyes like most of the others had. He moved around them slowly, as if checking suitability for work, or something worse.

"Who is leading this unfortunate party of rebels?"

"I am, my name is Captain Hayward." He then took a step forward.

The old priest slowly shuffled his way over to the captain like a flesh-eater moving in on his prey.

"Of course you are, *Captain*."

Captain Hayward did not know what the old man was insinuating by saying "Captain" in that way, but he stayed calm. He felt the breath of the priest against his face, before hearing him say, "I'm sorry Nazar is not here to welcome you." The Priest moved back a bit.

"I believe you wanted to find the home of our king?" He smiled, exposing his yellow teeth. "Well, here you are!"

He started to walk back to the chair. He then spoke in Russian to the gangly priest, telling him to pick three men. This priest's eyes lit up; he waltzed over to the group and looked at the men, but before he could even pick Captain Hayward, the old man shouted out, "Not the Captain."

First to be picked was a young private; he was tall and strong, and the soldier was told to walk over to the old man. The soldier looked back at Captain Hayward. The gangly priest then passed several more soldiers until he stopped at Benedict. "You do not look like a British soldier," he said, tapping him on the shoulder and telling him to join the other man by the chair. The gangly priest finished by standing next to Sergeant Butcher and Private Green. A finger was waving in the air between the two, but was stopped as the sergeant moved himself forward.

"Brave, but foolish. Join the others."

Captain Hayward moved towards the old man. Four destroyer drones burst forward and surrounded the captain.

"Why have you separated my men? There is a code of conduct with prisoners of war."

A ripple of laughter broke around the hall.

"In your world, yes, but that is coming to an end." Sweeping his hair back, the old man sat back. "They will now have to fight in the pit for their very lives."

Charles offered to fight instead of them, and said that only he should pay for them being here. This was greeted with mocking laughter. The priests started to come out of the shadows; they were of all different shapes and sizes. Some of the female priests were pretty and elegant, while others were disfigured and unsightly. Standing next to a particularly attractive female priest were two young boys. Charles saw them standing close to her, he guessed at them being around Arthur's age. His eyes were quickly drawn back to his men.

Sergeant Butcher and the other two were led through to another hall. Charles tried to resist but was held firmly by the four destroyer drones. "You can see for yourself, Captain, be patient."

"The rules are simple; if any of your men survive, you will not be flayed until tomorrow, if they fail, you will all be flayed tonight." He laughed, before continuing, "Maybe some of you will be eaten alive."

Charles and his men were led through to the second room. It smelt different to the main hall, rotten and dank. The torches were bigger and lit the room more brightly. In the centre was a large pit. Charles thought instantly of an illegal dog-fighting pit he had once witnessed in the East End. It was not somewhere he frequented, but he had been shown it by an old soldier who knew the area well. It was not something he enjoyed or wanted to see again.

He feared the worst as he looked down into the darkness of the pit. The soil underneath was bloodstained.

As the British soldiers lined up on one side and the priests on the other, servants lit the oil bowls below; this illuminated the fighting pit. Wooden stakes stopped anyone from climbing out, and people climbing in. Sergeant Butcher and the other two soldiers were led away. They soon appeared down below, carrying a sword or spear. The pit itself was a fair size and had three iron gates. It was not long before they started to rise. First to come out was a destroyer drone; he was around 6ft 6in, built like an ox and carrying an axe and shield. The second gate unleashed six flesh-eaters, and the third a long limb.

They did not all come at the three British soldiers at first; they waited as if controlled by the priests above.

Sergeant Butcher told the soldier and Benedict to stay calm and fight hard. He said this was not just for their own lives, but for the comrades above.

The gangly priest looked at Captain Hayward and smiled, he then looked at the high priest, who nodded.

"Let the battle commence!" shouted the gangly priest.

It was like a fuse being lit; the beasts came at them with death in their eyes. The young soldier took on the long limb; he had a spear and lunged at it, pushing it back. Benedict started swinging his sword at the flesh-eaters; he chopped a rotting female flesh-eater's arm off as she came at him. Behind her were several men; some looked like farm workers, while others were in various stages of decay and hard to distinguish.

Sergeant Butcher was going head to head with the destroyer drone; the drone let out a snarl and laughed at the sergeant.

"You're no match for me."

Sergeant Butcher said nothing, just tightened his grip on his axe and moved forward. The cheers and shouts of approval started to ring out from above. The British soldiers kept calm at first and looked at the action unfolding below. The priests were clearly excited about this event, and behaved in a manner of a frenzied crowd vying for blood.

Captain Hayward could not contain his anguish for his men in the pit and screamed out his support for them. This of course then opened the floodgates for his men to do the same. The priests looked surprised by this sudden outburst. Some even looked a little concerned by the emotion shown.

The high priest had already ordered for the drone soldiers to be doubled in the monastery. He did not want the British trying anything whilst the fight took place below. The tall, blond soldier was fighting well with the long limb, pushing it back towards its gate. He did not see a flesh-eater had broken off from attacking Benedict and was making a move for him. The flesh-eater woman with one arm sank her teeth into his tunic, her once blonde hair long and lifeless. Fortunately, her bite did not pierce his skin; the soldier was startled by this attack and swung around, and as this happened, the long limb lashed at his leg and sank its claws into his skin.

The flesh-eater was knocked off by the soldier, but he was dragged towards the long limb's gate. Lifting itself up, the flesh-eater woman with one arm started to stagger towards him. Benedict stopped her in her tracks, taking a leg and the other arm in one downwards swoop. He then tried to get to the soldier, but the other flesh-eaters grabbed him and the sword.

Sergeant Butcher could see what was unfolding to the side of him; he began to move over to help his fellow soldiers, but could see the beast in front of him waiting for his chance. It came. The destroyer drone saw that the sergeant was preoccupied enough to strike him; using his shield, he pushed forward, smashing him into the side of the pit wall. The sheer power and size of his opponent meant it knocked the wind out of the sergeant, who dropped down. Captain Hayward braced himself ready to jump down, but found that he had four swords aimed at his body and throat.

Sergeant Butcher felt himself being lifted off the floor and pinned against the wall. The high priest and the gangly priest were ecstatic; they were snorting and asking for wine. All around, the priests were laughing and celebrating as they felt the end was near.

The destroyer drone only made one mistake in his fight, and that was to look up at the high priest. In that short moment of taking his eyes off Sergeant Butcher, he was soon stumbling back. His nose broken and eyes blurry, the sergeant had headbutted him hard in the face and then pushed him back. In a flash, he picked up his axe and swung it down right between the drone's eyes, splitting his head in two. He did not stop there; soon his axe was cutting through the flesh-eaters on Benedict. The young lad had done well, and was still not bitten. Both of them now turned their attentions to the long limb, which had rolled the soldier over and was in the process of lowering its giant jaws onto his head.

A whoosh of air followed and then a thud. The long limb's body was still standing there, but its head was now at the sergeant's feet. The British soldiers erupted in euphoria and wild cheers and cries rung out.

The silence on the other side was deafening. The high priest was almost foaming at the mouth, his fists clenched.

"Do we have your word?" Captain Hayward wanted to act on the situation.

"My word, haaa!" He started to walk over to the captain.

"I can have you all executed now, or flayed or eaten alive!" Clearly angry, Charles did nothing to push him further.

"You can, but before I die, honour me with how Nazar and the priests became so powerful." Charles put the question to him as he stood ever closer.

"What does it matter to you now? Your world is finished and soon you will all be dead." The old man looked around, as if pondering an order.

"Because I'm interested to see what defeated us." Charles knew speaking in negative terms would spark some interest. "Finally, you admit you're beaten." He paused, before continuing, "Guards, take them back to the shed, the captain stays with me." He turned to the other priests. "They will be flayed alive tomorrow and then eaten." This brought a roar from the crowd and a nasty buzz of excitement.

Captain Hayward nodded to Captain Holfer; the Austrian could sense he was up to something. Sergeant Butcher, Benedict and the soldier were returned to their group. They all needed help being escorted down to the shed, leaving Captain Hayward alone with the gangly priest and the high priest.

"You may have won this battle, but you will lose the war," said the old priest.

He continued, "As you will die a horrible death tomorrow, Captain Hayward, I have something to show you."

He then raised his arm in the direction they should go. "Follow me," he said, and before Captain Hayward could even let his mind question this, he continued, "If you're thinking of trying to kill me and my fellow priest, think again." They were then joined by four guards. As they left the side of the pit, the dead bodies were being dragged out to be burnt.

The old priest took them down a side corridor; Charles frantically tried to remember everything and anything that could be useful should the old man be taking him to where he thought he would be going. Pushing through doors and continuing along this corridor was taking a lifetime. They finally came to a large door; the grain of the wood looked like oak. "The handle's made out of gold," chirped the old priest. He added as they pushed it open that it was made out of English oak, laughing as he did so. "The British Empire, we'll have to change a few names, eh?" Again, he sniggered to himself.

Charles's eyes closed momentarily as a roaring fire greeted them as they came into the room. He appreciated the heat; after spending time in the cold shed, it meant his body craved the warmth of a fire.

"Sit down, Captain!" the old man said abruptly.

The gangly priest poured them all a glass of whisky. The destroyer drones looked on, envious of the alcohol being consumed. Charles's first sip made him cough; his throat was dry and the harshness of this single malt reacted with it briefly. He soon knocked back the glass.

"Why have us killed when we can work as slaves for you?" Charles asked, as he was having his glass refilled.

"We have many slaves, and keeping soldiers alive is always dangerous," he replied, pausing while he took a swig of whisky, allowing the liquid to slosh around his yellow teeth in his mouth. "You and your men know how to fight." He took another swig, "The message is simple – those that defy us, die." The old priest slammed the glass onto the table in front of him.

"I will grant a condemned man a chance to see true power." He beckoned him over to a small chair and cabinet. He then pressed down hard on the floorboards by the chair. A wall to the side of the cabinet began to open; the gangly priest almost started to sway side to side, and the destroyer drones also started to twitch. Once it had opened fully, the old priest led them in. The corridor was narrow and dark; the torches that lit it were spread out. Charles felt uneasy in this darkness, but knew he needed to be shown what lay beneath their power.

Eventually, they came to a staircase; it was leading down into more darkness. The old priest was nimble considering he looked well into his seventies. Each step was chosen carefully, each foothold by Captain Hayward had purpose. If they had wanted to kill him, he thought, they could have done it at any time. He could not let his mind entertain the idea of being flayed alive.

Time passed slowly, and when they came to the bottom of the steps, Captain Hayward breathed out slowly.

"So much for being a fighting-fit soldier, Captain," the old man said, laughing, and took something from the wall. He walked over to a burning torch which lit the area around them; he then held what looked like a piece of wood with rags wrapped around it. They soon caught fire as the smell of burning oil filled Charles's nostrils. To the side of them was a track; he started to walk down to the left, and was instantly shouted at.

"That way goes to the lower courtyard!" The old priest did not hang around and turned and led them along the track. The tunnel was wide and structured. "Keep close, we do not want to surprise Colossus, he sleeps here in the evening."

They walked for another twenty minutes until they came to a large chamber. Sitting in the corner was a giant. He sat stirring a pot of steaming soup; when he saw the old priest coming, he got to his feet and lowered his head.

"My lord," he said in a deep, baritone voice.

His eyes then saw Captain Hayward's.

"I know you, you're the British officer I knocked off his horse." He smiled when he said this. The destroyer drones and gangly priest looked at the captain, as if a bully was playing up to his peer group.

"You did, Colossus," Charles replied, keeping a straight face.

The giant didn't like the fact he had said his name, he looked upset and angry.

"Calm down," said the old priest, "His time is coming to an end, he will be executed tomorrow." This brought a rueful smile back on to the giant's face.

"Until then, I am going to show him something, stand aside." The old priest gestured his hand as if to sweep him aside. Colossus stood still and did not move.

"Our king Nazar stated the enemy must never be allowed down there." He looked over to the carriage that was attached to metal chain pulleys and on a rail track that led into the darkness.
The old priest looked this oversized man in front of him up and down, and then said, "Do not question me again, Colossus, or you will be flayed with the captain tomorrow."

Colossus looked at the captain, who did nothing to antagonise the situation further; he then begrudgingly moved his giant frame to the side, letting the priest and the drones take Captain Hayward into the carriage. The mechanics of the pulley system were simple, one carriage would be released at the top or bottom, thus pulling one down and one up. The carriage itself could hold maybe thirty to forty people. It had oil lanterns which were lit. As the holding brake was released, the contraption kicked into action. The screeching sound was unsettling and the clunking of chains did not help his nerves. Captain Hayward looked at the sides of the tunnel as they moved downwards. The rock changed in colour the deeper they went; some areas were wet from water seeping through, while others were dry and rough.

He had visited a mine in Wales when he was a young man, but he wasn't too fond of the close-quarter conditions the miners had to work in. The pits were a dangerous place and he marvelled at the men who worked in them.

The conversation was sparse; the drones kept an eye on the captain and the priest seemed to allow himself to go into a trance. The gangly priest kept his eyes on the captain. Charles was not sure of how long they were in the carriage, but he reckoned on fifteen minutes or more. When they arrived at the bottom, more lanterns were burning; they lit up this chamber well. The first thing Charles realised was the size of the chamber; it was so much bigger than he thought it would be. They did not waste time and led him out. There were several corridors going off in different directions, but the old priest led them down the one straight in front of them.

They passed four more chambers of various sizes until they came to an opening, possibly the biggest of them all.

There, directly in front of Charles, was a huge rock. It wasn't like anything he'd seen before, it was a roundish shape, but the edges were rough. The surface of the rock looked to be steaming, and had many colours covering its outer exterior. The priests looked on like proud fathers; they could see the captain was awestruck.

"It's a special sight, isn't it, Captain?" The old priest shuffled closer to it. He cupped his hand and scraped off something which looked like a fungi that was growing on the surface of the rock. "Come closer and have a look."

Captain Hayward moved slowly forward; he did not trust his captors. The fungi were moving in the old priest's hand. It was as if the organisms were alive.

"So, this rock is behind your rise to power?" Charles was asked, still staring at the rock.

"Yes and no. It helped us work over hundreds of years on using its' substances to our advantage." He paused. "The creatures you now see walking this world are not from your god, they're from ours."

"What happens when you can no longer control the creatures?" Charles asked, taking a step back from the rock.

"Ha! That will never happen, and if it did, that would be our master's choice." The priest started to turn around and walk away from the rock.

"You mean the devil will? How can you go from following a god who stands for good, to one that knows only evil?" Charles was softly spoken as he asked this.

"Some things turn out that way, Captain Hayward." He clapped his hands together tightly. "The show is over; all that is left now is for you to be executed tomorrow." He smiled to the gangly priest as he said this.

Captain Hayward turned around and walked towards them. He kept a stony face. "You will fail in the end."

The priests laughed at him. "Take him back to the shed." As the captain was led back into the carriage to go back up, the gangly priest stood in front of him. "I'll enjoy watching you die tomorrow, Captain." The priests decided to stay a little longer with the rock.

Each side of the captain sat a destroyer drone; they said nothing to him as they all sat quietly rising back to the surface. When they arrived, Colossus was sleeping, and they walked past him softly. He stirred briefly, but was spoken to in Russian by a drone and fell back to sleep. Captain Hayward was already planning now; he noted they would have to get past Colossus, but he had also picked up on some other useful things.

When they arrived back at the shed, the soldiers were resting. Private Chamberlin came forward first. "Good to see you back, Captain."

"Good to be back, Private, we have work to do."

Chapter 41

Captain Hayward was joined by Corporal Heinz. He was still dressed as a drone and was playing the part. They spoke quickly about him coming back to them in an hour or so and that they would then go over his plan. In the meantime, he was asked to prepare the wagons with explosives and weapons, and also to find food and hay to take into the monastery.

Captain Hayward spoke to the officers first, giving a full description of what he had seen and his ideas on how they could get to the rock. When Corporal Heinz returned, he gathered the other soldiers and began to go over his plan. The officers were stationed as lookouts. The men listened intensely; Doctor Brown asked about Colossus and how they would get past him. Charles said he would confront the giant but would need help from Sergeant Butcher and Captain Holfer on taking him down. A soft whistle broke the meeting, everyone crouched down.

Loud voices could be heard outside; they were speaking Russian and their words sounded slurry.

"Drone soldiers," was the call that floated around. They crouched silently; no one could move a muscle. If they were found out now, all of them would be chained for the evening, meaning the flaying alive punishment would come true. The voices hung in the air for several more minutes before beginning to fade.

Corporal Heinz added that they must leave soon as he had overheard the destroyer drones would be taking over guarding the prisoners throughout the night. They had a small window now to move. The briefing was completed and the Engineers readied themselves. The wagons were brought around the back; fate was shining on them as most of the drone soldiers were still drinking at a barn, which had been converted into a beer venue. The priests had allowed them to unwind, as they wanted to keep their army happy. Slave women were also brought there for the soldiers; it was a desperate environment for them.

Private Alexander Chamberlin would be in the end wagon with a sharpshooter rifle. Benedict was told to keep with Doctor Brown. The British were in their khaki uniforms, and they were given their revolvers and rifles. Swords were also strapped over their backs. The general feeling was, if they were found out, they could at least die fighting, instead of being flayed alive for the enjoyment of the priests.

The blankets on the floor of the prison shed had been made to appear as if they were soldiers sleeping. No one knew how long this would give them, but the captain hoped it would be enough time.

The three wagons set off at a slow pace. They trundled along, passing rowdy drone guards and sleeping ones. Chained long limbs stirred a little as they passed, as if sensing something was not quite right with the wagons. They swept through the camp, with the soldiers holding on to the explosives tightly. If they were to get into a gun battle, it would not take much to send the three wagons into the heavens, along with all the British soldiers.

Soon they were climbing the hill towards the fort and monastery, and the camp started to look smaller behind them. Its size was illuminated by all the torches burning away. The wagons jumped on the odd stone in the track, but settled down as they approached the fort entrance.

"Halt, who goes there?" was the cry in Russian to Corporal Heinz; he replied and said that they had food and supplies for tomorrow's execution. This was a bluff; if one of the priests was around, it could easily be questioned and jeopardise the whole mission.

A clunking sound could be heard from the men crouching in the wagon, then there was the sound of a door being shook, indicating it was shut. Corporal Heinz waited with baited breath.

A short, bald drone soldier came out. He was not wearing his tunic and looked half asleep.

"It's two o'clock in the bloody morning, what do you want?" The drone soldier pulled up his trousers and scratched his head. Corporal Heinz was calm and said there was to be a large party tomorrow to celebrate the execution of the British prisoners. The guard looked half-interested, but asked why would they bring up the food now?

"Do you want to wake the high priest and ask him …? Well, do you? He will have you flayed with them." Corporal Heinz's forceful approach worked; the soldier shook his head as he thought about being slowly cut open.

"Ride with me so I don't have to go through this mess at every gate." The corporal gambled on this, but knew it could be decisive.

The drone guard opened the gates and waved the wagons in. He then shut the gates behind them; another drone came out of a turret to the side of the gate. He looked as though he had been sleeping. The short drone barked an order at him and then mounted the wagon to sit next to Corporal Heinz. They pushed on to the next courtyard. Each gate was met with trepidation; the sense of anxiety for the soldiers hiding in the wagon was huge. They could hear the soldiers speaking Russian, but the noises around the fort were relatively quiet.

The courtyard with the gate which had steps leading to the monastery was guarded by destroyer drones. Corporal Heinz said they would unload here and take the supply rail track to the monastery. The short, bald drone climbed down from the wagon; he added that he would get the keys to the doors for the supply track but told them to be quick, as they were ruining his sleep.

Captain Hayward was lying in the back of Corporal Heinz's wagon and listening to them speak.

"Bring the wagons to the right-hand side of the courtyard," Charles said, hoping he had guessed right where the rail track would be.

The guard came back and went to the right-hand side of the courtyard and moved into the darkness. He began fiddling with the keys, and soon two large doors opened; behind them several lanterns burned away. The light revealed the track and small coal-like trucks behind them.

"Make sure you lock those bloody gates or we'll all swing, and be quick," he said, and then left.

Charles and the other British soldiers had put mud on their faces and hands. This would help them be less visible to the enemy. The wagons were manoeuvred so that the back of each wagon pointed towards the stone walls. The two Russian soldiers kept an eye out whilst the British soldiers climbed out.

The plan was to locate the supply trucks on the rail track and load them as quickly as possible. Captain Hayward helped carry the boxes, which were loaded with explosives. One of the Engineers stumbled a little; he fell onto one knee, but kept the box from slamming into the ground. He puffed out his cheeks, got back up and continued.

Captain Hayward was more concerned about the noise of the boxes breaking on the ground rather than it exploding. Once all of the boxes were unloaded, he looked to his men. This was the signal for them to shut the wooden doors and continue to the rock that was buried deep in the darkness.

The wagons were left there; they did not know if they would be able to use them to escape out of the monastery and fort.

The torches flickered as the men moved past them. All of the soldiers pushed hard to get the supply trucks moving along on the tracks. Sergeant Butcher was bringing up the rear with Private Chamberlin and Private Green. The tunnel was a fair size and each fork in the track was treated with suspicion.

They began to see a larger chamber; Captain Hayward walked in front of his men, sensing this could be where Colossus guarded the carriage which led to the rock.

He raised his open hand, making the supply tracks come to a graceful stop. Colossus was not to be seen.

The decision was to try and get through this chamber and into the carriage or try to locate Colossus. Captain Holfer asked what they should do; Captain Hayward said they should leave the trucks in the semi-darkness and carry the boxes to the carriage.

Four of the soldiers led by Private Chamberlin took their rifles off their shoulders and took up defensive positions. Again, time was of the essence and they moved the explosives at a rapid rate, many sensing they were closing in on their goal. It took maybe five minutes to move them all. Once this was complete, they released the lever to allow the carriage to plunge them deep into the mountain.

The conversation was limited as they travelled down. It was as if no one wanted to jinx their mission so far. Charles spoke briefly to the officers, informing them that they would have to pass through several chambers before coming to the rock itself. When they arrived at the bottom, it was silent; again, a small unit was used as cover, and the rest of the men would have to cart the explosives over to the rock itself. They covered the ground well, but all of them stopped when they finally arrived at the rock. Its sheer presence had them standing with their mouths agape. The torches lit the rock well enough for them to see the fungi moving.

"Do not touch the rock, men. We do not know if it is poisonous to us or not." Captain Hayward was firm with this command.

The division of labour was then split into three teams; one to guard them, one to fetch the remaining explosives, and one to start laying the charges. There were other tunnels leading off from the rock, but Captain Hayward had no idea where they went. He had flashbacks to when they were escaping from Europe and the flesh-eaters they faced in the underground tunnels there. It was not the time to get spooked; they had to use this opportunity quickly or possibly regret it forever.

Each man set about their tasks in earnest. The noise of them moving backwards and forwards was quite loud. The priests had dug around the rock so that they could harvest the fungi which grew on it. This large object was only supported by the bottom of where it sat. Captain Hayward studied the rock with Sergeant Butcher, they could see cracks in the surface of the rock and openings which they could exploit. Charles spoke to Sergeant Butcher about getting the men to carefully place as much explosives as they could in these openings. They had gloves with them; Charles told him they were under strict instructions that should they get any of the fungi on the gloves, they must remove them immediately.

After he had spoken to the sergeant, Charles and the men went to work. Captain Hayward relayed the same message to Captain Holfer and Corporal Heinz. The fuses they had had a time lapse of around fifteen minutes; they could make them shorter or longer. He had to calculate the journey time up from the chambers below to the monastery cellars.

Charles checked his watch as the last of the explosives they had earmarked for the rock reached them. They could now be packed all over this strange object. Some of the gloves had been thrown to the base of the rock, with signs of fungi on them.

Captain Hayward did not know whether they could destroy it, but they would try at least to stop its usage for a while. The other explosives were being put in and around the tunnel and chambers leading to this power source.

Charles had explosives put at the bottom of the carriage entrance and they planned to attach the fuses on their trip back up. It was all going to be about the timing.

Fifteen minutes passed and the soldiers were finishing up. Private Chamberlin heard a soft groan and then a sound of something being dragged. He did not need to hear more. He called over to a soldier next to him, "Tell the captain we have flesh-eaters coming our way."

As soon as he had said those words, the first emerged out of one of the tunnels leading to the rock. He couldn't fully make out the face, as half of it was hanging off, but it seemed to pick up speed when it saw him. Its desire for flesh made it push on as fast as it could. Private Alexander Chamberlin was ready; he had attached his bayonet and let the flesh-eater come straight for him, then in one swift motion rammed the bayonet through its head. There was a ripping, gurgling sound; he then withdrew the blade quickly. As he did so, the creature fell forward to the cave floor below.

This was just the start of a wave of flesh-eaters now streaming in from the tunnels in front of them.

Captain Hayward ordered the fuses to be lit. He could not be sure if the priests knew they were down there and had started the flesh-eater attack, or whether these creatures were just wandering around in the darkness searching for their next meal.

The soldiers holding off the horde were just using bayonets, but they needed to take advantage of the Lee-Metford magazine, giving them the chance to fire quickly without the need to re-load straight away.

The first gunshot echoed down there, it was a huge *"Boom!"* killing a flesh-eater by taking its head clean off and knocking two down behind it.

This was the trigger for the soldiers to start firing; some withdrew their swords and waded in, slashing and cutting at what they could. Arms and heads began to roll, and blood spurted out of served limbs as the blades cut through flesh and bone.

"Fall back to the carriage!" Captain Hayward shouted out the order.

The numbers of flesh-eaters were swelling; their eyes shone as they passed the burning torches, giving them the appearance of a sea of death. The British soldiers were going back in a double line. One line was firing whilst the other retreated. They were almost totally swamped by the time they got to the carriage. Sergeant Butcher was standing next to Captain Holfer; they both used their rifles to push back the flesh-eaters. Corporal Heinz helped to gather the soldiers into the carriage. They began firing from the back of it; Charles called for the last of the men to fall in behind the officers.

They shut the carriage door with hundreds of arms coming through the windows, trying to grab at anything alive.

"Corporal, wounded report," Charles said, needing to know quickly.

"None, sir."

"Let's get moving!" Charles then said to Sergeant Butcher, as an Engineer at the front released the lever to send them rising upwards. Captain Holfer prepped the explosives, and asked, "What sort of fuse for the carriage, Captain?"

"Ten minutes if you can?" They were nearly at the top of the shaft when the order was given for the brake to be applied. The men all looked at each other; it was a strange moment, almost surreal. Moments earlier, they had been swamped by the living dead, and now they were sitting suspended three quarters of the way up a mineshaft.

"Corporal, lay the explosives. Time is against us."

The plan was simple – put what they had left around the track from the carriage and anything else they could attach explosives to. Corporal Heinz was excellent; he worked at great speed but was very composed. The fuse was lit and they were moving again.

It only took a few minutes for them to reach the top, but when they did, the men left the carriage at speed. Captain Hayward ordered his men to move to the wagons as fast as they could. They went past where Colossus would normally sleep but there was no sign of him. Charles was a little behind them as he brought up the rear and slung his rifle over his shoulder.

"Captain Hayward, trying to escape, are we?"

Charles turned around. He started to see this figure emerging from the darkness. His size and ominous power surrounded him. Captain Hayward did not run, but instead moved closer towards him.

"You may feel brave, but you are foolish," Colossus said, smiling. "I will not kill you, no; I will break you and then watch you die tomorrow." His english was laden with a heavy Russian accent.

"Colossus, you have failed as a guard and will die either way now." Charles smiled at him.

His eyes looked unsure. Then an almighty explosion shook the very ground they stood on. This was followed by another explosion from the mine shaft. Dust and debris came up from the shaft and drifted into the room.

"What have you done?" Colossus looked angry, but also concerned.

"I'd say your precious rock is in pieces." He then smiled again.

The giant did not say another word and lunged forward for Charles. His large fist missed Captain Hayward's head by inches; Charles darted forward, punching the leg of this oversized man, having little to no impact. Colossus laughed as he did so.

"This is not even a fight. You are so weak and puny."

The men moved around the chamber, Charles taking calculated sidesteps to avoid the reach of this beast of a man. Again, Colossus lurched forward to grab Charles; he slipped, stumbling to the ground. The British officer saw the chance to swing his rifle around; he took aim and squeezed the trigger. The bullet crunched into the giant's shoulder, sending flesh and blood flying into the air. Colossus let out a roar, before picking himself off the ground and charging at the captain. He was pulling back the bolt on his rifle, loading another bullet into the chamber, when he was hit hard. The knock sent the rifle spinning through the air and he followed with it.

He hit the ground hard. Charles gingerly tried to get on his feet, but felt himself flying through the air again into the far wall. Blood started to flow from his mouth; he could taste it, but in his dazed state could not find the cut.

Colossus came forward and picked him up by his shoulders. He looked him in the eyes.

"You put up a good fight, Captain, but it's time." He started to pull his arms out to the side. His plan was simple, rip Captain Hayward apart.

"Have you ever been to Africa, Colossus?"

The giant paused.

"What has that to do with anything?"

Charles smiled through the pain. To the corner of his eye he saw two figures moving from the tunnel his men had gone down.

"Large animals are brought down by small creatures."

Colossus looked puzzled.

Then two figures emerged from the darkness, running at Colossus and finally jumping in the air before sticking their swords into both of his thighs. The whole action was slick; it caused the giant to fall forward onto his hands and knees, forcing him to let go of Captain Hayward, who in turn fell to the ground. When Colossus looked up, his eyes met Captain Hayward's.

He did not say another word, as he could see in the eyes of his opponent what was about to happen. Charles withdrew his sword quickly from his back and brought it around hard, taking Colossus's head clean off. The body was left almost in the same position, with blood gushing from the wound.

"We must move," Charles said to Private Chamberlin and Corporal Heinz. He also thanked them as they left to join the others.

Chapter 42

A rider was allowed to pass into the fort. He said he carried a message from Nazar. The destroyer drones took him straight to the old priest. The gangly priest and old priest were up and about, concerned with the explosions. The rumbles had stirred the monastery and fort; it was starting to come to life. He ordered two priests to check on the rock and then took the message from the rider.

It was a short message.

We are making good progress in capturing Great Britain, but be warned. There is a group of British Engineers being led by a Captain Hayward, who we believe are trying to locate the rock. They should be stopped at all costs.

The old priest let the message slip out of his hand before bellowing out a massive cry. "Sound the alarm!" he shouted, his eyes rolling. "Bring me their heads, BRING ME THEIR HEADS!!!"

Priests and guards started to run off in different directions, but there was one walking towards the old priest.

"My lord, I have news of the rock. It's been destroyed." As the priest came closer, the old man looked down. He waited until the younger priest was at arm's length and then lunged a knife, which he had taken from his belt, into his stomach. He twisted it hard and stared at the shocked eyes of the young priest.

"Nazar will kill us all for this." He slowly pulled the knife out, letting the young priest fall to the floor.

There was a thunderous crack outside; the old priest stepped over the body and moved towards the monastery courtyard. He called over to a drone soldier by the door to the courtyard; the soldier looked at the dead priest lying on the floor before awkwardly going over. The old man asked what was happening now. His response was that they were being shelled.

"Prepare my horse and guards." The old priest could not hide his anger and left to get his sword.

Captain Hayward gathered his men by the wagons, it was still dusk outside.

"Captain, who is shelling the fort and monastery?" Captain Holfer looked hopeful, as if a large European army had landed and was now attacking the camp and fort.

"I'm not sure, but there was only one other force coming here and that was with Major Sherborne." He did not want to waste any more time, and said they must use this moment to get back to the boat. His plan was clear – whilst the shells were falling, get to the stables.

In the confusion, Corporal Heinz and the two Russian allied soldiers gathered drone overcoats for the British soldiers. This would help them as they moved through the fort. Once the men were ready, they moved out. The shelling had lulled a little. Corporal Heinz accompanied Captain Hayward alongside the left-hand side of the fort. They paused by the buildings and waited for everyone to group; there were soldiers moving around, but their focus was now on the enemy outside. They had not fully got the instructions to hunt for Captain Hayward and his men.

The stables were a flurry of activity, but there were enough horses for Captain Hayward's men to take. Several shells started to land outside again, which was perfect timing; three drone cavalry were killed in a direct hit and two buildings were now on fire.

Charles was aware he didn't want his men being killed in this shelling, but they would only have a short amount of time before the enemy located the mortars and captured those who were firing them.

Corporal Heinz led them to the gate leading out of the fort. Charles's heart was racing; this was their moment to escape. A guard came down to them; he shouted something in Russian to Corporal Heinz, who then shouted something back. A tense minute followed before the huge gate began to open. The soldiers galloped towards it at speed. They still had to get out of the main entrance to the camp, but they hoped the shelling would cause enough confusion to allow this. Their first thoughts were the mortar fire coming from along the riverside. Moving along the track, they could hear gunfire, even the crackle of a machine gun.

The guards on the main gate to the camp pointed in the direction of the riverside, thinking they would follow the other drones that had left. Private Chamberlin looked over his shoulder, and more cavalry was coming out of the fort. This time, there were a number of priests with them. He quickly glanced towards the camp. It was a sight he feared – hundreds of drone soldiers marching their way. Destroyer drones were riding a group of razor tooths, and to the side of them were priests herding flesh-eaters and long limbs. The final sight was coming along the east wall – Lagorians being ridden by the giants. He quickly relayed what was occurring to the others.

"We must be quick, head to the gunfire," Captain Hayward said as he led them out, and as soon as they were clear of the gunfire, he told them to put the drone cloaks in their saddlebags. He did not want them being killed by friendly fire.

It did not take them too long to find the river and start making their way along it. Roughly 100 yards in front of them were the corpses of thirty or more drone cavalry. Some of the drones were starting to change into flesh-eaters; others had been hit in the head by bullets and were not changing.

"Do not shoot, we're British Engineers," Captain Hayward called out.

Within seconds of this happening, a voice replied in English for them to come forward. They moved through the bushes, and sitting behind a makeshift barricade were four Marines and a Maxim machine gun; to the side of them were four more crouching down. Captain Hayward moved his horse and his men to the side of them.

"Captain Hayward," said Captain Brewer, lowering his rifle. There was a moment when the soldiers started to reach for their revolvers and rifles. "It's alright, we'll hold them off whilst you get to your boat."

Charles leaned forward and asked why the change of stance. Captain Brewer apologised for everything they had done in the past. They had followed Major Sherborne blindly, but being in Europe had shown them that the world had changed. It needed men like Captain Hayward, who would take on this enemy and beat them. He realised that some of their actions were unforgivable, but the only way to redeem themselves was to sacrifice their very lives for the Empire. Charles said the whole camp was coming their way, and they should not be taken alive. He added that they could mount up and leave with them now. Captain Brewer said he had discussed this with his men, and they were ready to fight to the end. He said that Captain Fairbrook was further down the river with a handful of soldiers and several mortars. Major Sherborne was somewhere along the river in a drunken state.

Charles saluted them as he rode past them, and his men did the same. They again picked up speed, galloping alongside the river's edge. The crackle of the machine gun started letting them know the enemy were close. As Charles led his men to the inlet where their boat was moored, they could see cavalry attacking a small hill half a mile away. They believed this was where Captain Fairbrook was with the mortars.

As their boat came into sight, Captain Hayward saw a horse tethered near a tree. He said to Sergeant Butcher that the men should leave their horses by the boat and get on board. He added that if he wasn't back in ten minutes, then to leave without him. With that, he turned his horse and galloped over to the riverbank.

The horse that was tethered to the tree was agitated. Captain Hayward could see flesh-eaters moving towards them in the distance, slowly gaining ground in their own menacing way. He tied his horse to an alder tree branch, and pushed his way through some bushes at the water's edge. The weather had changed over the past few days; the wind carried an icy feel to it.

Sitting against a rotting larch tree was Major Sherborne; he was talking to himself and drinking after every pause. He did not notice Captain Hayward approaching him.

"Major Sherborne."

He looked over at Captain Hayward.

"You, You … You just won't die, will you?" He took a long swig from his whisky bottle and tried to stand up, but failed miserably. He fell to the ground several times before eventually managing to haul himself up.

"You have made our Empire weak; your type has lost us the war in Europe and probably the war at home." The Major steadied himself as he got his balance back. His eyes were puffy and red, he had tears flowing from his eyes, rolling down his dirty face onto the ground below. His hair looked greasy and unclean.

"I have come to punish you for the death of my men," said Charles.

He sharply withdrew his sword. His eyes were as cold as the river that ran past them.

The Major stood there looking sorry for himself; "I did not mean for it to turn out like this." He dropped the whisky bottle on the soil below and stood staring blankly at the captain.

Charles gripped his sword tight. He wanted to thrust it into the man who had taken so much from them, and had never been held accountable for his actions, but he couldn't do it, he just couldn't do it. If Major Sherborne had come at him with his sword or had drawn his revolver, it would have been different. Instead, he was a broken man, a drunk who had lost everything; even his men no longer followed his orders.

A familiar sound then homed in on them. A flesh-eater staggered from the bushes to the side of them, breaking a branch as it moved in for fresh meat. Charles took a step to the side and swung his sword around, taking the flesh-eater's head clean off. The body fell at the feet of the major, which seemed to spark him into action. He bent down and frantically tried to roll the body. When he succeeded, he laughed out loud and then grabbed the whisky bottle which had being lying underneath.

"Goodbye, Major Sherborne." Charles turned and walked back to his horse. As he mounted the animal, three more flesh-eaters had closed in on them. The major's horse panicked and broke free, leaving him stranded. He did not try and run; he sat back and carried on drinking. Charles looked back one last time and saw the major bringing his revolver to his head. The flesh-eaters were almost upon him. He pulled the trigger, resulting in a loud retort; it was not enough to stop the flesh-eaters ripping into his warm, bloodied body. Charles kicked his horse on and galloped to join his men. The distant fire of the machine gun had stopped and the mortars were no longing firing.

On arriving near to the boat, he jumped off his horse and rushed over to the river's edge. The boat had moved further out into the river. Charles waded into the water and swam over towards it. The Nazar flag was now flying from a pole near the wheelhouse, and all soldiers on top deck were dressed as drones. A rope was thrown down to him and he was hauled up. Soon they were away, leaving the smoke which was drifting from the fort and monastery down towards the river as a reminder of what had happened. The enemy was moving in large numbers in the fields and woods around the camp and fort. Priests were seen patrolling the river's edge, but for now it seemed they had made it out alive.

Each hour that passed help put the camp further away from them. They had not seen any boats or vessels coming up the river behind them, or faced a challenge in the villages they passed along the way. It seemed the old high priest was more interested in killing the Marines who had attacked the fort and monastery, than surveying the river. He might have presumed he would locate the rest of the enemy force, if he found Captain Hayward and his men. Either way, it had played into their hands.

The skeleton crew that was left behind was grateful to have their comrades back. It had been stressful waiting on the boat, not knowing whether they would capture Captain Hayward and his men. They had been joined by Major Sherborne's boat crew, once Captain Brewer had told them to save themselves.

Both crews took turns manning the vessel, whilst the soldiers who were with Captain Hayward on the mission were allowed to wash and eat below deck. Charles was given a large cup of tea. He sat back on a stool and watched the men tuck into some fresh bread and cooked meat. The warm tea was comforting, and made him think of home. When he closed his eyes, he pictured a Sunday morning full English breakfast with Rebecca and the children. A good read of *The Times* newspaper and then a stroll in Windsor Great Park.

Sadly, when he opened them again, he was still sitting on the stool, below deck, on a ship.

"Captain," said Corporal Heinz, who was stood eating a large slice of warm bread.

"Please sit down, Corporal. You did an excellent job out there," Charles said, whilst looking at the warm bread. The corporal broke a bit off for him and then said he had some news. He explained that he had spoken to a Danish man who was dying in the camp. The man was fearful at first, but when he heard the corporal speak German and tell them of their mission, it had brought a smile to his face. He said there were survivors in Denmark from Europe, and talked of some of them going to Nykøbing for the winter. He also said they may have sought refuge on an island off the Danish coast called Byrum.

Charles's eyes lit up; he didn't know what to think of what he was hearing. The corporal added that there was something else the man had said before he died. He believed there were English families who had fled Europe heading to that island.

Charles put down his tea and held his hands over his face. He took a deep breath. His thoughts wandered over whether he could ask his men to travel to the island to check.

"You know the men will want us to check for you?" Corporal Heinz had read his mind. He had been with him long enough to know what he was thinking.

"I will ask them during a meeting tonight. Thank you, Corporal. I really appreciate that." Charles went and got some food. He spoke with the soldiers and officers before returning to his room. Lying on the bunk, he allowed himself something he had not dared to do for a long time, dream of reuniting with his family.

They passed along the Vorkuta River without a problem, and then moved onto the Usa River. They felt nervous with every town they passed. If an artillery battery had been set up along the river's edge, they would have been in real trouble. With this in mind, it was "stand at the ready" as they passed every village. Charles took time between villages to speak to the officers and soldiers about his request to stop at the Danish island Byrum. He knew he would have to ask the captains of the HMS *Orontes* and HMS *Jumma* about travelling there, but it would still come down to him taking a small band of soldiers onto the island and doing a quick reconnaissance of it. A week passed and he hadn't let himself get too carried away yet, but as they slowly edged out of Russia and into the open sea, he thought about the possibility.

They sent out Morse code messages to say they were returning back. After a half day's sailing, they met up with HMS *Orontes* and HMS *Jumma*. Time was taken to hook up their boat to HMS *Orontes*. A discussion was had between the captains of both ships about travelling to the island. It was agreed that they would try their best to get them in there. Captain Hayward and Captain Holfer were shown to the captain's quarters of HMS *Orontes*. He poured a whisky for both men. Taking a swig, the captain steadied himself.

"Nazar has landed on British shores." He took another swig of whisky and said a British warship had passed by them whilst they were on the mission in Russia and brought news of the invasion. The British fleet had engaged Nazar's fleet, but later found out it had been a diversion. He had built a fleet of ships to be destroyed and a fleet of ships for an invasion. There were reports of the south coast falling and heavy fighting along the South Downs. This could be why the seas around Europe and Russia had not been crawling with enemy ships. With this in mind, the opportunity was open.

Chapter 43

As they were heading into autumn, the weather was changeable. Some days it was stormy in the North Sea and others it was unpredictably calm and tranquil. The captains of the ships were old hands at this and navigated the vessels smoothly through the choppy waters. They moved past the Norwegian coastline and into the Skagerrak straight between Norway and Sweden; following this they slipped into the Kattegat channel. This was the channel between Denmark and Sweden; it was also where the island of Byrum was sitting.

Captain Hayward said he would go alone so as not to risk anyone on this quest, but this was not accepted. He was to land with Sergeant Butcher, Corporal Heinz, Private Chamberlin and Private Green. Once both HMS *Orontes* and HMS *Jumma* had laid anchor, they took the smaller boat to the island. It was all done cautiously. Nazar had his forces all across Europe, but had pulled most of them for the invasion, leaving pockets of Europe poorly guarded. Charles kept the same procedure as before. They had five horses with them, and a small selection of firearms.

The island wasn't too big, so they figured it wouldn't take that long to find the inhabitants, or the other way around.

Once landed, they made their way to the woodlands, which covered most of the island. They were all still dressed in their khaki uniforms. Private Green had a British flag wrapped on a pole. He was told not to undo it yet, but once they had found the survivors, it would hopefully help them not to be fired upon.

The sun was shining down on them; the wind was cold, but fresh. Captain Hayward led from the front. Private Alexander Chamberlin had his rifle lowered over his waist as he rode. It had a telescopic sight attached to it, and he knew that if things turned ugly, he would take as many enemy troops with him as he could.

Moving along the open tracks and alongside the woodland edges helped them keep a good visual range. Corporal Heinz and Private Chamberlin were the first to spot smoke rising over a thicket of pine trees. Charles warned them to be ready.

A large man rode up to them; he had an axe strapped to his back. When Charles saw him coming, he gave the order for the British flag to be released by Private Green. He took the gamble that this was not a Nazar soldier. The rider rode straight up to them; he had a long beard and powerful presence. He introduced himself as Hagen. This was the signal for others to emerge out of the woods around them. They had rifles and bow and arrows; some had homemade spears and other weapons. Charles kept his calm and made no swift movements.

"So, the English have arrived." Hagen's spoke English in a Danish accent.

"My name is Captain Hayward, we've come to take all of you with us," Charles said softly.

Hagen nodded to one of his men, who was watching from the woodlands. "Is it safe to go to Great Britain?"

"We're not sure." Charles waited and then breathed out. "I'm wondering whether you have any survivors from Paris."

"Follow me, Captain." Hagen led the soldiers towards some bushes that had been woven together. These were pulled apart slowly, revealing a small encampment. The huts had been dug down into the soil and built into the side of the embankments which surrounded this area. Grass had been grown on the roofs to help disguise them.

The soldiers dismounted, and were instantly surrounded by the people from the camp. Charles looked in earnest for Rebecca and the children, but sadly his eyes fell on many other faces, and not the ones he truly wanted to see. Sergeant Butcher leaned in next to him and said, "Don't give hope, Charles."

Hagen was speaking with the British soldiers and bringing people up to them. They still had guns trained on them from raised ground to the left- and right-hand sides, but with each minute, the situation was getting more relaxed and was one almost of excitement and euphoria. The word was spreading about them being rescued. Hagen came towards Charles, and said, "I recognise your name, Captain." He was smiling as he said this. "Come with me." He led him away from the other soldiers as they were being handed warm soup in bowls.

Charles followed Hagen through a small cluster of birch trees and out to a stream. There were more groups of people, some washing clothes, others fishing. Children were playing in the woods alongside it.

Hagen stood and looked over to the nook in the stream. Charles followed the line of his sight. There kneeling by the water's edge was Rebecca.

Charles's eyes filled up, and his throat went dry. He wanted to call out, but found his emotions were too strong. Hagen looked at him and patted him on the shoulder. He turned and walked back to the main camp. With tears rolling down his cheeks, Charles felt a tug on his tunic. He looked down and saw something he had wanted to see for a very long time. Standing there was Emily and Arthur; they were almost exploding with excitement. "We've missed you, Daddy!" Emily blurted out; Charles crouched down and wrapped both his arms around them. Through the tears, he told them how much he loved them. Arthur said it was the best day of his life. He looked older, wiser now. Then a voice cried out; Rebecca had seen Charles from across the stream, and she leapt into the water and almost fell in her sheer determination to get to him. As he stood up, she burst into his arms. She was crying floods of tears and lost her voice in the moment. When it did come back, it was trembling with emotion.

"I love you, Charles, I love you!" She then began to kiss him on the lips unashamedly. They then embraced for what seemed like a lifetime.

"Father, are we going home now?" asked Arthur.

Charles looked down at his son. "I'm not totally sure, Arthur, but we will all be leaving this island." He then took Rebecca by the hand and led her and the children back to the others in the camp.

Preparations had started for them to load everyone onto the ships. Private Chamberlin had rode back to ask for more rowing boats to load civilians and supplies into. Rebecca and the children found it hard to leave his side. He took them for a short walk along the beach they had landed at. Then, finding a suitable place to sit, they had time to share the happenings of the past year and a bit. There were tears, and hugs, but it was a crucial piece of time they needed as a family.

Charles looked at Rebecca and told her how beautiful she was; he hadn't forgotten how her face looked, that was deeply embedded in his mind and soul, but her sheer radiance was stronger in person than mind. He remarked on how Arthur and Emily had grown, not just in size, but in stature. They gave him loving, warm smiles. "It is time to move now, children. We must spend the rest of the day loading the vessels." As he walked his family back, a rowing boat was coming towards them. It had Captain Holfer in it. When this landed, the captain walked over to Charles and saluted him; he also lowered his head to Rebecca and the children. The way Charles was smiling gave away the fact that he had found his prize asset. He introduced them to the Austrian captain.

"Sorry to interrupt at this special time, but we have received a Morse code that a British small convoy with battleships will be passing our way and can escort us past London and through the English Channel."

Charles thanked him and said they should double their efforts to meet that convoy and secure a safer passage. He did not know whether that meant Great Britain had fallen, but knew it was an opportunity not to be missed. Kissing Rebecca again, he went to join his men as they loaded supplies. Rebecca took the children to join the others and take what they could for the trip.

Chapter 44

The ground was shaking under the bombardment.

"My lord, are we not too close to the action?" General Tarasov asked cautiously. His uniform was covered in blood and soil from fighting, his hair unsightly and scraggy.

Nazar wiped the dirt and dust away from his eyes. "Why has it taken so long to capture London?" His voice grew stronger, and more menacing.

General Tarasov tried to find validation for his own upcoming answer by scurrying around for a map. He then found one and spread it out on a wall that had been partially destroyed by a shell, and was lying on the floor. "The enemy have dug in their heavy artillery around the south east of London." He paused to gauge Nazar's eyes, which seemed to show interest.

"We have lost a lot of men taking London; they fought hard, even women and children fought for this country of theirs." The general still kept on looking at Nazar.

"General Tarasov, get to the point, before a point finds you." Nazar felt at the sword by his side.

"Their queen is sitting in her castle in Windsor; maybe we can come from three angles and break them." The general pointed out his plan on the map. Nazar's long fingers and sharp nails brushed against the map. An explosion landed close enough to send fragments of dirt and debris over the general and Nazar. Nazar did not flinch, he just pondered over the map.

"We outnumber them fifty to one, there should be no more delays, take the castle." He turned and started to walk back to the other priests, who had gathered in the town hall. He stopped as the general called his name. Nazar looked down at the soil beneath his feet and then up to the blackened skies from the burning buildings. "What is it, General?" His patience was nearly gone.

"My lord, we will need more artillery if we are to take the castle quickly." The general was almost apologetic bringing this up. Nazar told him what he already knew, that the British cavalry had destroyed a lot of their artillery since they had landed along the south coast. There were more artillery pieces being used up in the north. He suggested messengers be sent as swiftly as possible; Oksana was using her cavalry to raid through the Midlands and into Wales.

"If you do not have the artillery, press ahead as planned. The castle must fall." Nazar tossed his cloak over his back and walked towards the building. General Tarasov knew he could not ask any more questions. He must now find a way to take Windsor Castle. It would mean losing thousands of men, but Nazar was not worried about that. He left to join his officers.

Chapter 45

"Colonel Adams." The dispatch rider looked tired and sorrowful. He passed over a letter.

The lieutenant colonel picked open the wax-sealed letter and read the news. He breathed in and then slowly out, it was as if his body let in the tiredness it had resisted for so long. He read the words over again in his head. London had almost fallen; hundreds of thousands had given their lives for their country in vain. This force of darkness was coming, like a sea of death sweeping over Great Britain. The letter was hard to digest.

He had a staff sergeant standing next to him, Henry Bowman. He was of medium height, and stocky build. What made him stand out were his twisted moustache ends. They were well kept, even in this time of trouble. He was a veteran of several Victorian wars and was a widower who had never had children.

Sergeant Bowman sensed something was wrong, the way Lieutenant Colonel Adams was reacting to what he was reading.

"Do we have long before they're knocking on our door, sir?"

"We need to spread the news and double the fortifications," the lieutenant colonel said, then made his way to his tent.

Queen Victoria had decided to stay in Windsor Castle whatever the outcome. Most of the young royals had been evacuated to America. She now had only her loyal aids who wanted to stay. The queen had summoned the senior officers she had left to discuss the defence of the castle. Lieutenant Colonel Adams was one of them.

The field artillery could be heard in the distance; the Royal Horse Artillery were using their mobility as much as they could. The River Thames had meant Nazar had to fight to get across every bridge that had not been destroyed. The last of the heavy artillery was placed around the hills near Windsor and Egham. The East Surrey Regiment had dug into the hills and was preparing the defence. Windsor Great Park was full of refugees and wounded soldiers. Nazar's forces were sweeping up through Farnborough and Aldershot. Oksana's forces had been engaging with the British troops around Oxford and Aylesbury.

Lieutenant Colonel Adams joined the others officers as they waited outside one of the reception rooms in the round tower. The dispiriting sound of shells landing ever closer filled the space around the officers. Large pictures hung all around them, some depicting great battles, others showing more peaceful times. James let his mind drift out of the window and to the gardens below. He pictured the royal family moving around, children playing and the queen sitting watching them all. He was brought out of his reverie by an aid to the queen calling the men in.

Queen Victoria was sitting on a modest chair dressed in black. She had worn black since Prince Albert had died. Her eyes looked tired, as if she was carrying the weight of the country on her shoulders.

She had recently finished a cup of tea and now wanted to discuss the mission to Russia and the defence of the castle. She started by thanking the soldiers, who were fighting to the bitter end.

The queen then turned to Lieutenant Colonel Adams and asked whether he had heard of news from the mission to Russia. He felt honored she was addressing him, but also saddened, as he had no news of what had happened to his brother-in-law and their mission. She understood he could not update her with further information

He was asked about the defensive preparations and how they were going. He was able to update her on how they were using everything they could to fortify the castle and the land around it. She was especially pleased with this, because it would give more time to her subjects, who were retreating to the coast. The British Navy was helping to evacuate civilians as swiftly as they could and take them to America. The other officers updated her with their various roles and responsibilities. They collectively urged their queen to think about leaving for the west coast and taking refuge in America. She flatly refused to do this and stated she was not a politician; she would die with the people and soldiers of the British Empire if she must.

It had been decided that the royal colours would be saved. The queen had thought long and hard about this and wanted them to be taken to America, where other members of the royal family were along with British refugees. Captain Kingsbury had been chosen to take the flag to Cornwall and take a ship from there to America. He would have five Lancers escorting it with him. They hoped the sight of the royal colours would stir the soldiers they passed and give hope that all was not lost. Some of the officers feared it might do the opposite, and asked if it would be wiser to keep the flag in a pouch.

The queen wanted the flag to be seen. The captain was chosen because of his reputation of fighting in Europe and his actions in the defence of Great Britain. He had lost his wife and daughter in a savage attack in Europe and was seen as the officer to save the flag or die trying. The plan was for them to change their horses along the route to the west coast. There were still garrisons holding key areas and they would assist with fresh horses for them to complete their journey.

There was a sombre feeling towards the end of the meeting; the end was near and hard decisions were being made daily. She thanked again the officers and their men for their gallant efforts; as the officers left, they saluted the queen and made their way back to their posts.

As Lieutenant Colonel Adams stood in the lower ward taking in what they had discussed, he heard horses' hooves coming from the Horseshoe Cloister to his left; it was Captain Kingsbury with the royal colours. He had several Lancers with him; as he rode past the lieutenant colonel, he lowered his head in a sign of respect.

Lieutenant Colonel Adams could see the soldiers around him shrink with the sight of the royal colours leaving the castle.

Captain Kingsbury came out of the King Henry VIII gate into the fading sun of the autumnal day; there was a breeze which was strong enough to lift the flag and show it in its full glory. As he rode down the roads and tracks towards the coast, many retreating soldiers and families saw the flag.

A small boy grabbed his mother's arms at the sight of the Lancer riding past. "It's alright, my love, it's one of our soldiers." The young boy still held her tight. "What is that flag, mother?" She paused as a tear rolled down her cheek. She spoke softly as she struggled to let her words come out. "It's the royal colours; the country has fallen." She held her son tightly in her arms.

Captain Kingsbury could not look at the faces he passed. They were all carrying the same broken despair on seeing the royal colours passing them. He just rode hard, as his broken heart and anger threatened to swallow him whole.

He passed a group of soldiers from the 24th. A distressed cry went out for news of their queen. Captain Kingsbury could not answer; he just shook his head as he rode past. A soldier fell to his knees and took his helmet off, letting it fall into the dirt below him.

The group of Lancers with the flag looked around them as they rode; they found it hard to absorb the sadness as it played out to the backdrop of the dying light, which illuminated the quintessentially British countryside.

Nazar had been told by spies in the castle about the royal colours leaving. He arranged for High Priest Alekseev to set off after them with a detachment of destroyer drones. They would travel by boat to Brixham, then they would follow the coastline, and spies would update them along the way. News of refugees escaping to America from the west coast was known to Nazar. He had wanted to cut this escape route off, but did not have the ships or fighting force in place yet to do that. Once the British Army was defeated, he intended to secure Cornwall.

Chapter 46

A week passed whilst Nazar slowly overcame London and the forces defending it.

Horror stories were filtering into the castle from around Great Britain as it slowly fell to Nazar's hordes. It had a demoralising effect on soldiers and civilians alike. Losing a battle was one thing, losing your identity and country was soul-destroying.

Lieutenant Colonel Adams went back to his tent after finding he had no picture of his family in his tunic. He scrambled around for one in his trunk and searched like a madman all around his bed and table. Sergeant Bowman arrived and joined in the search, but sadly to no avail. James looked up, and in a moment of formality told Henry he would need his help.

"We need to go to Sunninghill to my sister's house," said James. He asked Henry to gather six men with horses and his own horse.

"Yes, sir," Sergeant Bowman said, leaving straight away. The plan from the lieutenant colonel was to find a picture of his family. He had made a decision and he needed a photograph to help this decision.

Private Brown was helping Heidi and some of the others load the wagons. They had been concerned with the rumours of London falling and mass executions. It had made the civilians around the castle start to flee to the coast; those that wanted to stay and fight were being armed. Windsor town was having small detachments of local militia and Coldstream Guards placed in different homes and hotels. Roads were being closed off and mortars set up in good locations to fire on the enemy. Snipers were being placed in all strategic high points. Private Thomas Farrell was one of these; he was a young man and had just seen his 21st birthday come and go. Private Brown had tried to help guide him where he could. He had even advised a local trip to Annabelle Watkins, a lady of the night, for a chance to be with a woman as the enemy drew in closer.

Private Brown had spoken to him about the heroics of Private Chamberlin. He pointed out how much fear a sniper can instil into an advancing enemy. He shook his hand as he left to climb the church tower at St John the Baptist Church. Private Farrell wanted to get the lie of the land and what firing positions were available. Once Private Farrell had left, Heidi found a corner by a house where she could pull John into; he looked around to make sure no one was coming. They quickly embraced and kissed each other. "I know we shouldn't, John, but time is running out."

"We might still make this, Heidi, never give up hope. Remember, if Captain Hayward and the others succeed, it could turn the war!" John kissed her on the lips passionately, before they returned to their duties.

He stood there looking at her for a second, as the autumn sun fell upon her pale skin. Her hair was not as vibrant as when they had first met and she had lost weight due to rationing, like they all had, but her eyes were alive and told a story of love.

As John put the last supply box onto the back of a wagon, Sergeant Bowman arrived on horseback with five others and two spare horses.

"Private Brown, the colonel needs you for a mission."

Heidi looked at the sergeant anxiously.

"It's to Sunninghill, my lady. Don't worry."

John touched her arm as he mounted his horse. He turned and nodded his head towards her. Then they left to join the lieutenant colonel.

Sergeant Bowman returned to Lieutenant Colonel Adams with six mounted soldiers; he was holding the reins to Lieutenant Colonel Adams's horse, whilst sitting in his saddle.

"Thank you, Sergeant. We must be quick as the enemy is on our doorstep."

They set off from the castle towards the bronze statue of the copper horse. This could be seen from the long walk, and was a direct route into the great park. They passed many defences and stockades. Maxim machine guns had been set up in some of the turrets and battlements. Field cannons were being placed in strategic positions and thousands of wooden stakes were hammered into the ground, creating the same effect as a hawthorn hedge, dense and menacing.

Lieutenant Colonel Adams called over to Private Brown and told him it was good to see a familiar face. They were greeted at the statue by a small detachment of the 11th Devonshire Regiment of Foot. They were guarding the long walk and had several sandbags and one Maxim machine gun covering the road.

The gunfire and pounding cannons could be heard closer there. One of the Devonshire soldiers said they had better be quick, as there were reports of flesh-eaters entering the park already. The lieutenant colonel thanked the guards and led his men across the fields towards Sunninghill. There was a lake in the park called Virginia Water Lake; they would come around the side of that and cross it before leaving the park. Then it would be a case of following a road past farmland to Sunninghill.

The men travelled at speed. They saw the odd farmhouse being fortified, and a selection of Royal Horse Artillery setting up on top of a hill. They were pleased to see the park was still in the control of the British at this moment in time. The trees were a mixture of deciduous and evergreens. The pine forests were thick and carried an air of something always watching them.

Moving along the road towards Sunninghill, a shell hit a field not too far from them. The explosion made the men lean low in their saddles; there was no sign of the enemy and they all hoped it was just a stray shell. Lieutenant Colonel Adams led the men down the road until they came to a crossroads. On the signpost it said they were less than a mile to Sunninghill village.

When they arrived in the village, it was deserted. Some doors were left open, and there were even supply boxes left standing in the street.

"Gentlemen, we must be quick. The enemy are close," James said, pushing his horse on; he knew the lanes around the village well, and got to his sister's house quickly. There, he dismounted and handed his reins over to Private Brown, who also dismounted.

Sergeant Bowman took two men and watched the lane further down from the house. The other soldiers dismounted. Private Brown handed the horse reins to one of the men and took his rifle off his shoulder. He told one of them to keep watch as he checked on the lieutenant colonel.

Inside the house, James had already found what he was looking for. It was a photo of his family. He sat in his brother-in-law's chair and found himself smiling at it.

He felt it hadn't been that long since they were sharing a drink together over Christmas, and now he was sitting in silence looking around this room filled with memories. He did not know if Charles had survived, or even if his sister and children had as well. It was hard to keep his thoughts together; it felt surreal sitting there, the environment was familiar, but something wasn't right. The life was no longer in the house; it was more like a museum now.

It was coming up to late afternoon, and the sun was starting to slowly sink. Private Brown was about to knock at the front door, when he heard a groaning sound. He did not think twice about reaching down and pulling out his bayonet; after attaching it to his rifle, he slowly breathed in and moved around the corner of the house. There were two overgrown bushes to the side of an outdoor table. The groans were coming from that direction. Private Brown edged closer, taking a cautious step each time. Something was thrashing around, it sounded like someone eating. Private Brown looked down to see blood leading to the bush. He was about five feet away when a snarl from his left caught him off guard. All he saw before it lunged at his body was huge teeth.

John managed to bring his rifle with bayonet around at the same time the creature leapt for him. The impact did not favour the wolf; its whimperings were short as the bayonet stuck through its neck. As this happened, the beast's body fell on top of Private Brown, pinning him to the floor; he tried to roll this large wolf off himself, but could not move it. His attention was soon brought back to the noise from the bushes, which were now to the side of him. The groaning was louder; a flesh-eater was starting to pull itself through the branches and leaves.

Private Brown tried to call out, but the weight of the animal on his chest stifled him. Every branch snapping sent a shiver down his spine, as the flesh-eater now came at him. It was a young man, who looked like he had only recently turned. He had bite marks on his face and arms, but his skin was not fully rotten.

Private Brown put in one last effort to roll the wolf's body off of his chest, and managed to push it away just in time; as he did so, the flesh-eater lunged at him. Private Brown stopped its teeth from biting his tunic with only inches to spare. The strength of this monster, when it sensed flesh, was surprising. He thought of Heidi and his family, but he could not adjust himself to stop the flesh-eater getting lower and lower to his stomach.

As its jaws widened to bite, a sword came from the side and pushed through the flesh-eater's head. Private Brown looked across with anxious eyes. Standing there was Lieutenant Colonel Adams.

"Time to go, soldier." He had a rueful smile on his face; he knew that it had been a close call. James helped push the flesh-eater's body off him and dragged the wolf off his legs, too. They joined the soldiers at the front of the house. As they mounted up, Sergeant Bowman came racing back with the other two soldiers.

"About 300 or more flesh-eaters coming our way, sir."

The lieutenant colonel gave a nod for them to leave. He looked over at the house one last time and then kicked on his horse.

Daylight was disappearing as they galloped along the lanes in the village. They could hear heavy gunfire coming from the direction of Sunningdale. The South Welsh Borders had been in charge of the defending of that village. The fighting had begun.

As they approached the gates leading into the park, the soldiers who had been guarding it were missing. The Maxim gun was still intact and there seemed to be no sign of action around it. Sergeant Bowman raised his hand, prompting the other riders to bring their horses to a halt. To the side of them, moving through beech trees, was a small detachment of drone cavalry mixed with long limbs. They had not seen the British soldiers yet. Lieutenant Colonel Adams pointed to the Maxim gun; he wanted to take this opportunity to attack this enemy group before they knew what was happening.

Dismounting with speed, Sergeant Bowman took three soldiers with him to the Maxim gun. The other soldiers knelt behind the sandbags, whilst two soldiers looked after the horses in the trees further behind them. The lieutenant colonel had a plan; he looked around to make sure his men were ready. He then shouted out, *'De fumo in flammam.'* And again in English, "Out of the smoke into the flame".

This was enough to get the drone cavalry to turn their way. A young priest rode to the front of the group, and before judging the situation, he charged. His men and long limbs followed. Lieutenant Colonel Adams held his hand to the side. "Wait for my signal, lads."

The enemy started to pick up speed. They withdrew their swords and the long limbs started to snarl and bellow out a deep, gravelly noise.

When they came within 300 yards, Lieutenant Colonel Adams dropped his hand, signalling to his men to open fire. The Maxim machine gun spluttered into life with devastating effect. Horses and long limbs began to fall, the bullets ripping through flesh and bone, no man or beast left untouched. The soldiers who were not manning the machine gun fired their rifles at the on-rushing cavalry. The priest and his men and creatures were all dead within a minute.

Smoke poured out of the Maxim gun barrel and rose gently into the dusk sky. The silence after the heavy gunfire was cathartic.

Lieutenant Colonel Adams told four of the men to fix bayonets and follow him to the dead or dying soldiers and long limbs. They quickly finished off those that were ready to pass over to the next world. When James came across the priest, he was shocked at how young he looked; he must have been no more than 16 at the most. He had been killed in the charge, but James felt sadness that this young man, who was not much older than his own son, had lost his life serving the dark lord.

Once they had checked over the bodies, James got the men to remount and move back to the castle. The young priest's face stayed in the lieutenant colonel's mind as they moved through the forests and woods in the park.

They arrived at the Copper Horse with the 11th Devonshire Regiment of Foot preparing the mortars. Lieutenant Colonel Adams told the officer in charge that they had engaged the enemy, and that they were coming their way. News was coming through that Sunningdale had fallen.

As they prepared to ride towards the castle, the Queen's 16th Lancers started to come towards them from the open plains; there was maybe 100 or more Lancers. Leading them was a captain who had fought at Box Hill. He rode over to the lieutenant colonel and saw Private Brown was with them.

He smiled and asked how they were. They were grateful to see this fearless officer, a young man who now had come to terms with his own fate and who others drew strength from. They had a quick conversation before the captain nodded his head, as if to move his men to the front.

"Sorry, Captain, I never got your name," Lieutenant Colonel Adams asked.

The captain looked back. "Andrew Harrington," he said, pausing for a moment. "Good luck to you all." There was something final in his words; he meant what he said sincerely, but there was a realisation of what he was saying, that this would be the final stand for the Empire.

When they arrived back in the castle, the last of the defences were been finished off. Sandbags were everywhere in Windsor, in cottage windows, in the town houses and even around the castle itself. A regiment of Grenadier Guards had arrived at the castle and was helping out across the town. The news about Sunningdale was filtering around the castle and town. Some of the Welsh Borders who had been fighting in Sunningdale were now joining the 11th Devonshire Regiment as they dug in around the hills overlooking Windsor.

It wasn't long before gunfire was heard coming from the Copper Horse. James looked at the sergeant. "Get some sleep; we do not know how long we have before they start knocking on the door."

The lieutenant colonel went to his tent and took off his tunic. He lit the log burner and laid down for a moment. He took out the picture of his family and held it tight to his heart, closing his eyes.

Heidi was happy to see John return. She had planned for them to go to an empty house in the town. John was given permission to take supplies with Heidi. The house wasn't too far from the castle, so he could report back quickly if the alarm was raised. She took medical supplies with her and got John to take a box with him. They would leave it with some Grenadier Guards and go to the house afterwards.

Heidi was excited to take John to the house; she quickly lit a lantern she had prepared earlier in the kitchen and took his hand as they walked through the front room. She then led him upstairs and lit several more candles. The bed was close to the window, and there was a small fireplace which was made out of cast iron next to the side of the bed. Heidi smiled at John and lit the kindling, which sat neatly in it. He sat there and looked at his beautiful girlfriend. She then began to undress; John gave her a look as if to say, *"Is this possible?"*

"It may be our last time." She said this as her nurse's shirt slowly came open, revealing her breasts. John sat and nodded his head in agreement, as she gently slid between the covers. "Come on, Englishman, we haven't got all night," she joked. John wasted no time in undressing and joined her. After making passionate love, they both lay in the bed looking at the fire. It crackled and popped as the wood slowly burnt. It was mesmerising, captivating, and helped John and Heidi lose themselves in the moment.

Unfortunately, the heavy fighting outside Windsor grew louder. To the north of Windsor, the fighting was intensifying around Slough. Eton Wick was a key defensive village as the River Thames split around it; the Black Watch were defending Eton Wick. Windsor was aided by the River Thames, and in truth it had stopped the mass invasion sweeping to them quicker. Nazar's army was suffering heavy losses crossing this river; the British forces had targeted this as an awkward hurdle to his conquest.

They both had fallen into a light sleep when a shell landing in the street near to the house woke them up. The house shook and the glass trembled. John was first to get himself out of bed and started dressing. Heidi knew she had to join him, but found it hard to leave the warm bed. She did eventually get herself up and ready to leave. The commotion outside was frantic; soldiers were leaving to reinforce different parts of the town.

Nazar had received news that Oksana was planning to cross into Eton Wick in the morning. This would coincide with his plans to cross at Staines. General Eltsina and General Georgiy were pushing hard in the hills above Windsor. They had four divisions of destroyer drones, mixed in with thousands of flesh-eaters and drone soldiers. General Eltsina was leading the cavalry and long limbs. This was backed up by wolves and razor tooths. There was a small detachment of bears with two heads; most of these, though, were with Nazar.

They had boats and rafts in great numbers. It was originally planned for a late evening attack, but this was changed as it could not be guaranteed that the hills around Windsor had fallen. The new idea was that a mass dawn attack would overstretch the remaining British forces and bring an end to the resistance in Britain.

Private Brown and Heidi made it back to the castle, John went back to helping with the defences, and Heidi returned to tending to the sick and wounded. The ebb and flow of injured soldiers had not been as intense yet; this was mainly down to the soldiers fighting to the death where they stood and Nazar's extermination policy with British soldiers, wounded or not.

Lieutenant Colonel Adams came out of a deep sleep to the sound of the call to arms. He was partially dressed as he had only laid down to catch forty winks, but had slept longer than he anticipated. By the time he came out of his tent fully dressed, the castle was a hive of activity. He felt in his left tunic pocket and realised that something precious had fallen out. Turning out of instinct, he rushed back in and saw the picture of his family on the side table next to his bed. He picked it up, kissed it and tucked it deep into his front left-hand tunic pocket.

He had his sword and revolver attached to his belt and put his Lee-Metford rifle over his shoulder. He made his way to the King Edward III Tower. This would give him a viewpoint on the fighting around the hills outside Windsor. As he approached the tower, Sergeant Bowman joined his side.

"Heavy fighting over at Elton Wick, Captain." The sergeant paused and added that the Black Watch was putting up an excellent fight. Oksana the warrior queen was losing troops by the thousands as they were mowed down trying to cross the Thames.

They both passed two Coldstream Guards and entered the tower. The stone walls inside looked sturdy and reassuring, and they both moved up the steps and towards the battlements. Once out on top of the tower, they felt an icy cold breeze brush across their faces and hands.

The lieutenant colonel was handed a pair of binoculars; he had to wipe his watery eyes with his sleeves as the cold wind whipped around them. He then pressed the binoculars to his eyes, scouring the hills for enemy movement. Plumes of smoke could be seen all along the horizon. The thunderous explosions could be heard all the time, like a non-stop storm raging relentlessly. He could see British forces reinforcing lines, and enemy attacks at key positions.

James handed the binoculars to Sergeant Bowman and asked him to have a look as well. He sighed as he followed the hill line. "Their attack is in full swing, then."

James breathed out and confirmed, "It is."

They spent a few more minutes looking at the horizon before joining some of the Royal Engineers and Grenadiers down outside St George's Chapel.

Standing there was Field Marshal Douglas Horatio Carrington. He had survived the fall of Box Hill and was now overseeing the last stand at Windsor Castle. He was glad to see Lieutenant Colonel Adams and wasted no time saying that he needed him to take a small squad and disable Eton Bridge.

He described the fighting around the outskirts of Windsor as desperate. The enemy had numbers that no army had faced before. "If there is a devil, he rides with Nazar today." The Black Watch were trying to repel an advancing detachment of drone cavalry and destroyer drones. They were being led by young officers, high on their conquests and junior priests. Oksana was still with her main force, trying to take Eton Wick.

Lieutenant Colonel Adams had around fifty men with him. Some of the Engineers, who were with Captain Hayward in Europe, were now helping the colonel.

The Grenadiers gave them that extra fighting edge. The soldiers were ready to move out, the Engineers had explosives with them, and the Grenadiers had plenty of grenades. Private Brown reported to the lieutenant colonel that several of the open areas around the north of the castle were now mined. He thanked him and asked to assist the other Engineers with the battlements.

With that, the group set off. The bridge could be seen from the castle, and even artillery was directed that way from the battlements. The decision to hold fire was on the grounds that the Black Watch had not lost total control of the island, and this was a skirmish group that was trying to secure the bridge for a larger attack party.

Lieutenant Colonel Adams was leading from the front; the men moved along the side of the castle for several minutes, such was the size of Windsor Castle. They would have gone out to the bridge through another gateway, but most were now secured for the impending attack. They wanted to make it as hard as possible for Nazar's army to take Windsor Castle. Some harboured hope that the Americans would join the war and help save the British Empire, but there was a lot of history between these powerful nations and America was already taking on board swaths of refugees with no long-term plan on how to feed them or house them.

There were some buildings around the foot of the bridge; this was the same for the Eton side. Drone cavalry were arriving at the same time as Lieutenant Colonel Adams and his men. A whizzing bullet fizzed past them as they moved rapidly towards the Thames. Sandbags had been put up alongside the river's edge and would offer good cover for the soldiers. There was also a large town house, which had been fortified. A small group of Coldstream Guards was returning firing from the windows higher up in the house.

The problem came as they got to the riverbank. They could see the drone soldiers taking up more firing positions and, to the side of them, destroyer drones carrying something into one of the buildings. Lieutenant Colonel Adams knew they had to place as much of the explosives around the base of the bridge and underneath it. The Grenadier Guards got themselves into good covering fire positions and began to shoot at the drone cavalry. Straight away, two drones slumped forward from their firing positions, blood pouring from their wounds.

Sergeant Bowman crouched next to the lieutenant colonel. Thuds of bullets pounding into the sandbags echoed around them. These defences were the only thing which separated them from death. James knew he had to get some of the explosives onto the bridge quickly, Eton Wick was already falling and, with the bridge intact, it would allow Oksana's army to sweep over from that side.

He hand-picked six men and told the sergeant to take another six should they all be killed. He laid his rifle down on the ground behind the sandbags and took one of the pouches loaded with dynamite.

They would have to move along the top and underneath using ropes. A small cannon was directed out of a lower window of a house close to the bridge and aimed across the river.

Small-arms fire continued to grow as the enemy advanced. Some of the Black Watch soldiers who were heavily involved in the fighting at Eton Wick tried to take back several buildings, but the enemy had gained key positions and were mowing them down as they poured forward. Lieutenant Colonel Adams waited a moment; he had given a quick outline of what they needed to do and wanted to pick the right point to go over the sandbags. It came in the form of the cannon being fired. The artillery shell pierced into the top left-hand corner of the house across the river, sending brick and masonry down onto the road below. It left a large hole in the building, which fire and smoke poured out of.

This was the moment James wanted to use. He gave a nod and over they went. Unfortunately, the object the destroyer drones had been carrying into a side house was a machine gun. The familiar sound of the *rat-a-tat-tat* started up. Its impact was instantaneous; two of the Grenadier Guards were hit in the shoulder and head and died as they charged forward. One of the Engineers was hit in the arm and leg, causing him to fall forward into the stone side wall of the bridge. Blood flowed from his wounds and soaked into his red tunic. Fortune had shone on them, as none of the explosives had been hit. These were kept in their pouches and backpacks.

Lieutenant Colonel Adams managed to get to the right-hand side with one Engineer. The other Engineer took up a position on the left. The machine gun continued to spray bullets down onto their position. Bits of stones and mud flung up around them. A large boom broke the *rat-a-tat-tat*, as the cannon fired a shell into the building that held the machine gun. This had the effect they wanted, killing the destroyer drones manning the gun and putting it out of action. Rifle fire continued, but this was the moment they had to take.

Moving the men roughly to the middle of the bridge, Lieutenant Colonel Adams attached the rope to his side, whilst the other soldier did the same on his left. With a quick look, they lowered themselves over. The Grenadiers tried to give them more covering fire from behind the sandbags and houses around the bridge.

The Engineers were now able to fix themselves onto the underside of the bridge. This was not going to be a precision job, they were to ram in as much of the explosives as possible and take the fuse from there. The Engineer, who was going to help pull the men up, fed the fuse back over the sandbags. He felt a nick to his side, and then sharp pain. He brought his right hand down as he sought cover behind a pillar. Blood was gushing from the wound. This did not stop him going back to help the lieutenant colonel and his fellow soldier. They waited for a second or two before making a dash to the sandbags.

The wounded soldier who had been hit earlier was lying motionless by the wall at the foot of the bridge. He had passed out; a third shell then hit the other side of the river. The smoke from this drifted across the bridge; they could almost taste the burning wood, was it Georgian or Victorian? Long gone were the thoughts for public property or landmarks.

Sergeant Bowman came over to the lieutenant colonel, but he did not have time to have a long conversation with him, as the lieutenant colonel hurtled over the bags again and towards the wounded soldier. He knelt down and managed to get the soldier over his shoulder, then moved back to British lines as quick as he could.

The soldier was then helped back to the medical ward in the castle. He was joined by a steady flow of injured soldiers. Back at the bridge, the fighting was still ferocious, and a collection of drone cavalry was preparing to charge over to the British lines. Lieutenant Colonel Adams sensed something was afoot; the amount of enemy fire on their positions was now concentrated. There had been no order to blow the bridge as of yet.
He sent a Grenadier Guard to speak to the soldiers camped in the houses near them, to warn them to be ready for an attack.

A young priest readied his men, who were out of sight, but his inexperience meant he was going to attempt to break into the enemy stronghold. The other young priest with him suggested they wait until Eton Wick had been secured and reinforcements had arrived. He sniggered at this and led his men out for the charge from behind a lane that was not in the firing line. The young priest had around twenty-five drone cavalry and fifteen destroyer drone cavalry. They withdrew their swords and charged en masse. Their pace gathered speed as they approached the bridge. Behind them, the Black Watch were moving into the positions they had vacated. The other young priest began to fall back.

As soon as the first horse touched the bridge, a machine gun that had been stationed at the top of the tallest building next to Eton Bridge began to open fire. The bullets rained down on charging men and horses. The effect was devastating; horses collapsed as they were hit and their riders were torn to shreds as the bullets broke through skin and bone. It did not take long for all of the drones, plus the young priest, to be lying on the bridge, either dead or dying.

The Black Watch were now pushing the other raiding party of soldiers back and gained control of the other side. A British flag was flown from a window to indicate the area was secure. Lieutenant Colonel Adams waited until he saw British soldiers moving along the river front on the other side before taking a small detachment to check the enemy dead. He withdrew his Enfield revolver and moved forward with several Grenadiers.

He ordered the soldiers to use their bayonets on the dying animals and drones, some of whom were already starting to turn. James walked over to a beautiful black horse, it was well groomed and lying motionless. Next to it was its rider, the young priest. He was dead from multiple hits to the body and head. James shook his head at this young, foolish charge, but knew this was now the start of the final chapter in the defence of the castle.

A voice broke the eerie silence.

"You should blow the bridge soon." It was an officer from the Black Watch.

James walked over to him. They shook hands and listened to the fighting in the background.

"You pull your forces onto this side of the river now." James was to the point.

"No, Oksana has crossed in multiple places and it's only a matter of time now." The Black Watch officer was dishevelled from the fighting; he had cuts and bruises over his face and his what looked like blond hair was now discoloured from masonry and blood.

"I'll send a message back to the castle," said James, calling over Sergeant Bowman and explaining that it was a matter of urgency that they get a response. He hand-picked a soldier, who sped off.

This left the officer and the lieutenant colonel talking in a moment of calm. He asked the man, who had a Scottish accent, whereabouts he was from. He replied Edinburgh. The conversation was cut short as the shells started to fall on Eton again. The bridge itself was shaking from the pounding.

A rider bolted towards the sandbags.

"The hills around Windsor have fallen. Waves of enemy regiments are coming towards the castle, sir." The rider then took a breath.

"The order is to destroy the bridge."

Lieutenant Colonel Adams sighed and looked over at the Scottish officer. His red tunic and tartan trousers helped distinguish him from other regiments fighting for the British Empire. The Black Watch was a fantastic regiment that had excelled themselves in many conflicts for the crown.

He felt his throat going dry as he saluted the soldier. "We will fight to the last man."

The officer saluted back. He also added, *"Nemo me impune lacessit,"* as he turned to walk back across the bridge.

"I pray the gods will be with us at the end," James said to the man as he disappeared into the smoke drifting across from Eton Wick.

The fighting had started to intensify on that side, and so had the shelling of Windsor. Sergeant Bowman came over with his rifle lowered, facing Eton.

"Shall we light the fuses, sir?"

"Yes, destroy the bridge." James took cover as the fuses were lit. The blast shook the buildings and ground around them; the explosives had done the trick regarding the bridge's infrastructure. It collapsed from the Windsor side and gave way in the middle. This was by no means a total destruction of the bridge, but would stop the enemy pouring straight over it.

James wasted no time taking his small detachment back to the castle.

Movements along the castle wall were carried out cautiously; all the soldiers were now on edge and James did not want his unit being shot by their own men. Once they had arrived through the King Henry VIII gate, they went quickly to report in.

Field Marshal Douglas Horatio Carrington had asked for reinforcements to be sent to the earth mounds. This defensive line was on the south-west side of the castle and faced the hills overlooking Windsor. It was effectively a buffer that helped protect the castle and town. The defences had been built with stones and soil, and had cannons directed towards the hills along the battlements. There were also machine guns spread out along the earth mound.

Lieutenant Colonel Adams had been given his orders, which were to reinforce the British defensive line. He proceeded towards King George IV gate; from there he reinforced his detachment up to 300 men. They had taken on more ammunition and quickly moved through the gates, and from there they would move further down to the British defences. There were other detachments standing behind the British line of defence, and Lieutenant Colonel Adams would be protecting the middle section.

The warfare was changing, meaning they could no longer just march directly into volley fire, especially with the arrival of magazine-loading rifles, or rapid-firing machine guns. This did not mean they would not take the enemy head on, it meant they had to think differently about their battle plans. Nazar was not as concerned with this; he had numbers to waste and was prepared to allow his forces to charge anything. He wanted the priests to use the flesh-eaters where possible, but would use drones none the less.

Lieutenant Colonel Adams slid his rifle over his shoulder and withdrew his revolver. "Move forward, men." A raucous call rose up from the hills in front of them. James got the soldiers to double their pace, as they went to stand behind the British defensive mounds.

Explosions ripped up soil and grass as they moved forward. A sea of faces was pouring towards the defences. The priests had sent drone soldiers, flesh-eaters and long limbs; this was assisted by bears with two heads. The British lines waited until they were in range, then the barrage began. The cannons from the castle opened up with a volley into the onrushing ranks of enemy soldiers.

This was followed up by the Maxim machine guns, which had been placed along the earth mounds. The heavy *rat-a-tat-tat* filled the air.

The enemy began to drop in mass numbers, blood spurting out of the wounds from soldiers charging into cannon- and machine-gun fire. The British riflemen waited until they were given the order to open fire. Even with the heavy numbers the enemy were suffering, they kept on pushing forward. The bears with two heads were soaking up bullets and cannon shot, often losing a head or part of their body until they would eventually capitulate and collapse into a heap on the floor.

The Grenadier Guards had faced many enemy armies, but nothing could size up to this relentless force of evil. They prepared their grenades for close-quarter combat. The earth mounds had wooden spikes rammed into them, meaning if attacked, they would have to overcome horrendous fortifications. The drone soldiers were often shot for retreating and then left infected to turn. This was already happening on the battlefield; some of the drone soldiers who had been killed were slowly coming back to life as flesh-eaters. "An army within an army," was one of the drone general's comments.

The enemy force was using ladders, made out of pine logs nailed onto wooden branches, to help scale the defences. With British soldiers firing at will, they shot down from the battlements at the enemy, whose ranks were swelling along the whole line. The artillery had to stop firing, otherwise they would kill their own men.

Lieutenant Colonel Adams's heart was pounding, and he ordered his men to attach bayonets.

They did this in unison as they moved forward, and Lieutenant Colonel Adams was proud of them. He looked at their red tunics gleaming in the late morning autumn sun. Soon they were standing at the ready behind the British defence works, acting as a reinforcement line.

The fighting was spilling onto the top of the earth mounds. The Grenadier Guards started hurtling grenades down onto Nazar's forces below. The explosions which followed tore off limbs and blew men and beasts to pieces, but they still kept on coming; once on top, the drone soldiers began using their bayonets to get a stronghold. Using the giant bears, they attached chains around the very spikes that were meant to fend off these creatures. Then they began to pull at the barricade. Slowly, but surely, some sections started to shift. The plan was to plant explosives in these damaged areas and then blow large gaps in these sections.

The Grenadiers were fighting hand to hand, with a level of determination that was shocking the priests, who were leading the drones and this attack. Many of the mortally wounded Grenadier Guards would take a grenade with them as their dying act to throw themselves into the enemy below. These acts of heroism were taking a good number of enemy lives. The flesh-eaters could not climb and many impaled themselves on the spikes. The priests on horseback tried to hold them back for a breach in the defence.

Long limbs were scrambling over other dead long limbs to get at the soldiers above. Just as it looked like the enemy line was starting to break, a horn sounding out broke through the gunfire and the mêlée. Coming through the smoke and over the fallen dead was another wave. It was full of destroyer drones; they also had wolves and giant riders of the north with them. The explosives were set off, killing everyone close to them, but crucially it started to create large enough holes in the defences to get through. This spurred on the other drones around them. Pouring over the top and through the gaps, the Grenadiers were slowly pushed back.

"At the ready," Sergeant Bowman said, bringing his rifle down with its bayonet pushing forward.

British soldiers began to fall back to Lieutenant Colonel Adams's line. Standing two deep, they prepared themselves. The earth mounds started to shake as the pressure of the force behind them grew. Some of the bears were being ridden by destroyer drones and they used them to dig at the soil and stones around the exploded sections, to make the openings wider. This was the signal for the flesh-eaters to start pouring through these gaps and make their way as one force to the British soldiers.

"Hold the line," shouted the lieutenant colonel.

All eyes focused on the flesh-eaters. This mass of wretched souls took centre stage. Many had blood-soaked hair and torn clothes, their mouths open, with rotten flesh hanging from their bodies, this army of dead moved towards the British line in a steady, unnerving motion.

James waited and withdrew his sword.

When they were close, he gave the order for the first rank to fire. The opening volley tore into the skin and bones of the flesh-eaters. In a lot of cases, the heavy rounds nearly cut them in two. Some of the beasts had recently turned and were more robust.

Sadly, they still came ever slowly forward.

As the creatures pushed into the British lines, Lieutenant Colonel Adams gave the order to use bayonets and give them hell. The soldiers lunged forward using their bayonets to ram into the flesh-eaters' heads. The effect was a straight kill, then advancing, they continued to stab and crush with their rifle butts anything in their way. The drone soldiers that were trying to push forward to help their attack got waylaid by the dead in front of them.

Lieutenant Colonel Adams used his sword to slash at the flesh-eaters around him. He cut two heads off in one clean blow, sending blood onto his tunic and face. An arm grabbed his, but he used his revolver to shoot in the forehead the flesh-eater who was trying to bite him. Two more were dispatched in similar fashion. The soldiers next to him fought like demented beasts, thrusting with their bayonets into the never-ending horde of flesh-eaters; slowly they began to come to the drone soldiers, and mixed in with them were destroyer drones. This now upped the fighting; they fought back with their bayonets and the destroyer drones used their strength to inflict damage in any way that they could. This included biting, clawing and anything available to them.

Bones were broken, flesh was torn open, and slowly the enemy started to gain the upper hand. A bear with two heads smashed through part of the earth mound and came at the British lines, knocking over and killing his own men to get at the British soldiers. Lieutenant Colonel Adams rammed his sword into the chest of a destroyer drone, and then used his foot to kick him back off it. His revolver was knocked out of his hand by a drone rifle, and the butt was then swung at his face. He ducked and pushed the man into a cluster of flesh-eaters. As this unfolded, the giant bear was upon them. Its two heads bit and gnawed at whatever was around it. Two British Grenadiers were picked up at the same time in the mouth of this beast; they were shaken like rag dolls and flung into the air. A swipe from one of the paws knocked five soldiers backwards, opening up a man's intestines as a claw sliced along his stomach.

The line had to fall back; riders of the north were now flowing through the holes made by the bears and several more openings were appearing. Two more bears pushed their way through. The lieutenant colonel swung his sword at the head of one of the bears as it picked at a carcass of a dead British soldier. The impact was severe, causing a huge cut down the side of the beast's neck. The animal spun around, knocking James to the ground. Before it could pounce on the lieutenant colonel, Sergeant Bowman pushed his bayonet into its side; this was followed by four more Grenadiers doing the same. Wounded, but not killed, the animal turned and started to flee.

James was still in the thick of it and was holding off a flesh-eater, which took advantage of him being knocked to the ground. It tried to feed on him whilst he was struggling on the floor. The destroyer drones and riders of the north had broken the British lines and a mêlée was now unfolding. Two priests rode in on horseback, one carrying the Nazar flag, the other a spear. They waved on their soldiers.

The smell of rotting flesh as the flesh-eater closed in on his face was sickening; James was tired, but was using all his strength to keep the creature from biting into his cheek. Sergeant Bowman and the soldiers around him could not get across as they were involved in their own fight for survival. James tried to throw off this flesh-eater, but he was a large man, with half his face missing, and his clothes were shredded, which indicated he had been dead for a while.

Rolling from side to side, James felt the moment to roll the creature; unfortunately, another came down trying to bite his legs. He frantically tried to kick it off. As the priests rallied their men, a bugler call went out. Coming from the side of the line was a large division of Lancers. They swept out of the castle's King George IV gate and took the enemy by surprise. Leading them was Captain Harrington; with his sword on his back and rifle close to his saddle, he led the Lancers with an imperious presence.

They caught Nazar's forces perfectly between scattering over the earth mounds and then being grouped together on the other side. This left the enemy flanks exposed; the riders of the north and the destroyer drones were now being attacked on the side with speed. The Lancers picked off the enemy soldiers with ease. The effect was enough to turn the tide of this attack. The priest carrying the Nazar flag turned to escape but two British Lancers slammed their lances into him, knocking him from his horse. They then withdrew their swords and joined in the fighting.

The enemy horn was blown for the retreat. Cannons from the castle began to fire on Nazar's soldiers, who were now retreating over the defensive line and across the open grassland in front of it. The flesh-eaters and bears were being led back, but were now exposed to cavalry. A Lancer picked off the two flesh-eaters on Lieutenant Colonel Adams with his sword. James got up and took his rifle off his back, fixed his bayonet and began killing flesh-eaters and helping out his fellow soldiers where he could. Captain Harrington drove his lance into the heart of a giant bear as the creature rose up to meet him head on. The lance snapped as the bear crashed to the ground, dying instantly on impact.

The Grenadiers had reformed their line, mixed in with some of the Royal Engineers. They began moving forward in a firing line formation and started to pick off any stragglers or enemy that was still fighting; a large wolf was feeding on a wounded soldier. It was shot in the hind leg and then set on with bayonets.

Once the soldiers were back on the earth mounds, they began to fire at will, as Nazar's forces retreated. Clumps of grass and soil shot up into the air, like a volcano erupting every time a shell landed. It also took many creatures and drone soldiers with it. The priest that had been leading the attack was trying to push through one of the gaps in the earth mound, but his horse had been hit in the hind legs, causing it to collapse in a sorry heap. The priest's leg was trapped underneath it. Lieutenant Colonel Adams arrived with Sergeant Bowman and several soldiers. The priest snarled at them and then laughed.

"Your pitiful Empire is finished!!"

The lieutenant colonel loaded a bullet into the breach, took aim and shot the priest in the head. The men around him looked a little shocked.

"They will spare no one," James said, then climbed the earth mound and took cover behind what was left of the defensive battlements. Many of the British soldiers were lifting their helmets as the enemy forces disappeared into the distance.

A young corporal spoke up. "Have we beaten them?"

"We've won this battle, but the war is still rumbling on." James was more realistic; he knew the fighting was taking place all around the castle and Windsor.

"Sergeant, get the wounded to the hospital and some men fixing these defences."

Lieutenant Colonel Adams took some time to walk along the British defences; in a surreal scene, part of the defensive line went in front of a cluster of trees, which backed onto cut lawns. This was previously a tranquil park, but now resembled a battlefield.

He wanted to visit the town to see how they were holding up. Private Brown and a small detachment of Royal Engineers joined him. A battalion of Royal Marines had arrived and were filtering into the town. The machine-gun ammunition was being transported by carts pulled by soldiers. All horses had been mobilised for the cavalry; even soldiers who were not cavalry-trained, but could ride, were mounted up.

Lieutenant Colonel Adams took time to look at the picture of his family, before climbing to a rooftop to survey over the town with his binoculars.

James sighed out loud, he did this without thinking. Private Brown was standing near him.

"Are you alright, Colonel?"

"I'm fine." He paused. "Nazar has arrived."

Chapter 47

"Should we attack now, my lord?" The drone captain was overexcited and brimming with confidence.

"We wait," said Nazar, his voice calm but aggressive. The captain did not say another word. Instead, he turned to join his men marching to the brim of the hillside.

General Tarasov and General Eltsina rode next to Nazar.

General Tarasov felt brave enough to ask about seizing the opportunity and attacking straight away with a detachment of razor tooths, Lagorians and giants.

"There is a mist coming, we will wait until dusk and then attack with force." Nazar looked along his lines and half-smiled at the sheer enormity of his army. "Bring what cannons we have to the front, they will be used to smash into the castle later."

News was brought to him that Oksana was now fighting for Eton Wick and her forces were amassing to attack the castle from the other side. Nazar dismounted from his horse and gave the reins of the animal to a destroyer drone that was guarding him. He was passed a pair of binoculars as he put out his hand. He then surveyed the town and castle. His eyes fell upon several figures on top of the roof of a house. He saw a flash of light, giving away that they were also surveying his army. Nazar did not know this was Lieutenant Colonel Adams; his eyes looked at the defences around the town. He then handed back the binoculars and walked over to his generals.

"Alekseev better retrieve the royal flag of this Empire." He took a swig of water out of his drinking canister. "Their queen will pay with her life, and her subjects will also suffer."

His generals were joined by high-ranking priests.

"We are on the verge of greatness;, the Dark Lord himself is riding with us. Death will come to those who stand in our way."

He then remounted his horse and rode along with his army with his sword high in the air, letting them see his presence. The roar that went up was deafening and could be heard clearly around the castle and Windsor.

Chapter 48

"Colonel, there seems to be a mist coming in over the fields." Private Brown was inside one of the town houses looking out over the hills around Windsor.

James was checking over a map of the town and castle as Private Brown muttered those words. He stopped what he was doing and came to the window. The mist was already licking at the bottom of the buildings and creeping up the street.

"The attack will begin soon." James stared out of the window as he said this.

There was a knock at the door; a guard let the messenger in. He was a Coldstream Guard from the castle. He was out of breath and needed a second to find his voice.

"Eton Wick has fallen and Oksana is crossing the river with her forces." As the soldier said this, artillery started firing from the castle. The soldier then excused himself to return to the front.

Lieutenant Colonel Adams led his officers to the roof again; they crouched down and looked over to the Windsor hills. The artillery had stopped firing, and there was an awkward silence. An icy blast from a gust of wind was enough to get the soldiers to shiver a little. It went through their tunics and into their skin beneath. The silence began to be broken by a soft murmur, which grew and grew with each second that passed. The noise grew as a collection of sounds, some voices, some growls. All of it could be heard coming out of the mist. The groans were a familiar noise and became the loudest sound. Flesh-eaters began to emerge from the darkness first; the smell of their rotting skin carried on the wind, then came the long limbs. They hit the defences hard, using their gangly bodies to scramble up the earth mounds.

The British machine guns began to open fire; this was joined in by the soldiers on the battlements. Flashing lights from the muzzles of their rifles lit up the late afternoon sky. Shells landed around the town, causing many of the buildings to shake. Mortar fire was largely behind it.

Destroyer drones had managed to get into the town. They were not there in heavy force, but there were enough to cause a distraction whilst the main force attacked. A small group of destroyer drones were trying to get into one of the houses close to Lieutenant Colonel Adams and his men. James took his Lee-Metford rifle and pressed it into his shoulder. The window to the building they were in was open, allowing him a clear shot at one of the drone soldiers. Taking aim, he squeezed the trigger. A destroyer drone fell into the wall, blood pouring from the head shot he had just received.

As the magazine held ten rounds, Lieutenant Colonel Adams began taking more shots; some thumped into the bricks around where the drones were, while another found the leg of a drone, causing him to yell out in pain.

They began to return fire. Lieutenant Colonel Adams had to crouch down as the bullets burst into the window frame and wall outside. Some of the soldiers with James found firing positions and joined in the gun battle.

More British soldiers began to open fire on the enemy from other houses and shops along the street. This made their position unattainable and forced the destroyer drones to retreat.

The fighting raged throughout the late afternoon and into the evening. The British were fighting hard, and many times the battle lines changed over the hours that passed. The mist was causing numerous problems; the British could fire into it, but ammunition could not be wasted.

The boats had started to cross the Thames again; Oksana was pushing hard from Eton Wick and along that stretch of river. The artillery from the castle rained down shells onto the boats that crossed. Many hit the water, causing large splashes to shoot up into the air. Those that found their targets had a destructive effect. Tearing the boats into smithereens, arms and legs ripped apart and were flung mercilessly into the water below. Any soldiers who survived were picked off as they swam towards the British side.

The earth mound defences were starting to buckle under the sheer numbers of enemy forces. Windsor began to burn as buildings caught alight from shelling or grenades. Hand-to-hand fighting from house to house was now common. There was little respite as the soldiers fought throughout the night. News was broken early to Lieutenant Colonel Adams that Field Marshal Douglas Horatio Carrington had been killed whilst fighting with his men. It was a big blow for the remaining regiments left fighting for Windsor.

Lieutenant Colonel Adams increased his forces in the houses they occupied. They had a machine gun on one of the higher floors looking down Peascod Street. Private Brown was joined with several other Engineers and Marines. There were also five Grenadiers spread out on two of the house rooves they were occupying. These soldiers were armed with grenades and a mortar.

The mist had eased a little in the morning, as the autumn's sun helped burn off some of the moisture in the air. Different parts of the town were embroiled in heavy fighting. James could see from his firing position in the window that long limbs were roaming up the street; some tried to break through doors or windows when they smelt fresh meat. The British soldiers in those houses fought back hard with bayonets and pikes.

By lunchtime, the enemy drone soldiers were moving up the street. Dismounted riders of the north, with their large frames, pulled two field cannons behind them. Coming over the roof tops were destroyer drones.

"Men, be ready! They will push for the castle!" James called out loud, and sent Private Brown to inform the soldiers on each floor and roof. As John Brown moved up and down the stairs, he paused for a second to look at a photo on the wall of a family that had lived in the house. They all looked contented and happy; he wondered where they were now, and if they were alive. This brought his thoughts on to Heidi; she was still in the castle helping the wounded. He tried not to think about death, but wanted to be with her at the end.

Bullets crunched into the brickwork as he moved towards the top of the house. There was a small passage with stairs which led to the roof. Jon kept his head down and moved up their cautiously.

As he slowly pushed the door to the roof open, he could see several Grenadiers throwing grenades down onto the enemy below. Unseen by them was a destroyer drone that had got into a shooting position and was preparing to squeeze the trigger on one of the British soldiers. Jon reacted with a deft move, letting his rifle slide off his shoulder and into arms. He quickly brought it up to his shoulder and looked down the sights. The bolt was rammed back, sending a bullet into the chamber, and the heavy round sat there waiting to be released.

Bang.

The bullet hit the destroyer drone through his left eye. He slumped forward, falling with his rifle. The Grenadiers nodded to Private Brown and continued fighting. He shouted at them that the big push was coming. Then he quickly went below to join the lieutenant colonel and others.

The enemy forces pushed up the street using carts loaded with sandbags as cover. The Maxim machine gun fired from the top floor of their building, often killing dozens in its deadly fire, cutting through flesh and bone indiscriminately. Lieutenant Colonel Adams was taking down drones and long limbs as they pressed ever forward.

The riders of the north had pulled the cannons into a covered part of the street. They had lost several men moving them and needed reinforcements to get them into a good firing point. For a short while, the enemy could not progress past Lieutenant Colonel Adams's occupied houses. Their covering fire and bloody determination was halting the enemy advancement.

This was short-lived. Coming up the street further back was Nazar on a horse. He was surrounded by priests and destroyer drones. To each side of him were giants riding Lagorians. The Lagorians' huge bodies had amour on, as did the giants. The guns they were carrying were modified grenade launchers. These giants also carried huge shields made out of metal. Bullets began to clank into them as the soldiers in the houses along the street tried to stop their advancement.

Nazar raised his sword and bellowed out "Charge!" to his men and beasts. At the same time, the riders of the north wheeled out the cannons, which had been primed. They knew their targets. The first puff of smoke from the nearside cannon sent its shell into the floor, where the British Marines were reloading the Maxim gun. It killed all of them on impact. The second shell crunched into the side of the house on the lower floor; the explosion shook the building and those in it. It left a hole in the wall, which the soldiers on the lower floor tried to find furniture to fill.

The exchange in gunfire intensified. This was followed by a massive roof attack from the destroyer drones. Slowly but surely, the town was falling. The giants had moved up the street and were now close to the lieutenant colonel's position. Streaming behind them were drones. They were shooting as they moved; many were dying from the returning fire, but their numbers could absorb the losses.

The lower floors of the town houses they were holding began to be assaulted. The giants dismounted and used their swords and body weight to pound the doors and walls. James went downstairs to the ground floor with Private Brown and three others. There were ten soldiers down there pressed against the doors and walls. Each thud shook the ceiling and the area around them. Pictures fell from their mounts and ornaments dropped off the cabinets.

Lieutenant Colonel Adams knew they did not have long in the building.

"Fall back to the first floor. We will cover you from the stairs." As soon as he had said this, the soldiers started to fall back. The doors shook on their very hinges. The first drone to climb through was shot in the chest by Private Brown. More followed and Lieutenant Colonel Adams and Private Brown covered as the other soldiers retreated up the stairs. Ammunition cases fell effortlessly onto the staircase, as the drones surged into the ground floor.

A giant took out the door and started to crawl through. His armour was thick and had bullets bouncing off it.

"Fall back!"

As they did, two of the soldiers with them were struck by bullets and fell down the stairs like rag dolls. The giant thrust his sword forward, missing Private Brown and the lieutenant colonel by inches. As he withdrew to strike again, they bolted up the stairs. James looked over at the two soldiers that had been struck and they were lifeless. As they reached the next floor, three Marines were ready with grenades.

"They're coming, light them," said the lieutenant colonel, spinning around and letting off a shot as the drones scrambled to get to the bottom of the stairs. The other soldiers up on the first floor had found furniture to throw down to help hinder their progress. The grenades were thrown instantly, and then the soldiers laid down covering fire.

"Get ready to crouch, men." James did not want any shrapnel injuring his own soldiers. As he said this, a huge sword went through the floor, impaling one of the Marines. This was followed by the grenades exploding.

The noise was deafening, and shook the house. James checked on the impaled Marine, but the sword had gone right through him and had killed him instantly.

He went to the streetside window and peered out, and a giant stumbled out of the ground floor; he had lost an arm and was bleeding heavily. This beast seemed to sense it was being watched and looked up at the window. Suddenly a shell from the castle landed where he was standing, blowing what was left of him into pieces around the street.

"We must keep moving, throw the rest of the furniture down the stairs and keeping moving up!" James said.

He then led his men up to the next floor. Bullets were now flying into every window. Glass or brick would fling up into the dust-filled rooms, causing the men to crouch as they moved.

A shout came from further up that destroyer drones were now on the roof and pressing to come in. They had to think quickly, so without wasting time, they began to use their bayonets to break through one of the walls on the second floor.

The enemy was trying to break the blockage on the stairs and smash their way down from the attic. The house was filled with a layer of smoke and gunpowder from the fire and rounds which had been dispensed. Once the hole was made in the wall, a Marine went through; he had called out to the soldiers in that house, as it was also occupied by British forces. Fortunately, they heard the calls and did not shoot or put a bayonet through the first British Marine to go through.

Once the men were all through, the smoke had started to become thicker. Lieutenant Colonel Adams ordered them to go into the third house in the street. The enemies outside were moving up along Peascod Street and would soon be upon the castle. In a frenzy of digging and bashing with their shoulders and anything else they could use, they broke into the third house. As this was unfolding, soldiers were shooting from the windows on two floors. The castle had begun firing its cannons down Peascod Street; this meant shops and houses were being hit. Masonry and debris were flying everywhere. It was having the desired effect, which was to slow down the advance.

They went down to the ground floor. The message was simple – they would have to make a run for it and get to the castle. Ammunition was checked, as were their backpacks, swords and re-sheathed revolvers.

"Ok, men, when we're out, stay close to the side of the street and make your way to the castle."

As soon as the soldiers burst onto the street, they came under fire. Three of them died in a hail of bullets. Lieutenant Colonel Adams told Private Brown to stay close to the edge of the houses and lead the way whilst he covered their retreat. He saw the flesh-eaters stumbling towards them; some looked like English civilians who had only turned recently, their eyes carrying the same menace and intent as the other millions of flesh-hungry souls.

James brought his rifle up and quickly pulled back the bolt on his Lee-Metford rifle before squeezing off a round, which raced into the head of a flesh-eater that was only 30 metres away. The soldiers moved at speed along the side of the street, and a roar rose up like a thunder behind them.

"Run for the main gate, it's now or never, men!" James flung his rifle over his shoulder and sprinted with the others across the road towards the castle. As they crossed, bullets whizzed past them, and a soldier to the right of Private Brown fell as he was hit in the leg. He looked back to see the Marine tell him to keep moving as he lay there on the ground. Private Brown glanced over shoulder for a split second and saw the street was moving like a wave of darkness towards them. He tightened his rifle over his shoulder and grabbed the wounded soldier, lifting him onto his back and beginning to run with him.

British soldiers from the castle saw their comrades running towards the gates and began to fire at the horde behind them.

As soon as they made it through the main gates, the portcullis was shut and the giant gates were pulled, too. Then, soldiers frantically began to blockade the gates with anything heavy they could find.

"Colonel, the town is nearly overrun; they are now attacking the north ramparts." The sergeant major was clear with his assessment; he turned and started to assist with the fortifications of the King Henry VIII gate.

"Sergeant Bowman, get the wounded to the hospital ward and then join us at the south tower." Lieutenant Colonel Adams then ordered the rest of the soldiers to follow him to one of the south towers overlooking Peascod Street. They took extra ammunition as they climbed the steep staircase and arrived at the top. On the way up, they could see many British soldiers firing out of the arrow slits and windows of the different rooms. At the top, the air was thick with smoke from the burning town. Bullets were flying through the air and the advice straight away was to keep their heads down.

For the next hour, Lieutenant Colonel Adams and his men fired down on the advancing Nazar forces. They came in waves with ladders and ropes. Maxim machine guns rained down terror upon those advancing towards the castle; thousands were dying in the streets leading towards the castle. The mortars and cannons fired without mercy, but the enemy kept on coming.

Lieutenant Colonel Adams looked up to see a bird of prey soaring high in the sky, as if looking down at the madness below. Shells were landing within the castle grounds and into the castle walls. A terrific explosion shook them in the tower they were in, which was followed by another loud, almost deafening explosion. The second made them look to the back of the castle. The round tower had been hit; it was on fire and burning brightly. Shouts from down below called for reinforcements to the north wall.

James took Sergeant Bowman and Private Brown, plus a handful of men, to assist with the north wall; as they reached the yard outside St George's Chapel, a soldier staggered towards them, he looked in shock and was just shaking his head. Sergeant Bowman took the man as he almost fell into his arms.

"She's dead, sir, they're all dead," he said, as his legs gave way.
"Who, my lad?"
The soldier looked up, and said, "Queen Victoria."

Sergeant Bowman felt his heart sink and lowered the soldier down. Lieutenant Colonel Adams had heard as well. The soldiers around him lowered their rifles; it was as if the energy was leaving them as they stood there, as if time stood still. The moment was broken by the sergeant major, who had helped them earlier.

"The wounded and nurses will leave now," the major said, looking down.

Lieutenant Colonel Adams composed himself and reached into his tunic.

"Private Brown." He looked at the young soldier.

"Yes, sir?"

"Take this to my wife and family, please." James handed over a letter.

Private John Brown knew what it meant, and took a moment before he could stretch out his hand to take it. "It doesn't have to be this way, sir." He shook his head.

"The wounded and other people retreating need time. Every minute will be precious, and it's my duty to give them that time." James was full of emotion; his voice wavered slightly, before he breathed in and ordered the soldier to go. Private Brown offered out his hand to shake the lieutenant colonel's. When James returned his, Private Brown grabbed it with his other arm. "We will meet again, maybe not in this world, but certainly in the next." He turned and left the lieutenant colonel.

The shelling was intensifying, and the roar of the enemy was growing ever stronger. James pulled out his revolver and waved his men on towards the north wall. They did not manage to get that far, as the noise from all around the castle vibrated off the very stones that held it together. The enemy was starting to flow over the north wall; the British regiments there were slowly getting pushed back. To their left, the enemy were coming over the magazine tower. In that moment, a soft breeze brushed across them, as they moved forward.

"Stand firm, men, this is our time. Fix bayonets!" James looked over to Sergeant Bowman. It was a look of encouragement.

Private Brown had joined Heidi in a tunnel that led them away from the castle. It was designed as an escape route, and would lead them far enough away from the castle to have a chance of making an escape to the west coast.

Chapter 49

"We have surrounded the castle, my king." The priest lowered his head as he said this.

Nazar was currently not at the frontline, he was instead in one of the half-destroyed hotels, overlooking the ruins of the burning town and feasting his eyes upon the castle.

"Take it now, and bring me their queen, dead or alive."

He also heard news of Oksana and how she was starting to get the upper hand on the north wall.

"Make sure we all attack at the same time from all sides," Nazar said, his long tongue coming out and licking his lips in an over-excited manner.

Drone General Georgiy, General Eltsina and General Tarasov joined him by his side.

"General Tarasov, lead the destroyer drones over the south wall, General Eltsina, the west, and Georgiy, you will come with me from the east. Attack now and destroy this Empire!"

Chapter 50

Lieutenant Colonel Adams had formed a line with the soldiers who had retreated from the walls. They were in the courtyard close to the burning round tower, with a large Union Jack flag flying on a pole next to them. There were many regiments mixed in together. A young drummer boy was standing next to the sergeant and lieutenant colonel. James had asked the lad why he did not retreat with the wounded. His answer was that he believed it was his duty to be with his regiment.

Nazar's forces were streaming over the walls; flesh-eaters and long limbs were pouring through the broken gates.

"Form a square!" shouted Lieutenant Colonel Adams.

They numbered 500 or more. There were soldiers fighting on the ramparts who would not be able to climb down, they would fight to the death where they stood. Sergeant Bowman barked out the orders for them to form three lines to each side of the square. A handful of orderlies managed to make it into the square with three wagons full of ammunition. They were on orders to distribute the bullets out as quickly as they could.

Oksana was on the north wall; she was a fierce fighter, knocking aside soldiers with her sword. She had been hit with bullets and blades, but she had the same healing powers as Nazar. This did not mean she could not be slowed down by a serious wound but she would have to lose her head to be killed. The British soldiers found out to their peril when fighting her, it would take something special to beat her.

Nazar rode through the King Henry VIII gate on the back of a razor tooth. He looked imperious with shield and large sword in hand. His soldiers swarmed in around him as they made their way to attack Lieutenant Colonel Adams's square.

"We have found the body of their queen, sire; she must have been killed by one of our shells." The young drone officer said this in a sheepish voice, not knowing Nazar's reaction. He snarled at the news, as if cheated out of the right to execute the queen of this Empire himself.

"Where is the body, then?" Nazar's eyes looked at the soldier as he said this.

"We believe it's still in the tower." The officer did not look him in the eyes.

"Retrieve it now!" He paused. Then he kicked on the beast he was riding. The young officer turned and ran to find the body straight away. If he failed to find it, he knew it would cost him his head.

As dust started to fall, the flames from the castle and town lit up the autumn sky. Screams and growls filled the air. Wolves, bears with two heads, flesh-eaters and long limbs joined the drone soldiers and giants. The riders of the north had dismounted and were coming over the walls with Oksana.

"Brace yourself, men!" James looked at the drummer boy as if to give him encouragement.

"They're coming now!" was the call that went out.

A roar that could be heard over the fighting was accompanied by loud drumming. This was the final push, and James knew it. The enemy was massing on all four sides; they came at them like a ferocious, rabid animal. A mixture of drones and creatures hurtling towards the British lines. The officers and sergeants that were left took a side each. Lieutenant Colonel Adams was with Sergeant Bowman on the south-facing line of the square.

"First rank, fire!" A thunderous, collective boom, as the mixture of Lee-Metford rifles and Martini–Henry rifles opened fire with their heavy rounds.

"Second rank, fire!"

"Third rank, fire!"

The effect on the on-rushing enemy was a powerful one; drones fell in their hundreds, beasts lost their footings and collapsed to the ground in the hail of bullets. This continued, but the problem was that the enemy could absorb the losses, and yet keep on coming.

Lieutenant Colonel Adams could see the long limbs and wolves still making into the lines of British soldiers. This of course was to tip the balance of the fighting; as the creatures tore into those around them, the lines broke to fight these insidious beasts. In the blink of an eye, the flesh-eaters and long limbs were now pushing into the square, followed by drone soldiers and destroyer drones. Several riders of the north rode razor tooths into the mêlée which was unfolding.

A large wolf knocked Sergeant Bowman down and proceeded to bite at his arm. Lieutenant Colonel Adams was quick to slash it with his sword; cutting the creature along the back, it screeched out in pain, before he drove his sword through its fur coat and into its heart. Bayonets were being used, as were swords. The fighting was frantic, and each British soldier had been told that the enemy would not spare their life. If they were to be captured, a certain death would await them.

Nazar was charging into the square; he had General Tarasov alongside him on horseback. The razor tooth flung soldiers in its path into the air like rag dolls. A giant followed behind Nazar, it carried a large axe and sword. Nazar made his way towards the Union Jack flag. This flag was situated next to Lieutenant Colonel Adams and Sergeant Bowman.

Nazar had two British Marines come at him, but dispatched them with a swipe of his sword, slicing one in half and the other across the chest. Many more bounced off his razor tooth as it came ever closer to the lieutenant colonel. As the beast raised itself up to bite James, a sergeant major who had been wounded in the fighting picked up a spear and thrust it into the creature's head. It was hit so hard that the spear passed through the creature's flesh and bone and came out the other side.

The razor tooth came to a crashing halt, falling on Nazar's leg and trapping him on one side. As the sergeant major moved forward to finish Nazar, a long limb came in from the side, biting into his shoulder and clawing at his stomach and leg. Sergeant Bowman shot the creature in the head, but it had already mortally wounded the sergeant major.

Lieutenant Colonel Adams holstered his revolver and made his way to stand on top of the razor tooth. Nazar's eyes looked up at him as he raised his sword. He smiled, showing his teeth. As James brought his sword down, it was blocked mid-flight. General Tarasov's sword blocked his master from death. "Haaa!" Nazar cried out, and then began to change. His face started to stretch and his body began to expand.

Lieutenant Colonel Adams brought his sword around sharply, but was blocked again by the general, who swung his sword low in return, but James was able to step back and avoid the swipe. The two men fought a fierce fight, punching and kicking as they both tried to gain the upper hand. Behind them, the razor tooth started to move. Nazar had doubled in size and strength; he let out a roar, which rallied his forces, and they began to swarm on the broken British square.

Whilst the general and lieutenant colonel fought, James did not see a flesh-eater come up from his left side and sink its teeth into his shoulder blade. He let out a scream of pain, before spinning around and pushing his sword into the flesh-eater's head. It slumped to the ground, but as he turned back, General Tarasov struck his sword into James's side, snarling as he did so. James held the sword in one hand, which took the general by surprise, and then thrust his sword into the general's throat. Blood started to trickle out of his mouth, before it began to flow.

Nazar was making his way across to James. A British soldier shot him with his Martini–Henry rifle, and then came at Nazar with his bayonet. It was not enough, as Nazar brought his sword around, cutting the rifle in half and then stabbing the soldier through the chest. As Lieutenant Colonel Adams pulled out the general's sword, he could see Nazar coming. Sergeant Bowman stood in front of James. He had his sword raised.

"You are the devil!" Sergeant Bowman shouted, showing his anger and disregard for this king.

"I am not the devil, although he does ride with me." He smiled and raised his sword. His voice had a growl to it, as now he looked part man, part beast. The sergeant ran at him, swinging his sword and bringing it down into the side of Nazar's neck and shoulder. In return, Nazar had brought his sword through Sergeant Bowman; it had come up through his stomach and out of his back. Nazar lifted him up, "Close." Then he let his lifeless body slide off his sword.

Lieutenant Colonel Adams, on seeing his sergeant and friend die, raised himself to his feet. Blood seeped from his wounds.

"Nazar, you will pay for your sins!"

Nazar smiled. "You are losing, Colonel. Just like your Empire and your queen."

Their swords came together in a heavy clash; Nazar's strength was energy-sapping, and he pushed the lieutenant colonel back. They fought hard across the battlefield, while the fighting raged around them, but their eyes were only transfixed on each other.

Lieutenant Colonel Adams saw an opportunity to swing for Nazar's leg; he did so, opening a large slice across his thigh, but Nazar's response was to catch the lieutenant colonel across the stomach. A drone soldier, who had just killed a British soldier, stepped forward to ram his bayonet into James, but Nazar was having none of it. He struck his sword into the drone soldier, who turned and looked confused. Nazar withdrew his blade and pushed the man over.

Again, the two of them clashed with swords, swinging hard; it was a series of attacks and counter attacks. Then there was a moment where both men squared off to each other. Nazar had been impressed with the lieutenant colonel's fighting skills, but he had no plans to spare anyone. They came at each other hard; James thrust his sword into Nazar's heart, and Nazar his into James's chest. They were inches away from each other, and blood started to pour from James's stomach and mouth. Nazar recoiled a little, but looked into James's eyes. "You fought well, Colonel." He pulled the sword from his own chest, then slowly let the lieutenant colonel fall to his knees with his sword still in him. "But I told you that you would lose."

James sighed, and with his shaking right hand, reached inside his tunic and pulled out the picture of his family. He smiled on seeing their faces, but felt his eyes growing heavy. He then fell forward and passed into the next world.

Nazar waited for a moment, surveying the battlefield. He then walked over and withdrew the sword; he was weakened by the fight, but knew only losing his head would kill him.

A small group of British soldiers now stood back to back. The drummer boy was one of them, spear in hand and tears running down his cheeks on seeing the death of the lieutenant colonel. The Union Jack was standing in the soil between them; a soft breeze gently rolled it out to show its full glory, before effortlessly falling back again. The drone soldiers now flanked them on all sides. The priests who had been fighting amongst the enemy held back the beasts and creatures.

Oksana rode over to her king and dismounted to stand next to him.

"Today you have a new ruler! I am your king!" he roared out his decree. "But I have no need for a British army." He nodded to General Georgiy. The general raised his hand, and then lowered it. The drone soldiers fired in unison. The thunderous fire ceased after one volley. The last of the British soldiers lay dead where they had put up a gallant fight.

Nazar was brought a horse. Oksana mounted, then came close and kissed her husband on the lips. "You must rest, my lord."

As he turned to leave, he ordered his generals to kill any British soldiers left on this island.

"What of the civilians fleeing to the west coast and America?" General Georgiy said, not wanting to displease Nazar after his victory.

Spitting out blood and returning to his normal size, he paused on his horse, before answering, "Let the army have its fill, then make examples of them." He moved forward slowly, continuing, "Reward those that helped us with this victory."

"Yes, my lord," General Georgiy said, lowering his head.

"Then we prepare for America," Nazar said, kicking on his horse and leaving the castle with Oksana.

Chapter 51

Passing along the coast, Captain Hayward and his family could see towns and cities burning. The small fleet of British ships sailed along unchallenged. They were wise enough not to get too close to the coast where the invasion had taken place, as Nazar could have field cannons or mortars, which they would use against them.

Small gunfire could be heard carried on the wind, as could roars and screams. By the afternoon, they had passed the Isle of Wight and the Dorset coastline. Arthur looked on as he pressed against the side of the boat. Rebecca had taken Emily below deck to rest.

"Do you think we will return one day, father?" Arthur asked, looking at the smoke rising from the villages and the shapes staggering along the coastal paths.

"Anything is possible in life, my son." He put his hand on his shoulder. "For now, we must settle in America." There was a silence as father and son looked out at the British coastline and the ever-unfolding story there.

"Should we be further away from the coastline, Father?" Arthur pointed to the flesh-eaters and long limbs moving in packs.

"We will be in the Atlantic Ocean soon enough, but there may be a chance for us to pick up more survivors." The further they got into Devon, the closer in they sailed. The small fleet had rescued several units of soldiers and many civilians as they moved along.

Captain Hayward felt a hand on his back, then a kiss on his neck. He turned to see Rebecca moving close to him. They kissed on the lips. "She is asleep now." Charles hugged her. "I have a lot to thank Hagen for." She nodded her head.

Hagen and the other survivors were busy working away; some were helping with the cleaning and cooking on the ship, others maintaining weapons.

"We will need people like him if we are ever to beat Nazar." He looked at Rebecca and smiled.

They moved along at a good speed. Some of the fleet would pass around to the west coast as a final sweep for survivors. Captain Hayward's ship and several others would venture on to America.

"We've just passed Burgh Island," Charles said to Arthur.

"Father, look." Arthur pointed to riders with a flag. Charles went to grab a pair of binoculars.

"My God, it's the royal colours," he said, pausing and then calling over a sailor. "Tell the captain we need to get in closer."

***

Captain Kingsbury was riding hard with the other five Lancers. They knew there was a chance they could get the colours to the west coast of Cornwall. Staying close to the coastline gave them a chance to look for British ships or boats.

They had spotted this small fleet and were making their way to the beach near Bigbury-on-Sea.

Closing in behind them was High Priest Alekseev, with around twenty destroyer drones.

"Captain, they're gaining on us." The corporal was riding alongside Captain Kingsbury.

"Stay with me, Corporal, we're nearly at the beach."

The royal colours flew outstretched behind him as the sun slowly started to sink in the skies.

"Ride, Captain, we will hold them off." The corporal signalled to the other soldiers before Captain Kingsbury could tell them otherwise. He knew their sacrifice would give him time, but it was something he did not want.

The five Lancers clashed well with the destroyer drones, killing five on impact with their lance spears. Then they reverted to swords. The high priest dismounted two Lancers as he rode past with his staff. He continued with five drones after Captain Kingsbury. The corporal and his remaining two riders tried in vain to pursue, but were simply outnumbered and continued the fight where they were.

Captain Kingsbury could hear the horses galloping behind him; he rode along the clifftops just ahead of the beach. As he came to a narrow edge, a destroyer drone came alongside him. He bumped and knocked into the captain with his horse, then swinging a fist and trying to knock the captain off his horse. Mud and grass sprayed up as their horses tore across the ground at great speed.

A savage blow to Captain Kingsbury's head drew blood, which gently flowed down his right ear and onto his blue tunic. He looked over quickly at the destroyer drone as they rode next to each other. The drone saw the flash of anger in his eyes. With his right arm he grabbed the drone, which was taken by surprise. He flung him backwards, sending him tumbling to the ground and over the cliff edge.

He had a plan. There was an area next to the clifftops in front of him where he would have more room. Riding to the very edge, he struck the royal colours into the ground. The wind of the sea lifted the flag, giving it almost lifelike qualities. It flapped backwards and forwards in a mesmerising fashion.

This brought to a halt High Priest Alekseev and his four destroyer drones. He smiled, showing off his yellow teeth.

"Haaaa haaa, you have nowhere to run now, Lancer!" The priest came forward slowly on his own. His sword still strapped to his back, he also tossed his cloak over his shoulder, showing his two daggers. "Leave the flag and I will give you a quick death."

"Your king's cousin of darkness killed my wife and daughter." Reaching to his side, Captain Kingsbury brought up his lance, which had been strapped across his back.

This took the smile off the priest's face. "So, you're the one who killed him? Your head will double my bounty. Kill him!" screamed the priest.

The four destroyer drones withdrew their swords and started to come at the captain. His horse looked down, scraping the ground underneath it. Then he launched forward, kicking his horse on. As the riders converged, Captain Kingsbury turned his lance to the side; this had the effect of knocking off two of the riders, slicing the throat of the one to the left and forcing the other to land heavily on the ground.

He circled around, again raising his lance; the two destroyer drones looked over to the high priest, who was angry that they had not dismounted or killed this soldier. The captain nodded to them and came again at speed. He touched the royal flag as he passed it; turning his horse to come in from the right, his lance pierced the chest of the drone on that side, sending him crashing to the ground with the lance sticking out of his chest and blood spurting out of his mouth.

The other drone swung his sword, catching the captain on the leg and opening up a deep wound, but as the drone moved to finish him off, Captain Kingsbury, having drawn his sword, thrust it forward into the drone's neck; it did not take his head off, but left it hanging on by flesh and bone. The drone was still holding on to his reins dead in his saddle as he passed the high priest.

Captain Kingsbury wiped the blood away from his mouth, then looked up at the high priest.

"You think this changes anything? Prepare to die, Lancer," said the high priest whilst withdrawing his sword and kicking on his horse.

Blood from Captain Kingsbury's leg wound was flowing down onto his horse and the ground below. He clenched his fist and gritted his teeth. Then he looked up and came at the priest. The two collided, clashing swords together; the priest tried to use his horse to bash into the captain's wounded leg, but as the two twisted around, swinging their swords together, they drew ever closer to the cliff edge.

The priest reached out as they passed the flag and grabbed it. It was a bold move, and one that the captain reacted to by putting his sword through the armpit of his attacker as it was left unguarded. He squealed out in pain, and dropped his sword, but kept hold of the flag. He reached inside his cloak and pulled out a dagger, and in a flash struck it into the chest of Captain Kingsbury. The pain caused the captain to recoil in his saddle, but he adjusted himself as they were now in a treacherous entanglement of death.

"You will never have our kingdom's colours." With that, he pulled the dagger from his chest and pulled the priest in close with his other hand. Then in a flash, he slammed the blade into the forehead of the priest. The shock in the eyes of his opponent was telling; unfortunately, they had fought to the edge of the cliff and as the blade went in, his horse started to fall over the cliff edge. Captain Kingsbury's last action was to grab the flag as he began to fall.

From his ship, Arthur saw the battle rage on the clifftop and then the horses and men fall into the sea below.

The tide had been in, but the drop was a significant one. Captain Hayward quickly called for a group of soldiers and sailors to get two boats in the water and go to the riders and royal colours. Arthur begged his father to let him go in the boat; Charles was reluctant, but Rebecca gave him a look and a nod.

"Stay close to me, Arthur." His son promised he would.

The rowing boats were lowered into the water and they set off at speed towards the riders who had fallen. The second rowing boat had Alexander and some of the other sharp shooters in it covering the clifftops. Sergeant Butcher joined Captain Hayward in his boat. As they approached the flag, Arthur jumped into the water and began to swim for it. Charles was about to shout out to him, and follow his son, when he saw a soldier in a blue tunic floating in the water. "Bring the boat around and pick Arthur up." He paused for a second. "Then come for me." Following that, he threw himself into the cold water. He was a good swimmer and got to the body quickly; he felt the man move a little as he turned him over and began to bring him towards the other boat, which had come closer to them.

Arthur was being hauled into the first rowing boat holding the flag; he was shaking and was wrapped in a blanket. He could see his father helping the British rider to be dragged into the second rowing boat. The man was barely alive, and was wrapped in a blanket. Charles was hauled out by Sergeant Butcher and given a blanket to warm him up. As they did this, they could see the other rider floating close to them. His dark clothes indicated he was probably a soldier of Nazar's. They moved closer and turned the body, revealing he was a priest. The blade that Captain Kingsbury had used was still sticking out of his forehead.

The two boats made it back to the ships and were raised out of the water. Captain Hayward was shocked that he recognised the Lancer as Captain Kingsbury. He was hanging on to life; Corporal Heinz went to get Doctor Brown, then helped the other soldiers take him below deck to be worked on by the doctor. Charles said he would check on him shortly.

The two horses which had fallen into the water with their riders had made their way to the beach and were seen galloping off into the fields behind.

Rebecca went to get Arthur fresh clothes; whilst she did so, he stood there with the blanket covering him from head to toe, but with both his hands wrapped around the royal colours. Charles smiled at his son; he was saddened to see the colours, but extremely proud to know they were in his son's hands and not in the enemy's.

Rebecca came back with fresh clothes and Arthur changed. The flag was stored below deck and the other ships in the small fleet signalled to each other that they would search the west coast for survivors before setting sail for America.

Charles spoke to Doctor Brown about the captain; he was hopeful that he would make it, but the voyage was a long one and only time would tell. Charles stood that evening holding Rebecca in his arms, and to her he said, "I pray God is with us, I have a feeling we'll need all the help we can get."

Chapter 52

Nazar returned to the hills overlooking Windsor. He had received a message regarding the royal colours. Oksana stood by his side, both had blood and sweat on them from the fighting; they watched the castle burn, along with the town in the evening sky.

"My lord, you should rest, the tent is ready and we have plenty of fresh meat."

He stared into the darkness.

"I have a feeling Alekseev failed." He let his cloak fall to the ground. "I hope he died trying, otherwise if he returns without it, he will be burned alive."

Oksana let her cloak slide off.

"Come, my lord; let's celebrate the end of the British Empire."

He turned and snarled, which was followed by a half-smile.

"Many of them escaped to America, and whilst that still stands, I cannot rest." He felt his wounds on his chest. "I want Captain Hayward." Nazar had been informed that the rock had been destroyed by him. "He has escaped my path once, but he will not escape again." Feeling his wound again, he looked at Oksana, and vowed, "He will suffer."

Nazar led Oksana into the tent, which had two large torches burning outside it, its ambers shooting into the skies above.

Smoke from Windsor was carried on the wind, and every forest and woodland now emanated an unnatural eeriness. Darkness had fallen on these lands.

Printed in Dunstable, United Kingdom